**Illinois Central College
Learning Resources Center**

*Critical Essays on
Salinger's*
The Catcher in the Rye

Critical Essays on Salinger's
The Catcher in the Rye

Joel Salzberg

G. K. Hall & Co. • Boston, Massachusetts

Library of Congress Cataloging in Publication Data

Critical essays on Salinger's The catcher in the rye / [edited by]
    Joel Salzberg.   p. cm.—(Critical essays on American literature)
    Includes bibliographies and index.
    ISBN 0-8161-8894-7 (alk. paper)
    1. Salinger, J. D. (Jerome David. 1919–   . Catcher in the rye.
I. Salzberg, Joel.   II. Series.
PS3537.A426C325   1989
813'.54—dc20   89-11202
                                                              CIP

This publication is printed on permanent/durable acid-free paper
MANUFACTURED IN THE UNITED STATES OF AMERICA

CRITICAL ESSAYS ON AMERICAN LITERATURE

This series seeks to anthologize the most important criticism on a wide variety of topics and writers in American literature. Our readers will find in various volumes not only a generous selection of reprinted essays and reviews but also original essays, bibliographies, manuscript sections, and other materials brought to public attention for the first time. This collection of reviews and essays traces the critical reputation of *The Catcher in the Rye*. It contains both a gathering of early reviews and a broad selection of modern scholarship from a variety of perspectives. Among the authors of reprinted articles are Bernard Oldsey, James E. Miller, Jr., Lilian R. Furst, Anne Goodman, James Bryan, John M. Howell, and Gerald Rosen. In addition to an important introduction by Joel Salzberg that surveys the history of scholarship on the novel are four original essays commissioned specifically for publication in this volume by A. Robert Lee, James M. Mellard, Siegfried Mandel, and Mary Suzanne Schriber. We are confident that this book will make a permanent and significant contribution to American literary study.

JAMES NAGEL, GENERAL EDITOR

Northeastern University

For Rachel and Graham

CONTENTS

INTRODUCTION

So often regarded as a minor classic, *The Catcher in the Rye*[1] has enjoyed a readership that has transcended the boundaries of age, education, and culture, a phenomenon unparalleled in the history of modern and contemporary literature. Its reputed charm has moved critics as totally opposite each other in background and personality as Sanford Pinsker and Ian Hamilton to recall with similar nostalgia their early enthusiasm for Salinger's only novel. For Pinsker, the initial impact and authority that *Catcher* had for him remains undiminished. "When those in the know about postmodern fiction," he declares, "wag their fingers at *The Catcher in the Rye* and call it 'counterfeit,' I continue to listen to the voices that mattered, and still matter—namely those in Salinger's novel."[2] For Hamilton, born and reared in Great Britain, the early experience with *Catcher* was even more compelling. "*The Catcher in the Rye*," he claims, "exercises a unique seductive power—not just for the young readers who discover it, but also for the millions or so original admirers like me who still view Holden Caulfield with a fondness that is weirdly personal, almost possessive."[3] The memories of Pinsker and Hamilton's youthful romance with *Catcher* have been carried over well into their middle years. In their different kinds of infatuation with Holden Caulfield, Pinsker and Hamilton illustrate the hold that the novel has had on the sensibilities of those who are otherwise separated from Holden Caulfield by a distinctly different cultural milieu or simply by the passage of the 1950s into history and memory.

One may now conjecture as to whether some of the earliest critics of *Catcher* who immediately condemned the book as insidious and corrupting were reacting to something more than the obvious display of sex talk and a new "youth" language. In their own negative way were they being sensitive to an infectiousness, a Pied Piper quality in the novel, that exists at some deeper level? Did they indeed exaggerate its potential for moral disruptiveness? Thirty years later the novel's latent infectiousness was to turn one of its most obsessive latter-day readers, Mark Chapman, into the murderer of John Lennon because of his belief that Lennon's authenticity had been replaced by a phoniness that was morally corrupting to the young. He too

1

attempted to become a catcher in the rye, and thereby contributed to one of the grim ironies involving the relationship of literature to life. How often has a work of fiction stimulated such an unexpected and volatile reader response and played such a deadly role in human affairs? Although it was the Book-of-the-Month Club selection for 1951, some readers nonetheless reacted with outrage, censorship, and even parody soon after it was published.[4] The usual effect that *Catcher* has on its readers has been benign, merely shocking them into a bittersweet recognition of Holden Caulfield as their adolescent double, in the same way that Salinger surely recognized Holden in himself. The powerful illusion of authenticity that he created through Holden, an illusion that has its imagined counterpart only in Twain's *Huckleberry Finn*, has been Salinger's great artistic achievement—an achievement unfortunately never as yet repeated by him.

If Salinger's creation of Holden Caulfield was an imaginative act less formidable than that of Flaubert's Emma Bovary or James's Isabel Archer, Salinger's character is no less complete within the range of his own human dimensions. Like the characters in Bernard Malamud's fiction, who, according to their author, were the products of "biographical [and autobiographical] essence," Salinger's Holden is also a distillation of his creator. Early in his career, in answer to one of his correspondents, Salinger acknowledged that Holden Caulfield was a self-portrait and went so far as to quote Holden's opinions as though he were a person rather than a character in fiction.[5] Indeed, Salinger's attachment to his character has a touch of literary fantasy about it. While J. D. Salinger, author, gradually disappeared from the literary scene, Holden Caulfield, his creation, gained ascendancy, much like Golyadkin junior in Dostoyevski's *The Double*, and has come to be regarded as Salinger's second self. It is not surprising then that Salinger critics tend to view *Catcher* both as Salinger's tomb and his monument, and in recent years some of the titles of articles on Salinger or *Catcher* have almost a reverential tone, as though they were ceremonial rituals of remembrance.[6]

Although the relation between Salinger's life and art still remains a tantalizing mystery, despite Ian Hamilton's recent attempt at writing Salinger's biography, *Catcher* pretends to be no such enigma. It is clear that Salinger intended to communicate the disorder and early sorrow of an American urban adolescence of the late 1940s (much of it reminiscent of his own) through accurately recalling and transcribing its colloquial style—the character of its vernacular, as well as its syntactical incompleteness—and capturing the cultural and geographical ambience of the New York City he knew intimately. But his accomplishment, in fact, was the result of artistic trial and error over a ten-year period in which he developed his ideal surrogate self. Appearing as an actual character in two earlier stories, "I'm Crazy" (*Collier's*, 22 December 1948) and "Slight Rebellion Off Madison" (*New Yorker*, 21 December 1946), this Holden Caulfield figure is merely a thin sketch, a prototype that eventually culminated in the Holden of *Catcher*.[7] While discovering the quintessential Holden, however, Salinger was finally able to bring into sharp focus, as

never before, his own hostility toward the spiritual squalor of American culture. Moreover, through Holden's repeated pronouncement of "phony" Salinger was also able to express an intuitive aesthetic as well as a moral inner light
under the guise of adolescent inarticulateness. As Salinger's ideas about these
matters began to crystallize, subsequently such pronouncements took the
form of religious conviction in, for example, *Seymour: An Introduction* and
Franny and Zooey, works that seem less like fiction and more like author
revelation. In his way, Holden Caulfield, the sensitive but semiarticulate
American adolescent, becomes for J. D. Salinger, on Salinger's own native soil
and on his own terms, what Steven Dedalus, a rising young Irish intellectual,
becomes for James Joyce—an engaging fictional embodiment of cultural disaf-
fection and subversion, and perhaps like Dedalus, an artist in the making.[8]
There is, of course, much more to Holden Caulfield than these labels suggest.
Because each decade has altered Holden's image according to its own literary
and cultural values, articles and chapters in books continue to contribute to
the scholarship on *Catcher*.

In 1963 an article comparing *Catcher* and *Lord of the Flies* was published in *America*, the same periodical in which a review of a new film,
David and Lisa, also appeared.[9] The film bore a number of resemblances to
Salinger's novel although to my knowledge no one has made the connection.
Based on a psychiatric history written by Dr. Theodore Rubin,[10] the film
portrayed a severely disturbed seventeen-year-old boy who obsessively fears
that the physical touch of another will bring about his own death. He is
committed to a home for disturbed adolescents where he encounters a
fifteen-year-old girl with schizophrenia to whom he extends himself in friendship. Moved by her vulnerability, David eventually allows Lisa to touch him
physically and is thereby rescued from his own dark obsession. Figuratively
speaking, both serve as catchers in the rye, each child-adolescent offering
the other human assistance. In her review in *America* Moira Walsh regarded
David and Lisa as a "remarkable low-budget film"[11] and the anonymous
reviewer in *Time* considered the film "a minor masterpiece."[12] (Skillfully
playing David, Keir Dullea might have easily been a suitable Holden Caulfield in a film version of *Catcher*, had Salinger approved the film adaptation
of his novel.) While *David and Lisa* faded into relative obscurity (although
Keir Dullea did not), *Catcher* continued almost uninterruptedly to garner
enthusiastic attention among popular readers all over the world and would
be discussed at length by academic critics for over thirty years. Eventually, it
received a form of canonization as a result of a *PMLA* article and rejoinder.[13]

Perceptive as some of the early reviewers of *Catcher* were, they were
generally brief and often highly subjective. Understandably, none of them
could foresee the unusual reception the novel would have, despite the fact
that most of the New York reviewers were already familiar with Salinger's
previously published short fiction in such magazines as *Collier's*, *Esquire*,
Harper's magazine, and the *New Yorker*. And these reviewers were expec-
tantly awaiting the publication of *Catcher*. Although many of them found

much to praise in the novel, their enthusiasm for it did not prevent them from criticizing what were presumably flaws. Anne L. Goodman in the *New Republic*, reflecting on Salinger's "A Perfect Day for Bananafish" and "For Esmé—with Love and Squalor," considered the final scene in *Catcher* ". . . as good as anything that Salinger has written," but faulted Salinger's "extraordinary portrait" of Holden because "there is too much of him."[14] Ernest Jones in the *Nation* recognized Salinger's skill and ingenuity but asserted that "the book as a whole is predictable and boring."[15] And William Poster in *Commentary* grudgingly admired Salinger's ability to render the current idiom and style of the Holden Caulfields in urban America but concluded that Salinger is "a well-paid satirist, with a highly developed technique, no point of view, and no target to aim at but himself."[16] Poster's very substantial review foreshadows the Marxian reading of Carol and Richard Ohmann[17] that would appear over two decades later. Other reviewers were more extreme in their responses. Harrison Smith in the *Saturday Review* was altogether positive, noting that "the magic of the novel does not depend on this boy's horrifying experience but on the authenticity of the language and the emotions and memories which overwhelm him."[18] And the anonymous reviewer of the Canadian periodical *Saturday Night* was equally enthusiastic: "Here is a novel that blends total adolescent recall and adult perspective so superbly that artistry—and, more important, life—leaps from every page."[19] In contrast, T. Morris Longstreth in the *Christian Science Monitor* remarked that *Catcher* might possibly lead to the creation of other Holden Caulfields "when immorality and perversion are recounted by writers of talent whose work is countenanced in the name of art or good intention."[20] Along the same lines, in a concise summary of the novel the anonymous reviewer for *Catholic World* concluded that it "is made monotonous and phony by the formidably excessive use of swearing and coarse language."[21] In short, from the praise, qualified and unqualified, and from those reviewers totally negative to the novel, the future of *Catcher*, and its inclusion in the mainstream of American literature, could in no way be foretold by these representative reviews.

In 1953 the publication of *Nine Stories*[22] gained Salinger praise equal to and often superior to that received for *Catcher*, a circumstance reminiscent of the enthusiastic reviews Bernard Malamud received for his first collection of stories, *The Magic Barrel* (1958), published a year after *The Assistant* (1957). In both instances the reviewers felt that each writer revealed his greatest skills in the creation of the short story rather than in the novel. Eudora Welty in reviewing *Nine Stories* in the the *New York Times Book Review* observed: "*The Catcher in the Rye* was good and extremely moving, although—for this reader—all its virtues can be held in a short story by the same author where they are somehow more at home."[23] Although *Catcher* began to attract a wide readership, especially among high school and college-age students—by 1961 sales had reached one and a half million copies in the United States alone[24]—a few more years would pass before the novel came to be regarded as a classic, eventually becoming required reading in some undergraduate literature courses in American colleges and universities. In addition to its commercial success among its many youthful admirers, academic critics of the late 1950s, who once had been counted among its youthful admirers, now discovered in *Catcher* a hero connected to the literary traditions of Europe and America and relevant to the interests of contemporary literary critics and theorists. Ever mindful of new critical paradigms that might prove useful in practical criticism, these academics must surely have felt indebted to R. W. B. Lewis's *The American Adam* (1955),[25] Richard Chase's *The American Novel and Its Tradition* (1957),[26] and R. W. B. Lewis's *The Picaresque Saint* (1958)[27]—even though these books, with the exception of Lewis's, did not deal directly with Salinger's fiction—for concepts that seemed to place *Catcher* within the mainstream of American literature as well as within the tradition of European literature. More specifically, Arthur Heiserman and James E. Miller, Jr., soon followed by other critics, began to use terms like myth, epic, quest, romance, and picaresque in their discussions of *Catcher* and helped to initiate the revaluation of *Catcher* that transformed it from a novel of some importance in 1951 to the status of a classic in their article, "J. D. Salinger: Some Crazy Cliff."[28] In their opening paragraph Heiserman and Miller asserted: "It is clear that J. D. Salinger's *The Catcher in the Rye* belongs to an ancient and honorable narrative tradition, perhaps the most profound in western fiction. The tradition is the central pattern of the epic and has been enriched by every tongue; for not only is it in itself exciting but also it provides the artist a framework upon which he may hang almost any fabric of events and characters."[29]

If the initial reviews of *Catcher* only brought academic critics to a simmer, the Heiserman and Miller article, followed soon after by others like it, surely brought them to a boil, for the opening paragraph of the article sounded like a proclamation and a call to celebration. As the article continued, it asserted Holden's affiliation to the questing heroes of ancient and modern literature—Ulysses, Aeneas, Aloysha Karamazov, Gatsby, Dedalus, Huck Finn, Ishmael, Hans Castorp—thereby placing Holden in a context of literary significance that, some argue, may well have inflated Holden's fictional stature. In the same year that the Heiserman and Miller article was published, Charles Kaplan's piece, "Holden and Huck: The Odysseys of Youth," appeared in *College English* and was in many respects similar to Heiserman and Miller's, so much so that Kaplan appended a note to his own indicating that it had been accepted in *College English* before theirs appeared in print.[30] Kaplan discussed *Catcher* and *The Adventures of Huckleberry Finn* as works that were mutually illuminating, particularly in view of Huck and Holden's quest for rebirth, and asserted, as well, that both works were "comic masterpieces." In 1957 Edgar Branch established additional points of contact between *Huckleberry Finn* and *Catcher* in his article, "Mark Twain and J. D. Salinger: A Study in Literary Continuity." concluding that *Catcher* "takes its place in that literary tradition—spreading beyond

Anderson, Lardner, Hemingway, Faulkner—that has one of its great sources in *Huckleberry Finn*."[31] It was inevitable that the richness Heiserman and Miller, Kaplan, and Branch had discovered in *Catcher* other critics would find lacking. John Aldrich was a case in point, dissenting from those critics who perceived in the novel a work of significant literary importance: Holden, he argued ". . . has objects for his contempt but no objects other than his sister for his love—no raft, no river, no Jim and no Tom. . . . Salinger had made the most of his subject but his subject was not adequate to his intentions, just as Holden's world is not adequate to his contempt."[32] Writing along the same lines, Maxwell Geismar in "J. D. Salinger: The Wise Child and the *New Yorker* School of Fiction" expressed his own skepticism regarding the relation between Salinger's intentions and his actual accomplishment. "*The Catcher in the Rye* protests to be sure against both the academic and social conformity of its period. But what does it argue *for*? . . . The real achievement of *The Catcher in the Rye* is that it manages so gracefully to evade just those central questions which it raises."[33]

Whatever serious reservations Aldrich and Geismar had about the achievement of *Catcher*—and those reservations were also shared by such critics as Harvey Swados[34] and George Steiner[35]—the flow of academic articles and books beginning in the late 1950s continued unabated. In 1957 Charles H. Kegel, in the article "Incommunicability in Salinger's *The Catcher in the Rye*," asserted that the Heiserman and Miller article would now force other critics to give *Catcher* careful critical attention.[36] Taking his own cue, Kegel proceeded to explore the pattern of communication failure that is so central to Holden's relations with adults and even to his own peers. Shortly thereafter Donald P. Costello introduced a linguistic perspective to the study of the novel—indeed the best one to date—and demonstrated that Holden Caulfield not only speaks an authentic teenage vernacular but also that Salinger uses it in order to establish Holden's characterization at a given moment in his narrative.[37] Legitimate as many of the articles were, so much had been written about Salinger and his work up to 1959 that George Steiner found it necessary to question whether Salinger's accomplishments truly justified the outpouring of criticism and commentary, or whether the "Salinger industry" was rather a matter of economic and academic opportunism involving easy publication for young academics.[38] Undeterred by such cynicism, academic critics throughout the 1960s and beyond continued to find more to say about *Catcher*, as well as about Salinger himself, although by 1963 the number of publications appearing on Salinger and his work had reached their peak and began to decline. Between 1962 and 1966, however, five collections of Salinger criticism appeared,[39] as well as two special issues on Salinger, the first in *Wisconsin Studies in Contemporary Literature*[40] and the second in *Modern Fiction Studies*.[41] Inevitably, the collections proved to be largely redundant, each repeating much of the material found in another, and almost all of them containing questions on Salinger's fiction intended to elicit critical essays from students studying Salinger's work. Of the five collections, two are especially useful. The first, *Salinger: A Critical and Personal Portrait*, edited by Anatole Grunwald, provides a biographical and critical introduction to Salinger's work. The essays themselves, some of which have been abridged for the collection, capture the spirit of the controversy surrounding *Catcher* and Salinger's shorter fiction. The second, *Studies in J. D. Salinger: Reviews, Essays, and Critiques of "The Catcher in the Rye" and Other Fiction*, edited by Marvin Laser and Norman Fruman, explores the publishing history of *Catcher* and discusses the early reviews of the novel. Similar to Grunwald's collection, Laser and Fruman's provides a cross section of the most important criticism on *Catcher* and Salinger's shorter fiction. Some essays, however, were also presented in an abridged form.

By the late 1950s Ihab Hassan had conveyed in his essay "J. D. Salinger: Rare Quixotic Gesture"[42] the dominant image of Holden Caulfield that was held through the 1960s by many academic critics, perhaps influenced by the recently published work of R. W. B. Lewis. Hassan asserts that all of Salinger's heroes are involved in a rare quixotic gesture—that is, "a gesture of protest and of prayer. . . . There is often something spontaneous about it, something . . . that revives our faith in the human spirit."[43] In short, Holden emerges as a kind of picaresque saint. Thus for Hassan Holden's concluding words, " 'About all I know is, I sort of *miss* everybody,' " amount to "an embarrassed testament of love." Following Hassan, Frederick L. Gwynn and Joseph L. Blotner in the first monograph on Salinger's work refer to Holden as a "saintly Christian person," but disappointingly they do so in only three pages of their section on *Catcher*.[44]

In the 1960s perhaps the fullest discussion of Holden as a saint figure is to be found in Jonathan Baumbach's essay "The Saint as a Young Man: A Reappraisal of *The Catcher in the Rye*."[45] Baumbach argued that Holden is involved in a central paradox: "He must leave innocence to protect innocence" and therefore suffer the effects of evil as it is experienced in this world. Although Baumbach's neo-Christian reading of Holden's character was virtually normative for this decade, Peter J. Seng's perception of Holden in "The Fallen Idol: The Immature World of Holden Caulfield" ran counter to it.[46] Instead of seeing Holden as the embodiment of saintliness, Seng judged Holden as "in some sense a tragic figure," possessed of a tragic flaw because of his inability to accept the world as it is. For Seng it is Holden's inability to compromise rather than his selflessness that is Holden's source of dignity. Both Baumbach and Seng, however, still reflected an idealized conception of Holden's character. Surely, it would have been something short of heresy to regard Holden Caulfield at this point in time as, in any appreciable way, meretricious.

To a large extent various aspects of the characterization of Holden dominated the interest of critics in the 1950s, Carl F. Strauch, however, in "Kings in the Back Row: Meaning through Structure—A Reading of Salinger's *The Catcher in the Rye*," declared that the criticism of the novel remained incomplete because it had failed to take into account "a symbolic structure of language, motif, and character" that encompasses an intense psychological drama.[47] Strauch's thesis is that Holden could be fully understood only when he is seen in relation to this structure. A convincing, insightful, and influential essay in formalist criticism, Strauch's work must be counted among the very best pieces on *Catcher* in the 1960s. Promising more than it delivers, Clinton W. Trowbridge's "The Symbolic Structure of *The Catcher in the Rye*"[48] claimed that prior to his article Salinger critics had not studied the symbolism of the novel closely, and pointed to the inadequacies of the work done by Heiserman and Miller, Fiedler[49] and Geismar on *Catcher*. Trowbridge, however, fails to acknowledge Strauch's important study of symbolic or metaphoric structure in the novel, while his own essay wanders from the intent suggested by his title. More successful than Trowbridge in exploring a pattern of interlinking symbolism is Kermit Vanderbilt in "Symbolic Resolution in *The Catcher in the Rye:* The Cap, the Carrousel, and the American West."[50] Focusing on Holden's cap and the two accompanying symbols, Vanderbilt demonstrates Salinger's self-conscious artistry in orchestrating these symbols in the text. According to Vanderbilt, "the cap works unobtrusively to suggest every aspect of Holden's thwarted search for external reality and private identity."[51] One of the more successful essays of its kind, Vanderbilt's study lucidly develops the argument implicit in the title and, like Strauch's, offers a close reading that is shrewd and convincing.

While Strauch and Vanderbilt found symbolic structures rising from the patterns intrinsic to the novel itself, John M. Howell in "Salinger in the Waste Land" claimed that Salinger consciously derived the controlling metaphor of the novel from T. S. Eliot's *The Waste Land*.[52] To establish his argument Howell appended three epigraphs to his essay from Salinger's fiction, two of which, "The Inverted Forest" and "A Perfect Day for Bananafish," do in fact make allusion to Eliot's poem. The third is a somewhat strained attempt to connect Holden's brother, D. B., to the impotent Fisher King. The substance of the article is an examination of themes and motifs from Eliot's poem reputedly adapted by Salinger for the novel. To read *Catcher* superimposed on *The Waste Land* may indeed reveal points of contact between these works, but whether or not all the parallels that Howell establishes are the result of Salinger's intentional orchestration or Howell's own ingenuity in close reading is a matter the reader alone must determine.

After ten years of spirited controversy and criticism, Salinger and his work would inevitably become the subject of a longer and more comprehensive treatment than articles or monographs could offer, and in 1963 with the appearance of Warren French's book, *J. D. Salinger*, such a study was now available, subsequently revised and published again in 1976 and followed by an altogether different version in 1988.[53] Acknowledging the difficulties of · establishing more than a rudimentary biographical section on Salinger—an exercise that proved to be even more frustrating for Ian Hamilton[54]—French nevertheless produced the best scholarly examination of Salinger's work available in the 1960s and 1970s. For those interested in the genesis of *Catcher*,

French identifies and discusses those stories leading up to the novel in which Salinger's tentative conceptions of Holden Caulfield appear.[55] Although he offers no new reading of *Catcher*, his chapter on the novel, "The Artist as a Very Nervous Young Man," attempts to fine-tune earlier structural analyses of the novel by outlining three interweaving patterns in the narrative: (1) Holden's physical breakdown; (2) his psychological breakdown; (3) and the story of Holden's maturation. It is disappointing, however, that the implications of the chapter heading, carried once again in a subsection with some variation, "*The Catcher in the Rye*, Artist in Embryo," are never really developed, for indeed Holden possesses the protean imagination of the artist and continually projects new images of himself to the reader: through the stylized manner he selectively records part of his "whole goddam autobiography,"[56] through his self-stylization in dress—"I swung the old peak way round to the back—very corny, I'll admit, but I liked it that way. I looked good in it that way" (18)—and in behavior—"I backed up a few feet and started doing this tap dance, just for the hell of it. . . . All I need's an audience. I'm an exhibitionist, 'I'm the God damn governor's son,' I said" (29). Holden's penchant for lying and "horsing around" are forms of adolescent art that playfully allow him to explore a variety of identities as a temporary respite from his own confusion, but they are also examples of a self-proclaimed exhibitionism, the manner by which Salinger's character attracts and is attractive to the reader. Holden engages our attention not only through his histrionic "cuteness,"[57] but also through his aesthetic and critical sensibility, which is itself cute. Early in Salinger criticism, Alfred Kazin observed that "we expect that boys of . . . [Holden's] age [to be] . . . consciously appealing and clever."[58] In this connection, Holden's ability to discriminate between good and bad art amounts to another, more subtle form of exhibitionism and cuteness. For Holden "the real thing" is recognized by a slight imperfection rather than by its perfection and is thereby authentically human. Consequently, the acting of the Lunts, of Sir Laurence Olivier, or the "tricky stuff" of Ernie's piano playing are for Holden versions of the "phony," somehow too perfect and unable to touch him. In his momentary guise as an adolescent Henry James, Holden is nothing if not fetching, beguiling the reader with a wisdom beyond his years. These remarks are intended to suggest a richness in Holden's characterization as artist-in-embryo that has remarkably been glossed over in the criticism on the novel during the last thirty years. Eugene McNamara's "Holden as Novelist"[59] and, to a lesser degree, Bernard S. Oldsey's "The Movies in the Rye"[60] have approached this topic, but only superficially. It has only been A. Robert Lee's essay " 'Flunking Everything Else Except English Anyway': Holden Caulfield, Author"[61] that has confronted Holden's role as artist in virtually all of its aspects and with an appropriate depth and detail.

The publication of James E. Miller, Jr.'s *J. D. Salinger* in the University of Minnesota Pamphlets on American Writers in 1965 was largely of an introductory nature, and the appearance of Salinger's name among the fifty-two other notable American writers listed in the series, situated between

Marianne Moore and Edward Taylor, served as another confirmation of his new importance and respectability in the canon of American literature.[62] There is a certain appropriateness in Miller's authorship of the pamphlet insofar as his first article with Heiserman inaugurated the beginning of serious criticism on Salinger in the 1950s. Miller's discussion of *Catcher*, reminiscent of his first article on the novel, judged *Catcher* not only as one of the funniest books in American literature but also as an influential work in the development of post–World War II "black" humor. In the 1970s Miller would again be heard from on *Catcher*, but this time in a spirited response to Carol and Richard Ohmann's Marxist critique of the novel.[63]

In the 1970s criticism of *Catcher* was put into several new perspectives, and the novel was variously read as Kafkaesque, Freudian, Marxian, and even Buddhist in substance, while the generally accepted view of Holden Caulfield's "saintliness" held by many critics in the 1950s and 1960s was challenged. Helen Weinberg in *The New Novel in America: The Kafkan Mode in Contemporary Fiction* contributed to the widening context in which Salinger in general and *Catcher* in particular would now be discussed.[64] "I have used Franz Kafka's novels," she observed, "as an index to the ways that the modern sensibility may yet write for the sake of life, not the sake of art, without self-deception or sentimentality: Kafka was the spiritual pioneer of the territory explored by the novelists of the fifties and sixties (Bellow, Mailer, Salinger, Malamud, Roth, Gold, Styron, Cassill), the territory of the quest for meaning, of the quest for the access to the spiritual world, and of the human assault on the divine."[65] In her brief remarks on *Catcher*, Weinberg argues that Holden is a protean hero, antisocial and existential, exploring the labyrinth of society—in short, that he is Kafkaesque. Although Holden's experiences may be likened to those of Joseph K. in *The Trial* or Karl Rossman in *Amerika,* Weinberg's actual discussion, as it applies to Holden, is carried by a rhetoric that never escapes from its own abstract formulations. To be fair to her thesis as it applies to Salinger, however, one must look at her analysis of *Seymour: An Introduction* to which she devotes more attention than she does to *Catcher*.

Although reading *Catcher* as one example of the Kafkan mode in American literature may have contributed to the increasing recognition of Salinger's relation to the modern imagination, the alignment of *Catcher* with other American novels in the Kafkan mode established no new critical breakthrough. Those in the 1970s and beyond who explored the psychological dimensions of Holden's experience offered more tangible insights to his character, or at least challenged critics to reexamine previously held conceptions about Holden's problems. For David Burrows in "Allie and Phoebe: Death in Love in J. D. Salinger's *The Catcher in the Rye*" the death of Allie, Holden's brother, is seen as the primal event in Holden's life that governs his unconscious, to the extent of tainting all of his adult experience with associations of death.[66] Although modest in scope, Burrows's essay drew attention to a topic that had not been fully treated in Salinger criticism and that would surface more frequently in subsequent articles in conjunction with different theoretical approaches to the novel.

On a more ambitious scale, James Bryan's *PMLA* article "The Psychological Structure of *The Catcher in the Rye*" advanced "a full fledged psychoanalytic reading" in which he discusses, in passing, Holden's association with sex and death as a reflection of an underlying guilt and Holden's unconscious sexual feeling for his sister, Phoebe.[67] According to Bryan, it is precisely this repression in Holden that leads to his sexual ambivalence toward all women. Examining the very same evidence that Bryan uses to establish his Freudian reading, Dennis Vail, in a rejoinder, countered with the argument that Holden shows no uneasiness about Phoebe in the bedroom scene when the two dance, and even when he pinches her behind, proposing that such contact is inherently innocent in the terms of its presentation.[68] For Vail, "the association of sex with death is not merely Holden's but the novel's." In the 1980s these and related issues would be confronted from a postmodern Freudian perspective and employ a different set of critical concepts.

Moving from Holden's psyche to Salinger's representation of society, Carol and Richard Ohmann examined *Catcher* from a Marxian perspective in their coauthored essay, "Reviewers, Critics, and *The Catcher in the Rye*."[69] Recounting the variety of critical approaches to the novel in over twenty years of criticism, the Ohmanns contend that *Catcher* has never properly been put into sharp critical focus because critics had written about Holden in generalizations that detached him from a social context. The Ohmanns asserted that although critics like James E. Miller, Jr., perceive that Holden is sickened by his experience with phoniness, they fail to take into account that "phoniness" is rooted in the economic and social arrangements of capitalism. Not only is Holden revolted by society, so the argument goes, but he also revolts against it, against bourgeois life in the United States around 1950 as the novel represents it.

In replying to the Ohmanns' criticism, James E. Miller, Jr., judged their reading of *Catcher* simplistic, while acknowledging that the political and economic implications of the novel had been slighted over the years. For Miller the restructuring of society would not cure Holden of his spiritual malaise, an inevitable consequence of his discovery of the human condition—sexuality, age, and death. Finally, Miller concludes that even in a socialist utopia love would have to be the glue that binds people together. Continuing the debate, the Ohmanns responded to Miller's criticism with the observation that adolescent behavior is not a universal condition but a result of the historical moment: "that Holden's experiences of old age, physical repulsiveness, sex, aloneness, and isolation and even death are embedded in his full experience of society."[70] For the Ohmanns, the disagreement with Miller was sharp and fundamental, and they argued that Miller's universals were not universals at all but "a special vocabulary of bourgeois thought." The issues that the Ohmanns raised were among the most important in the history of Salinger criticism, as well as for literary criticism in general, but the debate between the Ohmanns and Miller ended with the Ohmanns reply to Miller in *Critical Inquiry*.

Both Miller and the Ohmanns, despite their radically differing views of *Catcher*, generally accepted Holden at face value—as a painfully innocent and vulnerable adolescent either because his encounter with adult reality in its various forms was too overwhelming for him to bear or because his exposure to the phoniness inherent in an exploitive bourgeois society had bruised his psyche. Duane Edwards in "Holden Caulfield: " 'Don't Ever Tell Anybody Anything' " persuasively argued for another image of Holden, an ironic Holden who "shares in the phoniness he loathes," and for Edwards Holden inescapably "lives by his unconscious needs and not the value he espouses."[71] Consequently, Holden demonstrates his own capacity for exhibitionism and voyeurism while condemning it in others.

If it was time to revise or reassess the image of Holden Caulfield, surely it was also the right moment to reexamine *Catcher* as a whole, not only in the light of the amassed criticism but also in the context of the work subsequent to the novel, or so Gerald Rosen suggested in his essay, "A Retrospective Look at *The Catcher in the Rye*.[72] For Rosen, Salinger's work after *Catcher* is caught up in Eastern thought and religion, particularly Buddhism, and although *Catcher* itself does not explicitly address Buddhism, according to Rosen Holden's encounter with old age, sickness, and death are experiences as formative in his life as they were in the life of Buddha. Thus the renunciation of illusion so characteristic of Buddha is also a dimension of Holden's characterization that links *Catcher* much more closely with Salinger's later and more explicitly religious fiction, evolving in conjunction with Salinger's mythical Glass family. In finding a unity in *Catcher* and Salinger's later work, Rosen was, in fact, attempting to locate in it what Joseph J. Moldenhauer had tried to discover in all of Poe's work in the late 1960s—an intellectual coherence virtually governing it throughout, which critics had somehow failed to notice.[73]

In the meantime, however, "traditional" criticism continued in the 1970s and 1980s—as it had done in the 1950s and 1960s—to establish points of contact between *Catcher* and other works of fiction. Too often, however, these connections appeared superficial, as in the case of James E. Miller, Jr.'s first article on *Catcher*. But occasionally an essay would explore the relation of *Catcher* to another work of fiction—a proposed analogue of source—whose discussion carried within it unusual depth, plausibility, and significance. Lilian Furst's "Dostoyevsky's *Notes from Underground* and Salinger's *The Catcher in the Rye*" is just such an essay, and one of the better examples in the 1970s of a fruitful comparative analysis involving Salinger's novel against which similar comparative studies involving *Catcher* might be measured.[74] While acknowledging Salinger's roots to a native American tradition, Furst explores the connection between *Catcher* and *Notes from Underground*, and demonstrates, despite the differences of time and place that separate these works, striking resemblances in characterization, theme, rhetoric, and narrative form. When Furst concludes that *Catcher* can be read profitably within the context of world literature, as well as within the American literary tradition, her contention is not gratuitous, for her clear, detailed, and illuminating points of contact between Holden Caulfield and Dostoyevski's underground man underscore her assertion that Salinger's imagination in *Catcher* reveals a sensibility as modern as that of Sartre, Camus, or Svevo.

By the end of the 1970s the critical spectrum on *Catcher* seemed as broad as one might wish, or even possibly imagine, and the critical obsession with the novel began to level off, stimulating fewer superfluous pieces in the way of minor notes and reassessments so characteristic of the 1960s. Yet almost as though he were bearing witness to the indestructibleness of Salinger as the 1970s came to an end, James Lundquist in his book *J. D. Salinger* offered, as it were, a summing up of the criticism on *Catcher* in his chapter "Against Obscenity: *The Catcher in the Rye*."[75] Lundquist provides a synthesis of a number of critical positions taken on the novel over the years, but he goes on to propose that "the climate of ideas surrounding the novel" has been ignored or only treated superficially. It is only in the last third of his discussion of *Catcher* that Lundquist actually comes to grips with his thesis, arguing that the novel should be read against the intellectual currents of the 1950s embodied in the work of such figures as Margaret Mead, Ruth Benedict, Joseph Campbell, C. G. Jung, C. Wright Mills, and David Riesman, among others. The reader, however, is left with the impression that Lundquist has invoked these intellectual muses of the 1950s in the hope of renewing discussion of *Catcher* at a time when it had become increasingly difficult to say anything new about it.

During the 1980s the critical formulations that had been developing in the 1970s—structuralism, Lacanian criticism, gender criticism, and deconstruction—not only offered new and elaborate frameworks in which *Catcher* might be discussed, but also raised questions about the very motivations that had driven critics of earlier decades to write so persistently about the novel. Nevertheless, when critical or scholarly writing applied itself to questions other than an interpretation of *Catcher*, surely by now an exercise in redundancy, one might be less dubious of the result. For example, influence studies in which *Catcher* was recognized as a source of cross-cultural inspiration for the fiction of other writers sometimes proved to be mutually illuminating. The recent analyses produced by Walter Riedel[76] and Siegfried Mandel[77] explore the impact of *Catcher* on the postwar German literary imagination.

While Riedel considered the stylistic effectiveness of Heinrich Böll's translation of Salinger's novel, offering sample texts from the original and the translation for purposes of comparison, Mandel in a less technical and more wide-ranging discussion assesses the impact of Salinger's language and style—and Holden himself as a model of rebellion—for Böll and the East German Ulrich Plenzdorf, concluding that *Catcher* was a liberating influence on both writers at a time when each was seeking to escape the constraints of German formalism and earnestness, as well as the constraints of a recent German past that had insisted on unswerving loyalty to authority. One may hope that such revealing influence studies like Mandel's will continue, despite the changing trends of criticism, since *Catcher*, as the translations into nearly every major foreign languague testify, speaks with a voice that seems to be familiar, regardless of the language in which it is heard. Inevitably, future influence studies will represent an increasing proportion of Salinger criticism involving *Catcher*, since Holden Caulfield has undergone so many different cultural transformations.

Understandably, critics in the 1980s generally recognized that another close reading of *Catcher* was not what the decade needed, unless it offered the possibility of a new and potentially illuminating theoretical framework. As has been suggested earlier, A. Robert Lee's recent close reading of *Catcher* is a notable exception.[78] Consequently, the discussions of the novel, apart from those that were turned out as teaching aids, seemed to be of two distinctly different kinds: the one that was motivated largely by personal nostalgia, and the other that was the application of a postmodern critical theory. In the first instance Sanford Pinsker's essay "*The Catcher in the Rye* and All: Is the Age of Formative Books Over?" questions whether books still influence behavior, as they admittedly did for him in his own youth.[79] In the second instance, the recent work of Hubert Zapf and James M. Mellard illustrates the potential that some of the newer theoretical paradigms have for testing previously held assumptions about Holden Caulfield and the novel as a whole.

Zapf's short study "Logical Action in Salinger's *The Catcher in the Rye*," uses the *Catcher* as a way of illustrating the validity of structuralism itself as a descriptive device that explains the sequence and construction of a literary work.[80] For Zapf structuralism is a tool by which the basic principles of Salinger's compositional method are made visible. Accordingly, the representation of Holden's psychic state is logically connected to his relationships in the world, and Zapf supplies a chart in which Holden's psychic state and the relationships are represented as the governing structure of the novel, presumably making Salinger's compositional strategy more transparent.

The very word "structure" in the title of an academic article suggests a grasp of the principle in which a work is organized as though it were a Rosetta stone, the essential key by which the work is properly understood, and periodically commentators have variously ascribed different structures to the novel, sometimes a symbolic structure, either intrinsic or extrinsic to the novel, and at other times a psychological structure. Adding a new dimension to the critical writing on psychological structure of the novel, James M. Mellard's essay "The Disappearing Subject: A Lacanian Reading of *The Catcher in the Rye*" introduced a new paradigm against which the reader might perceive Holden's unconscious relationships.[81] Mellard's essay must be counted among the most sophisticated and the most demanding of theoretical approaches in its elaboration of an underlying structure based on Lacan's adaptation of Freud. Although both David Burrows[82] and Haviland Miller[83] considered the traumatic impact of Allie's death as the key to Holden's behavior, their approaches did not fully assess its consequences on Holden's conscious and unconscious relationships. Since the Lacanian terminology in Mellard's text and in his notes has not become as commonplace as classical Freudian terminology, however, the reader new to Lacan must be willing to risk what some might consider a painful rite of initiation.

While Mellard's elaborate Lacanian treatment of *Catcher* may well represent the outer limits of psychoanalytic criticism, Mary Suzanne Schriber, in a less demanding approach, confronts the psychology of the male critic in *his* response to *Catcher*, as that psychology is a reflection of gender. In her essay "Holden Caulfield, C'est Moi" Schriber asserts that the critics who have written about *Catcher* over the years have been predominantly male, narcissistically fall in love with Holden as a version of themselves, and regard his problems as unique to adolescent males.[84] Schriber cites several critics who confessed to having deep personal responses to the novel and to Holden himself when they first read *Catcher* as adolescents. As a result, Schriber argues, these critics have presumed that Holden's male adolescent experience is universal, and on that basis they have elevated the novel to the rank of a classic. Thus Schriber's probing into the psychology of the reader introduces a new turn in Salinger criticism as it edges toward the next decade.

If the 1980s revealed a broadening of the critical spectrum on *Catcher*, the decade also brought with it a badly needed research tool for those students and critics engaged in work on Salinger's fiction, as well as a biography. Jack R. Sublette's *J. D. Salinger: An Annotated Bibliography, 1938–1981*, is a gold mine of bibliographical information relating to *Catcher*, and includes reviews, articles, chapters in books, foreign criticism, translations of the novel into foreign languages, as well as peripheral writing to *Catcher* and Salinger himself.[85] In 1988 Ian Hamilton's biography *In Search of J. D. Salinger* was published after litigation initiated by Salinger against Random House prevented Hamilton's original biography, "A Writing Life," from being distributed.[86] Prior to Hamilton's biography, the chapter in Warren French's *J. D. Salinger*, appropriately titled " 'That David Copperfield Kind of Crap,' "[87] was the best biographical resource available without Salinger's assistance, but even that resource had to be considered cautiously inasmuch as it contained unauthenticated statements concerning Salinger's mother and grandfather.[88]

French wisely observed in the conclusion to the biographical chapter of his book that if a writer truly wished to remain anonymous, he ought to adopt a pseudonym in order to avoid an invasion of his privacy, a statement that may well have given Hamilton an added sense of justification on behalf of his own pursuit of Salinger's life. But aside from the legitimacy of literary biography as a genre—despite the reservations of such writers as Mordecai Richler, Bernard Malamud, and J. D. Salinger on the subject[89] (at least when their own lives have been the objects of scrutiny)—Hamilton seems to have been caught up by motives, as he himself confesses, that were at times less than scholarly and occasionally accompanied by an aggression that is difficult for him to repress. In pursuing Salinger's life, and citing his own recent involvement in it, Hamilton's biography sometimes sounds like a work of fiction with Hamilton himself as one of the protagonists. Indeed, the reader sometimes wonders who is the "hero" and who the antagonist. Consequently, the legitimate critical interest that one might have in how closely Salinger's own life contributes to *Catcher*, or how much is transformed in the artistic process, is compromised not only by Salinger's uncooperativeness but also by Hamilton's own annoyed response to it, carried in a tone that is reminiscent of a Holden Caulfield with whom Hamilton admittedly identifies and from time to time sounds like.

Although Hamilton was denied the use of Salinger's letters written between 1939 and 1962, many of which were quoted in the original biography, he was obliged to rescue his enterprise by approaching Salinger's life through contacting a few of those individuals with whom Salinger had either a personal or a professional relationship. Thus Hamilton's detective work brought him in touch with students who had been with Salinger at Ursinus College, where Salinger was an undergraduate, as well as such notable figures in publishing as Robert Giroux and Hamish Hamilton. Limited in scope by the injunction of the court, as well as colored by Hamilton's own sense of personal injury, the biography, by the very fact of its unavoidable omissions, nourishes the continuation of the Salinger mystique, even more than it adds to an understanding of the life. In his lawsuit against Random House and Ian Hamilton—copies of which the publisher has on file[90]— Salinger was successful in erecting a barrier that would keep the public at some distance from his life, to the extent that his life could be glimpsed in his letters. As Mark Pachter has observed in *Telling Lives*, "If certain lives have the power to touch and transform our own . . . to exalt or terrify us, then we, with the biographer as our representative, have a right to make sense of those lives, to their inmost nature."[91]

The issue as it pertains to Hamilton's biography of Salinger is perhaps reduced to its essence by Hamilton himself when he says: "Let it be confessed . . . [Salinger] is a writer whose work is more than usually powered by autobiography. It actually admits to being so."[92] Perhaps more than any other figure in twentieth-century American literature, Holden Caulfield, as a fragment of J. D. Salinger, has touched if not actually transformed the lives of those who have discovered him, if the testimony of one's students in the sophisticated decade of the 1980s, as well as those in earlier decades, is any measure. To desire some insight into the life and imagination behind such a powerful creation may be of secondary importance to experiencing that creation, but it is an urge that nevertheless follows close behind. With respect to *Catcher* Hamilton's index contains twenty-seven page references, the longest one running to nine pages of commentary, and occasionally they do, in fact, address the Salinger–Caulfield connection.

Other important aspects of Salinger's life, however, remain locked away from Hamilton and may be inaccessible for some time to come. As the son of a Jewish father and Scottish mother, Salinger leaves no trace of ethnic residue in his fiction, with the possible exception of the Glass family, an omission that seems most curious in the light of Hamilton's assertion that the fiction is "powered by autobiography." The emotional distance of Salinger from his own family history, his hostility to the cultural establishment, and the motives that govern his interior life make us pause to consider whether it is still J. D. Salinger about whom we speculate or Holden Caulfield.

No completely satisfactory explanation has been advanced to explain Salinger's transformation from a writer of fiction in *Catcher* to a spiritual guru after it, a change that many of his readers have found regrettable. While Holden Caulfield may not be as fully in and of the world as Bellow's Augie March, his alienation and anguish have an authority about them and continue to touch us, even though their sources in the novel remain oblique. Holden does return to the fallen world with all of its imperfections after his convalescence, and the changed Holden is now capable of expressing sentiments redolent of human love and reconciliation. But if Holden is, in a Wordsworthian sense, father to the man—rather to the author—it is ironically the earlier Holden who contributes to the making of the later J. D. Salinger, the Holden characterized by a "religious" sensibility and a taste for reclusiveness. Like Malamud's Arthur Fidelman in *Pictures of Fidelman*, who responds to W. B. Yeats's famous lines "The Intellect of man is forced to choose / Perfection of the life or work"[93] by wanting "both," Salinger also desires both. Hamilton observes that shortly after the publication of *Catcher*, Salinger began to regard his art and his life as religious vocations, each intertwined with the other.[94] In cultivating a fiction in which the felt life was almost entirely subordinated to religious vision—*Franny and Zooey, Seymour: An Introduction, Raise High the Roofbeams, Carpenters,* and finally, "Hapworth 16, 1924"— Salinger's characters, in their preciousness, sound less human, and begin to resemble Poe's spiritualized figures in the philosophical dialogues,[95] purged of all that is mundane and earthly. In *Catcher,* however, Salinger does capture the image, the imagination, and the emotions of an urban American adolescent in his time and place, as no one else before or since, and for that we still must give him tribute.

I am grateful to Kris C. McCusker of Norlin Library at the University of Colorado at Boulder for her efficient and untiring bibliographical assistance, and to my wife, Kathleen A. Salzberg, for her astute editorial suggestions.

JOEL SALZBERG

University of Colorado at Denver

Notes

1. For the sake of convenience, I will henceforth refer to *The Catcher in the Rye* as *Catcher*.

2. Sanford Pinsker, "*The Catcher in the Rye* and All: Is the Age of Formative Books Over?," *Georgia Review* 40, no. 4 (1986): 966.

3. Ian Hamilton, *In Search of J. D. Salinger* (New York: Random House, 1988), 4–5.

4. The history of the censorship surrounding *Catcher*, particularly in school settings, is amply covered in the citations supplied by Jack R. Sublette in *J. D. Salinger: An Annotated Bibliography, 1938–1981* (New York: Garland, 1984), 157–68. Holden's vernacular easily lends itself to parody by the sympathetic as well as the unsympathetic reader. The title of Sanford Pinsker's article (note 1) is an example of how even a friendly critic of the novel cannot resist the temptation to engage in parody, at least in passing. On the other hand, James Stern's early review of *Catcher* in the *New York Times* (15 July 1951, sec. 7, 15) is written in Holden's language as a way of deflating the book in lieu of responsible critical observation.

5. See Ian Hamilton's interview with Leila Hadley in *In Search of J. D. Salinger*, 126–27.

6. See, for example, Robert Coles, "Reconsideration: J. D. Salinger," *New Republic* 168, no. 3042 (1973): 30–32; Preston Thomas Roberts, Jr., "*The Catcher in the Rye* Revisited," *The Cresset* 40 (November/December 1976): 6–10; John Romano, "Salinger Was Playing Our Song," *New York Times Book Review*, 3 June 1987, 11, 48–49. Adam Moss, "*Catcher* Comes of Age," *Esquire* 96, no. 6 (December 1981): 56–60; Terry Teachout, "Salinger Then and Now," *Commentary* 84, no. 3 (June 1987): 61–64.

7. For discussion of the Holden Caulfield figure in Salinger's fiction prior to *Catcher*, see Warren French, *J. D. Salinger* (Boston: Twayne, 1976), 64–67.

8. French's chapter, "The Artist as a Very Nervous Young Man," in *J. D. Salinger*, often provokes but fails to satisfy the reader's curiosity about Holden. For example, in the subsection of that chapter, "*The Catcher in the Rye*—Artist in Embryo," French observes that "the novel is about a young man with an artistic bent" (124), but nothing more of Holden is said in this connection. As I suggest later in this discussion, Holden's creative imagination and critical sensibility have yet to be the subject of an extended analysis, with the exception of A. Robert Lee's article in this volume.

9. See Francis E. Kearn, "Salinger and Golding: Conflict on the Campus," *America* 108 (26 January 1963): 136–39, and Moira Walsh, "David and Lisa," *America* 108 (26 January 1963): 154.

10. Dr. Rubin's case study was actually called *Jordi: Lisa and David* (New York: Ballantine, 1962).

11. Walsh, "David and Lisa," 154.

12. Review of "David and Lisa," *Time* 80 (28 December 1962): 60.

13. See James Bryan, "The Psychological Structure of *The Catcher in the Rye*," *PMLA* 89, no. 5 (October 1974): 165–74, and Dennis Vail, "Holden and Psychoanalysis" 91, no. 3 (June 1976): 120–21. Both reprinted in this volume.

14. Anne L. Goodman, review of *The Catcher in the Rye*, *New Republic* 125 (16 July 1951): 20–21. Reprinted in this volume.

15. Ernest Jones, "Case History of All of Us," *Nation* 173 (1 September 1951): 176. Reprinted in this volume.

16. William Poster, "Tomorrow's Child," *Commentary* 13 (January 1952): 90–92. Reprinted in this volume.

17. Carol Ohmann and Richard Ohmann, "Reviewers, Critics, and *The Catcher in the Rye*," *Critical Inquiry* 3, no. 1 (Autumn 1976): 15–37. Reprinted in this volume.

18. Harrison Smith, "Manhattan Ulysses, Junior," *Saturday Review* 34 (14 July 1951): 12–13. Reprinted in this volume.

19. "Phoenix Burning," *Saturday Night* 66 (28 August 1951): 29.

20. T. Morris Longstreth, review of *The Catcher in the Rye*, *Christian Science Monitor*, 19 July 1951, 11. Reprinted in this volume.

21. Review of *The Catcher in the Rye*, *Catholic World* 174 (November 1951): 154. Reprinted in this volume.

22. J. D. Salinger, *Nine Stories* (Boston: Little, Brown, 1953).

23. Eudora Welty, review of *Nine Stories*, *New York Times Book Review*, 5 April 1953, sec. 7, 4.

24. For a discussion of the publishing history of *Catcher*, see Robert Gutwillig, "Everybody's Caught *The Catcher in the Rye*," *New York Times Book Review*, 15 January 1961, 38–39.

25. R. W. B. Lewis, *The American Adam: Innocence, Tragedy, and Tradition in the Nineteenth Century* (Chicago: University of Chicago Press, 1955).

26. Richard Chase, *The American Novel and Its Tradition* (New York: Doubleday, 1957).

27. R. W. B. Lewis, *The Picaresque Saint: Representative Figures in Contemporary Fiction* (Philadelphia: J. B. Lippincott, 1959).

28. Arthur Heiserman and James E. Miller, Jr., "J. D. Salinger: Some Crazy Cliff," *Western Humanities Review* 10, no. 2 (Spring 1956): 129–37. Reprinted in this volume.

29. Ibid., 129.

30. Charles Kaplan, "Holden and Huck: The Odysseys of Youth," *College English* 18, no. 2 (November 1956): 76–80. Reprinted in this volume.

31. Edgar Branch, "Mark Twain and J. D. Salinger: A Study in Literary Continuity," *American Quarterly* 9 (Summer 1957): 144–58.

32. John W. Aldridge, *In Search of Heresy: American Literature in an Age of Conformity* (New York: McGraw-Hill, 1956), 130–31.

33. Maxwell Geismar, "J. D. Salinger: The Wise Child and the *New Yorker* School of Fiction," *American Moderns: From Rebellion to Conformity* (New York: Hill & Wang, 1958), 198–99.

34. See Harvey Swados, "Must Writers Be Characters?," *Saturday Review* 43 (1 October 1960): 12–14, 50.

35. See George Steiner, "The Salinger Industry," *Nation* 199 (14 November 1959): 360–63.

36. Charles H. Kegel, "Incommunicability in Salinger's *The Catcher in the Rye*," *Western Humanities Review* 11 (Spring 1957): 188–90; see also Winston Weathers, "J. D. Salinger and the 'Nice Conversation' " in *The Broken Word: The Communication Pathos in Modern Literature* (New York: Gordon & Breach, 1981), 171–85.

37. Donald P. Costello, "The Language of *The Catcher in the Rye*," *American Speech* 34, no. 2 (October 1959): 172–81. Reprinted in this volume.

38. Steiner, "The Salinger Industry," 362.

39. See William F. Belcher and James W. Lee, eds., *Salinger and the Critics* (Belmont, Calif.: Wadsworth, 1962); Henry Anatole Grunwald, *A Critical and Personal Portrait* (New York: Harper & Brothers, 1962); Marvin Laser and Norman Fruman, eds., *Studies in J. D. Salinger: Reviews, Essays and Critiques of "The Catcher in the Rye" and Other Fiction* (New York: Odyssey Press, 1963); Malcolm M. Marsden, ed., *If You Really Want to Know: A Catcher Casebook* (Chicago: Scott, Foresman, 1963); Harold P. Simson and Philip E. Hager, eds., *Clamor vs. Criticism* (Boston: D. C. Heath, 1963).

40. "Special Number: Salinger," *Wisconsin Studies in Contemporary Literature* 4, no. 1 (Winter 1963).

41. *Modern Fiction Studies* 12, no. 3 (Autumn 1966).

42. Ihab Hassan, "J. D. Salinger: Rare Quixotic Gesture," *Western Review* 21 (Summer 1957), 261–28.

43. Ibid., 264.

44. Frederick L. Gwynn and Joseph L. Blotner, *The Fiction of J. D. Salinger* (Pittsburgh: University of Pittsburgh Press, 1958), 28–31.

45. Jonathan Baumbach, "The Saint as Young Man: A Reappraisal of *The Catcher in the Rye*," *Modern Language Quarterly* 25, no. 4 (December 1964): 461–72. Reprinted in this volume.

46. Peter J. Seng, "The Fallen Idol: The Immature World of Holden Caulfield," *College English* 32, no. 3 (December 1961): 203–9.

47. Carl F. Strauch, "Kings in the Back Row: Meaning through Structure—A Reading of Salinger's *The Catcher in the Rye*," *Wisconsin Studies in Contemporary Literature* 2, no. 1 (Winter 1961): 5–30. Reprinted in this volume.

48. Clinton W. Trowbridge, "The Symbolic Structure of *The Catcher in the Rye*," *Sewanee Review* 74 (July–September 1966): 681–93.

49. See Leslie Fiedler's earliest observations on *Catcher* in "Boys Will be Boys!," *New Yorker*, 28 April 1958, 23–26.

50. Kermit Vanderbilt, "Symbolic Resolution in *The Catcher in the Rye:* The Cap, the Carrousel, and the American West," *Humanities Review* 17, no. 3 (Summer 1963): 271–77.

51. Ibid., 271.

52. John M. Howell, "Salinger in the Waste Land," *Modern Fiction Studies* 12, no. 3 (Autumn 1966): 367–75. Reprinted in this volume.

53. French, *J. D. Salinger*. In his revised book, *J. D. Salinger Revisited* (Boston: Twayne, 1988), French, while recapitulating the salient biographical and critical issues of his previous books, also responds to some of the recent interpretation surrounding Salinger and his work. With regard to *Catcher* in particular, French considers (46) its underlying universal patterns perhaps the most important reason for its continuing ability to engage the contemporary reader.

54. Hamilton, *In Search of J. D. Salinger*.

55. French, *J. D. Salinger*, 64–67.

56. J. D. Salinger, *The Catcher in the Rye* (New York: Bantam Books, 1964), 1. Subsequent page references in the text are to this edition.

57. Alfred Kazin, "J. D. Salinger: 'Everybody's Favorite,'" *Atlantic* 208 (August 1961): 27–31, was probably the first critic to perceive how "cuteness" is an integral part of Salinger's characterization of his fictional children and young adults, particularly in the case of Holden Caulfield.

58. Ibid., 29.

59. Eugene McNamara, "Holden as Novelist," *English Journal* 54, no. 3 (March 1965): 166–70.

60. Bernard S. Oldsey, "The Movies in the Rye," *College English* 23, no. 3 (December 1961): 209–15. Reprinted in this volume.

61. A. Robert Lee's essay " 'Flunking Everything Else Except English Anyway': Holden Caulfield, Author" was written specifically for this volume.

62. James E. Miller, Jr., *J. D. Salinger* (Minneapolis: University of Minnesota Press, 1965).

63. See James E. Miller, Jr., "*Catcher* in and out of History," *Critical Inquiry* 3, no. 3 (Spring 1977): 599–603. Reprinted in this volume.

64. Helen Weinberg, *The New Novel in America: The Kafkan Mode in Contemporary Fiction* (Ithaca, N.Y.: Cornell University Press, 1970).

65. Ibid., x.

66. David Burrows, "Allie and Phoebe: Death in Love in J. D. Salinger's *The Catcher in the Rye*," in *Private Dealings: Modern American Writers in Search of Integrity* (Stockholm: Almqvist and Wiksell, 1969).

67. Bryan, "The Psychological Structure of *The Catcher in the Rye*," 1065–74.

68. Vail, "Holden Caulfield and Psychoanalysis," 120–21.

69. Ohmann and Ohmann, "Reviewers, Critics, and *The Catcher in the Rye*," 15–37.

70. Carol Ohmann and Richard Ohmann, "Universals and the Historically Particular," *Critical Inquiry* 3, no. 4 (Summer 1977): 773–77. Reprinted in this volume.

71. Duane Edwards, "Holden Caulfield: 'Don't Ever Tell Anybody Anything,' " *English Literary History* 44, no. 3 (Fall 1977): 554–65. Reprinted in this volume.

72. Gerald Rosen, "A Retrospective Look at *The Catcher in the Rye*," *American Quarterly* 29, no. 5 (Winter 1977): 547–62. Reprinted in this volume.

73. See Joseph J. Moldenhauer, "Murder as a Fine Art: Connections between Poe's Aesthetics, Psychology, and Moral Vision," *PMLA* 83 (1968): 284–97.

74. Lilian Furst, "Dostoyevsky's *Notes from Underground* and Salinger's *The Catcher in the Rye*," *Canadian Review of Comparative Literature* 5, no. 1 (Winter 1978): 72–85. Reprinted in this volume.

75. James Lundquist, *J. D. Salinger* (New York: Frederick Ungar, 1979), 37–68.

76. Walter Riedel, "Some German Ripples of Holden Caulfield's Goddam Autobiography: On Translating and Adapting J. D. Salinger's *The Catcher in the Rye*," *Canadian Review of Comparative Literature* 7, no. 2 (Spring 1980): 196–205.

77. Siegfried Mandel's essay "Salinger in Continental Jeans. The Liberation of Böll and Other Germans" was written specifically for this volume.

78. A. Robert Lee, "Flunking Everything Else Except English Anyway."

79. Pinsker, "*The Catcher in the Rye* and All," 953–67.

80. Hubert Zapf, "Logical Action in Salinger's *The Catcher in the Rye*," *College Literature* 12, no. 3 (1985): 266–71.

81. James M. Mellard's essay "The Disappearing Subject: A Lacanian Reading of *The Catcher in the Rye*" was written specifically for this volume.

82. Burrows, "Allie and Phoebe," 106–14.

83. Edwin Haviland Miller, "In Memoriam: Allie Caulfield in *The Catcher in the Rye*" *Mosaic* 15, no. 1 (Winter 1982): 129–40.

84. Mary Suzanne Schriber's essay "Holden Caulfield, C'est Moi" was written specifically for this volume.

85. Sublette, *J. D. Salinger: An Annotated Bibliography*.

86. According to a press release from Random House, bound galleys of "A Writing Life" had already been mailed to reviewers on 7 May 1986.

87. French, *J. D. Salinger*, "That David Copperfield Kind of Crap," 21–35.

88. In his biographical chapter on Salinger, French indicates that Salinger's father, Sol Salinger, was said to have been the son of a rabbi and that Salinger's Scots-born mother, Marie Jillich, had changed her name to Miriam. This information was attributed to an article by Ernest Havemann, "The Search for the Mysterious J. D. Salinger: The Recluse in the Rye" (*Life*, 3 November 1961), but Havemann, according to Ian Hamilton, was never able to verify the source.

89. Mordecai Richler's review of Ian Hamilton's *In Search of J. D. Salinger* in the *New York Times Book Review* (5 June 1988, 7) is illustrative of the sentiments on literary biography reflected in statements on the subject by both Malamud and Salinger. Richler asserts that literary biography is usually a dubious enterprise and tends to satisfy a taste for gossip rather

than to illuminate a writer's work. According to Richler, "the most prevalent form of literary biography does not set out to illuminate but to level."

90. Annik LaFarge, the publicity manager at Random House, kindly made available to me a chronological synopsis of the *Salinger* v. *Random House* and Ian Hamilton litigation, along with transcripts of the hearings.

91. Mark Packer, *Telling Lives: The Biographers' Art* (Philadelphia: University of Pennsylvania Press, 1981), 6.

92. Hamilton, *In Search of J. D. Salinger*, 11.

93. From "The Choice," in Yeats's *The Winding Stair and Other Poems* (1933).

94. See Hamilton, *In Search of J. D. Salinger*, 126.

95. See Edgar Allan Poe's "The Conversation of Eiros and Charmion," "The Colloquy of Monos and Una," or "The Power of Words."

The Fifties

Mad about Children

Anne L. Goodman*

In "A Perfect Day for Bananafish," the first of J. D. Salinger's remarkable short stories to attract widespread attention, a young veteran recovering from a nervous breakdown in Florida takes a little girl out swimming, in a charmingly described interlude, and then goes to his hotel room and shoots himself when he is confronted by his shallow wife. In "For Esmé—With Love and Squalor," one of the best and most moving of all his stories, an American soldier in Germany suffering from an extreme case of combat fatigue is brought back by a message from a little girl he had met in England. And in the climactic scene of his first novel, *The Catcher in the Rye*, the sixteen-year-old hero who has been wandering around New York alone for three days, ever since his expulsion from boarding school, in a state somewhere between reality and unreality, abandons his dream of running away to the West and goes home (and subsequently to a sanitarium) when his ten-year-old sister, whom he has met secretly, is clearly broken-hearted at the thought of his leaving.

In all three cases the children and the boy-men are exceedingly well done. In each case, despite the similarity and situation, they are quite different and distinct individuals. The final scene in *The Catcher in the Rye* is as good as anything that Salinger has written, which means very good indeed. So are a number of other episodes. But the book as a whole is disappointing, and not merely because it is a reworking of a theme that one begins to suspect must obsess the author. Holden Caulfield, the main character who tells his own story, is an extraordinary portrait, but there is too much of him. He describes himself early on and, with the sureness of a wire recording, he remains strictly in character throughout:

> I shook my head. I shake my head quite a lot. "Boy!" I said. I also say "Boy!" quite a lot. Partly because I have a lousy vocabulary and partly because I act quite young for my age sometimes. I was sixteen then, and I'm seventeen now, and sometimes I act like I'm about thirteen. It's really ironical because I'm six foot two and I have gray hair. I really do. The one side of my head—the right side—is full of millions of gray hairs. I've had

* Reprinted by permission from the *New Republic* 125 (16 July 1951): 20–21.

them ever since I was a kid. And yet I still act sometimes like I was only about twelve.

In the course of 277 pages the reader wearies of this kind of explicitness, repetition and adolescence, exactly as one would weary of Holden himself. And this reader at least suffered from an irritated feeling that Holden was not quite so sensitive and perceptive as he, and his creator, thought he was. In any case he is so completely self-centered that the other characters who wander through the book—with the notable exception of his sister Phoebe— have nothing like his authenticity. *The Catcher in the Rye* is a brilliant tour-de-force, but in a writer of Salinger's undeniable talent one expects something more.

Case History of All of Us   Ernest Jones*

Echoes reach me of the popularity of "The Catcher in the Rye." Why has this unpretentious, mildly affecting chronicle of a few days in the life of a disturbed adolescent been read with enthusiasm by Book-of-the-Month Club and lending-library adults ordinarily concerned with fiction as a frivolous diversion or as a source of lofty, incontrovertible platitudes?

Entirely, I think, because, like many contemporary and highly praised novels written on the assumption that the mere record of budding sensitiveness automatically results in fiction, the book is a mirror. It reflects something not at all rich and strange but what every sensitive sixteen-year-old since Rousseau has felt, and of course what each one of us is certain he has felt.

Mr. Salinger attempts to make his story specific, but it is constantly escaping into generalities. Holden Caulfield is friendly, "democratic," well-bred, and snobbish in ways peculiar to adolescence. He has the beginnings of taste; "corny" is a term frequent in his speech. A virgin, he never knows exactly what any girl may be expecting of him and is afraid to make love to the prostitute supplied by an obliging bellhop. He mistakes whatever is spontaneous in his behavior for madness: "But I'm crazy. I swear to God I am"; if he acts on impulse he feels guilty, though also boastful: "I'm the most terrific liar you ever saw in your life." Bravado and buffoonery imperfectly disguise his conviction of madness and guilt.

His sense of alienation is almost complete—from parents, from friends, from society in general as represented by the prep school from which he has been expelled and the night-club and hotel world of New York in which he endures a week-end exile while hiding out from his family. With his alien-

* Reprinted from the *Nation* 173, no. 9 (1 September 1951): 176, by permission of the Nation Company, Inc. Copyright 1951.

ation go assorted hatreds—of the movies, of night clubs, of social and intellectual pretension, and so on. And physical disgust: pimples, sex, and old man
picking his nose are all equally cause for nausea. It is of little importance that
the alienation, the hatreds, and the disgust are those of a sixteen-year-old.
Any reader, sharing or remembering something like them, will agree with
the conclusion to be drawn from this unhappy odyssey: to borrow a line from
Auden, "We must love one another or die." After every other human being
has failed him, Caulfield still has his loving ten-year-old sister to love; she
embodies the innocence we all hope we have preserved and the wisdom we
all hope we have acquired.

The skill with which all this has been worked into 277 pages is most
ingenious. But as it proceeds on its insights, which are not really insights
since they are so general, "The Catcher in the Rye" becomes more and more
a case history of all of us. Radically this writing depends on the reader's
recollection of merely similar difficulties; the unique crisis and the unique
anguish are not re-created. These emotional ups and downs become increasingly factitious—so much must be included to elicit memories of so many
callow heartbreaks—and though always lively in its parts the book as a whole
is predictable and boring.

Tomorrow's Child   William Poster*

The hallmark of a certain kind of art, it used to be said, is the shock of
recognition. But the fantastically rapid movement of present-day life has
altered matters somewhat. Mr. Salinger's novel gives us what amounts to a
series of shocks of precognition, quick anticipations of life presented in a
lightly organized cluster. Its most immediate effect is of being magically on
top of contemporary life, catching events in the making and plucking phrases
right out of the mouth of social history. This febrile power of observation,
amounting to a kind of genius, is a trait displayed in much popular American
art, a trait manifested not so much in the creation of a single character or
work as through an infinite number of small touches fitted into the interstices
of popular novels, comic strips, movies, and radio serials. This kind of observation is not, oddly enough, of the naturalistic documentary variety, though
a certain quantum of sheer recording ability is involved, nor does it depend
primarily on an overwhelming familiarity with an environment. The data go
beyond experience and habit to become clues to trend. The peculiarly brilliant effect imparted as one comes across the turn of speech, gesture, or
incident that only yesterday seemed to mark a significant change in group
mores is due to the slightly eery sensation one has of finding the future

* Reprinted by permission from *Commentary* 13, no. 1 (January 1952): 90–92.

crystallized. It is the natural talent, developed to a preternatural extreme, of entertainers whose most harrowing fear is that of finding themselves suddenly, instantaneously *démodé*, stranded by the unpredictable tides of American taste and predilection.

Thus, the language of Mr. Salinger's sixteen-year-old narrator-protagonist is something of a phenomenon in itself and carries most of the weight of the story: "I was feeling sort of tired from the trip to New York and all, and I started yawning. Then I started horsing around a little bit. Sometimes I horse around quite a lot, just to keep from getting bored. What I did was, I pulled the old peak of my hunting hat around to the front, then pulled it way down over my eyes. That way I couldn't see a goddam thing. 'I think I'm going blind,' I said in this very hoarse voice. 'Mother darling, everthing's getting so dark in here.' "

It is not merely the current idiom and style of this particular breed of American adolescent that is being rendered but yesterday's or rather today's served up through all the complex processes of writing and publishing as fresh as frozen vegetables. It is a *tour de force* the American fiction writer will probably find himself increasingly doomed to attempt if he does not wish to lag behind, much as the designer of military airplanes has to shape his plans to meet future rather than present conditions. Mr. Salinger's extended, perfectionist handling of contemporary idiom is indeed the literary equivalent of our time-defying technological innovations and one which will have far-reaching though not necessarily happy consequences.

Similarly, Mr. Salinger picks up his narrating hero with all the intimate ease and bounce of a comic-strip artist and carries him through the incidents typical of his milieu in a thin, adroit fashion that seems able, effortlessly, to maintain itself forever—as long, that is, as the environment holds out. The incidents—and they seem within a narrow compass to contain every adolescent highlight: the bad boy of the school breaking wind in assembly, brushes with a homosexual and a prostitute, an awkward fight between roommates, embarrassing intimacies with a teacher—are of a different kind from those that are permitted in our mass entertainments. Nevertheless, what fundamentally distinguishes *The Catcher in the Rye* from such comic strips as *Our Bill* and *Penny*, with which it has much in common, is not superior depth but a different kind of selectivity and a different set of conventions.

The machinery of the comic strip is geared to churn the life of the average American into a pure froth of light amusement, and its artifices are the result of mutual understanding between the audience and the creator and necessary to the effect. The machinery of novels like Mr. Salinger's is tooled to turn out supposedly unique heroes, fashionable departures from current norms who arouse envy and admiration through the author's advertisement of virtues of sensibility and intransigence which in fact they do not possess. Money, looks, "background," and a petty scrape or two are neatly blended to shape an imitation Byronic rebel. In the comic strip the audience is in on the rules of the game and identified with the character; in the novel the audience is excluded and tricked. Both phenomena result from the American failure to integrate and maintain a democratic aesthetic. Our popular arts split up repeatedly into the complementary extremes of mass egalitarianism and pseudoelite snobbery, with the lower-caste forms having the greater vitality and coherence.

It is the very American, very successful New York upper middle class (or lower upper class—the income bracket is somewhere between thirty and a hundred thousand dollars a year) adolescent prep-school student that Mr. Salinger epitomizes in the person of Holden Caulfield (the name is an instance of the author's shrewd selectivity). Holden is typical not so much of this adolescent class as a whole, but of a specific and extensive part of it, namely, those individuals who think of themselves as exceptions to the class by virtue of their superior taste. Salinger tries to pass Holden off as tragically isolated through excessive sensibility, but never shows him as in any way distinct from the hords of crew-cutted, Ivy League *aficionados* who used to turn up at Village jam sessions, thereby playing a large role in the breakdown of a once flourishing school of American music. Holden's disenchantment with the activities of his group, with education, patriotism, school spirit, literature, art, etc., would have some virtue if it had better logic and were not part of an indiscriminately squeamish lack of appetite for any aspect of life whatsoever. It would be easier to credit his detestation of the "phony slobs" who surround him if he were distinguished from them in any way but the weakness of his stomach.

Essentially, this negativism derives not so much from social reality as from the predicament of the sophisticated writer nearing the end of his resources. The cool, objective, humorous treatment of contemporary eccentricity which is characteristic of the *New Yorker* (where Mr. Salinger publishes his short stories) has run down because it cannot be recharged from the battery of some viable, positive approach to culture, morals, religion, or politics. Any literary attitude that contains fixed principles of detachment or exclusion is bound to wither in a society that pulls organically in the opposite direction. And *New Yorker* literature suffers not only from the desiccation common to every artificially constituted American elite, but also from some special ailments; the natural objects of its satire have disappeared, partly as a result of social change, partly because so many have become, themselves, *New Yorker* subscribers and exemplars of its approach. The ennui, heartburn, and weary revulsions of *The Catcher in the Rye* are the inevitable emotions, not of an adolescent, however disenchanted, but of a well-paid satirist with a highly developed technique, no point of view, and no target to aim at but himself.

The author's predicament does enable him to project, by a kind of transposition, something of the malaise of those scions of the upper classes who, as a result of excessive wealth, leisure, a secure social position, guilt, and the debilitated rudiments of sensibility, have nothing further to strive for within their class and cannot accept its usual goals. Lacking the discrimination and vigor necessary to create new forms of life, they can only dream fitfully and unpoetically of implausible escapes. Only Mr. Salinger tries to convince us that Holden's fearfully mawkish and ugly fantasies are the exquisite reveries of a soul tormented by sheer love of the beautiful and genuine, and that a mere prematurely withered casualty of history is one of its nobler tragedies.

Manhattan Ulysses, Junior   Harrison Smith*

That there is something wrong or lacking in the novels of despair and frustration that many of our younger writers are turning out has long been apparent. The sour note of bitterness and the recurring theme of sadism have become almost a convention, never thoroughly explained by the author's dependence on a psychoanalytical interpretation of a major character. The boys who are spoiled or turned into budding homosexuals by their mothers and a loveless home life are as familiar to us today as stalwart and dependable young heroes were to an earlier generation. We have accepted this interpretation of the restlessness and bewilderment of our young men and boys because no one had anything better to offer. It is tragic to hear the anguished cry of parents: "What have we done to harm him? Why doesn't he care about anything? He is a bright boy, but why does he fail to pass his examination? Why won't he talk to us?"

A remarkable and absorbing novel has appeared, J. D. Salinger's "The Catcher in the Rye," which may serve to calm the apprehensions of fathers and mothers about their own responsibilities, though it does not attempt to explain why all boys who dismay their elders have failed to pass successfully the barrier between childhood and young manhood. It is a profoundly moving and a disturbing book, but it is pathetic rather than tragic, and it is not hopeless. Holden Caulfield, sixteen years old and six foot two inches in height, narrates his own story from the time when he was dismissed from his third private school to return, ill and in a state of physical and mental shock, to the shelter of his home in New York three days later. What happens to him is heart-rending. To many readers some of his words and the accidents that befall him may seem to be too raw to be expressed in the words of a childish youth. If readers can be shocked in this manner they should be advised to let the book alone.

What was wrong with Holden was his moral revulsion against anything that was ugly, evil, cruel, or what he called "phony" and his acute responsiveness to beauty and innocence, especially the innocence of the very young, in

* Reprinted by permission form the *Saturday Review* 34, no. 28 (14 July 1951): 12–13.

whom he saw reflected his own lost childhood. The book is full of the voices
and the delightful antics of children. Especially he adored his stalwart and
understanding little sister, who in the end undoubtedly saved him from
suicide. And there were the memories of his dead brother, whom he had
loved, and a teacher in the first school from which he was dismissed. He had
no other friends, dead or alive. He accepted his parents, whose union had
been happy, as one of the stable factors in a devastating world. When he ran
away from school he knew that he had three days before they would hear of
his dismissal from the headmaster. His desire to escape from the ordeal of
their disappointment in him and to hide in New York, to go underground, is
understandable. Not every boy would have done it, but the reader is convinced that Holden would and that his behavior throughout the book is
equally natural and inevitable.

The magic of this novel does not depend on this boy's horrifying experience but on the authenticity of the language he uses and the emotions and
memories which overwhelm him. Without realizing it he is seeking the
understanding and affection which adults could give him—or even his classmates, who are perhaps an unreasonably repulsive lot of lads. But how could
they be fond of this overgrown, precocious, and yet childish boy? His roommate was an arrogant hunter of girls; the boy next door never brushed his
teeth and was always picking at his pimples; the group of "intellectuals," the
grinds, and the athletes were all phonies to him. But Holden's sense of the
phoniness is never contempt. It is worse; it is despair.

When he fled to New York he had plenty of money: a doting grandmother who seemed to think that he had a birthday every three months had
sent him some, and he had also roused a rich boy out of bed and sold him a
costly new typewriter for twenty dollars. On the train he met the mother of
one of his least attractive classmates and lied to her about her son to make
her happy. The hotel he went to was crawling with prostitutes and "queers."
In spite of his height waiters would not serve him a drink. Three older
women left him their check to pay; a prostitute came to his room and took ten
dollars away from him for five minutes' distraught conversation. He wan-
dered through the city night and day like a lost soul.

He slipped into his parent's apartment after midnight to look at his
sleeping little sister and then visited the one teacher he thought could help
him. The man was slightly intoxicated, and he told Holden, "This fall I think
you are riding for—is a special kind of fall, a horrible kind. The man falling
isn't permitted to feel or hear himself hit bottom. He just keeps falling and
falling." He writes out a text for the boy to remember: "The mark of the
immature man is that he wants to die nobly for a cause, while the mature
man wants to live humbly for one." None of this is any use to Holden, who
simply wants to know what makes him find so many people false and ignoble
at the same time that he is aware of his own capacity for love.

Whatever effect the man's wisdom might have had is ruined when the
boy wakes up in the night in horror to find the man stroking his head.

Holden dashes into his clothes and escapes. "Boy, I was shaking like a madman."

"The Catcher in the Rye" is not all horror of this sort. There is a wry humor in this sixteen-year-old's trying to live up to his height, to drink with men, to understand mature sex and why he is still a virgin at his age. His affection for children is spontaneous and delightful. There are few little girls in modern fiction as charming and lovable as his little sister, Phoebe. Altogether this is a book to be read thoughtfully and more than once. It is about an unusually sensitive and intelligent boy; but, then, are not all boys unusual and worthy of understanding? If they are bewildered at the complexity of modern life, unsure of themselves, shocked by the spectacle of perversity and evil around them—are not adults equally shocked by the knowledge that even children cannot escape this contact and awareness?

[Review of *The Catcher in the Rye*]   T. Morris Longstreth*

Mr. Salinger is a war veteran in his early thirties who has written short stories for the *New Yorker* and other magazines. This, his first novel, is the mid-summer selection of the Book-of-the-Month Club. A sixteen-year-old schoolboy, Holden Caulfield, tells the story—with the paradoxical result that it is not fit for children to read.

Mr. Salinger says, "All of my best friends are children. It's almost unbearable to me to realize that my book will be kept on a shelf out of their reach." Many adults as well will not wish to condition themselves to Holden's language. Indeed, one finds it hard to believe that a true lover of children could father this tale.

Twice there is a reminder of Shakespeare. It comes near Macbeth's despairing definition of life, "a tale told by an idiot . . . signifying nothing." And Salinger has taken a more sensitive than normal child, just as Shakespeare took a more than normally sensitive man in Hamlet. It could be debated long just how irrational is Holden Caulfield, as likewise, Hamlet.

Holden, who is the clown, villain, and even, moderately, the hero of this tale, is asked not to return to his school after Christmas. This is his third expulsion and he cannot endure to face his parents, so he hides out in New York, where his conduct is a nightmarish medley of loneliness, bravado, and supineness. Jerome David Salinger is an extremely skillful writer, and Holden's dead-pan narrative is quick-moving, absurd, and wholly repellent in its mingled vulgarity, naivete, and sly perversion.

"The Catcher in the Rye" purports to be the "Seventeen" of our times,

*Reprinted by permission from *Christian Science Monitor* 19 July 1951. Copyright 1951 the Christian Science Publishing Society. All rights reserved.

though it is as remote in conception from the Tarkington masterpiece, still much alive, as the television age from Indiana in 1916.

Holden Caulfield is so supersensitive to others' faults that he has no friends, among boys at least. He is as unbalanced as a rooster on a tightrope. He asks a girl to elope with him and then calls her names. He suffers from loneliness because he has about shut himself away from the normal activities of boyhood, games, the outdoors, friendship.

He is capable of love for a dead brother, for a lively younger sister, for all young things, as his explanation of the book's title makes clear—an oddly psychopathic one, it must be noted. (For Holden has mistaken the words of "Coming Through the Rye," as "If a body *catch* a body," and fancies himself the heroic rescuer of children in danger of plunging over a cliff in the field.)

But he is also capable of wholesome revulsion from contact with the human dregs, and impulsively seeks a kind of absolution by offering help to others. He hates what is wrong with the movies and in the end he forgets himself and his hoped-for escape into freedom to help his sister. He is alive, human, preposterous, profane and pathetic beyond belief.

Fortunately, there cannot be many of him yet. But one fears that a book like this given wide circulation may multiply his kind—as too easily happens when immorality and perversion are recounted by writers of talent whose work is countenanced in the name of art or good intention.

[Review of *The Catcher in the Rye*]   Anonymous*

Holden Caulfield, an artist at getting himself thrown out of prep schools and all, is the ribald narrator of this account of academic and social shortcomings. Like Charles Lamb, he is a victim of some very imperfect sympathies; he hates phonies, teachers ('You don't have to think too hard when you talk to a teacher'), and, well phonies. He wants to protect people, especially "little kids"; most of the time he finds himself acting "like a madman."

The Catcher in the Rye tells of the madman's week end he has in New York, after walking out on prep school. It's a mad mélange of ice-skating at Radio City, interviewing a prostitute in his hotel room, escaping from a homosexual, and so on. Not only do some of the events stretch probability, but Holden's character as iconoclast, a kind of latter-day Tom Sawyer or Huck Finn, is made monotonous and phony by the formidably excessive use of amateur swearing and coarse language.

*Reprinted by permission from *The Catholic World* 174, no. 1040 (November 1951): 154.

J. D. Salinger:
Some Crazy Cliff

Arthur Heiserman and
James E. Miller, Jr.*

It is clear that J. D. Salinger's *The Catcher in the Rye* belongs to an ancient and honorable narrative tradition, perhaps the most profound in western fiction. The tradition is the central pattern of the epic and has been enriched by every tongue; for not only is it in itself exciting but also it provides the artist a framework upon which he may hang almost any fabric of events and characters.

It is, of course, the tradition of the Quest. We use the medieval term because it signifies a seeking after what is tremendous, greater than the love of a woman. The love of woman may be part of the seeking, part even of the object sought, for we have been told that the Grail has gender and Penelope did wait in Ithaca. But if the love of woman is essential to the seeking or to the object sought, we must call the search a romance. These two terms (quest and romance) distinguish thematic patterns, and have nothing to do with tragic or comic effects. Furthermore, the same plots, characters, and idioms might be employed inside either pattern. But somewhere upon the arc of the Quest, the love of woman must be eschewed or absorbed: the hero must bind himself to the mast, or must seek his Ducalinda because she is Virtue, not because she is Female.

There are at least two sorts of quests, depending upon the object sought. Stephen Dedalus sought a reality uncontaminated by home, country, church; for like Eugene Gant and Natty Bumppo he knew that social institutions tend to force what is ingenious in a man into their own channels. He sought the opposite of security, for security was a cataract of the eye. Bloom, on the other hand, was already an outcast and sought acceptance by an Ithaca and a Penelope which despised him. And, tragically enough, he also sought an Icarian son who had fled the very maze which he, Bloom, desired to enter. So the two kinds of quests, the one seeking acceptance and stability, the other precisely the opposite, differ significantly, and can cross only briefly to the drunken wonder of both heroes. Bloom, the protagonist of *The Waste Land*, the Joads, Alyosha Karamazov, Aeneas, Ulysses, Gatsby—those heroes seek acceptance, stability, a life embosomed upon what is known and can be trusted. Dedalus, Huck Finn, Ishmael, Hans Castorp, Huxley's heroes, Dostoevski's Idiot—these protagonists place themselves outside the bounds of what is known and seek not stability but a Truth which is unwarped by stability.

American literature seems fascinated with the outcast, the person who defies traditions in order to arrive at some pristine knowledge, some personal integrity. Natty Bumppo maintains his integrity out-of-doors only, for upon the frontier a man must be a man or perish. For Huck Finn both sides

*Reprinted by permission from *Western Humanities Review* 10, no. 2 (Spring 1956): 129–37.

of the Mississippi are lined with fraud and hatred; and because the great brown river acts as a kind of sewer, you're liable to find murderers and thieves afloat on it—even the father whom you fled might turn up dead in it, as though the river were a dream. But in the middle of the great natural river, when you're naked of civilization and in company with an outcast more untarnished and childlike than yourself—*there* is peace. And in northern Mississippi, in the ante-Snopes era, frontiersmen conquer the wilderness using only their courage and their fury; and they behave, even when civilization has almost extinguished them, with the kind of insane honor that drives Quentin Compson outside of society and into suicide. And the hunter, as he tracks the great mythic bear or the incredible whale, must leave behind whatever is unnatural or convenient. Similarly, when the bull charges, you are faced with the same compulsion for integrity as is required by the wilderness, the whale, the bear, the river; and very often, the world so botches things that you must "make a separate peace" in order to maintain your moral entity intact.

All the virtues of these American heroes are personal ones: they most often, as a matter of fact, are in conflict with home, family, church. The typical American hero must flee these institutions, become a tramp in the earth, cut himself off from Chicago, Winesburg, Hannibal, Cooperstown, New York, Asheville, Minneapolis. For only by flight can he find knowledge of what is real. And if he does not flee, he at least defies.

The protagonist of *The Catcher in the Rye*, Holden Caulfield, is one of these American heroes, but with a significant difference. He seems to be engaged in both sorts of quests at once; he needs to go home and he needs to leave it. Unlike the other American knight errants, Holden seeks Virtue second to Love. He wants to be good. When the little children are playing in the rye-field on the clifftop, Holden wants to be the one who catches them before they fall off the cliff. He is not driven toward honor or courage. He is not driven toward love of woman. Holden is driven toward love of his fellow-man, charity—virtues which were perhaps not quite virile enough for Natty Bumppo, Ishmael, Huck Finn, or Nick Adams. Holden is actually frightened by a frontier code of masculinity—a code which sometimes requires its adherents to behave in sentimental and bumptious fashions. But like these American heroes, Holden is a wanderer, for in order to be good he has to be more of a bad boy than the puritanical Huck could have imagined. Holden has had enough of both Hannibal, Missouri, *and* the Mississippi; and his tragedy is that when he starts back up the river, he has no place to go—save, of course, a California psychiatrist's couch.

So Salinger translates the old tradition into contemporary terms. The phoniness of society forces Holden Caulfield to leave it, but he is seeking nothing less than stability and love. He would like nothing better than a home, a life embosomed upon what is known and can be trusted; he is a very wise sheep forced into lone wolf's clothing; he is Stephen Dedalus and Leopold Bloom rolled into one crazy kid. And here is the point; for poor

Holden, there is no Ithaca. Ithaca has not merely been defiled by a horde of suitors; it has sunk beneath waves of phoniness. He does, of course, have a Penelope who is still intact. She is his little sister Phoebe whom he must protect at all costs from the phantoms of lust, hypocrisy, conceit and fear—all of the attributes which Holden sees in society and which Huck Finn saw on the banks of the Mississippi and Dedalus saw in Dublin. So at the end, like the hero of *Antic Hay,* Holden delights in circles—a comforting, bounded figure which yet connotes hopelessness. He breaks down as he watches his beloved little Phoebe going round and round on a carousel; she is so *damned* happy. From the lunatic delight in a circle, he is shipped off to the psychiatrist. For Holden loves the world more than the world can bear.

Holden's Quest takes him outside society; yet the grail he seeks is the world and the grail is full of love. To be a catcher in the rye in this world is possible only at the price of leaving it. To be good is to be a "case," a "bad boy" who confounds the society of men. So Holden seeks the one role which would allow him to be a catcher, and that role is the role of the child. As a child, he would be condoned, for a child is a sort of savage and a pariah because he is innocent and good. But it is Holden's tragedy that he is sixteen, and like Wordsworth he can never be less. In childhood he had what he is now seeking—non-phoniness, truth, innocence. He can find it now only in Phoebe and in his dead brother Allie's baseball mitt, in a red hunting cap and the tender little nuns. Still, unlike all of us, Holden refuses to compromise with adulthood and its necessary adulteries; and his heroism drives him berserk. Huck Finn had the Mississippi and at the end of the Mississippi he had the wild west beyond Arkansas. The hero of *The Waste Land* had Shantih, the peace which passes human understanding. Bloom had Molly and his own ignorance; Dedalus had Paris and Zurich. But for Holden, there is no place to go.

II

The central theme of Salinger's work is stated explicitly in one of his best short stories, "For Esme—with Love and Squalor." Salinger quotes a passage from Dostoevski: "Fathers and teachers, I ponder 'What is Hell?' I maintain that it is the suffering of being unable to love."

The hero of "For Esme" is an American soldier who, driven too near psychosis by five campaigns of World War II and a moronic jeepmate, is saved in an act of childish love by two remarkable English children. Just as surely as war and neurosis are both manifestations of the lack of love, the soldier discovers peace and happiness are manifestations of love's presence. This Love must be spelled with a capital; for it is not the alienated, romantic love of the courtly romances and "Dover Beach"—a love which is tragic because it is founded upon Eros; but rather it is the expansive, yea-saying love of all Creation which we find in the saints and which is never tragic because it is founded upon Agape. This love is the dominant trait of all

Salinger's heroes, and when it is thwarted the hero either shoots himself, as does the veteran with "battle fatigue" in "A Perfect Day for Bananafish," or goes berserk or melancholic as do the heros of *The Catcher in the Rye* and "Uncle Wiggly in Connecticut." But when, on the other hand, a person finds a way to love the world, then that person is saved from madness and suicide as is the soldier in "For Esme." Salinger thus diagnoses the neurosis and fatigue of the world in one simple way: if we cannot love, we cannot live.

Childhood and the loss of innocence have obsessed much of western literature at least since the Enlightenment, when man was declared innately good, corrupted only by his institutions. If we could return to childhood, or to noble savagery; or if we could retain the sponaneity of childhood, our social and personal problems would disappear. Emile, Candide, the young Wordsworth, Huck Finn, Holden Caulfield—all lament or seek a return to a lost childhood for precisely the same reasons that one is forced to make peace with one's childhood on the analyst's couch, or that the Marxist must look with a sigh upon Eden, where the fruits of production were consumed entirely by their tenders. Each of us does indeed carry an Adam inside us, whether he is Original Sin or Innocence: and the modern world has for the most part judged him innocent. Yet the clouds of glory which we trailed dwindle and turn back in adulthood; for when the world was new, before the pimples appeared, it was with us not too much but utterly and we could live it innocently, without fear. Of course, what Wordsworth remembered above Tintern Abbey, what Clemens recalled in New York, what Rousseau attempted to breed in France, what modern art attempted to recreate from Negro and Oriental models, never really existed in pure form in the first place. How horrified Wordsworth would have been had he learned what romanticism's dank blossom, Freud, discovered in the dictum that "the child is father of the man"! Nevertheless, as Freud made Childism clinical he also made it rampant; and the initiation story, the fable of Innocence Lost, has developed into a dominant motif in contemporary fiction.

The flight out of the world, out of the ordinary, and into an Eden of innocence or childhood is a common flight indeed, and it is one which Salinger's heroes are constantly attempting. But Salinger's childism is consubstantial with his concern for love and neurosis. Adultism is precisely "the suffering of being unable to love," and it is that which produces neurosis. Everyone able to love in Salinger's stories is either a child or a man influenced by a child. All the adults not informed by love and innocence are by definition phonies and prostitutes. "You take adults, they always look lousy when they're asleep with their mouths open, but kids don't . . . They look all right." Kids like Phoebe shut up when they haven't anything to say. They even say "thank you" when you tighten their skates, and they don't go behind a post to button their pants. The nuns expect no swanky lunches after standing on a corner to collect money. Young James Castle would not go back on his word even though he had to jump from a window to keep it.

Holden is the kind of person who feels sorry for the teachers who have to flunk him. He fears for the ducks when the lagoon freezes over, for he is a duck himself with no place to go. He must enter his own home like a crook, lying to elevator boys and tip-toeing past bedrooms. His dad "will kill" him and his mother will weep for his incorrigible "laziness." He wants only to pretend he is a deaf-mute and live as a hermit filling-station operator in Colorado, but he winds up where the frontier ends, California, in an institution for sick rich kids. And we can see, on the final note of irony in the book, that the frontier west which represented escape from "sivilization" for Huck Finn has ended by becoming the symbol for depravity and phoniness in our national shrine at Hollywood.

III

The most distinctive aspect of Salinger's humor is its invariable effect of intensifying poignance and even horror. At the end of "A Perfect Day for Bananafish," Seymour Glass, the sensitive young protagonist, is unable to reconcile himself to the evil adult world into which he has been thrust, with its brutal wars and sordid and even hateful relationships with a shallow-headed wife and her self-centered family. Even the steadying influence of the genuine innocence of little Sybil Carpenter is not sufficient to deter Seymour from his will to self-destruction. As he is on his way to his room at the end of the story, he boards the hotel elevator and believes that one of his fellow passengers is scrutinizing him. "I see you're looking at my feet," he says, and the startled woman with zinc salve on her nose replies, "I *beg* your pardon?" But the young man has become acutely sensitive: "If you want to look at my feet, say so. . . . But don't be a God-damned sneak about it."

The story at this point is simultaneously at its funniest and its most poignant. In less than one brief page the young man is dead: "Then he went over and sat down on the unoccupied twin bed, looked at the girl, aimed the pistol, and fired a bullet through his right temple." The close juxtaposition of these two passages, the one a height in comic incongruity, the other a depth in tragic action, works a unique effect. The comic element intensifies rather than relieves the tragic. As we observe the young man raise the pistol to his head, we are horrified that we have just been laughing at his extreme sensitivity about his feet. Perhaps we even have the guilty feeling of having ridiculed a deformity—a deformity of the spirit. In any event we are stunned into a keen realization of the tragic human plight.

It is this poignance which characterizes all of Salinger's humor, this catch in the throat that accompanies all of the laughs. Holden Caulfield is no clown nor is he a tragic hero; he is a sixteen-year-old lad whose vivid encounter with everyday life is tragically humorous—or humorously tragic. At the end of the novel, as we leave Holden in the psychiatric ward of the California hospital, we come to the realization that the abundant and richly varied humor of the novel has reenforced the serious intensity of Holden's frantic flight from Adultism and his frenzied search for the genuine in a terrifyingly phony world.

Holden Caulfield, like Huckleberry Finn, tells his own story and it is in the language of the telling in both books that a great part of the humor lies. In the nineteenth century, Huck began, "You don't know about me without you have read a book by the name of *The Adventures of Tom Sawyer:* but that ain't no matter." The English of Huck's twentieth century counterpart, Holden Caulfield, is perhaps more correct but none-the-less distinctive: "If you really want to hear about it, the first thing you'll probably want to know is where I was born, and what my lousy childhood was like, and how my parents were occupied and all before they had me, and all that David Copperfield kind of crap, but I don't feel like going into it, if you want to know the truth."

The skepticism inherent in that casual phrase, "if you want to know the truth," suggesting that as a matter of fact in the world of Holden Caulfield very few people do, characterizes this sixteen-year-old "crazy mixed up kid" more sharply and vividly than pages of character "analysis" possibly could. In a similar manner Huck's "that ain't no matter" speaks volumes for his relationship to the alien adult world in which he finds himself a sojourner. But if these two boys lay their souls bare by their own voices, in doing so they provoke smiles at their mishandling and sometimes downright mangling of the English language.

Huck's spelling of *sivilization* gives the word a look which makes what it stands for understandably distasteful. Holden's incorrectness frequently appears to be a straining after correctness ("She'd give Allie or I a push. . . . ") which suggests a subconscious will to non-conformity. But the similarities of language of Huck and Holden are balanced by marked differences. Both boys are fugitives from education, but Holden has suffered more of the evil than Huck. Holden's best subject in the several schools he has tolerated briefly is English. And, too, Holden is a child of the twentieth century. Mark Twain himself would probably be startled not at the frankness of Holden's language but at the daring of J. D. Salinger in copying it so faithfully.

But of course neither J. D. Salinger nor Mark Twain really "copied" anything. Their books would be unreadable had they merely recorded intact the language of a real-life Huck and a real-life Holden. Their genius lies in their mastery of the technique of first person narration which, through meticulous selection, creates vividly the illusion of life: gradually and subtly their narrators emerge and stand revealed, stripped to their innermost beings. It is a mark of their creator's mastery that Huck and Holden appear to reveal themselves.

It is not the least surprising aspect of *The Catcher in the Rye* that trite expressions and metaphors with which we are all familiar and even bored turn out, when emerging from the mouth of a sixteen-year-old, to be funny. The unimaginative repetition of identical expressions in countless situations intensifies the humor. The things in Holden's world are always jumping up and down or bouncing or scattering "like madmen." Holden always lets us know when he has insight into the absurdity of the endless absurd situations which make up the life of a sixteen-year-old by exclaiming, "It killed me." In a phony world Holden feels compelled to reenforce his sincerity and truthfulness constantly with, "It really is" or "It really did." Incongruously the adjective "old" serves as a term of endearment, from "old" Thomas Hardy to "old" Phoebe. And many of the things Holden does, he does, ambiguously, "like a bastard."

Holden is a master of the ludicrous irrelevancy. Indeed, a large part of *The Catcher in the Rye* consists of the relevantly irrelevant. On the opening page, Holden says, "I'm not going to tell you my whole goddam autobiography or anything. I'll just tell you about this madman stuff that happened to me around last Christmas. . . . " By the time we have finished *Catcher* we feel that we know Holden as thoroughly as any biography could reveal him, and one of the reasons is that he has not hesitated to follow in his tale wherever whim and fancy lead him. For example, in the early part of the novel, Holden goes at some length into the history of the Ossenburger Memorial Wing of the new dorms, his place of residence. Ossenburger, we are told, was the Pencey alumnus who made a "pot of dough" in the undertaking business, and who, after giving money to Pencey, gave a speech in chapel "that lasted about ten hours." "He told us we should always pray to God— talk to Him and all—wherever we were. He told us we ought to think of Jesus as our buddy and all. He said *he* talked to Jesus all of the time. Even when he was driving his car. That killed me. I can just see the big phony bastard shifting into first gear and asking Jesus to send him a few more stiffs." Ossenburger, of course, had nothing to do, directly, with the "madman stuff" that happened to Holden around Christmas; but Holden's value judgment of the phony Ossenburger is certainly relevant to Salinger's purpose, the revelation of Holden's character.

When Holden refuses to express aggressive dislike of the repulsive Ackley, the pimply boy whose teeth "looked mossy and awful," he is not being facetious nor is he lying. He is simply expressing an innocence incapable of genuine hatred. Holden does not suffer from the inability to love, but he does despair of finding a place to bestow his love. The depth of Holden's capacity for love is revealed in his final words, as he sits in the psychiatric ward musing over his nightmarish adventures: "If you want to know the truth, I don't *know* what I think about it. I'm sorry I told so many people about it. About all I know is, I sort of miss everybody I told about. Even old Stradlater and Ackley, for instance. I think I even miss that goddam Maurice. It's funny. Don't ever tell anybody anything. If you do, you start missing everybody." We agree with Holden that it is funny, but it is funny in a pathetic kind of way. As we leave Holden alone in his room in the psychiatric ward, we are aware of the book's last ironic incongruity. It is not Holden who should be examined for a sickness of the mind, but the world in which he has sojourned and found himself an alien. To "cure" Holden, he must be given the contagious, almost universal disease of phony adultism; he must be pushed over that "crazy cliff."

Holden and Huck:
The Odysseys of Youth   Charles Kaplan*

Henry Thoreau, himself an interior traveler of some note, says in *A Week on the Concord and Merrimac Rivers:* "The traveller must be born again on the road, and earn a passport from the elements, the principal powers that be for him." In Mark Twain's *Adventures of Huckleberry Finn* (1884) and in J. D. Salinger's *The Catcher in the Rye* (1951) we meet two young travelers—travelers in their native land and also in the geography of their souls. Their narratives are separated in time by almost seventy years, but the psychic connection between them eliminates mere temporal distance: Huck Finn and Holden Caulfield are true blood-brothers, speaking to us in terms that lift their wanderings from the level of the merely picaresque to that of a sensitive and insightful criticism of American life.

Each work, to begin with, is a fine comic novel. Each is rich in incident, varied in characterization, and meaningful in its entirety. In each the story is narrated by the central figure, an adolescent whose remarkable language is both a reflection and a criticism of his education, his environment, and his times. Each is fundamentally a story of a quest—an adventure story in the age-old pattern of a young lad making his way in a not particularly friendly adult world. An outcast, to all intents without family and friends, the protagonist flees the restraints of the civilization which would make him its victim, and journeys through the world in search of what he thinks is freedom—but which we, his adult readers, recognize to be primarily understanding. Society regards him as a rogue, a ne'er-do-well whose career consists of one scrape after another; but the extent to which he is constantly embroiled with authority is exactly the index of his independence, his sometimes pathetic self-reliance, and his freedom of spirit. He is a total realist, with an acute and instinctive register of mind which enables him to penetrate sham and pretense—qualities which, the more he travels through the adult world, the more he sees as most frequently recurring. He has somehow acquired a code of ethics and a standard of value against which he measures mankind—including, mercilessly, himself. There are many people and things—not many, however—that are (in Holden's term) "nice"; there are many more that are "phony." He does not understand the world, but he knows how one should behave in it. The comic irony that gives each novel its characteristic intellectual slant is provided by the judgements of these young realists on the

*Reprinted by permission from *College English* 18, no. 2 (November 1956): 76–80.

false ideals and romanticized versions of life which they encounter on their travels.

The slangy, idiomatic, frequently vulgar language which Twain and Salinger put in the mouths of their heroes is remarkable for the clarity of the self-portraits that emerge, as well as for the effortless accuracy of the talk itself. F. R. Leavis describes Huck's colloquial language as a literary medium that is "Shakespearian in its range and subtlety." Likewise, Holden's twentieth-century prep-school vernacular, despite its automatic and somehow innocent obscenities and its hackneyed coinages, also manages to communicate ideas and feelings of a quite complex sort within its sharply delimited boundaries. The language, in each case, is personal, distinctive, and descriptive of character. Holden and Huck are moralists as well as realists: each has a deep concern with ethical valuation, and each responds fully to the experiences which life offers him. It is the tension between their apparently inadequate idiom and their instinctively full and humane ethics that both Twain and Salinger exploit for comic purposes.

"The traveller must be born again," said Thoreau; and Huck's voyage down the Mississippi is a series of constant rebirths, a search for identity. Beginning with the elaborately staged mock murder with sets him free from the clutches of Pap, Huck assumes a series of varied roles, playing each one like the brilliant improviser that he is. Twain counterpoints Huck's hoaxes against the villainous or merely mercenary pretenses of the Duke and the Dauphin; the boy's sometimes desperate shifts are necessary for his survival and to both his moral and physical progress. The series reaches a climax in the sequence at the Phelps farm, when Huck is forced to assume the identity of Tom Sawyer—when, for the first time, he cannot choose his own role.

This, it seems to me, is a significant variation, pointing to the world which begins to close in upon Huck toward the end of the novel. Not only is an identity forced upon him, but with the appearance of the real Tom Sawyer upon the scene, Huck surrenders the initiative in planning and, in effect, loses control of his own fate. This is the tragedy of Huckleberry Finn: that he has gone so far only to surrender at the end to the forces which have been seeking to capture him. For despite the apparent similarities, there is a vital difference between Huck and Tom: Tom behaves "by the book"; Tom relies on historical precedent; Tom operates within the conventions of the civilized world, accepting its values and standards, and merely play-acting at rebellion—Tom, in short, is no rebel at all, but a romanticizer of reality. Huck's term to describe Tom's method of doing things is that it has "style." Style it may have, but it lacks design. Huck's willingness to let Tom take over Jim's rescue indicates Twain's final acquiescence to the world which has been criticized throughout. True, Huck is going to light out again, he tells us in the last lines: "Aunt Sally she's going to adopt me and sivilize me, and I can't stand it. I been there before." But, despite the expression of sentiments pointing to another future escape—and the fact that the limiting article is not part of Twain's title— Huck, by the end of the novel, has been trapped. I should like to add my bit to the perennial debate concerning the artistic validity of the final sequence, and suggest that it is both ironical and true to life. Tom's play-acting before Huck sets off down the river—his ambuscade of the "A-rabs," for example—seems innocent and amusing; but the rescue of Jim seems, as I think it is meant to seem, tedious and irrelevant. After all, something has happened to Huck— and to us—between chapters 3 and 43.

Huck is trapped by a society whose shortcomings he sees, and he says, "I can't stand it." Holden's terminology is "It depresses me" and "It kills me." Ironically, he is revealed as telling us his narrative from an institution of some kind—psychiatric, we are led to suspect—having also been trapped by the people who want to "sivilize" him.

Holden's instinctive nonconformity asserts itself early in the novel. He has been told by one of the masters at Pencey Prep, from which he is about to be dismissed, that life is a game. "Some game," Holden comments. "If you get on the side where all the hot-shots are, then it's a game, all right—I'll admit that. But if you get on the *other* side, where there aren't any hot-shots, then what's a game about it. Nothing. No game." At the age of seventeen he has learned to suspect the glib philosophies of the elders, and to test the coin of experience by determining whether it rings true or false for him, personally.

Like Huck, Holden is also a refugee. He flees the campus of Pencey Prep before he is formally expelled, and returns to New York City to have three days of freedom before rejoining his family. Pencey Prep is merely the most recent in a series of unsatisfactory academic experiences for him. "One of the biggest reasons I left Elkton Hills was because I was surrounded by phonies. That's all. They were coming in the goddam window. I can't stand that stuff. It drives me crazy. It makes me so depressed I go crazy."

Also like Huck, Holden assumes a series of guises during his lone wanderings. "I'm the most terrific liar you ever saw in your life. It's awful. If I'm on the way to the store to buy a magazine, even, and somebody asks me where I'm going, I'm liable to say I'm going to the opera. It's terrible." In a sequence which reminds one forcibly of Huck Finn, Holden finds himself in conversation with the mother of one of his classmates, Ernie Morrow, whom he describes as "doubtless the biggest bastard that ever went to Pencey, in the whole crumby history of the school." But Holden, adopting the name of "Rudolf Schmidt" (the janitor), tells her what she wants to hear about her son, to her wonder and delight. Holden's comment is "Mothers are all slightly insane. The thing is, though, I liked old Morrow's mother. She was all right." His imagination rampant, Holden tells her a cock-and-bull story which includes an impending brain operation and a trip to South America to visit his grandmother, but he stops just short of revealing himself completely. It is a wonderfully funny scene, showing Holden in several aspects: his instinctive evaluation of the mother's "rightness" overcoming his profound distaste for her son, his adolescent imagination in a frenzy of wild invention, and his own awareness of the limits to which he can act his suddenly-adopted role of Rudolf Schmidt.

Huck's tortured decision not to "turn in" Jim is made on the basis of his own feelings, which he automatically assumes to be sinful since they have so often put him at odds with society. His personal moral code seems always to run counter to his duty to society, a conflict which serves to confirm him in the belief that wickedness is in his line, "being brung up to it." In the crucial moral act of the novel, Huck must "decide, forever, betwixt two things, and I knowed it. I studied a minute, sort of holding my breath, and then says to myself, 'All right, then I'll *go* to hell.' " Huck's humanity overcomes the so-called duty to society. Holden, also, is "depressed" by the notion that he is somehow a misfit, that he does strange, irrational things, that he is fighting a constant war with society—but his awareness of his own weaknesses (his compulsive lying, for example) is the result of his searching honesty.

The yardstick which Holden applies to the world is a simple one—too simple, perhaps, too rigorous, too uncompromising, for anyone but an adolescent (or, as the popular phrase has it, "a crazy mixed-up kid") to attempt to apply to a complex world: it is the test of truth. The world is full of phonies—so Holden dreams of running away and building his own cabin, where people would come and visit him. "I'd have this rule that nobody could do anything phony when they visited me. If anybody tried to do anything phony, they couldn't stay."

Huck's world, realistically depicted as mid-American in the middle of the nineteenth century, is also the world where the established codes are penetrated as being either hypocritical or superficial; Huck finds peace and reassurance away from the haunts of man, out on the river. After the waste and folly of the Grangerford-Shepherdson sequence, for example, Huck retreats to the river:

> Sometimes we'd have that whole river all to ourselves for the longest time. Yonder was the banks and the islands, across the water; and maybe a spark—which was a candle in a cabin window; and sometimes on the water you could see a spark or two—on a raft or a scow, you know; and maybe you could hear a fiddle or a song coming over from one of them crafts. It's lovely to live on a raft.

But the idyll is interrupted shortly thereafter with "a couple of men tearing up the path as tight as they could foot it"—the Duke and the Dauphin imposing their unsavory world upon Huck's.

Holden's world is post-war New York City, from the Metropolitan Museum to Greenwich Village, during Christmas week, where, in successive incidents, he encounters pompous hypocrisy, ignorance, indifference, moral corruption, sexual perversion, and—pervading all—"phoniness." Holden's older brother, a once promising writer, is now a Hollywood scenarist; the corruption of his talent is symptomatic to Holden of the general influence of the movies: "They can ruin you. I'm not kidding." They represent the world at its "phoniest" in their falsification of reality; in addition, they corrupt their audiences, converting them into people like the three pathetic girls from

Seattle who spend all evening in a second-rate night club looking for movie stars, or like the woman Holden observes at the Radio City Music Hall. She cries through the entire picture, and "the phonier it got, the more she cried. . . . She had this little kid with her that was bored as hell and had to go to the bathroom, but she wouldn't take him. . . . She was about as kind-hearted as a goddam wolf."

Holden's awareness of sham sensitizes him to its manifestations wher-ever it appears; in the pseudo-religious Christmas spectacle at Radio City ("I can't see anything religious or pretty, for God's sake, about a bunch of actors carrying crucifixes all over the stage"); in ministers with "Holy Joe" voices; in magazine fiction, with its "lean-jawed guys named David" and "phony girls named Linda or Marcia"; and in the performance of a gifted night-club pianist as well as that of the Lunts. His reaction to the performances of all three is a comment on the relationship between virtuosity and integrity: "If you do something *too* good, then, after a while, if you don't watch it, you start showing off. And then you're not as good any more." Both mock humil-ity and casual bravura are dangerous to the integrity of the individual: Holden finds no "naturalness" in the finished and most artistic performers in his world. His world, he comes to feel, is full of obscenities, both figurative and actual; even a million years would be inadequate to erase all the obsceni-ties scribbled on all the walls. His week-end in New York reminds him of the time an alumnus of Pencey visited the school and inspected the doors in the men's toilet to see if his initials were still carved there. While he searched for this memento of his past, he solemnly gave platitudinous advice to the boys. The glaring disparity between what even "good guys" say and what they do is enough to make Holden despair of finding anyone, except his sister Phoebe, with whom he can communicate honestly.

A few things Holden encounters on his voyage through the metropolis make him "feel better." Like Huck, who has to retreat regularly to the river, to reestablish his contacts with his sources of value, Holden several times meets perfectly "natural" things which delight him: the kettle-drummer in the orchestra, who never looks bored, but who bangs his drums "so nice and sweet, with this nervous expression on his face"; a Dixieland song recorded by a Negro girl who doesn't make it sound "mushy" or "cute"; and the sight of a family coming out of church. But these incidents merely serve to reveal in a sharper contrast the phoniness and the tinsel of the adult world which seeks to victimize Holden, and which, in the end, finally does. Like Huck, he finds himself at the mercy of the kindly enemy. The realist's sharp perceptions of the world about him are treated either as the uncivilized remarks of an ignorant waif or—supreme irony!—as lunacy.

In addition to being comic masterpieces and superb portrayals of per-plexed, sensitive adolescence, these two novels thus deal obliquely and poetically with a major theme in American life, past and present—the right of the nonconformist to assert his nonconformity, even to the point of being "handled with a chain." In them, 1884 and 1951 speak to us in the idiom and accent of two youthful travelers who have earned their passports to literary immortality.

Note: An article by Arthur Heiserman and James E. Miller, Jr., entitled, "J. D. Salinger: Some Crazy Cliff," *WHR*, X (Spring 1965), 129–137, which relates the adventures of Holden and Huck to the traditional theme of the Quest, places them in the company of Stephen Dedalus, Ishmael, Hans Castorp, and Dostoievski's Idiot, and contains many illuminating comparisons. My article having been accepted by *CE* before the appearance of the Heiserman-Miller article, the numerous parallels between the two can be attributed only to coincidental simultaneous generation.

The Language of
The Catcher in the Rye
Donald P. Costello*

A study of the language of J. D. Salinger's *The Catcher in the Rye* can be justified not only on the basis of literary interest, but also on the basis of linguistic significance. Today we study *The Adventures of Huckleberry Finn* (with which many critics have compared *The Catcher in the Rye*) not only as a great work of literary art, but as a valuable study in 1884 dialect. In coming decades, *The Catcher in the Rye* will be studied, I feel, not only as a literary work, but also as an example of teenage vernacular in the 1950s. As such, the book will be a significant historical linguistic record of a type of speech rarely made available in permanent form. Its linguistic importance will increase as the American speech it records becomes less current.

Most critics who looked at *The Catcher in the Rye* at the time of its publication thought that its language was a true and authentic rendering of teenage colloquial speech. Reviewers in the Chicago *Sunday Tribune*, the London *Times Literary Supplement*, the *New Republic*, the New York *Herald Tribune Book Review*, the *New York Times*, the *New Yorker*, and the *Saturday Review of Literature* all specifically mentioned the authenticity of the book's language. Various aspects of its language were also discussed in the reviews published in *America*, the *Atlantic*, the *Catholic World*, the *Christian Science Monitor*, the *Library Journal*, the Manchester *Guardian*, the *Nation*, the *New Statesman and Nation*, the *New York Times Book Review*, *Newsweek*, the *Spectator*, and *Time*.[1] Of these many reviews, only the writers for the *Catholic World* and the *Christian Science Monitor* denied the authenticity of the book's language, but both of these are religious journals which refused to believe that the "obscenity" was realistic. An examina-

*Reprinted by permission from *American Speech* 34, no. 3 (October 1959): 172–81. © 1959 by Donald P. Costello.

tion of the reviews of *The Catcher in the Rye* proves that the language of Holden Caulfield, the book's sixteen-year-old narrator, struck the ear of the contemporary reader as an accurate rendering of the informal speech of an intelligent, educated, Northeastern American adolescent.[2]

In addition to commenting on its authenticity, critics have often remarked—uneasily—the "daring", "obscene," "blasphemous" features of Holden's language. Another commonly noted feature of the book's language has been its comic effect. And yet there has never been an extensive investigation of the language itself. That is what this paper proposes to do.

Even though Holden's language is authentic teenage speech, recording it was certainly not the major intention of Salinger. He was faced with the artistic task of creating an individual character, not with the linguistic task of reproducing the exact speech of teenagers in general. Yet Holden had to speak a recognizable teenage language, and at the same time had to be identifiable as an individual. This difficult task Salinger achieved by giving Holden an extremely trite and typical teenage speech, overlaid with strong personal idiosyncrasies. There are two major speech habits which are Holden's own, which are endlessly repeated throughout the book, and which are, nevertheless, typical enough of teenage speech so that Holden can be both typical and individual in his use of them. It is certainly common for teenagers to end thoughts with a loosely dangling "and all," just as it is common for them to add an insistent "I really did," "It really was." But Holden uses these phrases to such an overpowering degree that they become a clear part of the flavor of the book; they become, more, a part of Holden himself, and actually help to characterize him.

Holden's "and all" and its twins, "or something," "or anything," serve no real, consistent linguistic function. They simply give a sense of looseness of expression and looseness of thought. Often they signify that Holden knows there is more that could be said about the issue at hand, but he is not going to bother going into it:

> . . . how my parents were occupied and all before they had me (5).[3]
> . . . they're *nice* and all (5).
> I'm not going to tell you my whole goddam autobiography or anything (5).
> . . . splendid and clear-thinking and all (6).

But just as often the use of such expressions is purely arbitrary, with no discernible meaning:

> . . . he's my *brother* and all (5).
> . . . was in the Revolutionary War and all (6).
> It was December and all (7).
> . . . no gloves or anything (7).
> . . . right in the pocket and all (7).

Donald Barr, writing in the *Commonweal*, finds this habit indicative of Holden's tendency to generalize, to find the all in the one:

Salinger has an ear not only for idiosyncrasies of diction and syntax, but for mental processes. Holden Caulfield's phrase is "and all"—"She looked so damn *nice*, the way she kept going around and around in her blue coat and all"—as if each experience wore a halo. His fallacy is *ab uno disce omnes;* he abstracts and generalizes wildly.[4]

Heiserman and Miller, in the *Western Humanities Review*, comment specifically upon Holden's second most obvious idiosyncrasy: "In a phony world Holden feels compelled to reenforce his sincerity and truthfulness constantly with, 'It really is' or 'It really did.' "[5] S. N. Behrman, in the *New Yorker,* finds a double function of these "perpetual insistences of Holden's." Behrman thinks they "reveal his age, even when he is thinking much older," and, more important, "he is so aware of the danger of slipping into phoniness himself that he has to repeat over and over 'I really mean it,' 'It really does.' "[6] Holden uses this idiosyncrasy of insistence almost every time that he makes an affirmation.

Allied to Holden's habit of insistence is his "if you want to know the truth." Heiserman and Miller are able to find characterization in this habit too:

> The skepticism inherent in that casual phrase, "if you want to know the truth," suggesting that as a matter of fact in the world of Holden Caulfield very few people do, characterizes this sixteen-year-old "crazy mixed up kid" more sharply and vividly than pages of character "analysis" possibly could.[7]

Holden uses this phrase only after affirmations, just as he uses "It really does," but usually after the personal ones, where he is consciously being frank:

> I have no wind, if you want to know the truth. (8).
> I don't even think that bastard had a handkerchief, if you want to know the truth. (34).
> I'm a pacifist, if you want to know the truth. (44).
> She had quite a lot of sex appeal, too, if you really want to know. (53).
> I was damn near bawling, I felt so damn happy, if you want to know the truth. (191).

These personal idiosyncrasies of Holden's speech are in keeping with general teenage language. Yet they are so much a part of Holden and of the flavor of the book that they are much of what makes Holden to be Holden. They are the most memorable feature of the book's language. Although always in character, the rest of Holden's speech is more typical than individual. The special quality of this language comes from its triteness, its lack of distinctive qualities.

Holden's informal, schoolboy vernacular is particularly typical in its "vulgarity" and "obscenity." No one familiar with prep-school speech could seriously contend that Salinger overplayed his hand in this respect. On the contrary, Holden's restraints help to characterize him as a sensitive youth who avoids the most strongly forbidden terms, and who never uses vulgarity in a self-conscious or phony way to help him be "one of the boys." *Fuck*, for example, is never used as a part of Holden's speech. The word appears in the novel four times, but only when Holden disapprovingly discusses its wide appearance on walls. The Divine name is used habitually by Holden only in the comparatively weak *for God's sake, God,* and *goddam*. The stronger and usually more offensive *for Chrissake* or *Jesus* or *Jesus Christ* are used habitually by Ackley and Stradlater; but Holden uses them only when he feels the need for a strong expression. He almost never uses *for Chrissake* in an unemotional situation. *Goddam* is Holden's favorite adjective. This word is used with no relationship to its original meaning, or to Holden's attitude toward the word to which it is attached. It simply expresses an emotional feeling toward the object: either favorable, as in "goddam hunting cap"; or unfavorable, as in "ya goddam moron"; or indifferent, as in "coming in the goddam windows." *Damm* is used interchangeably with *goddam;* no differentiation in its meaning is detectable.

Other crude words are also often used in Holden's vocabulary. *Ass* keeps a fairly restricted meaning as a part of the human anatomy, but it is used in a variety of ways. It can refer simply to that specific part of the body ("I moved my ass a little"), or be a part of a trite expression ("freezing my ass off"; "in a half-assed way"), or be an expletive ("Game, my ass"). *Hell* is perhaps the most versatile word in Holden's entire vocabulary; it serves most of the meanings and constructions which Mencken lists in his *American Speech* article on "American Profanity."[8] So far is Holden's use of *hell* from its original meaning that he can use the sentence "We had a helluva time" to mean that he and Phoebe had a decidedly pleasant time downtown shopping for shoes. The most common function of *hell* is as the second part of a simile, in which a thing can be either "hot as hell" or, strangely, "cold as hell"; "sad as hell" or "playful as hell"; "old as hell" or "pretty as hell." Like all of these words, *hell* has no close relationship to its original meaning.

Both *bastard* and *sonuvabitch* have also drastically changed in meaning. They no longer, of course, in Holden's vocabulary, have any connection with the accidents of birth. Unless used in a trite simile, *bastard* is a strong word, reserved for things and people Holden particularly dislikes, especially "phonies." *Sonuvabitch* has an even stronger meaning to Holden; he uses it only in the deepest anger. When, for example, Holden is furious with Stradlater over his treatment of Jane Gallagher, Holden repeats again and again that he "kept calling him a moron sonuvabitch" (43).

The use of crude language in *The Catcher in the Rye* increases, as we should expect, when Holden is reporting schoolboy dialogue. When he is directly addressing the reader, Holden's use of such language drops off almost entirely. There is also an increase in this language when any of the characters are excited or angry. Thus, when Holden is apprehensive over

Stradlater's treatment of Jane, his *goddams* increase suddenly to seven on a single page (39).

Holden's speech is also typical in his use of slang. I have catalogued over a hundred slang terms used by Holden, and every one of these is in widespread use. Although Holden's slang is rich and colorful, it, of course, being slang, often fails at precise communication. Thus, Holden's *crap* is used in seven different ways. It can mean foolishness, as "all that David Copperfield kind of crap," or messy matter, as "I spilled some crap all over my gray flannel," or merely miscellaneous matter, as "I was putting on my galoshes and crap." It can also carry its basic meaning, animal excreta, as "there didn't look like there was anything in the park except dog crap," and it can be used as an adjective meaning anything generally unfavorable, as "The show was on the crappy side." Holden uses the phrase *to be a lot of crap* and *to shoot the crap* and *to chuck the crap* all to mean "to be untrue," but he can also use *to shoot the crap* to mean simply "to chat," with no connotation of untruth, as in "I certainly wouldn't have minded shooting the crap with old Phoebe for a while."

Similarly Holden's slang use of *crazy* is both trite and imprecise. "That drives me crazy" means that he violently dislikes something; yet "to be crazy about" something means just the opposite. In the same way, to be "killed" by something can mean that he was emotionally affected either favorably ("That story just about killed me.") or unfavorably ("Then she turned her back on me again. It nearly killed me."). This use of *killed* is one of Holden's favorite slang expressions. Heiserman and Miller are, incidentally, certainly incorrect when they conclude: "Holden always lets us know when he has insight into the absurdity of the endlessly absurd situations which make up the life of a sixteen-year-old by exclaiming, 'It killed me.' "[9] Holden often uses this expression with no connection to the absurd; he even uses it for his beloved Phoebe. The expression simply indicates a high degree of emotion—any kind. It is hazardous to conclude that any of Holden's slang has a precise and consistent meaning or function. These same critics fall into the same error when they conclude that Holden's use of the adjective *old* serves as "a term of endearment."[10] Holden appends this word to almost every character, real or fictional, mentioned in the novel, from the hated "old Maurice" to "old Peter Lorre," to "old Phoebe," and even "old Jesus." The only pattern that can be discovered in Holden's use of this term is that he usually uses it only after he has previously mentioned the character; he then feels free to append the familiar *old*. All we can conclude from Holden's slang is that it is typical teenage slang: versatile yet narrow, expressive yet unimaginative, imprecise, often crude, and always trite.

Holden has many favorite slang expressions which he overuses. In one place, he admits:

> "Boy!" I said. I also say "Boy!" quite a lot. Partly because I have a lousy vocabulary and partly because I act quite young for my age sometimes. (12)

But if Holden's slang shows the typically "lousy vocabulary" of even the educated American teenager, this failing becomes even more obvious when we narrow our view to Holden's choice of adjectives and adverbs. The choice is indeed narrow, with a constant repetition of a few favorite words: *lousy, pretty, crumby, terrific, quite, old, stupid*—all used, as is the habit of teen-age vernacular, with little regard to specific meaning. Thus, most of the nouns which are called "stupid" could not in any logical framework be called "ignorant," and, as we have seen, *old* before a proper noun has nothing to do with age.

Another respect in which Holden was correct in accusing himself of having a "lousy vocabulary" is discovered in the ease with which he falls into trite figures of speech. We have already seen that Holden's most common simile is the worn and meaningless "as hell"; but his often-repeated "like a madman" and "like a bastard" are just about as unrelated to a literal meaning and are easily as unimaginative. Even Holden's nonhabitual figures of speech are usually trite: "sharp as a tack"; "hot as a firecracker"; "laughed like a hyena"; "I know old Jane like a book"; "drove off like a bat out of hell"; "I began to feel like a horse's ass"; "blind as a bat"; "I know Central Park like the back of my hand."

Repetitious and trite as Holden's vocabulary may be, it can, neverthe-less, become highly effective. For example, when Holden piles one trite adjective upon another, a strong power of invective is often the result:

He was a goddam stupid moron. (42).
Get your dirty stinking moron knees off my chest. (43).
You're a dirty stupid sonuvabitch of a moron. (43).

And his limited vocabulary can also be used for good comic effect. Holden's constant repetition of identical expressions in countless widely different situa-tions is often hilariously funny.

But all of the humor in Holden's vocabulary does not come from its unimaginative quality. Quite the contrary, some of his figures of speech are entirely original; and these are inspired, dramatically effective, and terribly funny. As always, Salinger's Holden is basically typical, with a strong overlay of the individual:

He started handling my exam paper like it was a turd or something. (13)
He put my goddam paper down then and looked at me like he'd just beaten the hell out of me in ping-pong or something. (14)
That guy Morrow was about as sensitive as a goddam toilet seat. (52)
Old Marty was like dragging the Statue of Liberty around the floor. (69)

Another aspect in which Holden's language is typical is that it shows the general American characteristic of adaptability—apparently strengthened by his teenage lack of restraint. It is very easy for Holden to turn nouns into adjectives, with the simple addition of a *-y:* "perverty," "Christmasy," "vomity-looking," "whory-looking," "hoodlumy-looking," "show-offy," "flirty-looking," "dumpy-looking," "pimpy," "snobby," "fisty." Like all of English, Holden's language shows a versatile combining ability: "They gave Sally this little blue butt-twitcher of a dress to wear" (117) and "That magazine was some little cheerer upper" (176). Perhaps the most interesting aspect of the adaptability of Holden's language is his ability to use nouns as adverbs: "She sings it very Dixieland and whorehouse, and it doesn't sound at all mushy" (105).

As we have seen, Holden shares, in general, the trite repetitive vocabulary which is the typical lot of his age group. But as there are exceptions in his figures of speech, so are there exceptions in his vocabulary itself, in his word stock. An intelligent, well-read ("I'm quite illiterate, but I read a lot"), and educated boy, Holden possesses, and can use when he wants to, many words which are many a cut above Basic English, including "ostracized," "exhibitionist," "unscrupulous," "conversationalist," "psychic," "bourgeois," Often Holden seems to choose his words consciously, in an effort to communicate to his adult reader clearly and properly, as in such terms as "lose my virginity," "relieve himself," "an alcoholic"; for upon occasion, he also uses the more vulgar terms "to give someone the time," "to take a leak," "booze hound." Much of the humor arises, in fact, from Holden's habit of writing on more than one level at the same time. Thus, we have such phrases as "They give guys the ax quite frequently at Pencey" and "It has a very good academic rating, Pencey" (7). Both sentences show a colloq_ial idiom with an overlay of consciously selected words.

Such a conscious choice of words seems to indicate that Salinger, in his attempt to create a realistic character in Holden, wanted to make him aware of his speech, as, indeed, a real teenager would be when communicating to the outside world. Another piece of evidence that Holden is conscious of his speech and, more, realizes a difficulty in communication, is found in his habit of direct repetition: "She likes me a lot. I mean she's quite fond of me" (141), and "She can be very snotty sometimes. She can be quite snotty" (150). Sometimes the repetition is exact: "He was a very nervous guy—I mean he was a very nervous guy" (165), and "I sort of missed them. I mean I sort of missed them" (169). Sometimes Holden stops specifically to interpret slang terms, as when he wants to communicate the fact that Allie liked Phoebe: "She killed Allie, too. I mean he liked her, too" (64).

There is still more direct evidence that Holden was conscious of his speech. Many of his comments to the reader are concerned with language. He was aware, for example, of the "phony" quality of many words and phrases, such as "grand," "prince," "traveling incognito," "little girls' room," "licorice stick," and "angels." Holden is also conscious, of course, of the existence of "taboo words." He makes a point of mentioning that the girl from Seattle repeatedly asked him to "watch your language, if you don't mind" (67), and that his mother told Phoebe not to say "lousy" (160). When the prostitute says, "Like fun you are," Holden comments:

It was a funny thing to say. It sounded like a real kid. You'd think a prostitute and all would say "Like hell you are" or "Cut the crap" instead of "Like fun you are" (87).

In grammar, too, as in vocabulary, Holden possesses a certain self-consciousness. (It is, of course, impossible to imagine a student getting through today's schools without a self-consciousness with regard to grammar rules.) Holden is, in fact, not only aware of the existence of "grammatical errors," but knows the social taboos that accompany them. He is disturbed by a schoolmate who is ashamed of his parents' grammar, and he reports that his former teacher, Mr. Antolini, warned him about picking up "just enough education to hate people who say, 'It's a secret between he and I' " (168).

Holden is a typical enough teenager to violate the grammar rules, even though he knows of their social importance. His most common rule violation is the misuse of *lie* and *lay*, but he also is careless about relative pronouns ("about a traffic cop that falls in love"), the double negative ("I hardly didn't even know I was doing it"), the perfect tenses ("I'd woke him up"), extra words ("like as if all you ever did at Pencey was play polo all the time"), pronoun number ("it's pretty disgusting to watch somebody picking their nose"), and pronoun position ("I and this friend of mine, Mal Brossard"). More remarkable, however, than the instances of grammar rule violations is Holden's relative "correctness." Holden is always intelligible, and is even "correct" in many usually difficult constructions. Grammatically speaking, Holden's language seems to point up the fact that English was the only subject in which he was not failing. It is interesting to note how much more "correct" Holden's speech is than that of Huck Finn. But then Holden is educated, and since the time of Huck there had been sixty-seven years of authoritarian schoolmarms working on the likes of Holden. He has, in fact, been overtaught, so that he uses many "hyper" forms:

I used to play tennis with he and Mrs. Antolini quite frequently. (163)
She'd give Allie or I a push. (64)
I and Allie used to take her to the park with us. (64)
I think I probably woke he and his wife up. (157)

Now that we have examined several aspects of Holden's vocabulary and grammar, it would be well to look at a few examples of how he puts these elements together into sentences. The structure of Holden's sentences indicates that Salinger thinks of the book more in terms of spoken speech than written speech. Holden's faulty structure is quite common and typical in vocal expression; I doubt if a student who is "good in English" would ever create such sentence structure in writing. A student who showed the self-consciousness of Holden would not *write* so many fragments, such after-thoughts (e.g., "It has a very good academic rating, Pencey" [7]), or such repetitions (e.g., "Where I lived at Pencey, I lived in the Ossenburger Memorial Wing of the new dorms" [18]).

There are other indications that Holden's speech is vocal. In many places Salinger mildly imitates spoken speech. Sentences such as "You could tell old Spencer'd got a big bang out of buying it" (10) and "I'd've killed him" (42) are repeated throughout the book. Yet it is impossible to imagine Holden taking pen in hand and actually writing "Spencer'd" or "I'd've." Sometimes, too, emphasized words, or even parts of words, are italicized, as in "Now *shut up*, Holden. God damn it—I'm *warn*ing ya" (42). This is often done with good effect, imitating quite perfectly the rhythms of speech, as in the typical:

> I practically sat down on her *lap*, as a matter of fact. The she *really* started to cry, and the next thing I knew, I was kissing her all over—*anywhere*— her eyes, her *nose*, her forehead, her eyebrows, and all, her *ears*—her whole face except her mouth and all. (73)

The language of *The Catcher in the Rye* is, as we have seen, an authentic artistic rendering of a type of informal, colloquial, teenage American spoken speech. It is strongly typical and trite, yet often somewhat individual; it is crude and slangy and imprecise, imitative yet occasionally imaginative, and affected toward standardization by the strong efforts of schools. But authentic and interesting as this language may be, it must be remembered that it exists, in *The Catcher in the Rye*, as only one part of an artistic achievement. The language was not written for itself, but as a part of a greater whole. Like the great Twain work with which it is often compared, a study of *The Catcher in the Rye* repays both the linguist and the literary critic; for as one critic has said, "In them 1884 and 1951 speak to us in the idiom and accent of two youthful travelers who have earned their passports to literary immortality."[11]

Notes

1. See reviews in *America*, LXXV (August 11, 1951), 463, 464; *Atlantic*, CLXXXVIII (1951), 82; *Catholic World*, CLXXIV (1951), 154; Chicago *Sunday Tribune*, July 15, 1951, Part 4, p. 3; *Christian Science Monitor*, July 19, 1951, p. 9; *Library Journal*, LXXVI (1951), 1125; *Times* [London] *Literary Supplement*, September 7, 1951, p. 561; Manchester *Guardian*, August 10, 1951, p. 4; *Nation*, CLXXIII (September 1, 1951), 176; *New Republic*, CXXV (July 16, 1951), 20, 21; *New Statesman and Nation*, XLII (August 18, 1951), 185; New York *Herald Tribune Book Review*, July 15, 1951, p. 3; *New York Times Book Review*, July 15, 1951, p. 5; *New York Times*, July 16, 1951, p. 19; *New Yorker*, XXVII (August 11, 1951), 71–76; *Newsweek*, XXXVIII (July 16, 1951), 89, 90; *Saturday Review of Literature*, XXXIV (July 14, 1951), 12, 13; *Spectator*, CLXXXVII (August 17, 1951), 224; *Time*, LVIII (July 16, 1951), 96, 97.

2. If additional evidence of the authenticity of the book's language is required, one need only look at the phenomenal regard with which *The Catcher in the Rye* is held by today's college students, who were about Holden's age at the time the book was written. In its March 9, 1957, issue, the *Nation* published a symposium which attempted to discover the major influences upon the college students of today. Many teachers pointed out the impact of Salinger. Carlos Baker, of Princeton, stated: "There is still, as there has been for years, a cult of Thomas Wolfe. They have all read J. D. Salinger, Wolfe's closest competitor." Stanley Kunitz, of Queens

College, wrote: "The only novelist I have heard praised vociferously is J. D. Salinger." Harvey Curtis Webster, of the University of Louisville, listed Salinger as one of the "stimulators." R. J. Kaufman, of the University of Rochester, called *The Catcher in the Rye* "a book which has complexly aroused nearly all of them." See "The Careful Young Men," *Nation*, CLXXXIV (March 9, 1957), 199–214. I have never heard any Salinger partisan among college students doubt the authenticity of the language of their compatriot, Holden.

3. Whenever *The Catcher in the Rye* is substantially quoted in this paper, a page number will be included in the text immediately after the quotation. The edition to which the page numbers refer is the Signet paperback reprint.

4. Donald Barr, "Saints, Pilgrims, and Artists," *Commonweal*, LXVII (October 25, 1957), 90.

5. Arthur Heiserman and James E. Miller, Jr., "J. D. Salinger: Some Crazy Cliff," *Western Humanities Review*, X (1956), 136.

6. S. N. Behrman, "The Vision of the Innocent," *New Yorker*, XXVII (August 11, 1951), 72.

7. Heiserman and Miller, *op. cit.*, p. 135.

8. See H. L. Mencken, "American Profanity," *American Speech*, XIX, (1944), 242.

9. Heiserman and Miller, *op. cit.*, p. 136.

10. *Ibid.*

11. Charles Kaplan, "Holden and Huck: the Odysseys of Youth," *College English*, XVIII (1956), 80.

The Sixties

The Saint as a Young Man:
A Reappraisal of
The Catcher in the Rye Jonathan Baumbach*

J. D. Salinger's first and only novel, *The Catcher in the Rye* (1951), has undergone in recent years a steady if overinsistent devaluation. The more it becomes academically respectable, the more it becomes fair game for those critics who are self-sworn to expose every manifestation of what seems to them a chronic disparity between appearance and reality. It is critical child's play to find fault with Salinger's novel. Anyone can see that the prose is mannered (the pejorative word for stylized); no one actually talks like its first-person hero Holden Caulfield. Moreover, we are told that Holden, as poor little rich boy, is too precocious and specialized an adolescent for his plight to have larger-than-prep-school significance. The novel is sentimental; it loads the deck for Holden and against the adult world; the small but corrupt group that Holden encounters is not representative enough to permit Salinger his inclusive judgments about the species. Holden's relationship to his family is not explored: we meet his sister Phoebe, who is a younger version of himself, but his father never appears, and his mother exists in the novel only as another voice from a dark room. Finally, what is Holden (or Salinger) protesting against but the ineluctability of growing up, of having to assume the prerogatives and responsibilities of manhood? Despite these objections to the novel, *Catcher in the Rye* will endure both because it has life and because it is a significantly original work, full of insights into at least the particular truth of Holden's existence. Within the limited terms of vision, Salinger's small book is an extraordinary achievement; it is, if such a distinction is meaningful, an important minor novel.

Like all of Salinger's fiction, *Catcher in the Rye* is not only about innocence, it is actively for innocence—as if retaining one's childness were an existential possibility. The metaphor of the title—Holden's fantasy-vision of standing in front of a cliff and protecting playing children from falling (Falling)—is, despite the impossibility of its realization, the only positive action affirmed in the novel. It is, in Salinger's Manichean universe of child angels and adult "phonies," the only moral alternative—otherwise all is cor-

*Reprinted by permission of the editor of *Modern Language Quarterly* and the author from *Modern Language Quarterly* 25, no. 4 (December 1964): 461–72.

ruption. Since it is spiritually as well as physically impossible to prevent the Fall, Salinger's idealistic heroes are doomed either to suicide (Seymour) or insanity (Holden, Sergeant X) or mysticism (Franny), the ways of sainthood, or to moral dissolution (Eloise, D. B., Mr. Antolini), the way of the world. In Salinger's finely honed prose, at once idiomatically real and poetically stylized, we get the terms of Holden's ideal adult occupation:

> Anyway, I keep picturing all these little kids playing some game in this big field of rye and all. Thousands of little kids, and nobody's around—nobody big, I mean—except me. And I'm standing on the edge of some crazy cliff. What I have to do, I have to catch everybody if they start to go over the cliff—I mean if they're running and they don't look where they're going I have to come out from somewhere and *catch* them. That's all I'd do all day. I'd just be the catcher in the rye and all. I know it's crazy, but that's the only thing I'd really like to be. I know it's crazy.[1]

Apparently Holden's wish is purely selfless. What he wants, in effect, is to be a saint—the protector and savior of innocence. But what he also wants, for he is still one of the running children himself, is that someone prevent *his* fall. This is his paradox: he must leave innocence to protect innocence. At sixteen, he is ready to shed his innocence and move like Adam into the fallen adult world, but he resists because those no longer innocent seem to him foolish as well as corrupt. In a sense, then, he is looking for an exemplar, a wise-good father whose example will justify his own initiation into manhood. Before Holden can become a catcher in the rye, he must find another catcher in the rye to show him how it is done.

Immediately after Holden announces his "crazy" ambition to Phoebe, he calls up one of his former teachers, Mr. Antolini, who is both intelligent and kind—a potential catcher in the rye.

> He was the one that finally picked up that boy that jumped out of the window I told you about, James Castle. Old Mr. Antolini felt his pulse and all, and then he took off his coat and put it over James Castle and carried him all the way over to the infirmary. (p. 226)

Although Mr. Antolini is sympathetic because "he didn't even give a damn if his coat got all bloody," the incident is symbolic of the teacher's failure as a catcher in the rye. For all his good intentions, he was unable to catch James Castle or prevent his fall; he could only pick him up after he had died. The episode of the suicide is one of the looming shadows darkening Holden's world; Holden seeks out Antolini because he hopes that the gentle teacher— the substitute father—will "pick him up" before he is irrevocably fallen. Holden's real quest throughout the novel is for a spiritual father (an innocent adult). He calls Antolini after all the other fathers of his world have failed him, including his real father, whose existence in the novel is represented solely by Phoebe's childish reiteration of "Daddy's going to kill you." The fathers in Salinger's child's-eye world do not catch falling boys—who have been thrown out of prep school—but "kill" them. Antolini represents Holden's last chance to find a catcher-father. But his inability to save Holden has been prophesied in his failure to save James Castle; the episode of Castle's death provides an anticipatory parallel to Antolini's unwitting destruction of Holden.

That Antolini's kindness to Holden is motivated in part by a homosexual interest, though it comes as a shock to Holden, does not wholly surprise the reader. Many of the biographical details that Salinger has revealed about him through Holden imply this possibility. For example, that he has an older and unattractive wife whom he makes a great show of kissing in public is highly suggestive; yet the discovery itself—Holden wakes to find Antolini sitting beside him and caressing his head—has considerable impact. We experience a kind of shock of recognition, the more intense for its having been anticipated. The scene has added power because Antolini is, for the most part, a good man, whose interest in Holden is genuine as well as perverted. His advice to Holden is apparently well-intentioned. Though many of his recommendations are cleverly articulated platitudes, Antolini evinces a prophetic insight when he tells Holden, "I have a feeling that you're riding for some kind of terrible, terrible fall"; one suspects, however, that to some extent he is talking about himself. Ironically, Antolini becomes the agent of his "terrible, terrible fall" by violating Holden's image of him, by becoming a false father. Having lost his respect for Antolini as a man, Holden rejects him as an authority; as far as Holden is concerned, Antolini's example denies the import of his words. His disillusionment with Antolini, who had seemed to be the sought-for, wise-good father, comes as the most intense of a long line of disenchantments; it is the final straw that breaks Holden. It is the equivalent of the loss of God. The world, devoid of good fathers (authorities), becomes a soul-destroying chaos in which his survival is possible only through withdrawal into childhood, into fantasy, into psychosis.

The action of the novel is compressed into two days in which Holden discovers through a series of disillusioning experiences that the adult world is unreclaimably corrupt. At the start of the novel, we learn from Holden that he has flunked out of Pencey Prep for not applying himself; he has resisted what he considers foolish or "phony" authority. Like almost all of Salinger's protagonists, Holden is clearly superior to his surroundings; he functions by dint of his pure sight, his innocence and sensibility, as initiate in and conscience of the world of the novel. Allowing for the exaggerations of innocence, we can generally accept Holden's value judgments of people and places as the judgments of the novel. For example, when Holden observes about this seventy-year-old, grippe-ridden history teacher that

> Old Spencer started nodding again. He also started picking his nose. He made out like he was only pinching it, but he was really getting the old thumb right in there. I guess he thought it was all right to do because it

> was only me that was in the room. I didn't *care*, except that it's pretty
> disgusting to watch somebody pick their nose. (pp. 13–14)

he is not being gratuitously malicious; he is passing what amounts to a moral judgment, although he is consciously doing no more than describing his reactions. Whereas the adult observer, no matter how scrupulous, censors his irreverent or unpleasant responses because he is ashamed of them, the child (Holden is sixteen) tells all.

Like Jane Austen, Salinger treats fools, especially pretentious ones, mercilessly. Though Spencer is seventy years old and for that reason alone may be worthy of respect, he is nevertheless platitudinous and self-indulgent, interested less in Holden than in pontificating before a captive audience. In a world in which the child is the spiritual father of the man, old age represents not wisdom but spiritual blindness and physical corruption. Spencer is not only foolish and "phony" ("Life *is* a game, boy"), but in his self-righteous way also actively malicious. Though Holden's is ostensibly a social visit, the old man badgers the boy about having failed history ("I flunked you in history because you knew absolutely nothing") and then insists on reading aloud Holden's inadequate exam.

> He put my goddam paper down then and looked at me like he'd just
> beaten hell out of me in ping-pong or something. I don't think I'll ever
> forgive him for reading me that crap out loud. I wouldn't've read it out loud
> to *him* if *he'd* written it—I really wouldn't. (p. 17)

In this confrontation between Holden and Spencer, there is an ironic inversion of the traditional student-teacher, son-father relationship which extends throughout the novel and throughout Salinger's fictional world. While Spencer, out of a childish need for personal justification, insensitively embarrasses Holden (already wounded by his expulsion from Pencey), the boy is mature enough to be kind to his conspicuously vulnerable antagonist. Holden accepts the full burden of responsibility for his scholastic failure so as to relieve Spencer of his sense of guilt.

> Well, you could see he really felt pretty lousy about flunking me. . . .
> I told him I was a real moron, and all that stuff. I told him I would've done
> exactly the same thing if I'd been in his place, and how most people didn't
> appreciate how tough it is being a teacher. That kind of stuff. The old bull.
> (p. 17)

In protecting his teacher's feelings, Holden performs the role of wise father; he is here a kind of catcher in the rye for a clumsy old child. His compassion is extensive enough to include even those he dislikes, even those who have hurt him. As he tells Antolini later in the novel:

> But you're wrong about that hating business . . . What I may do, I may
> hate them for a *little* while, like this guy Stradlater I knew at Pencey,
> and this other boy, Robert Ackley. I hated *them* once in a while—I

admit it—but it doesn't last too long, is what I mean. After a while, if I
didn't see them, if they didn't come in the room . . . I sort of missed
them. (p. 243)

Both Antolini and Spencer are too corrupt to notice that Holden is unable to
cope with the world not because he hates, but because he loves and the
world hates.

Spencer symbolizes all the stupid and destructive teacher-fathers at
Pencey Prep, which is in microcosm all schools—the world. In the short
scene between Holden and Spencer, Salinger evokes a sense of Holden's
entire "student" experience in which flunking out is an act of moral will
rather than a failure of application. Here, as throughout the novel, the wise
son resists the initiatory knowledge of the false ("phony") father and, at the
price of dispossession, retains his innocence. Holden is not so much rebelling against all authority, or even false authority, as he is searching for a just
one. That there are no good fathers in the world is its and Holden's tragedy.
It is the tragedy of Salinger's cosmos that the loss of innocence is irremediable. Ejected from the fallow womb of the prep school, Holden goes out alone
into the world of New York City in search of some kind of sustenance. His
comic misadventures in the city, which lead to his ultimate disillusion and
despair, make up the central action of the novel.

Holden not only suffers as a victim from the effects of the evil in this
world, but for it as its conscience—so that his experiences are exemplary. In
this sense, *Catcher in the Rye* is a religious or, to be more exact, spiritual
novel. Holden is Prince Mishkin as a sophisticated New York adolescent; and
like Mishkin, he experiences the guilt, unhappiness, and spiritual deformi-
ties of others more intensely than he does his own misfortunes. This is not to
say that Holden is without faults; he is, on occasion, silly, irritating, thought-
less, irresponsible—he has the excesses of innocence. Yet he is, as nearly as
possible, without sin.

The most memorable love affair Holden has experienced had its fruition
in daily checker games with Jane Gallagher, an unhappy, sensitive girl who
was his neighbor one summer. She had become the symbol to him of romantic love, that is, innocent love. When Holden discovers that his "sexy" roommate Stradlater has a date with her, he is concerned not only about the
possible loss of Jane's innocence, but about the loss of his dream of her—the
loss of their combined checker-playing, love-innocence. Holden has had one
previous emotional breakdown at thirteen when his saint-brother, Allie,[2]
died of leukemia. In Allie's death, Holden first recognized the fact of evil—of
what appears to be the gratuitous malevolence of the universe. Allie, who
was, Holden tells us, more intelligent and nicer than anyone else, has become for Holden a kind of saint-ideal. By rejecting an English theme on
Allie's baseball glove that Holden has written for him, and by implying that
he has "given Jane Gallagher the time," Stradlater spiritually maims Holden.
Holden's sole defense, a belief in the possibility of good in the world, col-

lapses: "I felt so lonesome, all of a sudden. I almost wished I was dead" (p. 62).

It is in this state of near-suicidal depair that Holden leaves for New York. That Stradlater may have had sexual relations with Jane—the destruction of innocence is an act of irremediable evil in Holden's world—impels Holden to leave Pencey immediately (but not before he quixotically challenges the muscular Stradlater, who in turn bloodies his nose). At various times in New York, Holden is on the verge of phoning Jane, and actually dials her number twice—that he is unable to reach her is symbolic of his loss of her innocence. The sexually experienced Stradlater, who is one of Holden's destructive fathers in the novel, has destroyed not Jane's innocence so much as Holden's idealized notion of her.[3]

Obliquely searching for good in the adult world, or at least something to mitigate his despair, Holden is continually confronted with the absence of good. On his arrival in the city, he is disturbed because his cabdriver is corrupt and unsociable and, worst of all, unable to answer Holden's obsessional question: where do the Central Park ducks go when the lake freezes over? What Holden really wants to know is whether there is a benevolent authority that takes care of ducks. If there is one for ducks, it follows that there may be one for people as well. Holden's quest for a wise and benevolent authority, then, is essentially a search for a God-principle. However, none of the adults in Holden's world has any true answers for him. When he checks into a hotel room, he is depressed by the fact that the bellboy is an old man ("What a gorgeous job for a guy around sixty-five years old"). As sensitized recorder of the moral vibrations of his world, Holden suffers the indignity of the aged bellhop's situation for him, as he had suffered for Spencer's guilt and Ackley's self-loathing. Yet, and this is part of his tragedy, he is an impotent saint, unable either to redeem the fallen or to prevent their fall.

If the world of Holden's school was a muted purgatory, the world of his New York hotel is an insistent Hell. The window of his room provides him with a view of the other rooms in the hotel. In one, he sees a man dress himself in women's clothes, and in another, a man and woman who delight (sexually) in squirting water at each other from their mouths. This is the "real" world, with its respectable shade lifted, which fascinates and seduces Holden by its prurience. Having lost the sense of his innocence, he seeks sexual initiation as a means of redemption. His attraction to older women suggests that his quest for a woman is really a search for a mother whose love will protect him against the corrupt world as well as initiate him into it. Where the father-quest is a search for wisdom and spirit (God), the mother-quest is a search not for sex but ultimately for Love. They are different manifestations, one intellectual, the other physical, of the same spiritual quest. His search for sexual experience, Salinger indicates, is the only love alternative left Holden after he loses Jane. Once the possibility of innocent love ceases to exist, sexual love seems the next best thing, a necessary compensation for the loss of the first. However, Holden is only mildly disappointed when he is unable to arrange a date with a reputedly promiscuous girl whose telephone number he has inherited from a Princeton acquaintance. For all his avowed "sexiness," he is an innocent, and his innocence-impelled fear dampens his desire. Though the women he meets are by and large less disappointing than the men, they too fail Holden and intensify his despair. That they are not as good as he would like them to be seems to him *his* fault, *his* responsibility, *his* failure.

If Jane represents sacred love profaned, the prostitute who comes to Holden's room represents profane love unprofaned. After he has agreed to have her come to his room (the elevator operator, Maurice, is go-between), he refuses to make love to her once she is there. The scene is a crucial one in defining Holden's nontraditional sainthood. Holden refuses the prostitute not because of moral principle, but because the condition of her existence (she is about Holden's age and a kind of lost-innocent) depresses him.

> I took her dress over to the closet and hung it up for her. It was funny. It made me feel sort of sad when I hung it up. I thought of her going in a store and buying it, and nobody in the store knowing she was a prostitute and all. The salesman probably just thought she was a regular girl when she bought it. It made me feel sad as hell—I don't know why exactly. (p. 125)

He would save her if he could, but she is far too fallen for any catcher in the rye. But as child-saint, Holden is quixotic. In not sleeping with her, he means to protect her innocence, not his own; he is spiritually, hence physically, unable to be a party to her further degradation. The consequences are ironic. Holden as a saint refuses to victimize the prostitute, but he is victimized by the girl and her accomplice, Maurice. Though Holden has paid the girl without using her, Maurice beats Holden and extorts an additional five dollars from him. This episode is a more intense recapitulation of the Stradlater experience. In both cases Holden is punished for his innocence. If the hotel is a symbolic Hell, Maurice, as far as Holden is concerned, is its chief devil. In offering Holden the girl and then humiliating him for not accepting his expensive gift, Maurice is another of Holden's evil fathers.

After disillusionment with Antolini, who is the most destructive of Holden's fathers because he is seemingly the most benevolent, Holden suffers an emotional breakdown. His flight from Antolini's house, like his previous flights from school and from the hotel, is an attempt to escape evil. The three are parallel experiences, except that Holden is less sure of the justness of his third flight and wonders if he has not misjudged his otherwise sympathetic teacher.

> And the more I thought about it, the more depressed I got. I mean I started thinking maybe I *should've* gone back to his house. Maybe he *was* only patting my head just for the hell of it. The more I thought about it, though, the more depressed and screwed up about it I got. (p. 253)

The ambivalence of his response racks him. If he has misjudged Antolini, he has wronged not only his teacher, but he has wronged himself as well; he, not Antolini, has been guilty of corruption. Consequently, he suffers both for Antolini and for himself. Holden's guilt-ridden despair manifests itself in nausea and in an intense sense of physical ill-being, as if he carries the whole awful corruption of the city inside him. Walking aimlessly through the Christmas-decorated city, Holden experiences "the terrible, terrible fall" that Antolini had prophesied for him.

> Every time I came to the end of a block and stepped off the goddam curb, I had this feeling that I'd never get to the other side of the street. I thought I'd go down, down, down, and nobody'd ever see me again. Boy, did it scare me. You can't imagine. I started sweating like a bastard—my whole shirt and underwear and everything. . . . Every time I'd get to the end of a block I'd make believe I was talking to my brother Allie. I'd say to him, "Allie, don't let me disappear. Allie, don't let me disappear. Allie, don't let me disappear. Please, Allie." And then when I'd reach the other side of the street without disappearing, I'd *thank* him. (pp. 256–57)

Like Franny's prayer to Jesus in one of Salinger's later stories, Holden's prayer to Allie is not so much an act of anguish as an act of love, though it is in part both. Trapped in an interior hell, Holden seeks redemption, not by formal appeal to God or Jesus, who have in the Christmas season been falsified and commercialized, but by praying to his saint-brother who in his goodness had God in him.

Like so many heroes of contemporary fiction—Morris' Boyd, Ellison's Invisible Man, Malamud's Frank, Salinger's Seymour—Holden is an impotent savior. Because he can neither save his evil world nor live in it as it is, he retreats into fantasy—into childhood. He decides to become a deaf-mute, to live alone in an isolated cabin, to commit a kind of symbolic suicide. It is an unrealizable fantasy, but a death wish nevertheless. However, Holden's social conscience forces him out of spiritual retirement. When he discovers an obscenity scrawled on one of the walls of Phoebe's school, he rubs it out with his hand to protect the innocence of the children. For the moment he is a successful catcher in the rye. But then he discovers another such notice, "*scratched* on, with a knife or something," and then another. He realizes that he cannot possibly erase all the scribbled obscenities in the world, that he cannot catch all the children, that evil is ineradicable.

This is the final disillusionment. Dizzy with his terrible awareness, Holden insults Phoebe when she insists on running away with him. In his vision of despair, he sees Phoebe's irrevocable doom as well as his own, and for a moment he hates her as he hates himself—as he hates the world. Once he has hurt her, however, he realizes the commitment that his love for her imposes on him; if he is to assuage her pain, he must continue to live in the world. When she kisses him as a token of forgiveness and love and, as if in consequence, it begins to rain, Holden, bathed by the rain, is purified—in a sense, redeemed.

A too literal reading of Holden's divulgence that he is telling the story from some kind of rest home has led to a misinterpretation of the end of the novel. Holden is always less insane than his world. The last scene, in which Holden, suffused with happiness, sits in the rain and watches Phoebe ride on the merry-go-round, is indicative not of his crack-up, as has been assumed, but of his redemption. Whereas all the adults in his world have failed him (and he, a butter-fingered catcher in the rye, has failed them), a ten-year-old girl saves him—becomes his catcher. Love is the redemptive grace. Phoebe replaces Jane, the loss of whom had initiated Holden's despair, flight, and quest for experience as salvation. Holden's pure communion with Phoebe may be construed as a reversion to childlike innocence, but this is the only way to redemption in Salinger's world—there is no other good. Innocence is all. Love is innocence.[4]

The last scene, with Holden drenched in Scott Fitzgerald's all-absolving rain,[5] seems unashamedly sentimental. Certainly Salinger overstates the spiritually curative powers of children; innocence can be destructive as well as redemptive. Yet Salinger's view of the universe, in which all adults (even the most apparently decent) are corrupt and consequently destructive, is bleak and somewhat terrifying. Since growing up in the real world is tragic, in Salinger's ideal world time must be stopped to prevent the loss of childhood, to salvage the remnants of innocence. At one point in the novel, Holden wishes that life were as changeless and pure as the exhibitions under glass cases in the Museum of Natural History. This explains, in part, Holden's ecstasy in the rain at the close of the novel. In watching Phoebe go round and round on the carrousel, in effect going nowhere, he sees her in the timeless continuum of art on the verge of changing, yet unchanging, forever safe, forever loving, forever innocent.

Salinger's view of the world has limited both his productivity and his range of concerns. In the last nine years, he has published only four increasingly long and increasingly repetitive short stories, all of which treat some aspect of the mythic life and times of the Glass family, whose most talented member, Seymour, committed suicide in an early story, "A Perfect Day for Bananafish." But though Salinger may go on, as Hemingway did, mimicking himself, trying desperately to relocate his old youthful image in some narcissistic internal mirror, his achievement as a writer cannot be easily discounted. All his stories, even the least successful, evince a stunning and original verbal talent, despite some stylistic debt to Fitzgerald and Lardner. Like *The Great Gatsby*, which both Holden and Salinger admire, *Catcher in the Rye* is, as far as the human eye can see, a perfect novel; it is self-defining, that is, there seems to be an inevitability about its form. Although the craft of the author is unobtrusive, everything of consequence that happens in the novel has been in some way anticipated by an earlier episode or reference. The rain that baptizes Holden at the end is, in symbol, the same rain that had fallen on Allie's gravestone and had depressed Holden; the scurrying of the visitors as they left the cemetery to seek shelter in their cars had emphasized Allie's immobility, his deadness. In praying to Allie, Holden implicitly accepts the fact of his brother's immortality which his earlier response had denied. Through association, Salinger suggests that the purifying rain is a manifestation of Allie's blessed and blessing spirit. Like Phoebe's kiss, Allie's rain is an act of love.

Notes.

1. J. D. Salinger, *The Catcher in the Rye* (Boston, 1951), 224–25; all page references are to this edition.

2. Holden's relationship to Allie, though less intense, is the equivalent of Buddy's to Seymour in the several Glass family stories.

3. Another destructive father is Ackley, who refuses Holden solace after Holden has been morally and physically beaten by Stradlater. (The father concern is intentional on Salinger's part.) Both Ackley and Stradlater are two years older than Holden, and at one point Ackley reproves Holden's lack of respect, telling him , "I am old enough to be your father."

4. Like the narrator in "For Esmé—With Love and Squalor," Holden is redeemed by the love of an innocent girl. In both cases the protagonist is saved because he realizes that if there is any love at all in the world—even the love of one child—Love exists.

5. At the graveside service for Gatsby, as rain falls on his coffin, Nick hears someone say, "Blessed are the dead that the rain falls on." I suspect that Salinger had the Fitzgerald passage in mind.

Kings in the Back Row: Meaning through Structure—A Reading of Salinger's *The Catcher in the Rye*   Carl F. Strauch*

I

The impressive accumulation of critical views on Salinger's *The Catcher in the Rye* is a tribute not only to the exciting qualities of the book but also to the awareness and resourcefulness of academic commentators. It has been compared to other fictional treatments of the crushing moral problems of sensitive American adolescents confronted by a hostile society. Critics, for the most part, have lavished an affectionate understanding upon a Holden Caulfield who regards his fellows with religious compassion and at the same time, out of his own durable honesty, reacts against the phony in both institutions and people. On this score there has been, so far as I know, only one conserva-

*Reprinted by permission from *Wisconsin Studies in Contemporary Literature* 2, no. 1 (Winter 1961): 5–30.

tive protest, wholly unconvincing, against Salinger's alleged Rousseauistic philosophy.[1] In another quarter *The Catcher* has been regarded as itself a conservative protest, along with *The Great Gatsby*, *II . M . Pulham, Esq .*, and the work of William Faulkner, against the anarchic drift of society and the shortcomings of the "natural man"; but in this view *The Catcher* is dismissed as providing a merely negative answer to the question of social chaos, and the conclusion of the novel can hardly serve "as a creed to live by."[2] if such an undiscerning approach amounts to a begging of the question, several rewarding insights, on the other hand, have emerged from detailed analysis of parallels in narrative pattern and characterization in *Huck Finn* and *The Catcher*; and one judges that such expansive comparisons between Huck and Holden require correction only in several premature unfavorable impressions of Holden.[3] A profitable view has arisen from the exploration of the epic motifs of alienation and quest; and from this vantage point Holden is observed to keep company not only with Huck Finn but also with Ulysses, Aeneas, Ishmael, Alyosha, Stephen Dedalus, and Hans Castorp.[4] Still another view discloses Holden as an American Don Quixote, indulging with rare gestures of the spirit in "behavior that sings" and thus, in spite of his adolescent disaffiliation, affirming values of truth and imagination.[5]

There is, nevertheless, some critical unhappiness with a Holden who refuses to mature and with a distinctly unsatisfactory conclusion to the novel; and on both counts *The Catcher* suffers in comparison with *Huck Finn*. If Holden displays a superiority over Huck in certain traits of character, his neurotic psychology, intensified by sexual conflicts from which Huck was free and aggravated by a vulgar, dehumanized society, leads the boy to the psychoanalytical couch in a thoroughly pessimistic novel, whereas *Huck Finn* ends on a resolute note of courage in Huck's rejection of his society with his escape into the farther West.[6]

Thus we may summarize a commentary at once elaborate, precise, and generally correct as far as it goes; and yet all these approaches, however sophisticated the insight, remain discursively short of the critical goal because they fail to acknowledge the terms for understanding that the novel itself, as a work of art, has furnished. Except in scattered and fragmentary flashes, it has thus far escaped attention that Salinger sharply accentuates the portrayal of Holden with a symbolic structure of language, motif, episode, and character; and when the complex patterns are discovered, the effect is to concentrate our scrutiny on a masterpiece that moves effortlessly on the colloquial surface and at the same time uncovers, with hypnotic compulsion, a psychological drama of unrelenting terror and final beauty.

If Holden's suffering is the measure as well as the product, in part, of the outrageous assault on private innocence by social depravity, it does not follow that Salinger's philosophy is Rousseauistic. If we acknowledge that a personality has been split to the very core, such a discovery does not support the view that Holden, unlike the resourceful Huck, wishes to remain immature. Nor, as we shall learn, does the conclusion of *The Catcher* present a "creed" of any kind in the sense demanded by one critic; and the conclusion, furthermore, is neither pessimistic nor, for that matter, ironical in any sense perceived thus far. An immature Holden is not being delivered up to the unmerciful process of adjustment to a society he detests. The irony is profounder than that because the meaning is profounder: a Holden who has accepted both the mood and the act of responsibility with Phoebe does not require psychoanalytical therapy, for he has miraculously wrought his own cure and has thus spiritually escaped the social rigidities that would be imposed upon him. The conclusion is, therefore, optimistic and affirmative, not in any credal sense but in terms of the unconquerable resources of personality.

Now, the thesis of the present study is that all or most of this psychological and philosophical insight can be gained only through a recognition of the interlocking metaphorical structure of *The Catcher*. We may thus perceive that Salinger has employed neurotic deterioration, symbolical death, spiritual awakening, and psychologial self-cure as the inspiration and burden of an elaborate pattern—verbal, thematic, and episodic, that yields the meaning as the discursive examination of Holden's character and problem out of metaphoric context can never do. Structure *is* meaning.

As a start, the readiest way of understanding *The Catcher* lies in an awareness of the dualism or ambivalence of language, for Holden employs both the slob and the literate idiom. He mingles them so nicely, however, and with such colloquial ease that the alternating modes have heretofore escaped attention; and however we look at the two languages, each is, in effect, employed both realistically and metaphorically. Holden's slob speech is obviously justified as a realistic narrative device, since it is the idiom of the American male; yet from the psychological point of view, it becomes the boy's self-protective, verbalized acceptance of the slob values of his prep school contemporaries. He thus may justify himself in his overt being and may hope to secure immunity from attack and rationalize his "belonging"; slob language, therefore, hits off two important social themes—security and status. But the psychological intent becomes symbolical portent when we see that the mass idiom emphasizes a significant distinction between two worlds—the phony world of corrupt materialism and Holden's private world of innocence, which, in its corporate love, embraces a secret goldfish. Holden's dead brother Allie, his sister Phoebe (all children, in fact), Jane Gallagher, nuns, and animals (ducks and zoo animals, the Doberman that belonged to Jane's family, and the dog that Olivier-Hamlet patted on the head). For his private world Holden uses a literate and expressive English, and so the profounder psychological and symbolical purposes of slob language may be detected only as that idiom functions in polarized relationship with the other. We need not labor the point that the full range of Salinger's portrayal would never be disclosed without an awareness of the ambivalence of language.

The literary Salinger has, of course, created a literate and even literary and artistic Holden, capable of acute aesthetic as well as moral judgments. Thus, Ernie, the piano player in Greenwich Village, was phony in his mingled real snobbery and false humility, and the Lunts overdid their acting and were *too* good. It is such a perceptive Holden that opens the narrative on a confessional note—"all that David Copperfield kind of crap"; and it may be observed in passing, as a literary parallel, that if Dickens portrays a young Victorian immoralist, Steerforth, Salinger gives us Stradlater, a "secret slob" and "sexy bastard." Holden's literary taste provides depth of background for a boy who said of himself, "I'm quite illiterate, but I read a lot." Favorite authors are his own brother D. B., Ring Lardner, and Thomas Hardy. Holden dismisses Hemingway as phony but approves of Fitzgerald's *The Great Gatsby,* from which, amusingly, he has borrowed Gatsby's nonchalant and phony habit of address—"old sport"; thus Holden refers to "old Spencer," "old Mrs. Morrow," "old Ernie," "old Phoebe." If this literary borrowing represents merely Holden's linguistic "horsing around," there is, on the other hand, real bite to his reporting Allie's verdict that Emily Dickinson was a better war poet than Rupert Brooke, the idea being that imagination imparts meaning to experience; and the discerning reader will keep this in mind as a gloss for Holden's concluding observation on his traumatic adventures.

Presumably, Holden's literary judgments are as perceptive as Allie's. Holden "wouldn't mind calling . . . up" Isak Dinesen, the author of *Out of Africa;* and his reason, open to readers of the Danish noblewoman, springs from his own suffering, for a writer so warmly understanding of children and animals would make an appropriate *confidante.* The slob Holden is more prominent, but the literate Holden is more intrinsic, for like Isak Dinesen he can use language to express sensitive insights and humane joys. As we proceed we shall note that although some of the literary sophistication is solely for background, a few works enter into and reenforce the moral, psychological, and symbolic range of *The Catcher.*

The literary precision with which Holden employs slob language for a public world that is varyingly indifferent and cruel and usually phony and literate speech for his private world emerges beautifully when he explains how he met Jane Gallagher: "The way I met her, this Doberman pinscher she had used to come over and *relieve* himself on our lawn, and my mother got very irritated about it. She called up Jane's mother and made a big *stink* about it. My mother can make a very big *stink* about that kind of stuff" (italics mine).

Once we have recognized the ambivalence of language we are prepared to discover Salinger's elaborate use of several kinds of pattern that support and help to develop the narrative. The first verbal pattern to be examined stands in an ironic and mutually illuminating relationship with the image of the secret goldfish at the head of the narrative symbolizing Holden and his secret world. In D. B.'s short story "The Secret Goldfish" the boy would not let others see the goldfish "because he'd bought it with his own money." Holden likewise was to pay in far more than money for his secret world; and as a further parallel, nobody ever saw (or cared to see) this secret world, although Holden invites inspection in the confessional mode, "if you really want to hear about it." This mode is maintained throughout with frequent interpolations of "if you want to know the truth" or "if you really want to know." As the story uncovers more and more of Holden's dilemma, these phrasings, although employed in the most casual manner, transcend their merely conversational usage and become psychologically portentous. The inference is that society, including his own parents, has no desire to recognize the truth about Holden or its own obsessions. In the middle of the tale Holden learns from the psychoanalytical snob, Carl Luce, that his father had helped him to "adjust"; and the blunted resolution of the narrative on the Freudian couch represents society's final humiliating indifference to truth. Recognition of the truth would embrace the love and compassion that it has no time for but that Holden himself not only lavishes on his secret world but extends to the public world in episodes and reflections rounded off with a minor verbal pattern, "You felt sort of sorry for her" or "I felt sorry as hell for him." The confessional mode embraces still another verbal pattern put variously, "People never notice anything," "He wasn't even listening," "People never believe you," and morons "never want to discuss anything." The failure in communication could not be more bleakly confirmed; and there is an immense irony in the contrast between Holden's telling the truth and the indifference surrounding him. Note, then, that the confessional mode, developed by several verbal patterns, provides a beautifully formulated enclosing structure for the tale—with the symbolic image of the secret goldfish at the start and at the end the equally symbolic talking couch.

Two other patterns ironically reenforce the confessional mode. At Pencey Dr. Thurmer had talked to Holden "about Life being a game," and Mr. Spencer added for the truant's benefit, "Life *is* a game that one plays according to the rules." Toward the end Mr. Antolini sustained the cliché in his overblown rhetoric. Considering Holden's own honesty and the indifference of his seniors, "playing the game" becomes a grisly farce; and there is further irony in the fact that Holden is himself fervently devoted to the concept, first in his treasuring Allie's baseball mitt and then in his confiding in Phoebe that he would like to be a catcher in the rye to save children from falling off "some crazy cliff." And does he not wear his red hunting hat backwards like a catcher? Mr. Antolini, who speaks to Holden from a sophisticated height and warns him of a "terrible, terrible fall," a "special kind of fall," is capable, in these psychological terms, of no more than talk, for he arrived too late to catch young Castle, who jumped out the window to escape the persecution of his contemporaries. The second pattern furnishes an ironical grace note or two. At the beginning of the tale Holden thought that Mr. Spencer yelled "Good luck!" at him, and toward the close a teacher in Phoebe's school wished him "good luck." Unrelenting in its vision of the double-dealing society, *The Catcher* portrays teachers as sentimentalists and guardians of an exploded ethic; and one of them, Antolini, is a linguistic phony. In these enclosing patterns, then, the reverberations of irony appear to be endless, and the structure of language and motif is all the more impressive because everything is presented in such an artless and colloquial fashion.

II

If the design thus far disclosed may be construed as the motif of un-sportsmanlike sportsmanship and if the social corollary is that by playing the game (but what *are* the rules?) one may achieve security and status, it remains to be said that society reduces Holden to an ambivalence of accep-tance and rejection, of boastful claims and humiliating admissions that are, in effect, destructive of the integrity of his personality. Holden seeks status with his contemporaries by talking slob language, but he shows the same impulse with his elders in more subtle fashion. With "old" Spencer he readily condemns himself as a moron and suggests plausibly that his trouble with school-work must arise from his passing through a phase. If his remark that he is "probably the biggest sex maniac you ever saw" represents the sting of conscience, his pursuit of sex with the prostitute is patently for adolescent status; and he immediately admits, with his engaging candor, that he is a virgin. So nervously aware of status is he that he is careful to preserve it for others. His roommate Slagle had inexpensive suitcases, and Holden therefore hid his own leather luggage under his bed "so that old Slagle wouldn't get a goddam inferiority complex about it." But Holden's accep-tance of status is mere lip-service, and the intrinsic Holden emerges in the remark that he "wouldn't go to one of those Ivy League colleges if [he] was *dying*, for God's sake" and in his rejection of law because a lawyer, like his father, would not know whether he was being phony.

If society were no worse than a somewhat difficult but rational enough arrangement for status-seeking and if a person had merely to pay a stiff psycho-logical price in adjustment for the rewards, Holden's frequent charge of "phony" might be dismissed. But the matter goes far deeper than that: society, in the repulsive form of Stradlater, subjects Holden to humiliations that pass beyond the legitimacies of playing the game. Holden's career discloses intensi-fied patterns of ambivalence—withdrawal and aggression, guilt feelings, fanta-sies of mutilation, the death-wish; and the reason lies almost as much in the social encounter as in the death of his brother Allie. A society that ignores or rejects his gesture for understanding, that preempts his possessions, body, and mind, that invades and violates his inner being—such a society is not only status-seeking; it is actively and crudely anthropophagus and psychophagus. The vision of ugliness in *The Catcher* challenges anything else in the same genre. From the window of his New York hotel room, as from a box in a theatre, Holden witnesses an example of transvestism and sees a man and a woman spitting water or highballs at each other's face; "they were in hysterics the whole time, like it was the funniest thing that ever happened." The violent contrast between such a society and Holden's private world produces the psychological ambivalence mentioned above; hence, also, the importance of certain verbal patterns that may be identified by their key words—"madman," "crazy," "kill," and "yellow."

As we pursue the "madman" pattern through its emotive transmutations we can see how Salinger loads his narrative with verbalisms that by themselves impart a pervasively psychological tone. Thus although there is nothing particularly significant in the description of the snow as "still coming down like a madman," in the Stradlater episode we detect a note of hysteria when Holden says that "he went right on smoking like a madman." On three separate occasions he "apologized like a madman"—first, to one of the three girls whom he picked up in the hotel; secondly, to the nuns for blowing smoke in their faces; thirdly, to Sally Hayes for his rude behavior. In his hotel room the prostitute "looked at [him] like [he] was a madman." It is obvious from these few examples that in a highly charged emotional context the verbalism slips out of the innocuously colloquial into the psychologically meaningful; and in these moments, furthermore, the verbal patterns converge and intensify the encounter, as may be noted with the "madman" and "crazy" patterns in the scenes with Stradlater and Sally Hayes.

The somewhat less than twenty pages of chapters four and six, the Stradlater episode, provide a brilliant instance of Salinger's technical virtuosity. Here we have convincing evidence that this completely selfish and indifferent young animal did push Holden, in his already neurotic state, down the nightmarish incline toward the psychoanalytical couch. Unlike Ackley, who was a slob, visible to all, in his personal habits, Stradlater was "a secret slob," impressive in his appearance for public show (he is handsome in a Year Book way), but filthy in his private habits. His razor "was always rusty as hell and full of lather and hairs and crap." He was "madly in love with himself" and spent half his life in front of a mirror, and he could never whistle in tune. Since it is the despoiling and humiliation of Holden Caulfield, to cynically indifferent invasion and stripping bare of his person, property, and secret imaginative world that is the burden of this episode, we note with fascinated attention how Stradlater possesses himself of all things that are Holden's, one after another. He uses Holden's Vitalis on his "gorgeous locks," he borrows Holden's hounds-tooth jacket for his date, and yawning all the while, he expects Holden to write his theme for him. A sovereign indifference to all about him is Stradlater's salient characteristic. He could not be bothered to get Jane Gallagher's first name right; he called her Jean. When Holden, with his studious care for the other person, asked whether Jane had enjoyed the game, Stradlater didn't know. A bitter humiliation for Holden is that he must ask this gorgeous phony, who has made a theme-slave of him, not to tell Jane that he is being expelled from Pencey; most galling for the reader is Holden's admission that Stradlater probably won't tell "mostly . . . because he wasn't too interested."

It is, however, the imminently dangerous quality of sex that is frightening. In chapter four when Holden heard that Stradlater was to have a date with Jane Gallagher, he "nearly dropped *dead*"and "nearly went crazy," and in chapter six, through all the mounting ordeal, he "went right on smoking like a madman." The psychological significance of these verbalisms is unmistakable, for Stradlater has invaded Holden's secret world and violated a symbol of innocence and respect. Indeed, in the elaborate pattern of this episode, Stradlater, the "secret slob," matched Holden's secret world with his own, for when Holden was driven to ask the crude but important question, he announced with all the taunting impudence of his kind, "That's a professional secret, buddy."

When Holden recalls for this "sexy bastard" how he had met Jane and goes on to say that he used to play checkers with her, Stradlater's contemptuous comment is, "*Checkers*, for Chrissake!" This girl, who had had a "lousy childhood" with a booze hound for a stepfather running "around the goddam house naked," always kept her kings in the back row. As Holden put it, "She just liked the way they looked when they were all in the back row." Half earnestly, half facetiously, he requests Stradlater to ask Jane whether she still keeps her kings in the back row; the symbolism of this imagery, portraying defense against sexual attack, is the central motif of the episode. Stradlater cannot, of course, know what a shocking and menacing figure he has become, for on the simple realistic level the request is merely casual reminiscence; but in the psychological context danger signals have begun fluttering in Holden's mind. If the request may be construed as Holden's desire to send Jane a secret warning against the slob who would himself be the bearer of the message, this defensive gesture, nevertheless, cannot issue in decisive action, and it remains no less symbolical than Holden's wearing his red hunting hat "with the peak around to the back and all." But these gestures indicate, so early in the narrative, that Holden is unconsciously preparing for his subsequent role as a catcher in the rye. In chapter six the futile best that he can do is to invite a beating at Stradlater's hands, and after the struggle he cannot, for a while, find the hat. All the protective gestures have dissolved in impotence, and with his nose "bleeding all over the place" Holden has had a thorough lesson in the game of life.

This lesson is all the more pathetic because in chapter five we have the first full glimpse of Holden's secret world and hence some indication of how, given a chance, Holden would play the game. The subject of his theme is his dead brother Allie's outfielder's mitt that has "poems written all over the fingers and pocket and everywhere." The mitt symbolically indicates that Holden would like to play the game with sensitivity and imagination, and Stradlater's crude rejection of the theme is itself a symbolic gesture, and a final one, shutting off all hope of communication. Holden tears the theme into pieces. But it should be added that, like Jane's kings in the back row, Holden's private world is impotent, and the effort at self-revelation in the theme is of a piece with this futility. His rapidly worsening neurotic condition has frozen him in this posture of feebleness, and indeed Holden must take Antolini's "special kind of fall" and disappear into the museum room where the mummies are and thus symbolically encounter death before he may be reborn to an active defense of his world. But this is to anticipate; meanwhile, on the night of his humiliation, several hours later and many hours before the precious Antolini disgorged his wisdom, Holden reflected, "It just drove me stark staring mad when I thought about her and Stradlater parked somewhere in that fat-assed Ed Banky's car [Stradlater is the conscienceless, universal borrower]. Every time I thought about it, I felt like jumping out the window." Holden's fantasying about suicide (and young Castle *did* jump) provides final evidence of frozen impotence, and action is not outwardly directed but inwardly as an impulse toward self-destruction.

The "crazy" pattern continues throughout the middle portion of the book and reaches a climax in the Sally Hayes episode; thereafter, since Holden's neurosis has by then been established, it occurs less frequently, and other patterns come into prominence. Meanwhile in the lobby of the New York hotel Holden's obsessive imagination presents a picture to him of Stradlater with Jane that "almost drove [him] crazy." After the incident with the prostitute and Maurice, Holden's violent fantasying (of which, more later) compels him to say, "But I'm crazy. I swear to God I am." The literary talk with the nuns provides some relief before the scene with Sally Hayes, but even here Holden's reflections are violent, though interestingly varied from the obsession with Jane. The talk is about *Romeo and Juliet;* his favorite character, Mercutio, leads him to the private comment, "The thing is, it drives me crazy if somebody gets killed—especially somebody very smart and entertaining and all. . . ." It is part of Salinger's intricately patterned structure that Holden's favorite character in the play should have been killed in a duel and that Holden himself was the manager of the Pencey fencing team and had "left all the foils and equipment and stuff on the goddam subway." Of greater import is the recollection of Allie in Holden's words about Mercutio, "somebody very smart and entertaining and all." Furthermore, this brief literary interlude brings together the "crazy" and "kill" patterns; and in a moment we shall pursue the latter.

The episode with Sally Hayes provides an explosive self-revelation, in which Holden (we have previously noted his apologizing "like a madman") admits that he is crazy and swears to God that he is a madman. What is a madman? Earlier in the fight with Stradlater Holden was "practically yelling"; and here Sally must ask him twice to stop shouting. Certainly, in his neurotic condition, Holden is scarcely master of himself, and yet, for the reader's sake if not for Sally's, he expresses his urge to withdraw from society with some semblance of rational discourse. His proposal that Sally and he escape to New England on his small bank account is, of course, fatuous; but what lies behind the proposal is not fatuous, and Salinger, indeed, permits us to penetrate the moral quality of Holden's secret world. Earlier that world was presented largely in terms of pathetic sentiment and instinctive honesty, but now our view of it is compellingly moral. Whereas Holden is nervously protective in the Stradlater episode, he is now aggressive and attacks modern urban life and mores. He protests that he doesn't like automobiles, even "*old* cars." "I'd rather have a goddam horse. A horse is at least *human,* for God's sake." As Holden sees matters, life has become so inhumanly mechanized that in his secret world animals move up a notch to assume the status of humans. Swift would approve such misanthropy.

III

We observe, then, that the "madman" and "crazy" patterns are employed most effectively in episodes, chiefly in the first two thirds of the book, that reveal Holden's neurotic condition and, as above, his sense of alienation. The psychological substratum is the frightening ambivalence of fantasy, with all the highly charged emotional responses flashing back and forth between the negative and positive poles; and we must now explore this dominant pattern.

Holden's fantasy begins at the obvious and apparently extroverted level of "horsing around." With Ackley Holden pretends to be a "blind guy," saying, "Mother darling, give me your *hand.* Why won't you give me your *hand?*" Considering the view we get later of parental care *in absentia* or by remote control, and considering, furthermore, what has already been disclosed of the highly wrought design of *The Catcher*, we should not fail to note, so early in the novel, the motif of mutilation and the implied charge that a mother has not provided guidance and owes her son the hand that he has broken; with Holden the extroverted simply does not exist. Ackley's response is, "You're nuts, I swear to God." Ackley calls Holden's hat a "deer shooting hat," and Holden facetiously retorts, "I shoot people in this hat"; and once again, in the sequel, the facetious may be seen to envelop aggressive tendencies. The hat, indeed, is the central symbol of Holden's fantasy and so of the book—not only, as here, for aggression, but later for his humanitarian role, faintly foreshadowed, as we have already noted, in the Stradlater episode; and a third symbolic function of the hat is to hit off Holden's quest, which is in a large measure hysterical flight, as he rushes about New York before he comes home to Phoebe. Aggression and withdrawal follow each other rapidly in the opening scenes, the first with Stradlater when Holden leaps on him "like a goddam panther," and the second when he wakes up Ackley and asks about joining a monastery.

In his hotel room, after "old Sunny," the prostitute, has gone, he talks "sort of out loud" to Allie and expresses guilt feelings about his having refused to take Allie with him and a friend on a luncheon bike-trip because Allie was just a child. Since Allie's death, whenever Holden becomes depressed, he tries to make up for this past cruelty by saying that he may go along. Here, then, in his guilt feelings we have an explanation of why Holden broke his hand against the garage windows, and we may trace all the elements of his fantasying to this psychological cause. Mulitation is itself the physical symbol of a psychological state of self-accusation and self-laceration.

Hence, when Holden, after discovering that he cannot pray, reflects that next to Jesus the character in the Bible that he likes best is the lunatic that lived in the tombs and cut himself with stones, we observe a consistent psychological development of the motif of mutilation and, linked to it, the death-wish; and recalling the verbal patterns of "madman" and "crazy," we note further that Holden identifies himself with a madman. In *Mark*, V:1–20, we are told of the lunatic that broke all chains and fetters, for no man could tame him. Jesus drove the spirits that possessed him into the swine and told him to go home to his friends. If we are to comprehend what really happens in *The Catcher* we must attribute prime importance to this little scene of about two pages at the head of chapter fourteen; for Holden will subsequently break his morbid psychological fetters, he will go home to Phoebe, and, in a manner of speaking, he will be able to pray.

Before all this may occur, however, society in the form of Maurice, the "elevator guy," intrudes for his shake-down and sadistic treatment of Holden, who, in consequence, is plunged into his most elaborate fantasy of mutilation, death-wish, and aggression. He pretends that in a gun fight with Maurice he receives a bullet in his abdomen, and Jane Gallagher bandages him and holds a cigarette for him to smoke as he bleeds. "The goddam movies. They can ruin you. I'm not kidding." The function of Hollywood is to glamorize and distort and, in consequence, to disparage private suffering for an entranced national audience. This view is scarely fresh-minted in *The Catcher*, but it is substantially Holden's criticism in the comment above when he realizes that he has given his own genuine difficulty the *ersatz* Hollywood form.

As the supreme national incarnation of the phony, Hollywood (and by extension, California) figures prominently in the tale from first to last, for it provides another enclosing pattern. We learn quite early that D. B. has prostituted himself by going to Hollywood to write scenarios; and at the end we see Holden in the clutches of a California psychoanalyst, who is interested not in the cause of suffering, not even in the person suffering, but rather in the "desirable" social result of adjustment. The suffering, in any case, would not have arisen or assumed such neurotic proportions had there been parental care instead of a nomadic existence at expensive prep schools. As Phoebe tells Holden, "Daddy can't come. He has to fly to California."

When Holden visits Radio City he is confronted by a phony image of withdrawal and escape matching his own genuine urge. Indeed, the fantasy projected upon the screen also matches his own most persistent fantasy of mutilation, for the hero, "this English guy," who is Duke, suffers from the mutilation of amnesia. Furthermore, the adult audience is sentimentally phony, for sitting next to Holden is a woman who, weeping copiously, refuses to take her boy to the lavatory but keeps him squirming in his seat. "She was about as kindhearted as a goddam wolf." If Holden is sick and escapes into fantasy, so too the nation; and although it may be going too far to suggest that a movie touched off Holden's recovery, it is nonetheless true that in the last third of the narrative the emphasis is on maturity and an affirmative, curative psychology.

Following the movie, Holden meets Carl Luce in the Wicker Bar of the Seton Hotel, where Holden, at his most amusingly raffish, "horses around" conversationally to the boredom and vexation of his older prep school friend, who has taken up with Eastern philosophy and a Chinese mistress rather older than himself. Three separate times Luce is driven to comment on Holden's immaturity: "Same old Caulfield. When are you going to grow up?" After Luce has gone Holden starts "that stupid business with the bullets in [his] guts again," but quite likely the phony movie and Luce's rather exalted talk have helped to take some of the steam out of "that stupid business." Certainly, the reader is being prepared for a turning point. Before Holden leaves the hotel he is told five times to go home; the psychological direction of the novel, under the narrative surface, is by now unmistakable. Although Luce "couldn't care less, frankly" about Holden's growing up, Holden will mature, and in the terms supplied subsequently by Antolini out of Stekel: "The mark of the immature man is that he wants to die nobly for a cause, while the mark of the mature man is that he wants to live humbly for one."[7]

IV

The visit to Central Park and then home to Phoebe must be regarded as the two halves of a single, unfolding psychological experience; they provide the hinge on which *The Catcher* moves. Holden had started thinking about the ducks during his talk with "old" Spencer; and in New York he asked two cab drivers about what the ducks did in such wintry weather. Holden knew the park "like the back of [his] hand," for as a child he had roller-skated and ridden his bike there. But now, searching for the lagoon, he is lost, and, as he says, "it kept getting darker and darker and spookier and spookier." The park has become *terra incognita*. When at last he finds the lagoon there are no ducks. Meanwhile he has dropped and broken the *Shirley Bean* record that he had bought for Phoebe, but he carefully gathers up the pieces into his pocket. He sits down on a park bench and shivers "like a bastard" because back at the hotel he had sloshed water over his head, and "little hunks of ice" had formed on his back hair. He thinks of himself as dying of pneumonia and by easy stages gets on to Allie, whom, significantly, he seems to regard as alive, out there in the cemetery surrounded by "dead guys and tombstones." It nearly drives him crazy to think that visitors could run to their cars when it rained but Allie could not. To relieve his distress Holden skips what little change he has over the lagoon "where it wasn't frozen." Finally, the thought of Phoebe gives him courage to live. "So I got the hell out of the park, and went home."

The psychological and thematic components of this little scene are profoundly rich and yet beautifully simple. Central Park represents Holden's Dark Tower, Dark Night of the Soul, and Wasteland; the paradise of his childhood is bleak, and the ducks that, in his fantasy, he has substituted for the human, have vanished. In effect, Holden is finished with childhood and is prepared for the burdens of maturity. But all the same he gathers up the pieces to be treasured, and in a final act of childhood profligacy—skipping coins over the lagoon—he symbolically rejects the materialism of the adult world that he is about to enter.

The apartment episode with Phoebe is so brilliant and so densely packed that we must examine it in two stages, here largely from Holden's point of view and later from Phoebe's. The meeting between brother and sister is presented as a conspiracy, for Holden enters the building under false pretenses and slips into his own apartment "quiet as hell." "I really should've been a crook." The anti-social bond is confirmed when Phoebe tells Holden that she has the part of Benedict Arnold in a Christmas play and when he gives her his symbolical hunting hat. They are rebels and seekers both.

Almost the first thing that Holden notices in D. B.'s room where Phoebe ususally sleeps when D. B. is away is her fantasying with her middle name, which she changes frequently, the present one being "Weatherfield." The various kinds of fantasy have an important role in *The Catcher* and, in alliance with other motifs, hint at the philosophical question of the narrative: "What is the nature of reality?" From this point onward the novel converges upon the answer. Meanwhile, Phoebe's fantasying "killed" Holden; and in this and later scenes with children his mood is good humored, indulgent, and parental. The word "kill" is used throughout the novel in colloquial fashion, as here; but presently it reflects a rising hysteria when Phoebe exclaims again and again about Holden's leaving school, "Daddy'll *kill* you." Paradoxically, the terror exists not for Holden but for Phoebe, and the boy who had been fleeing from one physical and psychological terror after another now finds himself in the role of the elder who must reassure his younger sister that nobody is going to kill him.

The spotlight is, furthermore, powerfully focused upon Holden's problem when Phoebe acts out a killing. She had seen a movie about a mercy killing; a doctor compassionately put a crippled child (on his way up to the apartment Holden, continuing his mutilation fantasy, had been "limping like a bastard") out of its misery by smothering it with a blanket. In symbolic mimicry Phoebe places her pillow over her head and resists Holdens's plea to come out from under. Here, indeed, is killing—"mercy" killing, and assuredly one way of dealing with children. But it would be a "mercy" also to save children, to catch them as they are about to fall off "some crazy cliff," and this is the humanitarian solution that Holden expresses to Phoebe. The anti-social conspiracy has blossomed into a benevolent and protective order. Antolini's thesis, coming belatedly as it does, merely renders conceptually the courage and maturity that Holden, with his imaginative heart, had discovered in the stolen moments of domestic affection and security with Phoebe. Salinger is intimating that for the imaginatively endowed the living experience may become the source of precept and rule. The point is that Holden is way ahead of his elders.

Holden's image of salvation is a compound of his own anecdote to Phoebe of how James Castle plunged to his death and of the snatch of song Holden had heard, "If a body catch a body coming through the rye." From this point onward, however, there is a bifurcation in his development, for he is paradoxically headed for both physical capture and psychological escape. Holden's verbal slip with the song (and Phoebe corrects him) is a *leitmotif* for his mood of utter weariness as he leaves the apartment; he had entered as a "crook," and now he "didn't give much of a damn any more if they caught [him]." The weariness is evident, furthermore, in his being unable to concentrate both with Phoebe and with Antolini as a sense of the rigidity of life overwhelms him. With a last immense and frightened effort he rushes from Antolini's apartment, escaping what in his fevered imagination he takes to be Antolini's perverted advances on the living room couch, before society finally flings him upon the Procrustes bed of adjustment. Such a development being clearly established, we may follow Holden's escape into freedom.

Now Holden's fantasying will not be neurotically defensive, but rationally motivated and ethically directed; and the death-wish will disappear. On his walk up to Phoebe's school Holden fantasies about going west; he would pretend to be a deaf-mute, and if anybody wanted to talk to him the person would have to write the conversation on a piece of paper. Whereas earlier in his effort to communicate with society, as in the theme he wrote for Stradlater, society rejected him, he now rejects society. If there is to be no communication it is of his own free, rational choice and not a piece of neurotic withdrawal. At Phoebe's school he sees the obscene word twice inscribed on corridor walls; but now, if he says that it drives him almost crazy, it does so not with a neurotic and inwardly directed thrust, but in an outward direction in defense of Phoebe and other children, for he says that he could kill whoever did it.

On the way up Fifth Avenue Holden has a recurrence of a feeling expressed at the beginning: "I felt like I was sort of disappearing," he had said after crossing a road. Once again he feels that he will never get to the other side of the street; he breaks out into a sweat, and he talks to Allie, begging him not to let him disappear. When he has successfully negotiated a crossing he thanks Allie, who thus assumes his function as a guide, like Virgil for Dante, into the lower regions of the dead, as we are about to see. Hence, in the tremendous culmination of the narrative, the "yellow" pattern has a significance that is effectively all-embracing, and it advances our perceptions beyond the threshold of awareness permitted by the other verbal patterns.

From the start Holden is convinced that by either standard—society's or his own, he is a coward. On returning to his hotel from the Village through the cold night he thinks of his stolen gloves. He calls himself "one of these very yellow guys" and by way of proof explains his likely elaborate and cowardly handling of the affair had he known who the thief was. He would not offer fight, and he would therefore be "partly yellow" since, as he admits, "If you're supposed to sock somebody in the jaw" you should. But his trouble is that he "can't stand looking at the other guy's face"; and this, he concludes, as a veiled revelation to the perceptive reader, is a "funny kind of yellowness." Later when the prostitute and the "elevator guy" knock on his door Holden confesses that he is "pretty scared" and "very yellow about those things." These first two instances show the coercive social standard, but the third, in the apartment with Phoebe, gives us Holden's self-condemnation when he admits that he "was too yellow not to join" a secret fraternity. The final instance, unmistakably illuminating the climax of the book, shows that he is not a coward and that, in effect, he essentially has business to transact only with himself, and he must therefore stop running. In the museum of art when Holden walks down "this very narrow sort of hall" leading to the room containing the mummies, one of the two boys with him bolts and runs, the other says, "He's got a yella streak a mile wide," and then he also flees. Not Holden but society is yellow.

Since Holden's neurosis includes feelings of insecurity stemming from Allie's death and from Jane Gallagher's "lousy childhood" (like his own) and since both Allie and Jane have become inextricably bound together in his mind, Holden conquers the two-fold hysteria at one and the same moment. There is sexual imagery in "this very narrow sort of hall" and the room containing the mummies, especially since the obscene word is written "with a red crayon . . . right under the glass part of the wall." Once again as in Phoebe's school he reacts with weariness over the corruption of this world and solemnly reflects that if he ever dies and is buried, his tombstone will bear the ugly legend. Here, at last, the identity of the fear of death and the fear of sex is made clear, and these fears are to be seen, actually, as a pervasive fear of violence to body or spirit and the ensuing mutilation. If in the Stradlater episode and throughout the rest of the novel Holden is an innocent, he is so, not so much in terms of our popular literary tradition, but rather in a classical, Christian, or psychoanalytical schema. His very fears yield proof that his innocence represents a harmony of attributes and drives—intellectual, emotional, and physical, so that in the proper regulation of them harm will result neither for the person nor for others.[8] Holden's obsession about faces indicates this fastidious care; the Egyptians tried to conquer the final violence of death by mummification so that, as Holden says, the face "would not rot." In Holden's encounter it is important that the spirit should not rot.

For insight into the psychologically symbolic meaning of the museum episode we turn once again to the structure of the novel. Allie's death has been such a traumatic experience that all Holden knows is death, for when "old" Spencer, who makes him "sound dead," confronts him with the unsatisfactory results of the history examination, it is clear that his historical knowledge is limited to the subject of mummification. It is to this knowledge, at the close of the book, that he returns with a sense of how "nice and peaceful" it all is. The psychological journey from the fear of death to a calm acceptance of it is further highlighted at the beginning when we learn that Mr. Ossenburger, the mortician, has donated the dormitory wing named for him in which Holden has his room.

Holden's victorious encounter with death reveals psychological maturity, spiritual mastery, and the animal faith and resiliency of youth. The charmingly offhand and rather awesome conditional statement, "If I ever die" reminds the reader that in the last quarter of the book it is so difficult for Holden to think of Allie as dead that Phoebe must underscore the fact, "Allie's *dead*." Yet although Holden masters his neurosis he also falls victim to society, for in alternating stress the novel continuously presents two mingled actions—his own inner dealings with himself and society's brutal effect upon him. After his visit to the mummies Holden goes to the lavatory and proceeds to faint, i.e., symbolically dies; and his comment is that he was lucky in falling as he did because he "could've killed" himself. The parallelism with the earlier Stradlater episode leaps instantly to the mind, for then, as we recall, Holden "nearly dropped *dead*"; and the scene also took place in a lavatory—a fit symbol, in both instances, for a scatalogical society. Significantly, he feels better immediately after; and he is reborn into a new world of secure feelings and emotions, with himself fulfilling the office of catcher in his mature view of Phoebe. Thereafter the psychoanalytical couch can mean little to him, far less than Antolini's couch, to which it is thematically related.

V

The dense contrapuntal effect of the verbal patterns is, finally, enhanced by one that keeps a persistent drum beat in the background until the full thematic range of *The Catcher* is disclosed. If Holden symbolically and psychologically dies only to be reborn into the world of Phoebe's innocence and love, he has all through the novel been announcing the theme of regeneration in the "wake up" pattern. After the Stradlater episode Holden wakes up Ackley, then another schoolmate Woodruff (to sell him a typewriter), and as a derisive parting shot, "every bastard on the whole floor" with his yell, "*Sleep tight, ya morons!*" In New York he wakes up or provides the occasion for having wakened up Faith Cavendish (striptease), Sunny (prostitute: "I was *sleepin'* when that crazy Maurice woke me up"), Sally, Phoebe, and the Antolinis. To round out the pattern, Holden's father "won't wake up even if hit over the head with a chair." Obviously, the thematic implication of the pattern transcends both the episodes and the characters involved; in moral as well as psychological terms Salinger is suggesting that a brutalized society requires regeneration and must arouse itself from its mechanistic sloth.

In a development that parallels the "wake up" pattern Salinger shows that Holden, of course, must wake up in his own way; and it has been the thesis of this reading of *The Catcher* that he does effect his own psychological regeneration. Jane Gallagher's kings in the back row symbolize, as we have already noted, the impotence of Holden's secret world, for kings should range freely over the checkerboard. Similarly Holden has interpreted the Museum of Natural History in terms compatible with his own rigid posture. "The best thing, though, in that museum was that everything always stayed right where it was." But the exhibit in the Indian Room, of which Holden is especially fond, with its portrayal of a vanished life, simply mirrors his own death-wish and the death-like quality of his secret world. Actually, Holden's secret world fails the boy not only outwardly in the encounter with society, but also inwardly in his retreat from circumstance, for it is effectively sealed off, so that, as with the outside world, there is here likewise no communication. The pattern that discloses this aspect of Holden's isolation is "giving old Jane a buzz." Early in the novel Holden thinks of phoning Jane's mother; twice thereafter he thinks of phoning Jane, but instead phones Sally. On two separate occasions phoning Jane is part of his fantasy. Toward the close of the novel he thinks of phoning her before going out west, but this bit of fantasy does not reveal a need for her, since, as we have observed, Holden's mood has become rational and volitional. But in the violent Hollywood fantasy earlier in the middle of the book, Holden does phone Jane, and she does come to succor him; any comfort, however, that the boy might derive from Jane, who is one of the two nodal images in his private world (the other being Allie), is immediately destroyed by the *ersatz* sentimental form of the fantasy. Equally significant for Salinger's purpose in underscoring the psychological remoteness of the image of Jane is the one time when Holden does actually phone her; there is no answer. His own world fails to respond. Thereafter come the visit to Central Park, the return home to Phoebe, and a concomitant spiritual recovery.

We now approach the second and, possibly, profounder level of interpretation for the apartment scene. Phoebe wakes up easily; and after this moment of incitation the currents of life may flow, and the rigid, frozen posture yield to the genial warmth of the natural and simple. We become aware of the benevolent and protective order of rebels and seekers, symbolized by the hunting hat and underscored by Holden's parental view of Phoebe, through all the devices of language, gesture, image, and symbol; but to comprehend the deeper level of significance (where we are enabled, perhaps, to answer the question, "What is the nature of reality?") we must rely, in this scene, almost entirely on image and gesture, with little help from speech; and in the final, cryptic chapter this submerged level is brought to the surface of conscious thought in the manner of a riddle. As it is, the profoundest language of the moment we are reexamining lies in the occult and dramatic postures of a charmingly expressive girl.

Neurotic fixations give clues to healthy, natural emotional needs; and Holden, in his trance-like satisfaction with everything in its place in the Indian Room, is instinctively reacting against the chaos outside and inside himself. Things must be in their place; but the constellation must be living and dynamic, not dead, and life must have a magnetic center around which the affairs of life will arrange themselves. For Holden Phoebe provides that center.

From Alice Holmberg Phoebe had learned how to cross her legs in the Yogi manner, hold her breath, and by concentrating exert the influence of mind over matter. In this position, "smack in the middle of the bed," Phoebe represents the still, contemplative center of life; at the same time she is listening to dance music, and with the impulsiveness of the child she offers to dance with Holden. In this manner Salinger indicates the viable relationship between the contemplative and the active participation in the dance of life— a spiritual perception that is as ancient as the *Bhagavad-Gita*. Although the humanitarian role of saviour that Holden assigns himself stands in the foreground, we must nevertheless not fail to see that Phoebe is the essential source; and if Holden, on the path up out of spiritual dilemma and crisis, must find the verbal and conceptual means of expressing his innermost needs, Phoebe, as easily as she wakes up, expresses an even more fundamental insight through symbolic gesture. The charm of the scene, when fully comprehended from this point of view, lies in the mingling of the naive and childlike with the spiritually occult, in the immense discrepancy between means (a child) and ends (spiritual insight); for adults it is a rather puzzling and even terrifying charm, when they acknowledge it, discoverable in fairy tales and some of the teachings of Jesus.

The source of this dualism or polarity of contemplation and activity lies in the intuitive wisdom of the unfettered personality freely acknowledging that the best satisfaction of human nature lies in what Emerson called the law of undulation. Part of this larger spontaneity is the recognition that much of the mastery of life comes through indirection, and hence the preference for the expressive act over precept. Holden, for example, comments that although he had taught Phoebe how to dance when she was "a tiny little kid," "you can't teach somebody how to *really* dance." A far more dramatic defense of personality against restrictions comes in the following scene at Antolini's apartment when, out of a heightened awareness of his approaching crisis, Holden argues his schoolboy point that digressions should be allowed in Oral Expression; "what I mean is, lots of time you don't *know* what interests you most till you start talking about something that *doesn't* interest you most." Holden liked it when somebody got excited about something.

In Holden's maturing there is no repudiation of childhood or even of the secret world. In the organic processes of life the continuity between childhood and maturity, need not, must not be severed. If the child is father of the man, as Wordsworth said, assuredly society at large and parents in particular have scarcely encouraged this teenaged boy, well over six feet, with a crippled right hand and the right side of his head full of "millions of gray hairs," to think of his days in Wordsworthian fashion as "bound each to each by natural piety." For that reason his secret world, when released from the death-like enchantment of neurosis, may well have been, ultimately, the real source of his salvation. Certainly in the daylight return to Central Park with Phoebe Holden experienced the natural piety that Wordsworth celebrated, being at once child and parent with her, both in the zoo (he need no longer search for the ducks) and at the carrousel, watching Phoebe go round and round, another symbol for the circular activity of life. Here the sense of continuity that Holden demands in his surroundings, as we have noted in his feelings for the exhibit in the Indian Room—the harmonious relation between the private person and the public world, receives a living affirmation when he comments with so much satisfaction that the carrousel "played the same song about fifty years ago when *I* was a little kid." When, to the adult reader's further amusement, Holden, like any apprehensive parent, says that Phoebe will have to take her chances with falling off the horse when reaching for the ring, the boy has added a cubit to his psychological stature.

The short concluding chapter, far from being the lame and defective appendage to a charming book that some think it, is like so much else in *The Catcher*, a triumph of technical virtuosity. In this reading of the novel the conclusion is blunted, and interestingly so, only because we cannot say what society will do to impose adjustment upon a boy who has effected his own secret cure; and we therefore close the narrative not with psychoanalytical questions, but ethical. In rejecting the formalism of psychoanalytical technique for the spontaneous personality Salinger follows D. H. Lawrence; and in boldly proposing that the resources of personality are sufficient for self-recovery and discovery, his book will stand comparison with Hermann Hesse's *Steppenwolf*, whose protagonist, Harry Haller, rises above his own neurosis in a discovery, based on Buddhistic thought, that the potentialities of the soul are limitless. Altogether, in this reading the answer to the question, "What is the nature of reality?" is both complex and simple, residing in the living, organic relation between childhood and maturity, continuity and change, the contemplative and the active, the external world and the inner spirit. This reality is not a philosophical abstraction, but an existentialist datum of physical and emotional experience. Since the action of *The Catcher* takes place against the background of the approaching Christmas holidays, the answer is again suggested in the implied contrast between the birth of Jesus and the Egyptian art of mummification.

In the chapter under consideration, as well as in a number of short stories, Salinger has found his rationale in Buddhistic thought. The blunted conclusion is to be understood not only as a realistic narrative device but also as the paradoxical product of a tremendous leap in thought. In Zen Buddhism the koan or riddle lifts one above the level of the conceptualizing intelligence to that of immediate insight, as in the famous koan that Salinger affixed to his *Nine Stories:* "We know the sound of two hands clapping. But what is the sound of one hand clapping?" The Zen riddle presents an intellectual impasse "beyond assertion and denial"; and if the master's answer to the disciple's question often seems impertinent and even frivolous the purpose is to turn the question back upon the disciple to sharpen his awareness of "life's elusiveness and indefinability." As one authority puts it, "Thus when the disciple comes to the final point where the Koan absolutely refuses to be grasped, he comes also to the realization that life can never be grasped, never possessed or made to stay still. Whereupon he 'lets go,' and this letting go is the acceptance of life *as* life, as that which cannot be made another's property, which is always free and spontaneous and unlimited."[9]

Once again there is an immense discrepancy between means (a child) and ends (spiritual insight). When the psychoanalyst (in the role of disciple) asks Holden (the master) whether he intends to apply himself at school, and Holden replies that he doesn't know because you don't know "what you're going to do till you do it," the surface impression is that of a typically unsatisfactory answer from a teen-ager. When D. B. askes him what he thinks about "all this stuff [he] just finished telling . . . about" and Holden replies that he does not know what to think, the surface impression is the same. Finally, Holden proposes a riddle. He says that he misses everybody, even Stradlater, Ackley, and "that goddam Maurice." "Don't ever tell anybody anything. If you do, you start missing everybody." Here is a shock to the conceptualizing, precept-laden intelligence, a puzzle or paradox that will not yield to logical analysis but that, on the contrary, sends the mind back over the experience recorded, even into the depths of the unconscious where both the malady and the cure lay. In the large, Whitmanesque acceptance of evil there is affirmation of the life-process as the personality "lets go"; and such Zen riddling is easily translatable into existentialist understanding.

In its emphasis on the conflict between the organic and the mechanistic, the secret and the public, reality and appearance, awakening and death, *The Catcher* hits off the strongest Romantic affirmations from Goethe and Wordsworth down to Lawrence, Joyce, and Hesse. Whether at Walden Pond, at Weissnichtwo, or in New York hot spots, the problem of personality remains; one surmises that, after a century and more, as *A Portrait of the Artist* and *Steppenwolf* likewise indicate, the struggle has become intensified. At the close of *The Catcher* the gap between society and the individual has widened perceptibly; and far from repudiating Holden's secret world, Salinger has added a secret of psychological depth. A mechanistic society, represented just as much by Antolini as by the psychoanalyst, may with the glib teacher continue to ignore the boy and talk of "what kind of thoughts your particular size mind should be wearing"; we may all comfort ourselves with the reflection that, after all, Holden is another bothersome case of arrested development, albeit rather charming in a pathetic and oafish manner.

No doubt Salinger has overdrawn the portrayal, but a work of literature is not a statistic, it is a special vision. In its pathetic and sentimental tone *The Catcher* faithfully reflects the surface of American life, and insofar, therefore, as it lacks intellectual substance and a valid universality based on a cultural heritage, it falls far below the Romantic masterpieces to which I have made passing reference. But as I have tried to make clear, *The Catcher* is strongest where these are strongest. Whatever the dreadful odds, the human spirit, though slain, refuses to stay dead; it is forever hearing the cock crow, forever responding to the Everlasting Yea. So in *The Catcher;* and the blunted, ambiguous ending mingles with this affirmation the doubt whether now at last, in the long travail of the spirit, the odds have not become too dreadful. If, as this reading interprets the book, the scales tip in favor of the affirmation, it is so because the history of youth is almost always hopeful.

Notes

1. Albert Fowler, "Alien in the Rye," *Modern Age,* I (Fall, 1957), 193–97.

2. Hugh MacLean, "Conservatism in Modern American Fiction," *College English,* XV (March 1954), 315–25. See pp. 321–22 especially.

3. Edgar Branch, "Mark Twain and J. D. Salinger: A Study in Literary Continuity," *American Quarterly,* IX (Summer 1957), 144–58.

4. Arthur Heiserman and James E. Miller, Jr., "J. D. Salinger: Some Crazy Cliff," *Western Humanities Review,* X (Spring 1956), 129–37.

5. Ihab H. Hassan, "Rare Quixotic Gesture: The Fiction of J. D. Salinger," *Western Review,* XXI (Summer 1957), 261–80.

6. See especially Branch, pp. 147 *et passim*. For Branch Holden is "the sex-conscious boy who yearns for the uncomplicated state of Huck" (p. 147); the carrousel scene represents "a dynamic moment of happy, static immaturity" (p. 149); "the underlying despair of Salinger's book is that a privileged adolescent wants to act immaturely" (p. 150). For Heiserman and Miller, Holden "seeks the role of a child" (p. 131). This is substantially the view in Leslie A. Fiedler's *Love and Death in the American Novel* (New York, 1960). But see Charles H. Kegel's brief reply to Heiserman and Miller: "Incommunicability in Salinger's *The Catcher in the Rye,*" *Western Humanities Review,* XI (Winter 1957), 188–90. This excellent note fails, unfortunately, to present the full complexity of the problem; but Kegel does see that Holden matures.

7. Wilhelm Stekel (1868–1940), the colleague of Freud and Jung, was the author of numerous works, based on his own practice, in which infantilism and maturity are a frequent subject of interpretation and comment. Worthy of special mention here is the English translation by James S. Van Teslaar of his *Peculiarities of Behavior: Wandering Mania, Dipsomania, Pyromania and Allied Impulsive Acts* (New York, 2 vols., 1924 and 1943). I do not find Antolini's quotation in this or other works by Stekel, though there are passages in several volumes, in particular the *Autobiography* (New York, 1950), that hit off the same idea. Interestingly, Stekel is mentioned in Dashiell Hammett's *The Thin Man* (1934), in which two adolescents, Dorothy and Gilbert Wynant, exhibit psychological problems arising out of the social chaos around them similar to those of Jane Gallagher and Holden Caulfield. Among other parallels are the "lousy childhood" of Dorothy and Jane (involving a stepfather) and the wandering mania of Dorothy and Holden. Considering the critical emphasis on comparisons between Huck Finn and Holden, it may be plausibly urged that *The Thin Man* is just as acceptable a prototype for *The Catcher* as is *Huck Finn*.

8. By a "psychoanalytical schema" I mean, of course, psychotherapy with the sole purpose of exploring the psychological disturbance and restoring the invalid to his original health; I exclude the sociological motivation of "adjustment" to supposedly "desirable" social ends.

9. Alan W. Watts, *The Way of Zen* (New York, 1957), pp. 70, 75. See also Christmas Humphreys, *Zen Buddhism* (London, 1958), pp. 124–31.

Salinger in the Waste Land

John M. Howell*

"Not wasteland, but a great inverted forest with all foliage underground."

—Raymond Ford, "The Inverted Forest" (1947)

"Ah, Sharon Lipschutz, . . . How that name comes up. Mixing memory and desire. . . . Sybil, I'll tell you what we'll do. We'll see if we can catch a bananafish."

—Seymour Glass, "A Perfect Day for Bananafish" (1948)

"He wrote this terrific book of short stories, *The Secret Goldfish.* . . . Now he's out in Hollywood, D. B., being a prostitute."

—Holden Caulfield, *The Catcher in the Rye* (1951)

This brief dialogue is the essence of my argument that J. D. Salinger, "a dash man and not a miler,"[1] found in T. S. Eliot's *The Waste Land* a controlling metaphor for his only published novel to date, *The Catcher in the Rye*.

THEME

In 1946, Salinger had a ninety-page version of *The Catcher* accepted for publication—but then withdrew it for revision and expansion.[2] One year later he published "The Inverted Forest," the first story to make obvious use of the waste land motif. Raymond Ford, the protagonist, is, like Holden's brother, D. B., a successful writer—a poet who lives in an emotional limbo which he characterizes as "Not wasteland but an inverted forest / with all foliage underground."[3] As he says, "The place where Alph, the sacred river, ran—was found out not invented" (p. 124). To find the underground forest, he must "ford" the sacred river. This he cannot do. Ultimately, he deserts his wife, Corinne, whose resultant fantasy prefigures Holden's dream of being a "catcher in the rye"[4]: ". . . a gallant file of people was approaching the precipice of her brain. One by one—she couldn't stop them—they dived off" (p. 129).

Tom Davis points out that Holden's idealized role as "catcher" strongly resembles that of the bodhisattva in Mahayana Buddhism who devoted himself to helping mankind find release from the wheel of birth and death. He quotes a passage from the *Vajradhvaja Sutra*, which concludes, "I must rescue all these beings from the stream of Samsara. . . . I must pull them back from the great precipice."[5] Davis says that Samsara is the process of reincarnation, and that the carrousel that Phoebe rides at the end of the novel is probably an allusion to the Buddhist Wheel. He might also have mentioned, as Jessie L. Weston does in *From Ritual to Romance*, that in Mahayana scriptures the "Buddha is referred to as the Fisherman who draws

*Reprinted by permission from *Modern Fiction Studies* 12, no. 3 (Autumn 1966): 367–75.
© 1966 by Purdue Research Foundation, West Lafayette, Indiana.

fish from the ocean of Samsara to the light of Salvation."[6] Miss Weston was concerned, as I am, with the Fisher King; and it was from her, along with H. C. Warren's *Buddhism in Translation* and Sir James G. Frazer's *The Golden Bough*, that Eliot got his central motifs: Grail and Tarot cards, Fisher King and Grail Knight, waste land and regenerative water, Buddhist Wheel and Fire Sermon.

Like Raymond Ford, Seymour Glass is also searching for a forest; as his story begins we learn that he has previously almost killed himself by deliberately driving into a tree. Just as D. B. has his "goldfish," Seymour has his "bananafish," a fantasy creature which gorges itself on bananas, gets stuck in a hole, and dies of banana fever.[7] Like Aeneas, he has a companion named Sybil, but she comes from "Whirly Wood" rather than Nemi Wood, and there is no "Golden Bough" in sight. Seymour decides, ultimately, that it is a "perfect day for bananafish" (p. 13), a perfect day to end all "memory and desire" (p. 14) in suicide. Sybil, of course, lives on.

D. B.'s story is "about a little kid that wouldn't let anybody look at his goldfish because he'd bought it with his own money" (p. 5). At one point Holden says, "If we had any children, we'd hide them somewhere" (p. 179). But the significance of "fish" is most clearly dramatized by Holden's repeated questions about the frozen lagoon in Central Park, which functions, like Eliot's Thames in winter, as a pervasive symbol of sterility. In probably the single most amusing sequence in the novel, a taxi driver named Horwitz, in response to Holden's obsessive question about where the ducks go in the winter, answers, instead, just as compulsively about the fish: "They get frozen right in one position for the whole winter. . . . If you was a fish, Mother natur'd take care of *you*, wouldn't she? Right? You don't think them fish just die when it gets to be winter, do ya?" (pp. 76–77).

Holden's fantasy world is similarly frozen, and he finds his metaphor in the glass cases of the Indian Room at the Museum of Natural History. Here, in a huge aquarium where no fish swims, time is arrested as Holden would have it; a world where birds are always "flying south for the winter," where an Eskimo is always "fishing over a hole in this icy lake, . ." (p. 110). In a key thematic statement, Holden says "Certain things they should stay the way they are. You ought to be able to stick them in one of those glass cases and just leave them alone" (p. 111). This is, of course, the "immortality" that he would like to give Phoebe—the existence of the Sybil who begs for death in *The Waste Land*'s epigraph. A few years later, in "De Daumier-Smith's Blue Period," Salinger's protagonist looks into a glass case of medical supplies and says "I would always at best be a visitor in a garden of enamel urinals and bedpans, with a sightless wooden dummy-deity standing by in a marked-down rupture truss."[8] Holden is at best a visitor in a world of perpetual "winter," where a fisherman is always fishing, but catching no fish, and Allie is dead, and the people are spiritually sterile.

Although Holden does not recognize the sterility of his idealized world, he does see the sterility of D. B.'s: "The goddam movies. They can ruin you"

(p. 96). They have ruined D. B. , his brother, and they are now threatening Phoebe, who excitedly tells Holden about *The Doctor*, another obvious analogue to Holden's "catcher" fantasy: "It was all about this doctor . . . that sticks a blanket over this child's face that's a cripple and can't walk. . . . He was a mercy killer. Only, he knows he deserves to go to jail because a doctor isn't supposed to take things away from God" (p. 147). Implication almost becomes statement, a moment later, when Phoebe, learning that Holden has been kicked out of Pencey, flops on her bed and puts a "pillow over her head" (p. 149). The "Catcher," the "Eskimo," and the "Doctor" are at one with the "Sybil": the fish, once caught, is dressed in a shroud.

What is the proper way to "catch" fish? Allie, Holden's dead brother, has said that Emily Dickinson is a better war poet that Rupert Brooke (p. 127), and has left behind a baseball mitt covered with her poems (just as Seymour leaves a bedroom door covered with inspirational quotations[9]). Allie's glove is, then, a kind of spiritual gauntlet which Holden as "catcher" must carry into the waste land. But what of Allie himself? His death from leukemia, three years before, reaped a sterile harvest: D. B. sacrificed his "goldfish" for the movies; Holden crippled his hand on the garage windows— and one side of his head turned gray. Like Seymour, Allie remains in spirit as the essence of truth and innocence. It is only to the degree that Holden can see the spirit of the saintly Allie in humanity that he can forgive those who do not conform to his ideal; that he can become his own savior as well as a savior of others.

STRUCTURE

The Burial of the Dead

Before leaving Pencey, Holden goes to see Mr. Spencer, his history teacher, who initially resembles Eliot's Madame Sosostris in that both have bad colds which interfere greatly with their prophetic powers. Madame Sosostris tells the hero's fortune with a "wicked pack" of Tarot cards— associated historically with Egypt. Spencer tells Holden's fortune with his poorly answered examination on the Egyptians; all Holden can remember is how they bury their dead: "Modern science would still like to know what the secret ingredients were that the Egyptians used when they wrapped up dead people so that their faces would not rot for innumerable centuries. This interesting riddle is still quite a challenge" (p. 14). Holden, who has just that morning lost the fencing teams's foils, is told that "Life is a game" (p. 11); and later asked: "Do you feel absolutely no concern for your future, boy?" (p. 16). But the "boy" is, at this moment, thinking about the frozen lagoon, and wondering where the ducks go in the winter; all he knows is: "I didn't like hearing him say that. It made me sound dead or something" (p. 17).

Appropriately, Holden lives in the "Ossenburger Memorial Wing of the new dorms" (p. 18), named after an undertaker, a wealthy and hypocritical alumnus. Eliot's quester makes a grotesque joke with the character Stetson:

"That corpse you planted last year in your garden. / Has it begun to sprout? Will it bloom this year?" (ll. 71–72). (Eliot is referring to a hanged God—Christ, Attis, or Osiris, probably the latter.) A parallel is suggested when Holden says that Ossenburger "probably dumps them [the corpses] into the river," and talks "to Jesus all the time" (p. 18). The parallel is extended when Holden says that he talks to Allie (pp. 90, 178), who is "planted," but significantly vulnerable to water in Holden's mind: "twice—*twice*—we were there when it started to rain. It was awful. It rained on his lousy tombstone, and it rained on the grass on his stomach. It rained all over the place. All the visitors that were visiting the cemetery started running like hell over to their cars. That's what nearly drove me crazy. . . . I know it's only his body and all that's in the cemetery, and his soul's in Heaven and all that crap, but I couldn't stand it anyway. I just wish he wasn't there" (p. 141). Significantly, the only other corpse which Holden agonizes over is that of James Castle, who *falls* out a window while Holden "was in the *shower* and all, and. . . . could hear him land outside" (p. 153). Four years later Zooey says that "*isn't anyone out there who isn't Seymour's Fat Lady*" and that the "Fat Lady" is "Christ Himself . . ." (p. 200). In *The Catcher* Salinger has apparently chosen to dramatize a similar equation between Holden's "Allie" (Allah?) and James Castle ("J. C."?); that is, "Allie" is "Christ Himself."

A Game of Checkers

Like Holden, Jane Gallagher, one of the few "unphony" people in the book, is poor at games—specifically, the game of checkers, because she insists on keeping her kings in the back row (p. 32). Carl F. Strauch suggests that "the symbolism of this imagery, portraying defense against sexual attack, is the central motif of the episode."[10] Extending this analogue to Holden, he says, "Like Jane's kings in the back row, Holden's private world is impotent, and the effort at self-revelation in the theme is of a piece with his futility. His rapidly worsening neurotic condition has frozen him in this posture of feebleness"(p. 14). My immediate concern here is with Jane's obvious similarity to Eliot's lady in *The Waste Land,* who reflects both fear and lust as she plays "A Game of Chess." In this same section, we find allusions to the bewitched Prince Ferdinand, later identified with Phlebas the Phoenician, the "Death by Water" figure, and with Tiresias, the helpless "seer" of degeneration. Significantly, Holden, who tells us that he calls "people a 'prince' quite often when horsing around" (p. 25), pulls his red hat down over his eyes: "I started groping around in front of me, like a blind guy, but without getting up or anything. I kept saying, 'Mother darling, why won't you give me your *hand?*' " (p. 23). But, like Eliot's blinded heroes and Fisher King, Holden is caught in the "back row" of life; and it is at this point in the story that both his quest and his "fortunate fall" begin. With red hat on head, and Allie's "gauntlet" symbolically in hand, Holden sets out into the waste land, wounded in both spirit and body.

The Fire Sermon

Riding in a taxi near the frozen Central Park lagoon, Holden, like Eliot's heroes, is concerned with the ravages of nature, but he comments on the departure of ducks rather than nymphs. After reaching his hotel, he is even more concerned with the ravages of modern society, as he looks out his window at another wing of the building. Holden says that the lecherous Stradlater should be there: "He'd have been the king of the hotel" (p. 58). But Holden is "king," as he sees, in one room, "a gray-haired very distinguished-looking guy" take out "women's clothes, and put them on"; and, in the room below, "a man and woman [reminiscent of Sweeney and Mrs. Porter] squirting water out of their mouths on each other. It probably was highballs . . ." (p. 58). Then in the hotel lounge he meets three girls whom he affectionately calls the "three witches at the next table" (p. 65). They have come to see movie stars, but there are none there; and they, like Eliot's Thames and Rhine Maidens, are mourning their supposed loss, reminding the reader of D. B. 's sterile existence and the gold-fish he has lost. Later, in the elevator, the bellhop Maurice, like Eliot's Eugenides, offers the hero an evening's sex. Holden accepts, but the minute the young prostitute, Sunny, makes advances, he stops her, claiming that he is impotent, that he has had an "operation very recently" (p. 89). Again we are reminded of D. B. and the movies—and death by water—as Sunny tries to flatter Holden by telling him that he looks like a movie actor, "That one that was Mel-vine Douglas' kid brother? That falls off this boat?" (p. 89). But D. B. 's "kid brother" reaffirms his impotency, and Sunny exits in disgust, leaving him alone, trying to break his depression, first by talking to his dead brother, Allie, and then by praying—but all he can remember are the "Holy Joe voices" (p. 92) of those who, like Ossenburger, are more interested in sales than souls. Maurice, who is also interested in "profit and loss," comes to Holden's room with Sunny to demand another five dollars—which Sunny takes out of Holden's wallet. Then Maurice snaps "his finger very hard on [Holden's] pajamas" (p. 94), and answers Holden's outrage with a hard punch in the stomach: ". . . this time I thought I was dying. I really did. I thought I was drowning or something" (p. 95). Only love can repair the "blindness" of Tiresias, the "wound" of the Fisher King, or the "drowning" of Phlebas.

Death by Water

Finally, after another day in the unreal city, Holden, drunk, his head sopping wet, staggers into the park in search of the frozen lagoon and the ducks. Finding no ducks, and almost falling in, he sits down on a bench and begins to worry about the back of his hair, which, he says, is "full of little hunks of ice. That worried me. I thought probably I'd get pneumonia and die. . . . Boy, when you're dead, they really fix you up. I hope to hell when I *do* die somebody has sense enough to just dump me in the river or something. Anything except sticking me in a goddam cemetery" (p. 140). Then Holden's mind turns to Phoebe: he decides to go home.

But Holden's quest cannot end at this point; even more terrifying ordeals lie ahead—as they must, of course, if he is to win the Grail. Soon after his return home, he goes to the apartment of his former English teacher, Mr. Antolini, in what functions as a thematic repetition of his visit to Mr. Spencer's home in the beginning of the novel. Here, once again, we listen to dark prophecy of a tragic future. Antolini's advice appears to be less of a cliché than Spencer's, but it is still in the tradition of Madame Sosostris, a fortune told through "Rorschach cards" in the psychoanalytic jargon which for Antolini has great significance, but which means little to Holden. Then, ironically, Antolini, who seems himself to be caught in a sterile and loveless marriage, unites, in one metaphorical statement, all that the previous imagery has suggested: "This fall I think you're riding for—it's a special kind of fall, a horrible kind. The man falling isn't permitted to feel or hear himself hit bottom. He just keeps falling and falling" (p. 169). And so Holden does, "entering the whirlpool," moments later, when he is awakened by Antolini's ambiguously affectionate patting on his head. He has not yet found the Grail—only the impotent formulas and actions of sterile minds in a sterile society.

What the Thunder Said

Although "It sort of looked like it was going to rain" (p. 176), as Holden walks up the street a few hours later, it is quite obvious that the "Hanged God" has not "risen," when he hears two truckers unloading a big Christmas tree: " 'Hold the sonuvabitch *up!* Hold it *up,* for Chrissake!' It certainly was a gorgeous way to talk about a Christmas tree. It was sort of funny, though, in an awful way, and I started to sort of laugh. . . . the minute I started to laugh I thought I was going to vomit" (p. 177). And just as Eliot's quester on his journey to Emmaus calls out to the Hanged God, "gliding wrapt in a brown mantle . . ." (l. 363), so also does Holden call out to Allie, as each cross street becomes a terrifying abyss—each curb, the edge of a "cliff": "Everytime I came to the end of a block and stepped off the goddam curb, I had this feeling that I'd never get to the other side of the street. I thought I'd just go down, down, down, and nobody'd ever see me again. . . . I'd say to him, 'Allie, don't let me disappear'. . . . then when I'd reach the other side of the street without disappearing, I'd *thank* him" (p. 178).

Holden's "rebirth" begins when, after leaving a note for Phoebe at her school, he goes to the museum. Just inside the door he meets two small boys, who ask about the mummies in the Egyptian Room, leading him—and the reader—full circle to a discussion of how the Egyptians bury their dead. When they enter the narrow passage way to the Pharoah's tomb, the two boys flee; but for Holden there is no turning back. He must undergo further terrors of the spirit. Speaking of the Grail Knight's entry into the Perilous Chapel and Cemetery in *The Waste Land,* Grover Smith says, "It is in effect—and the mortuary atmosphere is indicative enough—a descent into the grave, into the regions of the dead, so that the initiate may achieve spiritual knowledge."[11] Holden, on entering the room "where the mummies were," at first finds it "nice and peaceful"; but then, suddenly, he sees the same sexual obscenity that had so disturbed him when he saw it on the walls of Phoebe's school (p. 183). He begins to realize the futility of protecting innocence in a "glass-case world"; to recognize that no one can ever escape such emotional sterility: that such an obscenity will probably appear on his own tombstone—as it does now, symbolically, "written with a red crayon or something, right under the glass part of the wall, under the stones" (p. 184). On leaving the tomb (or womb?) Holden faints and, in falling, symbolically repeats the trauma experienced when Allie died; when in despair he had broken the garage windows and "hurt" his hand (p. 38). Now, he says, "My arm sort of hurt, from where I fell, but I didn't feel so damn dizzy any more" (p. 184). At the time of his original trauma, psychoanalysis was recommended. But only the willingness to love can save him—the emotion he experiences but does not recognize as, looking through the "glass part of the door" he sees not death in life, but his sister Phoebe, a different kind of Sybil: "The reason I saw her, she had my crazy hunting hat on—you could see that hat about ten miles away" (p. 185); just as you could see Allie's red hair "about a hundred and fifty yards" across a golf course (p. 37).

If indeed Allie is a "Hanged God," then it is most appropriate that he should be so obviously identified with the color "red," the traditional symbol of rebirth. Apart from the red hat, and Allie's and Phoebe's red hair, we see the red-crayoned sexual obscenity on the walls of the Pharoah's tomb—dedicated, one assumes, to Osiris, whose color is also red, and whose procreative symbols would be equally as offensive to Holden. But now the color is identified with Phoebe, who suggests a Grail Bearer, "catching" Holden with the spirit of love symbolized by the red hat.

Rejecting Phoebe's offer to sacrifice everything and accompany him out West, Holden is himself rejected when she angrily throws the red hat in his face, and tells him to "shut up": "It sounded worse than swearing" (p. 187). Phoebe's innocence is already threatened, whatever the "obscenity." Still Holden makes another effort to "catch" her as she watches the sea lions being fed at the Zoo: ". . . a guy was throwing fish at them—so I went back. I figured it was a good chance to catch up with her and all. I went up and sort of stood behind her and sort of put my hands on her shoulders, but she bent her knees and slid out from me . . ." (p. 188). The "fish" cannot be caught.

Holden finally realizes this fact when he sits watching Phoebe on the carrousel (which turns like Eliot's "wheel"), endangering herself as she reaches out for the gold ring: "If they fall off, they fall off, but it's bad if you say anything to them" (p. 190). Then Phoebe gets off the carrousel and comes over and kisses him, and says, "It's raining. It's starting to rain" (p. 191). Reaching into his coat pocket, she takes out his red hat and puts it on his head; then returns to the carrousel. The waters are freed, and so are Holden's emotions, for the moment, as he sits crying with joy, watching Phoebe circle. But he does not "know why" (p. 191); like the Grail Knight, he fails to ask the right question, and we find him, at the end, sitting in a mental institution near the "unreal city" of Hollywood, the desert behind him, and the impotent "Fisher" D. B. at his side. Yet, in his "madness," Holden, like Eliot's Hieronymo, has a few inverted and ironic "fragments" to shore up his "ruin": "Don't ever tell anybody anything. If you do, you start missing everybody."

Notes

1. Quoted by Herschel Brickell in "Backstage with Esquire," *Esquire*, XXIV (October 1945), 34.

2. See William Maxwell's brief account of this event in "J. D. Salinger," *Book-of-the-Month Club News*, Midsummer, 1951, p. 6.

3. *Cosmopolitan*, CXXIII (December 1947), 115.

4. New York: Signet Books, p. 156.

5. "J. D. Salinger: 'Some Crazy Cliff' Indeed," *WHR*, XIV (Winter, 1960), 98.

6. Garden City, N. Y.: Anchor Books, 1957, p. 126.

7. *Nine Stories* (New York: Signet Books, 1954), p. 16.

8. *Nine Stories*, p. 116.

9. *Franny and Zooey* (New York, 1961), p. 175.

10. "Kings in the Back Row: Meaning Through Structure—A Reading of Salinger's *The Catcher in the Rye*," *Wisconsin Studies in Contemporary Literature*, II (Winter 1961), 13.

11. *T. S. Eliot's Poetry and Plays* (Chicago, 1961), p. 94.

The Movies in the Rye   Bernard S. Oldsey*

Several good novels—including F. Scott Fitzgerald's *The Last Tycoon*, Nathanael West's *The Day of the Locust*, and Budd Schulberg's *The Disenchanted*—have registered the effect of the movies, Hollywood style, on the American imagination. J. D. Salinger's *Catcher in the Rye* should be added to this list, since, in addition to its literary merit, it is as much a Hollywood product (that is to say, anti-Hollywood product) as we have had.

The unrecognized fact is that the movies constitute a major influence on Salinger's novel and play a peculiarly functional part in it. This is particularly true in respect to thematic development and character revelation rather than form.[1] Thematically, the novel is intent on exposing the phoniness of life in these United States, the tawdriness of a Barnum-and-Bailey world remade

*Reprinted by permission from *College English* 23, no. 3 (December 1961): 209–15. © 1961 by the National Council of Teachers of English.

by Metro-Goldwyn-Mayer. This antiphoniness theme is developed through a series of related character reactions and revelations—all filtered through the censuring lens of Holden Caulfield, who is himself not left unmarred in the process. The way individuals react to phoniness—of a dramatic and literary sort too,[2] but especially cinematic—becomes the infallible metric aid by which he assesses character.

Actually, the novel opens and closes on a note of character assessment, with Holden the reluctant and, at the end, unwitting re-assessor. In the very first paragraph, as he begins his story from inside a mental hospital, he exhibits great concern over what is happening to his older brother, D. B., in Hollywood (which is "not too far from this crumby place"). As the author of a "terrific book of short stories," D. B. has been Holden's idol; but the idol is crumbling, may even have crumbled, for D. B. has become a movie writer, or as Holden bluntly puts it: "Now he's out in Hollywood, D. B., being a prostitute."

In the last paragraph of the novel, this concern lingers wonderingly on. And it is easy to understand why: Holden has already lost one brother to death and is extremely reluctant to admit having lost the other to Hollywood. Nevertheless, he must report that on his last visit to the mental hospital, D. B., already equipped with one of those little Jaguars "That can do around two hundred miles an hour," has brought with him a familiar Hollywood opiate: "He drove over last Saturday with this English babe that's in this new picture that he's writing. She was pretty affected, but very good-looking." This may be but a final, weaker echo of the lines with which Holden leads into his story proper: "If there's one thing I hate, it's the movies. Don't even mention them to me" (p. 4).

Yet it is Holden himself who mentions the movies afterward, and keeps on mentioning them. As a child of his times he is automatically a child of the movies; even his name, one suspects, is an ironic amalgam of the last names of movie stars William Holden and Joan Caulfield.[3] His imagination—à la Mitty's—battens on the movies; his reveries revolve around them; and his narrative depends heavily upon them.

Holden has a habit for instance, whenever in trouble or "just horsing around," of slipping into a convenient movie role. One of the first times he does this is in watching his roommate shave; he gets bored just sitting there on a washbowl; so, urged on by the acoustics of the "stone" floor, he taps his way into a screen role:

> I started imitating one of those guys in the movies. In one of those *musicals*. I hate the movies like poison, but I get a bang imitating them. Old Stradlater watched me in the mirror. . . . "I'm the goddam Governor's son," I said. I was knocking myself out . . . "He doesn't want me to be a tap dancer. He wants me to go to Oxford. But it's in my goddam blood, tap dancing." Old Stradlater laughed. He didn't have too bad a sense of humor. . . . (p. 38)

Holden's favorite role, however, is not musical, but the kind made famous by James Cagney and Humphrey Bogart. He uses it several times, the first for Ackley's benefit: "What I did," Holden explains, "I pulled the old peak of my hunting hat around to the front, then pulled it way down over my eyes . . . 'I think I'm going blind,' I said in this very hoarse voice. 'Mother darling, everything's getting so *dark* in here' " (p. 23). He uses it again when slugged by Maurice, the elevator-operating pimp. Though not knocked unconscious (earlier he has informed us, when hit by Stradlater, that "It's pretty hard to knock a guy out, except in the goddam movies"), Holden is rather stunned by the blow to the stomach; his mind slips and he begins to imagine things:

> But I'm crazy. I swear to God I am. About halfway to the bathroom, I sort of started pretending I had a bullet in my guts. Old Maurice had plugged me. . . . I pictured myself coming out of the goddam bathroom, dressed and all, with my automatic in my pocket. . . . Then I'd walk down a few floors—holding onto my guts, blood leaking all over the place—and then I'd ring the elevator bell. As soon as old Maurice opened the doors, he'd see me with the automatic in my hand and he'd start screaming. . . . But I'd plug him anyway. . . . Then I'd crawl back to my room and call up Jane and have her come over and bandage up my guts. I pictured her holding a cigarette for me to smoke while I was bleeding and all.
>
> The goddam movies. They can ruin you. I'm not kidding. (pp. 135–36)

Once again Holden resorts to this role—after a dispiriting chat with an acquaintance named Carl Luce, who advises him to see a psychoanalyst and have "the patterns" of his mind clarified. Luce leaves him alone at the bar, and Holden goes on drinking: "When I was *really* drunk, I started that stupid business with the bullets in my guts again." The business includes the same ingredients as before—the supporting hand inside the jacket, the dripping blood, the hurried phone call to Jane (p. 195). Certainly by this time one of the patterns of Holden's mind has been clarified. It is a one-reeler starring Holden the wounded.

On numerous other occasions and in various ways Holden sees himself and others in relationship to the movies. For example, on Saturday night he considers going to Agerstown with Ackley and Mal Brossard to see a comedy starring Cary Grant. Eventually they eschew it for hamburgers; and Holden is just as glad, because he has been to the movies before with Ackley and Brossard, who laugh "like hyenas at stuff that wasn't even funny" (p. 48). Another evening, the night he meets Carl Luce, Holden has some time to kill and goes to the movies at Radio City. "It was probably the worst thing I could've done," he explains apologetically, "but it was near, and I couldn't think of anything else" (p. 177). On this occasion he sees the film version of James Hilton's *Random Harvest*.[4] Taking two and a quarter pages to outline its implausible, tear-jerking plot, he finishes with a short analysis of the maudlin woman who sits next to him during the performance. She cries throughout the show, but will not allow her suffering child to go to the toilet. "You take somebody that cries their goddam eyes out over phony stuff in the movies," Holden concludes, "and nine times out of ten they're mean bastards at heart."

His apologetic explanation for going to Radio City becomes clear when we consider what Holden has said about others on this score earlier. The three girls he dances with in the Lavender Room are all movie struck; their fondest hope, after coming all the way from Seattle, is to see some movie celebrities in New York. Until Holden meets them they have had little success, having caught sight only of Peter Lorre (so at least they claim). To revenge himself on one of them, the heavy-dancing Marty, Holden pretends to have spotted Gary Cooper on the opposite side of the dance floor and makes him disappear before the hopeful Marty can turn in that direction. Later, though, Holden feels sorry for the lot of them, when they announce they have to get up early next day to fulfill their intentions: If somebody . . . comes all the way to New York—from Seattle, *Washington*, for God's sake— and ends up getting up early in the morning to see the goddam first show at Radio City Music Hall, it makes me so depressed I can't stand it. I'd've bought the whole three of them a *hundred* drinks if only they hadn't told me that" (p. 98).

Lillian Simmons and Sunny, the youthful whore, also fall victim to Hollywood's attraction. Lillian an old girl-friend of D. B.'s, simply gushes when Holden informs her D. B. is in Hollywood writing for the movies (p. 113). Holden thinks her one of the biggest—in all respects but one—phonies he has ever met. Sunny is a more complicated case: She claims to be from Hollywood; she thinks Holden resembles this movie actor, Whosis (appeared in "that pitcher with Mel-vine Douglas"); and she confesses to having no other activities (besides those demanded by her profession) except sleeping and going to the movies. She depresses Holden even more than the Lavender Room girls: "*She* was depressing. Her green dress in the closet and all. And besides, I don't think I could ever do it with somebody that sits in a stupid movie all day long" (p. 125).

Holden considers two other girls—much more important to the novel than either Lillian or Sunny—in terms of the movies; namely, his sister, Phoebe, and the girl he really cares for, Jane Gallagher. Phoebe passes every test. Her innocence is proof against the phoniness of Hollywood. She tends toward foreign films and those with serious themes. She liked seeing *The Baker's Wife*, with Raimu; and her favorite is *The 39 Steps*, with Robert Donat. Holden has taken her to the latter at least ten times; she knows it so well that she can put in bits of dialogue and the missing-finger business at just the right places (pp. 88–89). When Holden first sees Phoebe after he has been dropped from Pencey, one of the first things she must tell him about is a problem movie, *The Doctor:* " 'It's a special movie they had at the Lister Foundation. Just this one day they had it. . . . ' " He tries several times to discuss more immediate problems, but Phoebe rushes on with her rapt summary: " 'It was all about this doctor in Kentucky and everything that sticks a blanket over this child's face that's a cripple and can't walk. Then they send him to jail and everything. It was excellent' " (p. 211).

This summary of *The Doctor*, with its central problem of euthanasia, underscores Holden's own problem. Like the doctor in the movie, he, too (though by different means), wishes to protect the young from the cruelties and indignities of the world. For their pains, the doctor goes to prison, Holden to a mental hospital.

The movie with the doctor in it also moves us closer to Jane Gallagher's problem. Jane is a strange, intelligent, attractive girl, whose muckle-mouth seems to go "in about fifty different directions" when she talks. The most peculiar thing about her, however, is that in playing checkers she never takes her kings out of the back row—a fact so significant as to be mentioned at least four times. In spite of these peculiarities, or probably because of them, Holden is very fond of Jane. He feels as protective toward her as toward Phoebe and the kids in the museum and the ducks on the pond. When his roommate, Stradlater, takes her lightly and hints of intimate relations with her, Holden flies into a quixotic rage and absorbs a physcial beating in her honor.

Actually, Jane is product of a movie and book. The stage is set for the main treatment of her in chapter eleven, where Holden declares, "I know old Jane like a book," and again—"I still couldn't get her off my brain. I knew her like a book" (p. 90). The movie and book in question, which concerns not one but three doctors, is Henry Bellaman's *Kings Row* (1940), a well-known novel that was made into a very popular and, in risking censorship, coura-geous movie in 1942. *Kings Row* shares with *The Catcher in the Rye* three notable elements: youthful innocence in a world of adult cruelty, possible confinement in a mental institution, and a muted theme of incest.[5]

Jane Gallagher, like Cassandra Tower and Louise Gordon of *Kings Row*, fills the role of the fearful daughter; only in her case incest possibilities are heightened by the fact that she is a stepdaughter. Keeping her kings in the back row has already been interpreted as a fear manifestation by Gwynn and Blotner.[6] But it is necessary to go an inferential step further and fill out the syndrome with incestuous qualification. If evidence for such a step seems at first highly circumstantial, there is additional support in Holden's account of a certain afternoon when he and Jane came closest to "necking." As he describes the situation—"It was a Saturday and it was raining like a bastard out, and I was over at her house, on the porch. . . . We were playing checkers. I used to kid her once in a while because she wouldn't take her kings out of the back row" (p. 101). There follows an explanation about how he dislikes kidding Jane too much because he senses something perhaps over-sensitized in her. "Anyway," he continues, "I was telling you about the afternoon. . . . It was raining like hell and we were out on her porch, and all of a sudden this booze hound her mother was married to came out on the porch and asked Jane if there were any cigarettes in the house" (p. 102).

Holden here provides another analysis of Jane's stepfather, Cudahy, whom he has already described for Stradlater as an alcoholic playwriter who runs "around the goddam house, naked" (p. 42). Then he goes on—"Anyway, old Jane wouldn't answer him when he asked her if she knew where there was any cigarettes. . . . Finally the guy went inside the house. When he did, I asked Jane what the hell was going on. She wouldn't even answer *me*, then" (p. 102).

Jane begins to cry, and one of her tears, a big one, plops right onto the checkerboard. Suddenly Holden finds himself comforting her, kissing her all over, except on the lips: "She sort of wouldn't let me get to her mouth." And finally, miraculous to say, they go to "a goddam movie," with Holden still in the dark as to what has happened between Jane and her stepfather: "I asked her, on the way, if Mr. Cudahy had ever tried to get wise with her. She was pretty young, but she had this terrific figure, and I would't've put it past that Cudahy bastard. She said no, though. I never did find out what the hell was the matter. Some girls you practically never find out what's the matter" (p. 103).

So the incestuous matter with Jane is left about as ambiguous as the homosexual matter with Mr. Antolini; but both contribute to the education of young Caulfield. It is an education which by now includes the matters of the transvestite and the water-squirting perverts at the Edmont Hotel, and the matter of Sunny and her finger-flicking friend, Maurice, as well as the matter of a single word, scrawled everywhere, reducing human relationships to the level of travesty. It is an education, moreover, that makes Holden more determined than ever to be a protector of innocence.

The movies are connected with Holden's protective desire to become a catcher in the rye. The idea comes to him while he watches a small boy walking perilously toward, or on, Broadway. The boy, oblivious to the traffic and crowds around him, sweetly sings what Holden takes to be "If a body catch a body coming through the rye" (p. 150). In contrast to the boy, who cheers him up, there are the mobs of people, who depress him, because "Everybody was on their way to the movies—the Paramount or the Astor or the Strand or the Capitol. . . . " It is by now a familiar form of depression; another pattern of Holden's mind is clarified: "I can understand somebody going to the movies because there's nothing else to do, but when somebody really *wants* to go . . . then it depresses hell out of me. Especially if I see millions of people standing in one of those long, terrible lines, all the way down the block . . ." (p. 151).

It is an unpleasant vista of mass man in pursuit of phoniness. Holden— whose favorite phrase is "if you *really* want to know"—is in revolt against this phoniness. As a Wordsworthian or Rousseauistic version of the little boy lost, Holden represents Romantic innocence in search of continuing truth. He seeks a truth as durable as that figuring with beauty on Keat's Grecian urn ("For ever warm and still to be enjoyed, / For ever panting, and for ever young . . ."). In fact, speaking of the displays at the Museum of Natural

History, he produces a modern version of Keats's "Ode," with truth and beauty held in kinetic bond: "The best thing, though, in that museum was that everything stayed right where it was. . . . You could go there a hundred times, and that Eskimo would still be just finished catching those two fish, the birds would still be on their way south, the deers would still be drinking out of that water hole . . . , and that squaw with the naked bosom would still be weaving that same basket. The only thing different would be you" (pp. 157–58).

Thus Holden is as anxious to hold onto beauty and truth as he is those children who might fall off a cliff into some abyss of death, or untruth. He explains most of his occupational desire to be a Protector to Phoebe, and he also explains what he does not want to be: he will not be a corporation lawyer, like his father; nor will he even chance being a lawyer who goes around saving "innocent guys' lives" (pp. 223–24). For this too might turn out to be phony, as it often does "in the dirty movies"; and Holden must be sure: "How would you know you weren't being a phony? The trouble is you wouldn't." He really suffers from a form of "phoni-phobia" and must keep checking himself. Once he almost succumbs when, as a very good golfer, he is asked to appear in a golfing short—"but I changed my mind at the last minute. I figured that anybody that hates the movies as much as I do, I'd be a phony if I let them stick me in a movie short" (p. 100).

He must be pure to be the catcher in the rye, saving little children who might be rushing to their doom, and living in his own peaceful cabin. There, one of his few visitors would be Phoebe. As for his brother D. B. , a proviso is necessary: ". . . I'd let D. B. come out and visit me for a while if he wanted a nice, quiet place for his writing, but he couldn't write any movies in my cabin, only stories and books. I'd have this rule that nobody could do anything phony when they visited me. If anybody tried to do anything phony, they couldn't stay" (pp. 265–66).

So the boy of sanity, of peace and truth and beauty, lights out for his own rye-covered territory and finds his own retreat, which ironically is "not too far" from Hollywood, as things turn out. There is a certain amount of literary ambiguity implicit in the geographical juxtapostion. Hollywood is not too far from insanity; but on the other hand, Holden's "insanity," or neurosis, or whatever it is that troubles him is not far removed from Hollywood. If someone were to ask him (as Captain Delano does Benito Cereno), "What has cast such a shadow upon you?" Holden might very well answer, "The movies." In fact, he has already given the equivalent answer with "If there's one thing I hate, it's the movies" and "The goddam movies. They can ruin you."

Notes

1. In form, the book is an extended flashback framed by an introductory paragraph and three short concluding paragraphs, and to some extent it does resemble a movie adaptation

script, with built-in camera angles, bare character suggestions, and fast scenic shifts. But of course the long interior ramble by which Holden tells his story not only subtly reveals his character and controls the thematic tone of the book, but also helps distinguish the novel from a movie script.

2. For comments on phoniness in drama and literature see *The Catcher in the Rye* (Boston, 1951), pp. 152–53, 164–65, 182. All references in parentheses are to this edition.

3. The plausibility of this conjecture is increased by the fact that these two actors costarred in the well-known 1947 movie version of *Dear Ruth,* the story of a juvenile girl who, in writing to a soldier overseas, tries to appear more mature than she actually is.

4. See Frederick L. Gwynn and Joseph L. Blotner, *The Fiction of J. D. Salinger* (Pittsburgh, 1958), p. 29.

5. The incest motif of *Kings Row* was a much discussed topic of the day; for critical commentaries on the handling of the problem in the movie version, see Russell Maloney, "A Good Movie," *New Yorker* (February 7, 1942), p. 56; and Otis Ferguson, "More Sound than Fury," *New Republic* (February 16, 1942), pp. 237–38.

6. *The Fiction of J. D. Salinger,* p. 30.

The Seventies

The Psychological Structure of
The Catcher in the Rye
James Bryan*

Standing by the "crazy cannon" on Thomsen Hill one sunless afternoon, listening to the cheers from a football game below, "the two teams bashing each other all over the place," Holden Caulfield tries to "feel some kind of a good-by" to the prep school he has just flunked out of:

> I was lucky. All of a sudden I thought of something that helped make me know I was getting the hell out. I suddenly remembered this time, in around October, that I and Robert Tichener and Paul Campbell were chucking a football around, in front of the academic building. They were nice guys, especially Tichener. It was just before dinner and it was getting pretty dark out, but we kept chucking the ball around anyway. It kept getting darker and darker, and we could hardly *see* the ball anymore, but we didn't want to stop doing what we were doing. Finally we had to. This teacher that taught biology, Mr. Zambesi, stuck his head out of this window in the academic building and told us to go back to the dorm and get ready for dinner. If I get a chance to remember that kind of stuff, I can get a good-by when I need one.[1]

A careful look at this first scene in the novel provides clues for interpretation, by no means crucial in themselves, but illustrative of a pattern of scene construction and suggestive imagery which does yield meaning. Appropriate is this adolescent's sense of his "darkling plain" where, if an extravagant metaphor be allowed, "ignorant football teams clash by afternoon." In a pattern repeated throughout the novel, he thinks back to a time when he and two "nice guys" passed a football around, shared rather than fought over it, though even then the idyllic state seemed doomed. Holden is poised between two worlds, one he cannot return to and the other he fears to enter, while the image of a football conflict is probably an ironic commentary on Holden's adolescence, football's being a civilized ritualization of human aggression.

What is forcing Holden's crisis? Everything in the idyllic scene points to the encroachment of time—the season, the time of day, even such verbal

*Reprinted from *PMLA* 89, no. 5 (1974): 1065–74, by permission of the Modern Language Association of America.

echoes from his friends' names as "ticking," "bell," and "pall." Accrual of this sort of evidence will justify what may seem overintepretation here, especially of the significance of a biology teacher's ending the boys' innocent pleasures—their idyll already sentenced by time, darkness. More than anything else Holden fears the biological imperatives of adulthood—sex, senescence, and death—which are delicately foreshadowed in the innocent October scene by the unwelcome call to dinner.

Much of the *Catcher* criticism has testified to Holden's acute moral and esthetic perceptions—his eye for beauty as well as "phoniness"—but the significance of his immaturity in intensifying these perceptions has not been sufficiently stressed nor explained. Precisely because this sixteen-year-old acts "like I'm about thirteen" and even "like I was only about twelve," he is hypersensitive to the exploitations and insensitivity of the postpubescent world and to the fragile innocence of children. A central rhythm of the narrative has Holden confronting adult callousness and retreating reflexively into thoughts and fantasies about children, childlike Jane Gallaghers, and especially his ten-year-old sister, Phoebe. These juxtapositions render both worlds more intensely and at the same time qualify Holden's judgments by showing that they are emotionally—or, as we shall see, neurotically—induced.

While a fair number of critics have referred to Holden's "neurosis," none has accepted Salinger's invitation—proffered in the form of several key references to psychoanalysis—to participate in a full-fledged psychoanalytical reading. The narrative, after all, was written in a mental hospital with Holden under the care of a "psychoanalyst guy." One problem is that Holden tells us very little about "what my lousy childhood was like" or the event that may have brought on the trauma behind all of his problems: the death of a younger brother when Holden was thirteen. We know little more than that the family has been generally disrupted since and that Holden has not come to grips with life as he should have. Allie's death takes place outside the province of the narrative, but a valuable psychological study might still be made of the progression of Holden's breakdown—how he provokes fights in which he will be beaten, makes sexual advances he cannot carry through, and unconsciously alienates himself from many of the people he encounters. As a step toward psychological understanding, I shall consider certain manifestations of Holden's disturbances. An examination of the structure, scene construction, and suggestive imagery reveals a pattern of aggression and regression, largely sexual, which is suggested in the Pencey Prep section, acted out in the central part of the novel, and brought to a curious climax in the Phoebe chapters.

I

One implication of the novel's main motif, that which polarizes childlike and adult responses, concerns the dilemma of impossible alternatives. Here characters suggest human conditions that Holden either cannot or must not make his own. In the novel's first paragraph Holden tells us that his brother D. B. has "prostituted" his writing talents by going to Hollywood—a failure implicitly contrasted throughout with the purity of Allie, the brother who died before the temptations of adulthood. Holden's first encounter is with Spencer, the old teacher who fills his mind with thoughts of age and death, while his last is with Phoebe, his emblem of unattainable childhood beauty. Stradlater and Ackley are antithetically placed to represent what Holden fears he may become if he is either sexually appropriative or repressed. Because the novel is built around these impossible alternatives, because Holden's world provides no one he can truly emulate, the many critics who read *Catcher* as a sweeping indictment of society have virtually drowned out those who attack Holden's immaturity. One feels the justice of this, yet the novel's resolution, like all of Salinger's mature fiction, transcends sociological indictment in affirming individual responsibility. When Holden answers for his own life as he verges toward some rather dreadful appropriation of his own, he begins to come to terms at once with himself and society.

At the outset of traditional quest narratives, the hero often receives sage advice from a wise old man or crone. The best old Spencer can do is to wish Holden a depressing "good luck," just as another agent of education, a woman "around a hundred years old," will do in the penultimate chapter. Spencer's plaintive "I'm trying to *help* you, if I can" and the old woman's irrelevant chatter near the end bracket the bulk of the narrative in which Holden seeks answers from without. And in both scenes the human resources that do see him through are dramatized in his compassion for the two old people.

Though the Spencer chapter serves notice that Holden has flunked the administrative requirements of education, we learn immediately that he draws sustenance from art. He returns to his room to reread in Isak Dinesen's *Out of Africa* that chronicle of sensitivity surrounded by primitive id forces. At this point he is interrupted by eighteen-year-old Robert Ackley, a grotesque possibility of what Holden may become if his manhood is similarly thwarted. Unleavened sensitivity will not be enough as we see Holden vacillating through five chapters between Ackley and Ward Stradlater, the equally unacceptable model of male aggressiveness. Stradlater's vitality is dramatized in his "Year Book" handsomeness, "damn good build," and superior strength, while Ackley's impotence is reflected in acned, unsightly looks, general enervation, and repulsive habits. Stradlater is slovenly too— Holden calls him a "secret slob"—but he elicits some admiration where Ackley is only pathetic.

Stradlater's date for the evening is Jane Gallagher, a girl with whom Holden has had a summer romance. That relationship was characterized by Jane's habit of keeping her kings in the back row when they played checkers—later on, Holden says specifically that their lovemaking never went beyond the handholding stage. In Holden's request that Stradlater ask

Jane if she still keeps her kings in the back row, one critic sees Holden signaling warnings about her "sexy" date.[2] Holden tells us in another chapter that Jane was the kind of girl you never wanted to "kid too much." "I think I really like it best," he goes on to say,

> when you can kid the pants off a girl when the opportunity arises, but its a funny thing. The girls I like best are the ones I never feel much like kidding. Sometimes I think they'd *like* it if you kidded them—in fact, I *know* they would—but it's hard to get started, once you've known them a pretty long time and never kidded them. (p. 101)

On an action level, of course, Jane did keep her checker kings in the back row and Holden is indeed talking about kidding. But such double entendres as "kidding the pants off a girl" reveal not only Holden's sexual preoccupations but the elaborate coding his mind has set up against recognizing such preoccupations for what they are. In the early parts of the novel, Salinger may be training the reader to see through Holden's words in these rather apparent ways, thus to prepare for the most subtle and crucial coding of all in the Phoebe section.

Stradlater's strength and sexuality cause Holden to discountenance his own. This night, for example, Stradlater uses Holden's "Vitalis" hair tonic and borrows his "hounds-tooth" jacket, leaving Holden "so nervous I nearly went crazy" as he thinks of this "sexy bastard" with Jane. Conversely, Holden this same night endures Ackley's droning narrative of his sexual exploits with a final comment, "He was a virgin if I ever saw one. I doubt if he ever even gave anybody a feel." Not until Holden faces the Ackley and Stradlater in himself will he be able to do any purgative writing that is of course the form of the novel itself. They are almost like doppelgangers; one will interrupt him when he reads to escape while the other rejects the composition he ghostwrites because it is escapist. Even when he attacks the cocksure Stradlater after the latter's date with Jane, Holden's brief blood initiation is, as we shall see, a needful battle against himself. Right after the fight, getting no consolation from that other polar figure, Ackley, Holden leaves Pencey Prep.

The five Stradlater and Ackley chapters make for closely woven, dramatized exposition of Holden's psychological quandary which prepares for the loose, episodic middle section of the novel where Holden goes questing after experience and wisdom. Rejecting the alternatives implicit in Stradlater and Ackley, Holden wants his life to be vital without appropriation, innocent without retrogression. In the Phoebe section where the novel tightens up again, we shall see that Holden nearly becomes *both* appropriate and retrogressive and that it is precisely Holden's awareness of this that points the way to maturity.

Immediately after arriving in New York and checking into a hotel room, Holden is treated to a fresh installment of the Ackley-Stradlater antithesis. Through one window across an airshaft he sees a transvestite dress himself and mince before a mirror, while in the window above a couple squirt water "out of their mouths at each other." Holden confesses at this point that "In my *mind*, I'm probably the biggest sex maniac you ever saw" and that he might enjoy such "crumby stuff" as squirting water in a girl's face. Characteristically, he decides to call his chaste Jane, thinks better of it, and phones Faith Cavendish, a stripper recommended to Holden as one who "didn't mind doing it once in a while." Her ritual objections to the late-hour call dispensed with, she suggests a meeting the next day. Holden declines, however, and "damn near" gives his "kid sister Phoebe a buzz," justifying the switch by describing Phoebe's charms at length. Later in a bar he is flanked on his left by "this funny-looking guy" nervously reciting to his date "every single goddam play" of a football game he had seen, and on the other side by a suave young man giving a beautiful girl "a feel under the table," over her embarrassed objections, "at the same time telling her all about some guy in his dorm that had . . . nearly committed suicide." All around him Holden sees distorted reflections of his own spasmodic aggression and withdrawal. And in the last instance cited we get an early hint of one of the most dangerous manifestations of his neurosis: his association of sex with death.

When he retreats in a panic to Grand Central Station, for example, he begins to read a discarded magazine to "make me stop thinking" about Antolini's apparent homosexual advances. One article convinces him that his hormones are "lousy" and another that he would "be dead in a couple of months" from cancer. What seems burlesque here ("That magazine was some little cheerer upper") becomes urgent in Holden's response to an obscene legend he sees shortly after in Phoebe's school:

> Somebody'd written "Fuck you" on the wall. It drove me damn near crazy. I thought how Phoebe and all other little kids would see it, and how they'd wonder what the hell it meant, and then finally some dirty kid would tell them—all cockeyed, naturally—what it meant. . . . I figured it was some perverty bum that'd sneaked in the school late at night to take a leak or something and then wrote it on the wall. I kept picturing myself catching him at it, and how I'd smash his head on the stone steps till he was good and goddam dead and bloody. But I knew, too, I wouldn't have the guts to do it. I knew that. That made me even more depressed. I hardly even had the guts to rub it off the wall with my *hand*, if you want to know the truth. I was afraid some teacher would catch me rubbing it off and would think *I'd* written it. But I rubbed it out anyway, finally. (pp. 260–61)

As we shall see, Holden is more repelled by the "obscenity" of the sexual act itself than by the obscene word. And his fear of being identified with the sort of "pervert" who planted it in Phoebe's school is reiterated when, in one more withdrawal, he goes to the mummy tomb in the museum and again finds the legend. At this point he decides,

> You can't ever find a place that's nice and peaceful, because there isn't any. You may *think* there is, but once you get there, when you're not looking,

somebody'll sneak up and write "Fuck you" right under your nose. Try it sometime. I think, even, if I ever die, and they stick me in a cemetery, and I have a tombstone and all, it'll say "Holden Caulfield" on it, and then what year I was born and what year I died, and right under that it'll say "Fuck you." I'm positive, in fact. (p. 264)

It is not enough to leave it that Holden's sickness has brought about this odd commingling of lovemaking and dying in his mind. Looking back at Holden's ostensibly random comments on various fascinations and aversions, one sees a subtle but coherent psychological pattern taking shape. Early in the novel we learn of his interest in Egyptian mummification and his particular fascination—mentioned again in the tomb scene—that the process ensured that "their faces wouldn't rot or anything." After watching the "perverts" squirt water in each other's faces, Holden reflects that

if you don't really like a girl, you shouldn't horse around with her at all, and if you *do* like her, then you're supposed to like her face, and if you like her face, you ought to be careful about doing crumby stuff to it, like squirting water all over it. (p. 81)

If there are sexual inhibitions reflected in Holden's curious concern with the "preservation of faces," they must also be implicit in his general and constant longing for a state of changelessness. He laments, for instance, that though his beloved museum never changed, he did:

The best thing, though, in that museum was that everything always stayed right where it was. Nobody'd move. You could go there a hundred thousand times, and that Eskimo would still be just finished catching those two fish, the birds would still be on their way south. . . . Nobody'd be different. The only thing that would be different would be *you*. Not that you'd be so much older or anything. It wouldn't be that, exactly. You'd just be different, that's all. You'd have an overcoat on this time. . . . Or you'd heard your mother and father having a terrific fight in the bathroom. . . . I can't explain what I mean. And even if I could, I'm not sure I'd feel like it. (pp. 157–58)

Readers experienced in the strategies of unreliable narration will suspect that Holden probably does somehow "explain" and that there must be a reason why he's not sure he'd "feel like it" if he could. One notices, as a possible clue, that the museum is associated here and elsewhere with Phoebe.

I kept thinking about old Phoebe going to that museum on Saturdays the way I used to. I thought how she'd see the same stuff I used to see, and how *she'd* be different every time she saw it. It didn't exactly depress me to think about it, but it didn't make me feel gay as hell, either. Certain things they should stay the way they are. . . . I know that's impossible, but it's too bad anyway. (p. 158)

Indeed, Holden's feelings about Phoebe may explain much that is puzzling in his narrative.

II

The expository sections of the novel dramatize Holden's problems as essentially sexual and moral. Yet most critical readings of the novel's ending either ignore these things or imply their absence by declaring that the resolution is "blunted" or else "humanly satisfying" while "artistically weak." Those critics who attest to a harmonious resolution generally do so on philosophical grounds, the effect being a divorce of theme from Holden's human situation. To deny a fused sexual and moral resolution of some sort in the closing emotional crescendo of the Phoebe section would, it seems to me, impugn the integrity of the novel.

I am suggesting that the urgency of Holden's compulsions, his messianic desire to guard innocence against adult corruption, for example, comes of a frantic need to save his sister from himself. It may be Phoebe's face that Holden unconsciously fears may be desecrated; hence the desire to protect Phoebe's face that compels his fascination with mummification. And it may be Phoebe who provokes his longing for stasis because he fears that she may be changed—perhaps at his own hand. Holden's association of sex with death surely points to some sexual guilt—possibly the fear that he or Phoebe or both may "die" if repressed desires are acted out.

I do not mean to imply that Holden's desires, if they are what I suggest, drive him inexorably to Phoebe's bed. The psychoanalytical axiom may here apply that a sister is often the first replacement of the mother as love object, and that normal maturation guides the boy from sister to other women. At this point in his life, Holden's sexuality is swaying precariously between reversion and maturation—a condition structurally dramatized throughout and alluded to in this early description:

> I was sixteen then, and I'm seventeen now, and sometimes I act like I'm about thirteen. It's really ironical, because I'm six foot two and a half and I have gray hair. I really do. The one side of my head—the right side—is full of millions of gray hairs. I've had them ever since I was a kid. And yet I still act sometimes like I was only about twelve. Everybody says that, especially my father. It's partly true, too, but it isn't *all* true. . . . Sometimes I act a lot older than I am—I really do—but people never notice it. (p. 13)

The narrator's overall perspective is thus mapped out: his present age representing some measure of maturity, and thirteen and twelve the vacillation that normally comes at puberty and that is so much more painful when it occurs as late as sixteen. This vacillation is somehow resolved in a climax beginning in Phoebe's bedroom (or rather the bedroom of D. B., the corrupt brother, where she sleeps) and ending at the carrousel after Holden has refused to let her run away with him. However one interprets the ending, it comes as a surprise which is dramatically appropriate precisely because it shocks Holden. Hence, also, the aptness of providing only scattered hints of things to come through the quest section, hints which, in my presentation, will necessarily seem tentative.

One notes in passing, for example, Holden's sudden infatuation with Bernice, one of the prosaic Seattle girls, while they are dancing. "You really can dance," he tells her. "I have a kid sister that's only in the goddam fourth grade. You're about as good as she is, and she can dance better than anybody living or dead." A possible association might be made of the name of the young prostitute, "Sunny," with "Phoebe."[3] Certainly Sunny's childlike aspects are emphasized throughout the episode:

> She was a pretty spooky kid. Even with that little bitty voice she had, she could sort of scare you a little bit. If she'd been a big old prostitute, with a lot of makeup on her face and all, she wouldn't have been half as spooky. (p. 127)

Holden has to beg off with the excuse that "I was a little premature in my calculations." His beating at the hands of Maurice, her pimp, suggests psychic punishment as well, particularly when Holden imagines that he's dying and pretends "I had a bullet in my gut."

More can be made of an assertion Holden is constrained to repeat that Phoebe is "too affectionate." After retreating from making the date with Faith, he describes Phoebe at length and tells the reader,

> She's all right. You'd like her. The only trouble is, she's a little too affectionate sometimes. She's very emotional, for a child. She really is. (p. 89)

Later, when Holden awakens Phoebe and "She put her arms around my neck and all," he blurts out:

> She's very affectionate. I mean she's quite affectionate, for a child. Sometimes she's even *too* affectionate. I sort of gave her a kiss. (p. 209)

One begins to recognize the brilliant stratagem of imprecise adolescent qualifiers such as "sort of," "I mean," "and all," and the nervous repetition of "affectionate" which dramatize Holden's confusion of restraint and desire. This confusion develops in the first passage as language moves from firm declaration to qualification; in the second, Phoebe's presence provokes even more qualified language.

Then, there is the curious matter of "Little Shirley Beans," the record Holden buys for Phoebe:

> It was about a little kid that wouldn't go out of the house because two of her front teeth were out and she was ashamed to. . . . I knew it would knock old Phoebe out. . . . It was a very old, terrific record that this colored girl singer, Estelle Fletcher, made about twenty years ago. She sings it very Dixieland and whorehouse, and it doesn't sound at all mushy. If a white

girl was singing it, she'd make it sound *cute* as hell, but old Estelle Fletcher knew what the hell she was doing, and it was one of the best records I ever heard. (p. 149)

The significance of the record is underscored by Holden's anxiousness to give it to Phoebe and his inordinate dismay when he breaks it:

Then something terrible happened just as I got in the park. I dropped old Phoebe's record. It broke into about fifty pieces. . . . I damn near cried, it made me feel so terrible, but all I did was, I took the pieces out of the envelope and put them in my coat pocket. (p. 199)

One wonders if the accident wasn't psychically determined. If the Shirley Beans affair were a subject of dream analysis, the missing teeth, the shame, and the translation through "whorehouse" jazz by a singer who "knew what the hell she was doing" would conventionally suggest the loss of virginity. Hence, Holden's unconscious forces would dictate the destruction of this "record" as well as its purchase. In the same vein is the information Holden passes on, as he sneaks into the apartment to see Phoebe, that the maid wouldn't hear "because she had only one eardrum. She had this brother that stuck a straw down her ear when she was a kid, she once told me."

At one point Holden hears a child singing the song that becomes the anthem of his savior fantasies: "If a body catch a body coming through the rye." Yet in the next paragraph he buys the "Little Shirley Beans" record—the pairing symbolically dramatizes his conflict of protecting and of violating. His thoughts turn to the Olivier *Hamlet* he and Phoebe had watched and he singles out this highly suggestive scene:

The best part in the whole picture was when old Ophelia's brother—the one that gets in the duel with Hamlet at the very end—was going away and his father was giving him a lot of advice. While the father kept giving him a lot of advice, old Ophelia was sort of horsing around with her brother, taking his dagger out of the holster, and teasing him and all while he was trying to look interested in the bull his father was shooting. That was nice. I got a big bang out of that. But you don't see that kind of stuff much. The only thing old Phoebe liked was when Hamlet patted his dog on the head. (pp. 152–53)

In all of these early clues, one notices that the nearer Holden's desires come to surfacing, the more hesitant his language and behavior become. When the dreadful suggestions have the protective coloration of, say, the art of "Little Shirley Beans" or *Hamlet*, he is not so uneasy: "That was nice. I got a big bang out of that."

After a series of abortive adventures with women, Holden rather desperately seeks the counsel of a former classmate who was regarded as the dormitory's resident expert on sexual matters. Luce is too pompous to help, but his cutting assessments are probably accurate. He tells Holden that his "mind is immature" and recommends psychoanalysis, as he had done the last time they had talked. Holden's self-diagnosis at this point—that his "trouble" is an inability to get "sexy—I mean really sexy—with a girl I don't like a lot"—raises questions when one recalls his fraternal affection for Jane Gallagher and the relatively sexy episodes with the likes of Sally Hayes and "a terrible phony named Anne Louise Sherman." A probable answer, as we shall see, lies in his confused feelings about Phoebe.

All chances for normal sexual expression or even sexual understanding now depleted, Holden gets drunk and goes to Central Park to find "where the ducks go in winter." One critic reads that episode, filled as it is with thoughts of death, as Holden's "dark night of the soul," after which the boy begins to gain in psychic strength (Strauch, p. 109). It ought to be pointed out that Holden's breakdown occurs after the events of the narrative. His desperation in the park is certainly one extreme of his vacillation, the withdrawing extreme which is imaged by coldness and thoughts of death. Finally, he decides to see Phoebe, "in case I died and all," more explicitly associating Phoebe with death.

Holden makes his way into the apartment furtively—ostensibly to keep his parents from learning that he had flunked out of school. Yet his guilt seems obsessive. "I really should've been a crook," he says after telling the elevator operator that he was visiting the "Dicksteins" who live next door, that he has to wait for them in their hallway because he has a "bad leg," causing him to limp "like a bastard." Though his mother "has ears like a goddam bloodhound," his parents are out and he enters Phoebe's room undetected.

Phoebe is asleep:

> She had her mouth way open. It's funny. You take adults, they look lousy when they're asleep and they have their mouths way open, but kids don't. Kids look all right. They can even have spit all over the pillow and they still look all right. (p. 207)

Suddenly Holden feels "swell" as he notices such things as Phoebe's discarded clothing arranged neatly on a chair. Throughout the Phoebe section, double entendres and sexually suggestive images and gestures multiply, most flowing naturally from Holden's mind while others, once the coding is perceived, become mechanical pointers to the psychological plot.

When Holden awakens Phoebe and is embarrassed by her over-affection, she eagerly tells him about the play in which she is "Benedict Arnold":

> "It starts out when I'm dying. This ghost comes in on Christmas Eve and asks me if I'm ashamed and everything. . . . Are you coming to it?" (p. 210)

When the Benedict Arnold image recurs at the end, we shall see the role of "traitor" is precisely the one she must play if her brother is to weather his crisis. Phoebe then tells him about *The Doctor*, a movie she has seen "at the Lister Foundation" about "this doctor . . . that sticks a blanket over this child's face that's a cripple and can't walk. . . . and makes her suffocate. Then they make him go to jail for life imprisonment, but this child that he stuck the blanket over its head comes to visit him all the time and thanks him for what he did. He was a mercy killer." (p. 211)

This suggestive plot points to a horrible psychological possibility for Holden. He may "kill" Phoebe, pay his penalty agreeably, and even receive the gratitude of his victim. If interpretation here seems hard to justify, especially the implications of *Phoebe's* having suggested all this to Holden, consider the climax of the chapter in which Phoebe puts "the goddam pillow over her head" and refuses to come out. "She does that quite frequently," Holden reassures us—and then takes it all back: "She's a true madman sometimes." However innocent, Phoebe's responses to Holden's secret needs become the catalyst for both his breakdown and recovery.

Through the next chapter Phoebe hears Holden out on his "categorical aversions," in Salinger's phrase, to all the "phoniness" that has soured his world. The conversation begins in a curious manner:

Then, just for the hell of it, I gave her a pinch on the behind. It was sticking way out in the breeze, the way she was laying on her side. She has hardly any behind. I didn't do it hard, but she tried to hit my hand anyway, but she missed.

Then all of a sudden, she said, "Oh, why did you *do* it?" She meant why did I get the ax again. It made me sort of sad, the way she said it. (p. 217)

Holden spells out his dissatisfactions at length—and indeed he cites valid and depressing instances of human failings—until Phoebe challenges him several times, "You don't like *anything* that's happening." "Name one thing," she demands. "One thing? One thing I like?" Holden replies. "Okay." At this point he finds he can't "concentrate too hot."

She was in a cockeyed position way the hell over the other side of the bed. She was about a thousand miles away. (p. 220)

He can't concentrate, I suggest, because the truth is too close.

About all I could think of were those two nuns that went around collecting dough in those beat-up old straw baskets. Especially the one with the glasses with those iron rims. And this boy I know at Elkton Hills. (p. 220)

Repression has transferred the true thing he "likes a lot" to a nun, an inviolable "sister," who, we remember, had embarrassed Holden by talking about *Romeo and Juliet*, "that play [that] gets pretty sexy in parts." It may also be significant that *Romeo and Juliet* involves forbidden love that ends tragically—especially significant in connection with the other "thing" Holden thinks about, James Castle, the boy who had killed himself wearing Holden's turtleneck sweater.

None of this will do for Phoebe and she repeats the challenge:

> "I like Allie," I said. "And I like doing what I'm doing right now. Sitting here with you and talking, and thinking about stuff, and—" (p. 222)

When she objects that "Allie's dead," Holden tries to explain but gives up:

> "Anyway, I like it now," I said. "I mean right now. Sitting here with you and just chewing the fat and horsing—" (p. 223)

Her insistence drives him to the loveliest—and most sinister—fantasy in the novel:

> "You know that song 'If a body catch a body comin' through the rye'? I'd like—"
> "It's 'If a body *meet* a body coming through the rye!' " old Phoebe said. (p. 224)

Holden proceeds to conjure up the daydream of himself as catcher in the rye, the protector of childhood innocence. As Phoebe implies, however, the song is about romance, not romanticism. Because he has to, Holden has substituted a messianic motive for the true, erotic one.

In the next chapter Holden and Phoebe seem to be acting out a mock romance, much the way Seymour Glass does with the little girl in "A Perfect Day for Bananafish." The episode is at once movingly tender and ominous. Holden finds Phoebe "sitting smack in the middle of the bed, outside the covers, with her legs folded like one of those Yogi guys"—an image one critic interprets as making her an emblem of "the still, contemplative center of life" (Strauch, p. 43). This may be valid for one level of Holden's mind. When he immediately asks her to dance, however, and "she practically jumped off the bed, and then waited while I took my shoes off," his excessive justifications point to guilt:

> I don't like people that dance with little kids. . . . Usually they keep yanking the kid's dress up in the back by mistake, and the kid can't dance worth a damn *any*way, and it looks terrible, but I don't do it out in public with Phoebe or anything. We just horse around in the house. It's different with her anyway, because she can *dance*. She can follow anything you do. I mean if you hold her in close as hell so that it doesn't matter that your legs are so much longer. She stays right with you. (p. 227)

After the dance, Phoebe "jumped back in bed and got under the covers" and Holden "sat down next to her on the bed again . . . sort of out of breath." " 'Feel my forehead,' she said all of a sudden." Phoebe claims she has learned to induce fever psychosomatically so that

> "your whole forehead gets so hot you can burn somebody's hand."
> That killed me. I pulled my hand away from her forehead, like I was in terrific danger. "Thanks for *tell*ing me," I said.
> "Oh, I wouldn't've burned *your* hand. I'd've stopped before it got too—*Shhh!*" Then, quick as hell, she sat way the hell up in bed. (p. 229)

The parents have returned and the scene that follows, Holden gathering up his shoes and hiding in the closet as the mother interrogates Phoebe about the (cigarette) "smoke" in the bedroom and asks "were you warm enough?" is reminiscent of nothing so much as that mainstay of French farce, the lover hiding in the closet or under the bed as the girl ironically "explains" to husband or parent. More important are the implications of Phoebe's "heat." Though she cannot really induce it, her innocent compliance in the whole sexual charade does place Holden "in terrific danger."

When the mother leaves, Holden emerges from his hiding place and borrows money from Phoebe. Phoebe insists that he take all of her money and Holden "all of a sudden" begins to cry:

> I couldn't help it. I did it so nobody could hear me, but I did it. It scared the hell out of old Phoebe when I started doing it, and she came over and tried to make me stop, but once you get started, you can't just stop on a goddam *dime*. I was still sitting on the edge of the bed when I did it, and she put her old arm around my neck, and I put my arm around her, too, but I still couldn't stop for a long time. I thought I was going to choke to death or something. Boy, I scared the hell out of poor old Phoebe. The damn window was open and everything, and I could feel her shivering and all, because all she had on was her pajamas. I tried to make her get back in bed, but she wouldn't go. (p. 233)

Holden's breakdown, his visiting of his own suffering on the child, the chill air, and the innocence of their intimacy in this moving scene signal his growing, frightening awareness of the other sort of intimacy. From now until he sees Phoebe again, Holden is in full flight. Nonetheless, their parting is filled with suggestions of a sort one might expect after a casual, normal sexual encounter. (The emphases in the following passage are my own.)

> then I *finished buttoning* my coat and all. I told her I'd *keep in touch with her*. She told me *I could sleep with her* if I wanted to, but I said no, that I'd better beat it. . . . Then I took my hunting hat out of my coat pocket and *gave it to her*. She likes those kind of crazy hats. She didn't want to take it, but *I made her*. I'll bet she *slept with it* on. She really likes those kinds of hats. Then I told her again I'd *give her a buzz* if I got a chance, and then I left. (p. 233)

It is almost as if Holden is acknowledging the real content of the sexual charade and escaping while he can. It would also seem that realization, however vague, is equated with deed as Holden immediately indicates that he wanted to be punished:

> It was a helluva lot easier getting out of the house than it was getting in, for some reason. For one thing, I didn't give much of a damn any more if they caught me. I really didn't. I figured if they caught me, they caught me. I almost wished they did, in a way. (pp. 233–34)

Holden leaves Phoebe to spend the night with Mr. Antolini, a former teacher who during the course of the evening offers sound if stilted assessments of Holden's future which become particularly relevant in the epilogue. Antolini has been drinking, however, and disrupts the peace he has provided (Holden feels sleepy for the first time) by awakening the boy with tentative homosexual advances. Certainly Holden is victimized ("I was shaking like a madman. . . . I think I was more depressed than I ever was in my life"), but the encounter may torment him most for its parallels to his own unconscious designs on a child. Now one begins to see the significance of Holden's unfounded suspicions about Jane Gallagher's stepfather and his murderous rage at the "perverty bum" who wrote the obscenity on Phoebe's school wall—inordinate reactions pointing to fears about himself.

At this point Holden's neurosis verges on madness. Each time he crosses a street, he imagines he will "disappear" and "never get to the other side of the street." I do not take this so much as a symbolic manifestation of "identity crisis" and of his fear that he "may never reach maturity"—although both are implicit—but rather as a literal, psychologically valid description of the boy's breakdown. He retreats into wild fantasies of running away forever, living in a cabin near, but not in, the woods ("I'd want it to be sunny as hell all the time"), and feigning deaf-muteness, all to escape the confusion about to engulf him. Phoebe betrays these plans—the first ironic level of the Benedict Arnold motif—by joining in his escape. When she appears, bag in hand and the hunting cap on her head, Holden reacts wildly:

> "I'm going with you. Can I? Okay?"
> "What?" I said. I almost fell over when she said that. I swear to God I did. I got sort of dizzy and I thought I was going to pass out or something again. . . .
> I thought I was going to pass out cold. I mean I didn't mean to tell her to shut up and all, but I thought I was going to pass out again. . . .
> I was almost all set to hit her. I thought I was going to smack her for a second. I really did. . . .
> "I thought you were supposed to be Benedict Arnold in that play and all," I said. I said it very nasty. "Wuddaya want to do? Not be in the play, for God's sake?" That made her cry even harder. I was glad. All of a sudden I wanted her to cry till her eyes practically dropped out. I almost hated her. I think I hated her most because she wouldn't be in that play any more if she went away with me. (pp. 267–68)

These near-hysterical responses can be understood, it seems to me, only in the context that Phoebe is the very thing he is fleeing. He somehow realizes that she *must* be his "Benedict Arnold."

Holden's fury at Phoebe having set the climax in motion, Salinger now employs a delicate spatial strategy. Phoebe returns the hat, turns her back on Holden, announces that she has no intention of running away with him, and runs "right the hell across the street, without even looking to see if any cars were coming." Positioning here signifies the end of their relation as possible lovers, but love remains. Holden does not go after her, knowing she'll follow him "on the *other* goddam side of the street. She wouldn't look over at me at all, but I could tell she was probably watching me out of the corner of her crazy eye to see where I was going and all. Anyway, we kept walking that way all the way to the zoo." They are still apart as they watch the sea lions being fed, Holden standing "right behind her."

> I didn't put my hands on her shoulders again or anything because if I had she *really* would've beat it on me. Kids are funny. You have to watch what you're doing.
>   She wouldn't walk right next to me when we left the sea lions, but she didn't walk too far away. She sort of walked on one side of the sidewalk and I walked on the other side. . . . Old Phoebe still wouldn't talk to me or anything, but she was sort of walking next to me now. I took a hold of the belt at the back of her coat, just for the hell of it, but she wouldn't let me. She said, "Keep your hands to yourself, if you don't mind." (pp. 271–72)

Holden promises not to run away and they rejoin as brother and sister in the presence of the carrousel—miraculously open in winter. Phoebe wants to ride and Holden finds a mature, new perspective:

> All the kids kept trying to grab for the gold ring, and so was old Phoebe, and I was sort of afraid she'd fall off the goddam horse, but I didn't say anything or do anything. The thing with kids is, if they want to grab for the gold ring, you have to let them do it, and not say anything. If they fall off, they fall off, but it's bad if you say anything to them. (pp. 273–74)

The substitution of a gold ring for the traditional brass one may point to Phoebe's future as a woman. In any event, Holden has renounced his designs on Phoebe and thus abrogated his messianic role. Another Salinger story has young de Daumier-Smith relinquish his sexual designs on a nun with the announcement, "I am giving Sister Irma her freedom to follow her destiny. Everyone is a nun." One need not search for literary sources to recognize that the carrousel finally represents everyone's sacred, inviolable human destiny.

III

Readers now dubious about this paper's clinical approach ("aesthetic pathology," Salinger has called it) may wonder why I have thus far neglected to make a masculine symbol of Holden's long-peaked hunting cap—which he purchased, one recalls, after losing the fencing team's foils in a subway. This rather mechanical symbol does partake of the boy's masculinity or sexuality. But more than that, it becomes the most reliable symbolic designation of Holden's psychic condition through the novel. Ackley points out that it is a deer hunter's hat while Holden maintains that "This is a people shooting hat. . . . I shoot people in this hat." When one remembers that hunters wear red hats to keep from being shot and that Holden usually wears his backwards in the manner of a baseball catcher, the symbol embraces Holden's aggressive and withdrawing tendencies as well as the outlandish daydreams of becoming the messiah in the rye.

Holden's masculinity is plainly involved in such instances as when he has to retrieve the hat from under a bed after the fight with Stradlater and when it is entrusted to Phoebe's bed, but the symbol becomes more encompassing when she "restores" the hat in the climactic carrousel scene.

> Then all of a sudden she gave me a kiss. Then she held her hand out, and said, "It's raining. It's starting to rain."
> "I know."
> Then what she did—it damn near killed me—she reached in my coat pocket and took out my red hunting hat and put it on my head. . . . My hunting hat really gave me quite a lot of protection, in a way, but I got soaked anyway. I didn't care, though. I felt so happy all of a sudden, the way old Phoebe kept going around and around. I was damn near bawling, I felt so damn happy, if you want to know the truth. I don't know why. It was just that she looked so damn *nice*, the way she kept going around and around, in her blue coat and all. God, I wish you could have been there. (pp. 274–75)

At its deepest level, the hat symbolizes something like Holden's basic human resources—his birthright, that lucky caul of protective courage, humor, compassion, honesty, and love—all of which are the real subject matter of the novel.

As the symbolic hat gives Holden "quite a lot of protection, in a way" and he gets "soaked anyway," those human resources do not prevent emotional collapse. In the epilogue we learn that Holden went West—"after I went home, and . . . got sick and all"—not for the traditional opportunity there but for psychotherapy. This would be a bleak ending were it not for the fact that Holden has authored this structured narrative, just as Antolini predicted he might:

> "you'll find that you're not the first person who was ever confused and frightened and even sickened by human behavior. You're by no means alone on that score, you'll be excited and *stimulated* to know. Many, many men have been just as troubled morally and spiritually as you are right now. Happily, some of them kept records of their troubles. You'll learn from them—if you want to. Just as someday, if you have something to offer, someone will learn something from you. It's a beautiful reciprocal arrangement. And it isn't education. It's history. It's poetry." (p. 246)

The richness of spirit in this novel, especially of the vision, the compassion, and the humor of the narrator reveal a psyche far healthier than that of the boy who endured the events of the narrative. Through the telling of his story, Holden has given shape to, and thus achieved control of, his troubled past.

Notes

1. J. D. Salinger, *The Catcher in the Rye* (Boston: Little, 1951), pp. 7–8. Page numbers from this edition will be cited in the text.

2. Carl F. Strauch, "Kings in the Back Row: Meaning through Structure—A Reading of Salinger's *The Catcher in the Rye*," *Wisconsin Studies in Contemporary Literature* 2 (Winter 1961), 5–30; rpt. in *If You Really Want to Know: A* Catcher *Casebook* (Belmont, Calif.: Wadsworth, 1962), p. 104.

3. Salinger may be echoing Phoebus rather than Phoebe, the personification of the moon; but he also may have in mind an antithesis between "Sunny" and Phoebe, the cool and chaste.

Holden and Psychoanalysis

Dennis Vail*

To the Editor:

I would like to comment on James Bryan's psychoanalytic reading of *The Catcher in the Rye* (PMLA,89, 1065–74). I pass by Bryan's silence about psychoanalysis as an object of satire in the novel and his dubious assumption that Holden is in a mental hospital, to remark on what seems to me his misreading of Holden's relationship with Phoebe.

During the bedrooom scene, Holden shows no uneasiness about his and Phoebe's being there together in their parents' absence, about dancing with her, or even about pinching her behind; and the fact seems hardly consistent with the intense and barely submerged sexual desires that Bryan attributes to him at this juncture. The point is that such contact need *not* be corrupt (and Holden's previous contact with Jane Gallagher demonstrates the same truth). If anything, Salinger is setting a trap and Bryan has taken the bait. Salinger's technique here constitutes a test (one of many) of the values and responses of the highly personal "you" to whom the novel is addressed. Holden's being "out of breath" after dancing with Phoebe is simply another indication of his lack of "wind," which suggests figuratively, throughout the novel, a lack of the psychological staying power that he will have to have to survive in the adult world.

Holden's taking the money from Phoebe is important. The corrupt Sunny (her name is partly ironic, but she does manifest the life principle of the corrupt adult world) has chiseled Holden out of more than the agreed upon amount, for which he gets no return anyway; the innocent and loving Phoebe insists that he take all she has. Holden is probably not conscious of the parallel, but we need not search for feelings of remorse over incestuous desires to explain his temporary emotional breakdown. It is quite enough that he has reached the pass of appropriating his little sister's "Christmas dough." Holden is being exploitive, all right, but not sexually so.

*Reprinted from PMLA 91, no. 1 (June 1976):120–21, by permission of the Modern Language Association of America.

On one level the money and the hat constitute an unconscious mutual pledge of fidelity. But on another, though related, level the hat is the badge of Holden's calling and responsibility. Phoebe has the hat only while Holden is planning to run away, and only when she puts it back on his head are things finally right. For Holden's responsibility is precisely for Phoebe and and for succoring the value that she represents. Holden must still wear the hat "for a while" (New York: Bantam, 1970, p. 212), for Phoebe is not ready to assume the responsibility herself, and her parents are manifestly incapable of doing so. Her presence in D. B.'s bedroom foreshadows the corruption that may well be her destiny if Holden reneges on this obligation.

Throughout the bedroom scene Phoebe keeps repeating, "Daddy's going to kill you," Daddy—the authority principle—has been trying to do that all along, and Holden is in considerable danger of his succeeding. When he responds, "I don't give a damn if he does" (p. 173), he shows the dangerous predilection that Mr. Antolini later puts his finger on. Holden may well die "nobly . . . for some highly unworthy cause" (p. 188), as James Castle does. It is this unacceptable kamikaze impulse that Phoebe forces Holden to face in himself when she says, "You don't like *any*thing that's happening," and the fact fully explains his discomfiture at trying to meet her challenge, "Name one thing."

Something very similar happens at the novel's climax. Phoebe does betray Holden's plans and thereby becomes the agent of his salvation (we recall Holden's assertion that Jesus wouldn't send Judas to hell). She forces him to face and to reject the escapist course to which he is now so intensely committed; hence his momentary rage and hatred for her. Only after this, by replacing an imaginary field full of anonymous children with the real live Phoebe as the object of his solicitude, does Holden establish the possibility of a genuinely effective life.

The gold ring is most directly a symbol of ideal perfection and truth, the imaginable state toward which all striving tends; and striving involves risks. Holden has been "trying to grab for the gold ring" throughout the novel, though in a self-destructive way. Mr. Antolini is afraid that Holden is "riding for some kind of a terrible, terrible fall" (p. 186), just as Holden is afraid that Phoebe will fall from the carrousel horse. Both falls (as well as the children's threatened fall from the cliff in Holden's "catcher" fantasy and James Castle's fall from the window) are the fall from life and innocence into death or corruption. Transcending the dilemma between physical death or insanity (escape) and spiritual death or corruption (capitulation) is Holden's essential problem. And the fact that he alone in the novel exhibits the problem (D.B. has accepted one of the alternatives) is emphatically to his credit.

The association of sex with death is not merely Holden's but the novel's. Holden says, "Sex is something I just don't understand. I swear to God I don't (p. 63). Even Mr. Antolini, who has tried to save D. B. and who tries to save Holden, exhibits the shoddy motive. "It's really too bad," but the sad fact is that in this fallen world "so much crumby stuff is a lot of fun some-times" (p. 62); and it is essential to the novel's effect that Holden remains a virgin throughout. The eros-agape opposition cannot be resolved through Luce's claptrap about psychoanalysis and Eastern philosophy. Maintaining one's essential innocence in full knowledge of and contact with an essentially corrupt world (that synthesis of innocence and experience represented by the "Little Shirley Beans" record and the nun who loves *Romeo and Juliet*) constitutes the only maturity worth having. It is this that promises to flower in Phoebe and that Holden himself finally shows promise of being able to achieve. It is rare; it is so painfully difficult as to be almost impossible. But nothing less is acceptable, for nothing less can lead to happiness. Everything else is death.

Reviewers, Critics, and *The Catcher in the Rye*

Carol Ohmann and Richard Ohmann*

On the day *The Catcher in the Rye* was published, on Monday, July 16, 1951, the *New York Times* reviewed it; a review in the Sunday *Times* had appeared the day before, and a rush of other reviews followed. Through the later fifties and on into the sixties, *Catcher* engaged academic critics, and it still does, although the novel generates criticism at a slower rate today than it used to. By 1963 Warren French supposed that critics had written more on *Catcher* than on any other contemporary novel, and in 1965 James E. Miller, Jr., claimed, reasonably enough, that Salinger had stirred more interest among the public and critics alike than any writer since Fitzgerald and Hemingway.[1] By 1961, *Catcher* had sold 1,500,000 copies;[2] by 1965, 5,000,000;[3] last year the total of its sales stood at more than 9,000,000.[4]

The Catcher in the Rye arrived to stay and is older now than most of its audience when they read it for the first time. That quarter century is time enough to allow us to generalize not only about the book's reception in 1951 but about the consensus of critical opinion that developed afterwards. We are concerned, in brief, with how *Catcher* became a classic: this is a case study of capitalist criticism. And in it, we shall have in mind the distinction Raymond Williams makes in *Culture and Society* between the lives books lead in the minds of readers and the lives their readers (and writers) live in particular historical times.

*Reprinted by permission from *Critical Inquiry* 3, no. 1 (Autumn 1976):15–37. © 1976 by the University of Chicago.

I

To return to July 16, 1951: on that Monday, the front page of the Times carried eleven news stories. The largest headline, with the text beneath breaking into two parts, concerned the war in Korea, then a year old: one part told that peace talks between United Nations negotiators and Communists had resumed in Kaesong (they would, of course, be unsuccessful), and the other reported with extensive quotation a speech Secretary of State Dean Acheson made in New York to book and magazine publishers on the meaning of the Korean conflict; the State Department had released the speech "at the request of a number of those" who were present to hear it. An account of the fighting itself with maps and communiqués from the field and a list of casualties appeared on page two. The front-page news was not, in other words, of the combat and its immediate consequences but of verbal maneuvering in the conflict between Communism and the Western world and of the ideological interpretation our leading spokesman in foreign affairs wished to give to events in Korea. Apart from stories on a flood in Kansas City, the weather in New York (hot, dry, and hard on the water supply), and a request for funding for new schools in the City, all the other articles on the front page bore on the struggle between East and West, of which events in Korea were simply for the moment the most dramatic and costly example: in Teheran, 10,000 "Iranian Reds" rioted to protest the arrival of Averill Harriman, who had come as Truman's special assistant to talk with the Shah's government about the Iranian-British oil dispute; Admiral Forrest P. Sherman, Chief of Naval Operations, left for a week in Europe, which would include discussion in Spain about possibilities of "joint military cooperation"; the United States asked for the recall from Washington of two Hungarian diplomats in retaliation for the expulsion of two American officials from Budapest; a Republican congressman protested that his party's opposition to Truman's proposal for continued price, wage, and credit controls was not "sabotaging" those controls but aimed at stopping "socialistic power grabs" on the part of the Administration.

The front page of the *Times* on July 16, 1951, serves to outline, quickly enough, the situation of the world into which *The Catcher in the Rye* made such a successful and relatively well-publicized entrance. The main action of the world, the chief events of its days were occurring within a framework of struggle between two systems of life, two different ways of organizing human beings socially, politically, economically. The opposition between East and West, between socialist and capitalist, was determining what happened in Kaesong, Budapest, Madrid, Teheran, Washington, New York. Name-calling the Administration, Republicans threw out the term "socialist," and the bid for millions to build schools in the five boroughs of New York would finally have to dovetail with allocations of taxes for defense.

The review of *The Catcher in the Rye* in the back pages of the *Times* made no mention of any of this. The kind of reality reported on the front page belonged to one world; the new novel was about to be assimilated into another, into the world of culture, which was split from politics and society. And this separation repeated itself in other reviews: typically, they did not mention the framework of world history contemporary with the novel; they did not try to relate *Catcher* to that framework even to the extent of claiming that there was only a partial relationship or complaining, however simplistically, that there was none. Our concern from here on will be to try to sketch what reviewers and what academic critics after them did see in the novel and what they might have seen in it. We are interested in the conceptual frameworks, the alternatives to history, they used to respond to and interpret *Catcher* as they passed it on to its millions of lay readers.

Before turning to the world of culture, though, it seems useful to turn back one last time to the news of July 16, 1951, for even as it was being reported it was, of course, already being interpreted. The Secretary of State's speech in New York and the lead editorial were especially rich in interpretive intent. Acheson placed the Korean War in the perspective of an *ongoing* conflict between the United States and Russia, and urged us to prevail in that conflict: "Korea's significance is not the final crusade. It is not finally making valid the idea of collective security. It is important perhaps for the inverse reason that in Korea we prevented the invalidation of collective security." Even if peace was made in Korea, we should not relax, because further dangers resided in the

> awakening of the vast populations of Asia, populations which are beginning to feel that they should have and should exercise in the world an influence which is proportionate to their numbers and worthy of their cultures. We must manage our difficulties so prudently that we have strength and initiative and power left to help shape and guide these emerging forces so that they will not turn out to be forces which rend and destroy.

What Acheson implied to be the eventual happy ending of our present and future efforts is obvious and familiar: we would not only retain our present advantages economically and politically but augment them. Nations emerging in Asia would do so in ways compatible with rather than antagonistic to our hegemony, hence to our own well-being. The fundamental value to which Acheson appealed in his speech, the goal and the sanction of all that he urges, is comprehended in the phrase "national interests." Our nationalism was not, in the language of his argument, aggressive but defensive. "A blow has been struck at us in Korea." Another might be struck in a year elsewhere if we slackened in our defense effort; Asian nations would rend and destroy us if we did not guide them otherwise.

The lead editorial supported Acheson's policies and yet at the same time shifted the mode of justifying them:

> We would be less than humane if we did not urge and support any course of action that can spare the loss of life. No honest person wanted a war in

Korea and all right-minded persons want to see it ended. Nevertheless, we are not willing to sacrifice honor and morality to our will to peace. The United Nations was right in the first place to resist aggression, and that rightness has not been changed. Obviously, the aggression that will have to be resisted now is political rather than military. Our defenses need to be as strong in one field as in the other.

The fundamental appeal here was to a timeless, extranational morality transcending particular interests. Sparing lives and living peacefully are good—everyone right-minded and honest and honorable believes that—but, regrettably and inexorably, the defense of freedom must come first. The United Nations was fighting for a self-determining, united Korea independent of foreign intrusion, and would go on fighting if that end was not achieved at the conference table in Kaesong.

In appealing to "national interests," Acheson did offer a justification, a definition of right, that is congruent with the historical moment; "national interests" fittingly named, though it certainly did not spell out, a clear-sighted interpretation of politico-economic realities in 1951: the United States, having determined the policy of the United Nations, was fighting in Korea to protect and eventually to extend America's post-World War II domination of the world's economic system. The editorial writer obscured the historical moment and mystified the Korean War: as an honorable nation, we were fighting north and south of the fortieth parallel to preserve morality. The transformation worked on historical fact between the front page and the editorial parallels, we think, the transformation reviewers and critics worked on *The Catcher in the Rye*. The novel does not, of course, mention the conflict between East and West. It does mirror a competitive, acquisitive society, where those who have, keep and press for more—the same society that put half a million troops on the field in Korea and sent Harriman to Teheran and Sherman to Madrid. *Catcher,* to anticipate our argument at this point, is precisely revealing of social relationships in midcentury America, and motives that sustained them, and rationalizations that masked them. In the hands of reviewers and critics, though, its precision and its protest were blurred and muted, masked not quite white but grayed by a steady application of interpretive terms that tended to abstract and merely universalize its characters and its action, dimming the pattern of their own historical time. As Acheson spoke of interests and the editorial writer of morality, Salinger wrote about power and wealth and reviewers and critics about good and evil and the problems of growing up.

From the *Times* directly or from other daily papers and from radio and television broadcasts purveying the same news, reviewers turned to *The Catcher in the Rye*. They were fairly consistent in their estimates of the novel; either they praised it or, finding some fault with it, they allowed that it was nonetheless brilliant or a tour de force or at the very least lively. What concerns us here, though, is not how the reviewers rated it but the categories under which they apprehended it. They viewed the novel as a novel, commenting especially on its most striking formal feature, Salinger's choice of a seventeen-year-old personal narrator and his matching of syntax and idiom to that choice. They were also concerned to label *Catcher* generically; they saw it as satire or comedy or tragicomedy, or at their most casual they called it funny or sad or both at once. And in a rudimentary way at least they positioned the novel in the history of fiction: it reminded them of Twain's work and Lardner's and Hemingway's. In other words, neither surprisingly nor inappropriately, the reviewers described *Catcher* as a literary work in itself and placed it vis-à-vis other works similar in genre and style. What they were concerned to do mostly, though, was to relate Catcher to life, and upon that relationship they hinged their estimates of its quality far more than they did on its stylistic or generic qualities. They assumed that a novel's most important function is mimetic and that insofar as it succeeds as representation, it succeeds as fiction. Theoretically, this standard might have integrated the two worlds which we have spoken of as separate. But in fact it did not because of the way the reviewers defined, and circumscribed, "life."

They were, first of all, concerned to describe Holden Caulfield as a person, and, doing that, they emphasized his youth; usually they went on to diagnose what ails him and, sometimes, to prescribe a cure and to guess what would happen to him next, beyond the point where the novel itself ends. In the *Times*, Nash K. Burger wrote: "Holden's mercurial changes of mood, his stubborn refusal to admit his own sensitiveness and emotions, his cheerful disregard of what is sometimes known as reality are typically and heartbreakingly adolescent."[5] Phrases similar to "typically and heartbreakingly adolescent" recur in other reviews: "[Salinger] charts the miseries and ecstasies of an adolescent rebel" (*Time*);[6] "[Holden is a] bright, terrible, and possibly normal sixteen-year-old" (Harvey Breit, *Atlantic*);[7] "Holden is not a normal boy. He is hypersensitive and hyper-imaginative" (S. N. Behrman, *New Yorker*);[8] "the reader wearies of this kind of explicitness, repetition and adolescence, exactly as one would weary of Holden himself" (Anne L. Goodman, *New Republic*).[9] The kind of typing implicit in these quotations is laid out plain in Ernest Jones' review: "[Catcher] is a mirror. It reflects something not at all rich and strange but what every sensitive sixteen-year-old since Rousseau has felt, and of course what each one of us is certain he has felt. . . . its insights . . . are not really insights; since they are so general, 'The Catcher in the Rye' becomes more and more a case history of all of us . . ." (*Nation*).[10] The reviewers differed on certain points: Holden is normal or he is not, but even those who say he is not or possibly not, have a norm in mind. They type Holden according to a timeless developmental standard. They do not fully agree on how to define adolescence, or on how far Holden fits the category (is he *hyper*sensitive? is he *especially* bright?), but they do agree that there is a norm or model and that Holden more or less matches it.

We would exaggerate if we said the reviewers had no awareness at all of

Holden Caulfield's time and place. They did address themselves to Salinger's representation of his hero's society, although much less emphatically than they set about describing the hero himself, but here again, they showed a common disposition to typify or to categorize and to do so in remarkably similar ways. Harvey Breit called *Catcher* "a crititique of the contemporary grown-up world" (*Atlantic*).[11] Harrison Smith referred to the "complexity of modern life" and "the spectacle of perversity and evil," which bewilder and shock Holden as they do so many youths (*Saturday Review*).[12] Both these reviewers alluded at least to the time of the novel's time. But Breit did not enlarge upon his point save to say that Holden is not a good observer, that we do not see the world through his eyes, only himself; the phrases Smith employed are very far from specific, and this disposition to abstraction is even more pronounced in some other reviews.

In S. N. Behrman's words, "[Holden] is driven crazy by 'phoniness,' a heading under which he loosely gathers not only insincerity but snobbery, injustice, callousness to the tears in things, and a lot more"; he is faced in the novel with "the tremendously complicated and often depraved facts of life" (*New Yorker*).[13] Burger, in the quotation above, attributed Holden's difficulties to "a world that is out of joint." In Virgilia Peterson's opinion, Holden "sees the mixtures, the inextricably mingled good and bad, as it is, but the very knowledge of reality is what almost breaks his heart" (*Herald Tribune Book Review*).[14] To say that modern life is complex is to say very little indeed about it, and to speak of "the tears in things" and "a world that is out of joint" and "reality" is to move *Catcher* altogether out of its contemporary setting, to see Holden's difficulties as everywhere and always the same. Even the reviews that make no explicit mention of modernity or of Holden's "world" imply by typing him as an adolescent that a sixteen-year-old's problems have been, are, and will remain the same.[15]

II

In the March 1957 issue of *The Nation*, David L. Stevenson remarked, "It is a curiosity of our age that J. D. Salinger . . . is rarely acknowledged by the official guardians of our literary virtue in the quarterlies."[16] That was accurate, though not perhaps so curious if, as we suppose to be the case, our official guardians then as now work primarily in our prestigious institutions of higher learning and work over a canonical list of English and American and other Western writers passed on down by those institutions. Although *The Catcher in the Rye* continued to very much read through the fifties, there was a lag between its date of publication and the appearance of very much professional or academic criticism about the novel. Two years after Stevenson's comment, however, *The Nation* carried an article by George Steiner titled "The Salinger Industry." "[Stevenson,]" Steiner wrote, "can now rest assured. The heavy guns are in action along the entire critical front."[17] What were they booming?

In Steiner's opinion, they were not only noisy but off target. He was concerned both to note the critical energy being expended on Salinger and to correct its aim. At the very time *Catcher* was being assumed into our literary canon, he was suggesting what bounds criticism should keep within and what conclusions it ought to be reaching. Salinger was a "gifted and entertaining writer with one excellent short novel and a number of memorable stories to his credit."

But criticism, Steiner complained, was busy comparing Salinger to *great* writers and speaking of his work in "complex" and "sublime" terms. Why so much activity, more than Salinger's merit (in Steiner's opinion) deserved, and why such exaggeration and pretension? Steiner gave two reasons, and to his mind they exposed what was wrong with criticism written in contemporary America: first, critics had grafted New Critical jargon onto Germanic scholarship and could no longer speak plainly; second, our academic institutions turned out too many critics, too many assistant and associate professors in need of promotions and fellowships and constrained to publish to get them. "Along comes a small though clearly interesting fish like Salinger and out go the whaling fleets. The academic critic can do his piece with few footnotes, it will be accepted by critical reviews or little magazines, and it is another tally on the sheet of his career."

Steiner's piece is in certain ways inaccurate. It tells what one might have expected to happen if one were predicting the nature of Salinger criticism in the later fifties from an exclusive and judgmental point of view of American academic institutions (too many critics on their way up the ladder, "too many critical journals, too many seminars, too many summer schools and fellowships for critics"); but it is skewed in its description of Salinger criticism as it actually did happen in the fifties. We have paused on Steiner because he did remark the arrival of the 'Salinger industry' and because the prejudices he brings into the play are commonly leveled against academics. We want to distinguish our quarrel with the critics from Steiner's. As we see them, they were generously intentioned and more sincere, less dominated by New Criticism or any other "school" and more subtle, than they appeared to be in Steiner's account of a "vast machine in constant need of new raw material." If, as we go on to argue, they underestimated or overlooked or misread Salinger's rendering of contemporary American life, they do not appear to us to have done so because they were time-serving drudges fattening their bibliographies for promotion.

It is true that critics exercised their professional training in writing on Salinger, as they might be expected to do. They spoke of the novel's style; an article in *American Speech*, for example, scrutinized Holden's vocabulary and grammar, considering how far they conformed to teenage vocabulary in the 1950s.[18] They clustered its images in significant patterns, interpreted its symbols, explained its literary allusions, brought to light principles of narrative repetition and variation that govern its structure, spoke of its time scheme, saw Holden in California as a novelist of sorts himself, looking back on his expertise and shaping it to try to understand it. They paid, un-surprisingly, more precise and lengthier attention to the novel as a work of art than its reviewers had is 1951. And they cared much more than the reviewers about positioning *Catcher* with reference to other literary works, finding generic and literarily historical lodgings for it. In a particularly influ-ential article in 1956, Arthur Heiserman and James E. Miller, Jr., identified *Catcher* as belonging to "an ancient and honorable narrative tradition" in Western literature, "the tradition of the Quest."[19] Other critics reiterated the idea of the quest, or they spoke of Holden's trip to New York as a journey to the underworld or through the waste land, or they called his series of adven-tures picaresque. And yet, academics though they were, the critics as a whole were less concerned, really, with typing the novel and less employed, even, with explication as an activity in itself than they were with elucidating the novel's rendering of human experience and evaluating its moral atti-tudes. In this they were close to the original concerns of the reviewers. And they give the impression less of elaborately trained professionals eager to display their learning and methodological expertise (while hungering after advancement) than they do of serious common readers approaching *Catcher* for what it reveals of life and offers in the way of wisdom.

We shall lower here a very plain but, we hope, serviceable grid on a number of critics and ask how they saw *Catcher* answering two questions: what went wrong with Holden, propelling him from Pencey Prep to New York to a psychiatrist's couch in California, and what, if anything, could have been, or could be, done about it?

One group of critics located the causes of Holden's predicament alto-gether or mainly in himself, in his soul or in his psyche. Flunking out of his third prep school, Holden is responding to inner rather than outer pressures; "he is a victim not so much of society as of his own spiritual illness" which forbids his discarding any of his experiences and condemns him to carry the burden of indiscriminate remembrance.[20] Or else he is saintly in his sensitiv-ity, suffering and yet blessed in his inability to withhold either empathy or compassion.[21] Or else Holden is immature or spoiled, an adolescent who is too absolute in his judgments, too intolerant of human failings[22] or an "upper-class New York City boy" who is a "snob."[23] For his spiritual illness, there can be no cure unless he grows into spiritual perfection, finding God and living by His injunction to love. His immaturity calls for growth, for matur-ing into an acceptance of things as they are, and so does his snobbery.[24] These critics differed as to whether or not Holden is left arrested in his difficulties or moved toward or even through redemption or initiation or acceptance or adjustment. But in any case, these views of his predicament all imply that the answer to it, whether that answer is realized in the action of the novel or not, lies in some inward movement of the soul or psyche, a kind of resource that might be available to anyone any time and just as timelessly necessary to saints and sinners as bewildered young men.

More often than they held Holden responsible for his fate, for his breakdown and the events that led him to it, critics saw it derived more emphatically from external causes; they were disposed to blame the world instead of or along with the hero. For some, Holden collides with an unchanging set of antagonists which they speak of in religious or philosophical terms. Holden confronts "evil,"[25] an "immoral world,"[26] a "mutable and deceitful world";[27] his is, as everyman's always is, the existential condition. Like Hamlet, he "stand[s] aghast before a corrupt world."[28] He is "sickened by the material values and the inhumanity of the world."[29] In other readings, his antagonists are more particularly named American and modern. Holden is seen facing, and breaking on, forces characteristic of American life and, more particularly, twentieth-century American life. The people he meets are "innocently imperceptive and emotionally dead"; they impose standards of conformity, as they did on Thoreau and Henry Adams.[30] Or, Holden's society, worse than Thoreau's, and Adams' (and Huck Finn's), is complex, urbanized, dehumanized and dehumanizing; his is the condition of "contemporary alienation."[31] Holden is encircled by "phoniness, indifference and vulgarity"; "as a 'neo-picaresque,' [Catcher] shows itself to be concerned far less with the education or initiation of an adolescent than with a dramatic exposure of the manner in which ideals are denied access to our lives and the modes which mendacity assumes in our urban culture."[32] Contemporary America is afflicted with "neurosis and fatigue."[33] Society is "sick"; "our national experience hurtles us along routes more menacing than the Mississippi."[34] The critic who cast his net widest, aiming at both the enduring and the timely explanation, drew in the most reasons for Holden's fate, for the fact that his retrospective narration issues from a California institution for the mentally ill: "Holden could not face a world of age, death, sickness, ugliness, sex and perversion, poverty, custom, and cant."[35]

Most of these terms, we need hardly emphasize, conceptualize Holden's world in a general way. Many have a moral frame of reference (evil, deceit, corruption, inhumanity, mendacity); many have a psychological or emotional frame of reference (the individual feels the pressure to conform, or society is tired and disturbed). In either case, they tend away from precise description of the society Salinger renders in Catcher.

When Catcher's society did draw pointed comments from critics, they were apt to be negative. Maxwell Geismar, for example, admired Salinger's creation of Pencey Prep, with "all the petty horrors, the banalities, the final mediocrity of the typical American prep school," but faulted his portrayal of Holden's family and class as vague and empty. Holden, he argued, comes to us from "both a social and a psychological void"; Salinger makes no reference to the "real nature and dynamics" of the hero's urban environment.[36] And Ihab Hassan conceded that Catcher is not a "sociological" novel: "No doubt social realities are repressed in the work of Salinger—note how gingerly he handles his Jews."[37] There is an assumption here that a novel that is satisfyingly realistic mirrors society sweepingly and fully, follows Mr. Caulfield into his corporate office and introduces the maid who lives in the room behind Phoebe's. And that assumption, we think, worked to obscure how much Salinger did represent of the contemporary world in *Catcher*, and how far he understood what he represented.

And when Holden's predicament *was* given external cause, at least in part, what could be done about it? What resolution if any did these critics see the novel reaching or at least implying? For certainly a difference in diagnosis would seem to entail a difference in prescription, especially when critics did invoke historical time and place to account for Holden's misadventures. They did not, however, differ very much from the critics above who addressed themselves primarily to the state of Holden's soul or psyche. Holden was searching, as they saw it, for truth or for wisdom or for personal integrity. And beyond reaching understanding and achieving his own identity, he needed to communicate and to love or to find an object for the love he was able to feel at least as the novel ended if not before. In *Catcher* Salinger showed that "the resources of the personality are sufficient for self-recovery and discovery."[38] Or they saw *Catcher* posing Holden's predicament without offering or even implying its solution. More rarely, they touched on the question of how society itself might change along with or apart from any change Holden might manage within his own psychic territory. America had lost its own innocence and, like Holden himself, needed to "face [the] problems of growing up."[39] Although facing them was more likely to lead to "despair" than to "hope."[40]

Of this common intellectual strategy, we can take James E. Miller's criticism as typical. In 1965, almost ten years after his article with Heiserman appeared, Miller wrote again about *Catcher*, this time in the Minnesota pamphlet series on American writers, where his responsibility was in part to voice the critical consensus that had developed. He did so in language that is by now familiar. Holden is on a threefold quest: for "the innocence of childhood," for "an ideal but un-human love," and for "identity." His is "the modern predicament." He is up against "the world as it is," and "the fundamental physicality of the human predicament," which is "a phenomenon of all human relationships, all human situations, by their very nature of being human." In spite of the word "modern," and some references to the atom bomb ("contemporary horrors"), Miller's epitomizing language takes the novel quite out of real history and makes it an eternal story of "death and rebirth."[41] This critical transformation, evidently, was what it took in the academic American fifties and sixties to claim for a literary work the status of a classic.

We fix on Miller, not because he was an inept critic, but because, on the contrary, he was one of the best. In 1965, had we written the Minnesota pamphlet, we surely would have written it in the same ideological key—and less well than Miller. But through another decade of history the book has come to lead a different kind of life in our minds, and it is to our present understanding that we now turn.

III

For us, as for almost all readers, Holden's sensitivity is the heart of the book, that which animates the story and makes it compelling. Events are laden with affect for Holden. He cannot speak of an experience for long in a neutral way, apart from judgment and feeling. And of course those judgments and feelings are largely negative. Not so entirely negative as Phoebe says—"You don't like *any*thing that's happening"—but this novel is first the story of a young man so displeased with himself and with much of the world around him that his strongest impulse is to leave, break loose, move on. From his pain follows rejection and retreat.

But what exactly is it that puts Holden out of sorts with his life? What does he reject? The critics answer, as we have seen, phrases that universalize: an immoral world, the inhumanity of the world, the adult world, the predicament of modern life, the human condition, the facts of life, evil. As we see it, the leap is too quick and too long. Holden lives in a time and place, and these provide the material against which his particular adolescent sensibility reacts.

Holden has many ways of condemning, and an ample lexicon to render his judgments. Some people are bastards, others jerks. The way they act makes you want to puke. What they do and say can be—in Holden's favorite adjectives—depressing, corny, dopey, crumby, screwed-up, boring, phony. "Phony" is probably Holden's most frequent term of abuse, definitely his strongest and most ethically weighted. For that reason his application of the word is a good index to what he finds most intolerable in his life. And Holden is quite consistent in what he calls phony.

Holden says he left Elkton Hills, one of the schools he attended before Pencey, because he was "surrounded by phonies," in particular Mr. Haas the headmaster, "the phoniest bastard I ever met in my life." Haas earned this label in the following way:

> On Sundays [he] went around shaking hands with everybody's parents when they drove up to school. He'd be charming as hell and all. Except if some boy had little old funny-looking parents. You should've seen the way he did with my roommate's parents. I mean if a boy's mother was sort of fat or corny-looking or something, and if somebody's father was one of those guys that wear those suits with very big shoulders and corny black and white shoes, then old Haas would just shake hands with them and give them a phony smile and then he'd go talk, for maybe half an *hour*, with somebody else's parents. I can't stand that stuff.[42]

In a word, snobbery. Haas toadies to those who comfortably wear the uniform of their class—some register of high bourgeois—and snubs those with padded shoulders and unfashionable shoes who have come lately to their money, or not at all. His gestures to the latter are inauthentic, and such contempt can wound. But only because class does exist: Haas is not just

personally mean; his phoniness and his power to hurt depend on an established class system that institutionalizes slight and injury.

Just a bit later Holden tells of another phony, an old Pencey grad named
Ossenburger who has "made a pot of dough" through a chain of "undertaking
parlors all over the country that you could get members of your family buried
for about five bucks apiece." Holden has little respect for Ossenburger's
enterprise: "He probably just shoves them in a sack and dumps them in the
river." Nonetheless, Ossenburger is an eminence at Pencey, to which he has
given "a pile of dough," and where Holden's dormitory is named after him.
On a football weekend Ossenburger comes to the school in "this big goddam
Cadillac," receives an obligatory cheer at the game, and gives a speech in
chapel "that lasted about ten hours." It is a pious affair, making obliquely the
Calvinist connection between wealth and virtue. Ossenburger extols prayer:

> he started telling us how he was never ashamed, when he was in some kind
> of trouble or something, to get right down on his knees and pray to
> God. . . . He said *he* talked to Jesus all the time. Even when he was
> driving his car. That killed me. I can just see the big phony bastard shifting
> into first gear and asking Jesus to send him a few more stiffs. [Pp. 16–17]

Holden demystifies in the telling, better than if he had said, "this man claims
legitimacy for his money, his Cadillac, his business ethics, his eminence and
class privilege, by enlisting religion on his side." Again, phoniness is rooted in
the economic and social arrangements of capitalism, and in their concealment.

But a second motif in these scenes also deserves comment. The clues to
phoniness lie in outward forms of conduct. Haas' phony smile follows an
external convention, but accords poorly with emotional reality. His hand-
shakes imply equality, but thinly hide the reverse of equality. Ossenburger
talks within a framework of conventions: he is in chapel; he gives a sermon;
he speaks of prayer. Holden's revulsion attends, in part, on ceremony itself:
on prescribed forms that shape the flow of our words and movements. A
smile, a handshake, a chapel assembly with boys seated in rows, a sermon, a
prayer: none of these is a spontaneous expression of the self; all impose limits
and bear conventional meaning. Holden resents these constraints, and delights in release from them. Hence:

> The only good part of [Ossenburger's] speech was right in the middle of it.
> He was telling us all about what a swell guy he was, what a hot-shot and all,
> then all of a sudden this guy sitting in the row in front of me, Edgar
> Marsalla, laid this terrific fart. It was a very crude thing to do, in chapel
> and all, but it was also quite amusing. Old Marsalla. [P. 17]

We won't offer a disquisition on old Marsalla's fart, but these things may be
noted: a fart is the antithesis of ceremony (in this society, anyhow). It asserts
the body, assaults manners and convention. Here, it shatters Ossenburger's
hypocrisy and boastfulness. But it also strikes at the social idea behind a
"speech" itself. It mocks the meaning of "sitting in the *row*." It is a "crude

thing to do, in *chapel* and all." In brief, it is commendable ("quite amusing") because it challenges, not only Ossenburger's false ideology, but also the very existence of social forms.

These twin themes run through the book. When a situation or act seems phony to Holden, it evidences bad class relationships, or public ritual, or both. The first theme is foregrounded when Holden stigmatizes the word "grand," or the phrase "marvelous to see you"; the second when he notes the hollow formality of "glad to've met you." The first theme unites the Wicker Bar at the Seton Hotel, ambitious lawyers, the fashionable opinion that the Lunts are "angels," Spencer's deference to headmaster Thurmer, the night club set's public affection for pseudoculture (cute French songs), the "dirty little goddam cliques" at boy's schools (where "all you do is study so that you can learn enough to be smart enough to be able to buy a goddam Cadillac some day"), Andover, "Ivy League voices," men in "their goddam checkered vests, criticizing shows and books and women in those tired, snobby voices." The second theme is foregrounded in Sally Hayes' *letter,* inviting Holden to help trim the *Christmas tree;* in the black piano player, Ernie, and his "very phony, *humble*" *bow* to his philistine audience; in that audience's *applause;* in *actors'* conventional representation of people: in ministers' *sermons* ("they all have these Holy Joe voices. . . . I don't see why the hell they can't talk in their natural voice"); in Stradlater's *hello* to Ackley: in Holden's *handshake* with Ackley; in phony *parties* and smoking for show and *conversations* about art.

Holden rounds on mores and conventions that are a badge of class. He also revolts against convention itself. We would remark here that although these two feelings often blend, they have quite different origins. Society is imaginable without privilege, snobbery, unequal wealth. To banish *all* convention would be to end society itself. More of this later.

For now, we want to underline the first of the two conclusions we have reached by looking at what Holden calls phony. The novel's critique of class distinction may be found, not just between the lines of Holden's account, but in some of his most explicit comment on what's awry in his world. We must quote at some length from his digression on suitcases. When Holden meets the two nuns in the sandwich bar, their suitcases prompt him to say,

> It isn't important, I know, but I hate it when somebody has cheap suitcases. It sounds terrible to say it, but I can even get to hate somebody, just *looking* at them, if they have cheap suitcases with them. Something happened once. For a while when I was at Elkton Hills, I roomed with this boy, Dick Slagle, that had these very inexpensive suitcases. He used to keep them under the bed, instead of on the rack, so that nobody'd see them standing next to mine. It depressed holy hell out of me, and I kept wanting to throw mine out or something, or even *trade* with him. Mine came from Mark Cross, and they were genuine cowhide and all that crap, and I guess they cost quite a pretty penny. But it was a funny thing. Here's what happened. What I did, I finally put *my* suitcases under *my* bed,

instead of on the rack, so that old Slagle wouldn't get a goddam inferiority complex about it. But here's what he did. The day after I put mine under my bed, he took them out and put them back on the rack. The reason he did it, it took me a while to find out, was because he wanted people to think my bags were his. He really did. He was a very funny guy, that way. He was always saying snotty things about them, my suitcases, for instance. He kept saying they were too new and bourgeois. That was his favorite goddam word. He read it somewhere or heard it somewhere. Everything I had was bourgeois as hell. Even my fountain pen was bourgeois. He borrowed it off me all the time, but it was bourgeois anyway. We only roomed together about two months. Then we both asked to be moved. And the funny thing was, I sort of missed him after we moved, because he had a helluva good sense of humor and we had a lot of fun sometimes. I wouldn't be surprised if he missed me, too. At first he only used to be kidding when he called my stuff bourgeois, and I didn't give a damn—it *was* sort of funny, in fact. Then, after a while, you could tell he wasn't kidding any-more. The thing is, it's really hard to be roommates with people if your suitcases are much better than theirs—if yours are really *good* ones and theirs aren't. You think if they're intelligent and all, the other person, and have a good sense of humor, that they don't give a damn whose suitcases are better, but they do. They really do. It's one of the reasons why I roomed with a stupid bastard like Stradlater. At least his suitcases were as good as mine. [Pp. 108–9]

The source of Holden's feeling could hardly be clearer, or related with more social precision. He belongs by birthright at Elkton Hills; Dick Slagle pre-sumably does not. Their situation—living together—calls for an equality of human beings. (School itself, the American institution that most supports our myth of equal opportunity, carries the same hope.) Likewise, Holden's desires point him toward a world in which human qualities like intelligence and a sense of humor would be the ground of relatedness, rather than Mark Cross luggage and the money that stands behind it.

Both boys are deformed by what they bring with them to their room from the social order outside. Holden is depressed, and wishes to find the right gesture (throw the suitcases away, trade with Slagle) to deny their socially imposed difference. He is hurt by Slagle's resentment, when it becomes more than kidding, and he finally gives up on the relationship. Slagle, naturally, suffers more. Shame over his suitcases is one thing. But worse are the contradictory feelings: he hates the class injustice, and strives through the word "bourgeois" ("He read it somewhere") for the ideas that would combat it; yet at the same time he longs to be on the *right* side of the barrier, to *benefit* from class antagonism by having others think he owns the Mark Cross suitcases. Clearly Holden understands all this; we can only suppose that Salinger does too.

It was the nuns' suitcases, and their straw baskets, that reminded Holden of Dick Slagle, and the nuns also stir in him reflections about money and the expression of social feeling. He tries to imagine women from his own class "collecting dough for poor people in a beat-up old straw basket," but it's "hard to picture." His aunt is "pretty charitable," but always dressed in a way that emphasizes her condescension. "I couldn't picture her doing anything for charity if she had to wear black clothes and no lipstick. . . ." As for Sally Hayes' mother: "Jesus Christ. The only way *she* could go around with a basket collecting dough would be if everybody kissed her ass for her when they made a contribution." If they didn't, she'd get bored and "go someplace swanky for lunch. That's what I liked about those nuns. You could tell, for one thing, that they never went anywhere swanky for lunch. It made me so damn sad . . ." (p.114). At the root of Holden's sadness are lives confined by poverty, the loss of human connectedness, the power of feelings distorted by class to overcome natural bonds of affinity and friendship. In the end, one chooses to room with "a stupid bastard like Stradlater," whose suitcases are as good as one's own.

So we hold that the text of this novel, and the experience of it, warrant a formulation of what wounds Holden quite a lot more precise that the one given it by phrases like "the complexity of modern life," "the neurosis and fatigue of the world," or "our collective civilized fate." These epitomes are in fact strongly ideological. They displace the political emotion that is an important part of Salinger's novel, finding causes for it that are presumed to be universal.

Likewise, the majority opinion on what Holden yearns for—ideal love, innocence, truth, wisdom, personal integrity, etc. Let's examine one such idea in detail. James Miller writes, "Perhaps in its profoundest sense Holden's quest is a quest for identity, a search for the self. . . ." Holden tries various disguises, but "the self he is led to discover is Holden's and none other. And that self he discovers is a human self and an involved self that cannot, finally, break with what Hawthorne once called the 'magnetic chain of humanity.' . . ."[43] Miller writes of the self as if it were innate, genetically coded, yet somehow repressed. When Holden does rediscover it, it is "human" and "involved."

These rather vague characterizations lack social content. Yet we doubt that Miller or anyone else believes the identity of a person to lie beyond social influence, not to say definition. Any society provides identities for its members to step into; Holden's is no exception. We can hardly consider his quest for identity apart, for instance, from the fact that his father is a corporate lawyer ("Those boys really haul it in") on the edge of the ruling class, who has tried, however fruitlessly, to open for Holden the way to a similar identity by apprenticing him in a series of private schools. For Holden, such an identity is imaginatively real, and coercive. He gives it a reasonably concrete description when Sally Hayes refuses his invitation to go live by a brook in Vermont. She says there will be time for such pleasures later, after college. Holden:

No, there wouldn't be. There wouldn't be oodles of places to go at all. It'd be entirely different. . . . We'd have to go downstairs in elevators with suitcases and stuff. We'd have to phone up everybody and tell 'em good-by and send 'em postcards from hotels and all. And I'd be working in some office, making a lot of dough, and riding to work in cabs and Madison Avenue buses, and reading newspapers, and playing bridge all the time, and going to the movies and seeing a lot of stupid shorts and coming attractions and newsreels. [P. 133]

Holden understands well enough that such an identity is incompatible with the spontaneous feeling and relatedness he wishes for.

But what vision can he entertain of some alternate self? Here imagination darkens. Holden has no idea of changing society, and within the present one he can see forward only to the bourgeois identity that waits for him. So he fantasizes another identity which fulfills desire by escaping society almost entirely. He would hitchhike out West to "where it was pretty and sunny and where nobody'd know me," get a (working class) job at a filling station, and build a cabin at the edge of the woods. He would "pretend I was one of those deaf-mutes," thereby ending the necessity of having "goddam stupid useless conversations with anybody." If he married, it would be to a beautiful deaf-mute, and if they had children, "we'd hide them somewhere . . . and teach them how to read and write by ourselves" (pp. 198–99). No corporate structure and no Madison Avenue; but also no social production, no school, and no talk. In short, an identity for Holden that erases human history.

Here is the main equivocation of the book, and it seems to be both Holden's and Salinger's. We argued a while back that the force of Holden's severest judgment is divided. "Phony" stigmatizes both the manners and culture of a dominant bourgeoisie—class society—and ceremonies and institutions themselves—any society. As long as we listen to critical themes of the novel, the equivocation doesn't matter much: after all, the only society around *is* bourgeois society. But when we listen to those hints in the novel of something better, of alternative futures, of reconstruction, it makes a great deal of difference. Given Salinger's perception of what's wrong, there are three possible responses: do the best you can with this society; work for a better one; flee society altogether. Only the second answers to the critical feeling that dominates the book, but Salinger omits precisely that response when he shows Holden turning from that which his heart rejects to that which has value, commands allegiance, and invites living into the future without despair. So, when Holden imagines an adult self he can think only of the Madison Avenue executive or the deaf-mute, this society or no society.

And what does he like in the present? Phoebe accuses him of not liking anything, but he likes much: his dead brother Allie, for inscribing poems on his baseball mitt; Jane Gallagher, for keeping her kings in the back row at checkers. Both violate convention, and show a disdain for winning. Richard Kinsella, who broke the rules of the Oral Expression class, and digressed about his uncle's brace when he should have been telling about his father's farm. The nuns with their straw baskets, poor but outside competitive society. James Castle, who refused even the minimal compromise with society that would have saved his life. The Museum of Natural History, where the Eskimos remain as changeless as figures on a Grecian urn, and so defy historical process. For Holden, images of the valuable are generally images of people withdrawn from convention—people who are private, whimsical, losers, saints, dead. Holden's imagination cannot join the social and the desirable. At the beginning and again at the end of the novel he has the illusion of disappearing, losing his identity altogether—both times when he is crossing that most social of artifacts, a street.

So long as the choice is between this society and no society, Holden's imagination has no place to go. He wants love and a relatedness among equals. These do not thrive in the institutions that surround him, but they cannot exist at all without institutions, which shape human feeling and give life social form. When Phoebe retrieves Holden from nothingness and despair she draws him, inevitably, toward institutions: the family, school, the Christmas play, the zoo in the park, the carrousel where "they always play the same songs." In short, toward the same society he has fled, and toward some of its innocent social forms, this time magically redeemed by love.

Holden returns to society, the only one available. It is unchanged; he has changed somewhat, in the direction of acceptance. To go the rest of the way back, he requires the help of another institution, and a psychoanalyst. Society has classified him as neurotic—a fitting response, apparently, to his having wanted from it a more hospitable human climate than it could offer. He will change more. Society will not. But that's all right, in the end: the very act of telling his story has overlaid it with nostalgia, and he misses everybody he had told about, "Even old Stradlater and Ackley, for instance. I think I even miss that goddam Maurice. It's funny. Don't ever tell anybody anything. If you do, you start missing everybody" (p. 214). In a word, *Art* forms the needed bridge between the desirable and the actual, provides the mediation by which social experience, rendered through much of the story as oppressive, can be embraced.

IV

The Catcher in the Rye is among other things a serious critical mimesis of bourgeois life in the Eastern United States, ca. 1950—of snobbery, privilege, class injury, culture as badge of superiority, sexual exploitation, education subordinated to status, warped social feeling, competitiveness, stunted human possibility, the list could go on. Salinger is astute in imagining these hurtful things, though not in explaining them. Connections exist between Holden's ordeal and the events reported on the front page of the *Times*, and we think that those connections are necessary to complete Salinger's understanding of social reality. Iran and Korea and the hard-pressed New York school system express the hegemony of Holden's class, as do Broadway and

Pencey and Stradlater. Salinger's novel makes no reference to the economic and military scope of that class's power, but the manners and institutions he renders so meticulously are those of people who take their power for granted, and expect their young to step into it.

We say, further, that these themes are not just discernible to the eye of an obsessed political reader, as one might strain to give *Catcher* an ecological or existential of Seventh Day Adventist reading. They are central to the book's meaning and to the impact it has on us and other readers. Its power is located, all agree, in Holden's sensitivity, keen observation, and moral urgency, and in the language with which he conveys these in relating his story. For all his perceptiveness, though, he is an adolescent with limited understanding of what he perceives. Readers (adults, at least) understand more, and in this gap a poignancy grows. Most readers share or are won to Holden's values—equality, spontaneity, brotherhood—but sense that these values cannot be realized within extant social forms. The novel draws readers into a powerful longing for what-could-be, and at the same time interposes what-is, as an unchanging and immovable reality.

It does so in a way that mirrors a contradiction of bourgeois society: advanced capitalism has made it imaginable that there could be enough "suitcases" for everyone, as well as spontaneity and brotherhood, and it feeds these desires at the same time that it prevents their fulfillment. Only a few can hope for suitcases and spontaneity, at the expense of the many, and enjoyment of them depends on shutting out awareness of the many. Furthermore, even the few are somehow blocked from enjoyment by the antagonistic striving required to secure one's suitcases, by the snotty human relationships of the Wicker Bar and Madison Avenue, by what Philip Slater calls "our invidious dreams of personal glory." In short, the esthetic force of the novel is quite precisely located in its rendering a contradiction of a particular society, as expressed through an adolescent sensibility that feels, though it cannot comprehend, this contradiction. Short of comprehension, both Holden and Salinger are driven to a false equation—to reject this society is to reject society itself—and a false choice—accept this society or defect from society altogether.

It is here that the novel most invites criticism, informed by history and politics. But the critics have instead, with few exceptions,[44] followed Salinger's own lead and deepened the confusion of the novel with the help of mystifications like "the adult world," "the human condition," and so on. Pressing for such formulations, they have left history and the novel behind. They have failed both to understand its very large achievement—for we consider it a marvelous book—and to identify the shortcomings of its awareness and its art. And in this way they have certified it as a timeless classic.

We have been speaking of "readers," "critics," and "criticism." This is itself, needless to say, a mystification. Most readers and almost all critics belong to the professional and managerial strata between the high bourgeoisie and the working class. Almost all the critics have been college teachers, and at a time when their (our) lives were affected dramatically by the course of American capitalism. Specifically, in the fifties and the sixties, these conditions wrought a significant change in the position of academic intellectuals: (1) America preserved, with great success at first, the world hegemony of capitalism through a policy of "containment" (Korea, etc.). (2) This achievement, along with rapid technical development and corporate expansion, allowed unprecedented use of the world's markets and resources (e.g., Iranian oil) for the enrichment of the American economy: both the new imperialism and new technical development (television, computers, military hardware, etc.) resulted in a rapidly increasing demand for college trained people and for research. Hence the enormous expansion of the university system. (4) This happened just when new teachers had to be recruited from the small cohort of depression babies, while the *student* population began to swell as the much larger cohort born after the war reached school and college. In short, there was a sharp increase in demand for college teachers, and a corresponding improvement in our absolute and relative position in the society. Not great wealth, to be sure, but modest prosperity, quick advancement, more prestige, confidence and a new self-esteem.

Here we must leave the argument without perfect closure. It would be vulgar determinism to hold that from these economic conditions followed a "bourgeoisification" of the academic mind, and from that a capitalist misreading of *The Catcher in the Rye*. For one thing, this picture ignores McCarthyism, the pressure toward liberal conformity in the university, and the sweet, secret inducements proffered to intellectuals by the CIA through the Congress for Cultural Freedom, *Encounter*, *Partisan Review*, and all the instruments of cooptation.

But common sense and a belief in real connections betwen people's ideas and their material lives are enough, we think, to make it seem natural for a critical establishment so located in American capitalism to interpret and judge literary works in a way harmonious with the continuance of capitalism.

We need hardly say that the world is a different place in 1976 than it was in 1951 or 1971. Even from the American academy, capitalism now seems a less inevitable and friendly part of the landscape. Academic criticism, and indeed literary study, hold a less favored position than they did even five years ago, and all indications point to a further decline. As thousands of people in our field join the unemployed or ill-employed, it will be surprising if most teachers of English maintain a separation of culture from society, and keep on writing the kind of criticism that mediated *Catcher's* acceptance as a classic.

Notes

1. Warren French, *J. D. Salinger* (New York, 1963), p. 102; James E. Miller, Jr., *J. D. Salinger* (Minneapolis, 1965), p. 5.

2. Robert Gutwillig, "Everybody's Caught 'The Catcher in the Rye,' " *New York Times Book Review*, Paperback Book Section, 15 January 1961, p. 38.

3. Alice Payne Hackett, *70 Years of Best Sellers: 1895–1965* (New York, 1967), p. 13.

4. Our estimate, based on this information: Bantam has sold just over 5,000,000 copies since it became sole publisher of the novel in April, 1964 (thanks to Peter McCue of Bantam for this figure). Assuming that about 1,000,000 of these were sold before the end of 1965, we conclude that over 4,000,000 have been sold since Alice Payne Hackett's tally (see n.3). *Catcher* was twelfth among all novels in American sales by 1965; our guess is that it is third or fourth now, and will soon be at the head of the list.

5. Nash K. Burger *New York Times*, 16 July 1951, p. 19.

6. "With Love & 20-20 Vision," *Time*, 16 July 1967, p. 96.

7. Harvey Breit, *Atlantic* 188 (August 1951): 82.

8. S. N. Behrman, "The Vision of the Innocent," *New Yorker*, 11 August 1951, p. 71.

9. Anne L. Goodman, "Mad About Children," *New Republic*, 16 July 1951, p. 21.

10. Ernest Jones, "Case History of All of Us, *Nation*, 1 September 1951, p. 176.

11. Breit, p. 82.

12. Harrison Smith, "Manhattan Ulysses, Junior," *Saturday Review*, 14 July 1951, p. 13.

13. Behrman, pp. 71–75.

14. Virgilia Peterson. *Herald Tribune Book Review*, 15 July 1951, p. 3.

15. An exception is the review by William Poster, "Tomorrow's Child," *Commentary* 13 (January 1952):90–92. He places Holden in the upper-middle or lower-upper class, estimates Mr. Caulfield's income at between $30,000 and $100,000 a year, and calls Holden "typical not so much of this adolescent class as a whole, but of a specific and extensive part of it, namely, those individuals who think of themselves as exceptions to their class by virtue of their superior taste," those who "have nothing further to strive for within their class and cannot accept its usual goals." We do not entirely agree with this account, as will become evident later; but at least Poster sees the book as socially precise.

Other reviews appeared in *America*, 11 August 1951: *Catholic World*, November 1951; *Harper's*, August 1951; *New Statesman and Nation*, 18 August 1951; *Spectator*, 17 August 1951; *TLS*, 7 September 1971.

16. David L. Stevenson, "J. D. Salinger: The Mirror of Crisis," *Nation*, 9 March 1957, p. 215.

17. George Steiner, "The Salinger Industry," *Nation*, 14 November 1959, p. 360. Further quotations are from pp. 360–63, passim.

The first entries under Salinger in the *MLA International Bibliography* appeared in 1956. Each succeeding year has carried entries, whose number crested at 33 in 1963, when *Wisconsin Studies in Contemporary Literature* gave an entire issue to Salinger, as *Modern Fiction Studies* was to do in 1966. Both the *WSCL* and *MFS* issues included bibliographies of criticism on Salinger.

18. Donald P. Costello, "The Language of 'The Catcher in the Rye,' " *American Speech* 34 (October 1959):172–81.

19. Arthur Heiserman and James E. Miller, Jr., "J. D. Salinger: Some Crazy Cliff," *Western Humanities Review* 10 (Spring 1956):129.

20. William Wiegand, "J. D. Salinger: Seventy-Eight Bananas," *Chicago Review* 9 (Winter 1958):4.

21. Donald Barr, "Saints, Pilgrims and Artists," *Commonweal*, 25 October 1957, pp. 88–90.

22. Peter J. Seng, "The Fallen Idol: The Immature World of Holden Caulfield," *College English* 22 (December 1961):203–9.

23. Frederic I. Carpenter, "The Adolescent in American Fiction," *English Journal* 46 (September 1957):314–15.

24. Unless of course Salinger himself was seen not only to have drawn an adolescent hero, but to have endorsed his attitudes in which case critics addressed themselves to the writer's shortcomings, e.g., Maxwell Geismar in "The Wise Child and the *New Yorker* School of Fiction," *American Moderns: From Rebellion to Conformity* (New York, 1958), pp. 195–209.

25. Jonathan Baumbach, "The Saint as a Young Man: A Reappraisal of *The Catcher in the Rye*," *Modern Language Quarterly* 25 (December 1964):467.

26. Paul Levine, "J. D. Salinger: the Development of the Misfit Hero," *Twentieth-Century Literature* 4 (October 1958):97.

27. Kermit Vanderbilt, "Symbolic Resolution in *The Catcher in the Rye:* The Cup, the Carrousel, and the American West," *Western Humanities Review* 17 (Summer 1963):272.

28. George R. Creeger, *"Treacherous Desertion": Salinger's* The Catcher in the Rye (Middletown, Conn., 1961), p. 8.

29. Dan Wakefield, "Salinger and the Search for Love," *New World Writing* 14 (1958):70.

30. Arthur Mizener, "The Love Song of J. D. Salinger, *Harper's*, February 1959, p. 90.

31. Stevenson, p. 216.

32. Ihab Hassan, "The Rare Quixotic Gesture," in *Salinger*, ed. Henry Anatole Grunwald (New York, 1962), pp. 148–49. Reprinted from Hassan's *Radical Innocence* (Princeton, 1961). First appeared in the *Western Humanities Review*, 1957.

33. Heiserman and Miller, p. 132.

34. Edgar M. Branch, "Mark Twain and J. D. Salinger: A Study in Literary Continuity," *American Quarterly* 9 (Summer 1957):157

35. Donald P. Costello, "Salinger and His Critics," *Commonweal*, 25 October 1963, p. 133.

36. Geismar, pp. 197–98.

37. Hassan, in Grunwald, p. 139.

38. Carl F. Strauch, "Kings in the Back Row: Meaning Through Structure—A Reading of Salinger's *The Catcher in the Rye*," *Wisconsin Studies in Contemporary Literature* 2 (Winter 1961):27.

39. Carpenter, p. 316.

40. Branch, p. 154.

41. Miller, pp. 12–17.

42. *The Catcher in the Rye* (New York, 1964), pp. 14–15. Future page references to *Catcher* are in the text.

43. Miller, p. 13.

44. Notably these: (1) In " 'Franny and Zooey' and J. D. Salinger," (*New Left Review* 15 [May–June 1962]:72–82), Brian Way argued that *Catcher* is one of the few "contemporary American novels that have recreated in twentieth-century terms that simultaneous sense of character and society of the great nineteenth-century realists." School, he pointed out, "is the agency by which America more than most countries consciously socializes the immature for entry into the approved adult activities: and so a boy's relation to school becomes a microcosm of the individual's relation to his society. In this concentration upon a manageable network of representative relationships, we see at work the only method by which a novel can create with any living force the pressures of a society. . . ." Way went on to analyze both the successes and failures of the book in these terms, in an admirable essay. (2) Writing mainly about *Franny and Zooey*, but with reference to *Catcher* as well, Paul Phillips emphasized that "What Salinger's sensitive characters find so consistently repulsive is the vulgarity, the rampant selfishness, the

fundamental hypocrisy and foulness of bourgeois conventions." We agree, though perhaps with milder epithets; and we think Phillips was nearly right in holding that "Salinger's major limitation as a satirist is that he is generally unconcerned with world issues" ("Salinger's *Franny and Zooey*," *Mainstream* 15 [January 1962]:32–39). (3) Three years earlier, also in *Mainstream*, Barbara Giles said of Holden, "In a vague sort of way he senses that the mannerisms and general make-believe he hates would not be worth hatred if they didn't proceed from a system in which the 'dirty movies' and the Broadway productions that his father, the corporation lawyer, helps to finance, play a directly debasing role. In the helplessness of his hatreds he may even be said to sense, still more vaguely, the extent of a power and corruption he cannot name." She went on to say that Salinger's young people reject this system, "but with it they reject any further study of motive itself, demanding only certificates of purity from themselves" ("The Lonely War of J. D. Salinger," *Mainstream* 12 [February 1959]:2–13). We would note that all three articles appeared in left wing journals, well out of the *academic* mainstream. Establishment critics did not take up their lead. We had not heard of the three articles before we set out to write this piece.

Catcher in and out of History   James E. Miller, Jr.*

Carol and Richard Ohmann, in "Reviewers, Critics, and *The Catcher in the Rye*" (*Critical Inquiry*, Autumn 1976), remind us that J. D. Salinger's youthful novel is a quarter century old. The reminder comes as a shock to me personally, inasmuch as I find myself given some prominence among those "Critics" of the title: as the co-author, with Arthur Heiserman, of one of the first critical essays on *Catcher* ("J. D. Salinger: Some Crazy Cliff," 1956) and as the author of the 1965 Minnesota pamphlet on Salinger. The Ohmanns treat both the article and the booklet with great tact and tenderness, while at the same time using them as focal points for their considerable disagreements. I do not want to come to the defense of these aging critical works, although I am tempted to identify in the early essay the flashes of genius in the passages written by the late Arthur Heiserman when he was young and energetic and we both were afire with ideas and plans. Both of us were bemused as we watched our essay become enshrined in a succession of Salinger casebooks: it had the distinction of being singled out as a target by George Steiner in a blast against the university critical enterprise in a piece entitled "The Salinger Industry." As the Salinger mania faded, Arthur and I sighed to ourselves that at least the anti-academic critics would not have our article to kick around anymore.

My Minnesota pamphlet on Salinger came after Salinger's lapse into silence, and soon after its appearance, Salinger seemed to fade from the public consciousness. But though he no longer appeared on the covers of *Time*, his novel was still and still is avidly read, especially by high school students at the age of Holden Caulfield (16–17). I found this out when students coming into my contemporary American novel courses demon-

*Reprinted by permission from *Critical Inquiry* 3, no. 3 (Spring 1977): 599–603. © 1977 by the University of Chicago.

strated such familiarity with *Catcher* that I dropped it from my reading list. I long ago assumed that *Catcher,* like *Billy Budd* and *Turn of the Screw,* had been so intensively examined by critics that little if anything was left to say. But I clearly reckoned without the Ohmanns, and what might be termed a Marxist or neo-Marxist approach.

The Ohmann essay begins its argument by quoting headlines and editorials that appeared the day of *Catcher's* publication (stories and commentaries revolving around the hot war in Korea and the cold war with Russia) and then goes on to show how the reviews of *Catcher* (and the critical essays on it) ignored the novel's relation to its moment in time and in effect "removed it from history" by concentrating on its universal elements. The essay can best speak for itself: *Catcher* is defined in essence as "a serious critical mimesis of bourgeois life in the Eastern United States, ca. 1950—of snobbery, privilege, class injury, culture as a badge of superiority, sexual exploitation, education subordinated to status, warped social feeling, competitiveness, stunted human possibility, the list could go on. Salinger is astute in imaging these hurtful things, though not in explaining them." These themes, we are told, are "central to the book's meaning and to the impact it has on us." The book's readers ("adults, at least") are "won to Holden's values— equality, spontaneity, brotherhood—but sense that these values cannot be realized within extant social forms. The novel draws readers into a powerful longing for what-could-be, and at the same time interposes what-is, as an unchanging and immovable reality."

Although the Ohmanns introduce some qualifiers in these summary generalizations, their reading of *Catcher* and their view of its limitations are in reality comprehensive and exclusive. If the reader grants their generalizations, he is likely to find that other views or approaches embodying his experience of the novel are no longer tenable. A close glance at the Ohmann reading reveals it as simplistic: Holden's warm, human values are pitted against a cold, selfish society; Holden's (and Salinger's) main failure (the "confusion of the novel") is in choosing only between rejoining or dropping out from this bourgeois, capitalistic society instead of opting for radical—that is, socialist—change.

Few would want to deny a political-economic dimension to *Catcher,* and it is possibly true that this dimension has been slighted in past criticism. But to see Holden's malaise of spirit solely or even mainly caused by the evils of a capitalistic society is surely myopic; and to envision a utopian socialistic society (even were we to grant its possible creation) as miraculously erasing all the problems Holden faces is naive. The problems of a sensitive and perceptive adolescent moving painfully to maturity can never be solved by restructuring society politically and economically.

Early in the novel we hear Holden on his history teacher, "Old Spencer": ". . . you wondered what the heck he was still living for. I mean he was all stooped over, and he had very terrible posture, and in class, whenever he dropped a piece of chalk at the blackboard, some guy in the first row always had to get up and pick it up and hand it to him."[1] We learn that Holden's brother Allie died of leukemia some years before the novel opens, and that Holden had kept his memory alive through his baseball mitt on which Allie had copied out Emily Dickinson poems. In the dormitory room next to Holden's lives the unfortunate Robert Ackley, with "lousy teeth" that "always looked mossy and awful," who had "a lot of pimples" and a "terrible personality"—a "sort of nasty guy" (p. 19). When Holden's roommate Stradlater refuses to tell Holden whether he made it or not with Holden's friend Jane Gallagher, Holden strikes out and is struck down, bleeding. Over and over again Holden complains that nobody ever gives your message to anybody. Over and over again we hear Holden cry out: "I felt so lonesome, all of a sudden. I almost wished I was dead" (p. 48).

This catalogue of characters, incidents, expressions could be extended indefinitely, all of them suggesting that Holden's sickness of soul is something deeper than economic or political, that his revulsion at life is not limited to social and monetary inequities, but at something in the nature of life itself—the decrepitude of the aged, the physical repulsiveness of the pimpled, the disappearance and dissolution of the dead, the terrors (and enticements) of sex, the hauntedness of human aloneness, the panic of individual isolation. Headlines about Korea, Dean Acheson and the cold war seem, if not irrelevant, essentially wide of the mark—if we define the mark as the heart and soul of *Catcher*.

The important comic scene in which Holden is victimized by the elevator operator Maurice and the prostitute Sunny surely must be read as something more than a revelation of "sexual exploitation" in a capitalistic society. The economic-political reading of the novel tends to pass over without mention Holden's groping about in desperation to come to terms with his sexuality, which both fascinates and threatens, lures and depresses him. His sexual feelings are central to the maturing process he is undergoing, and they lie obscurely behind his tender feelings for (and secret envy of) the various children he encounters: they remain in the pre-adult world of unsullied innocence. The title of the novel itself directs attention to Holden's dream, which he reveals to Phoebe, of standing on the edge of "some crazy cliff" near a playing field of rye, catching the kids before they fall over the cliff: the fall would surely be into sexuality, experience, adulthood.

It is difficult to see how the Marxist reading might come to terms with the crucial scene near the end of the novel, when Holden wakes up in fright to find his old and trusted teacher, Mr. Antolini, patting him on the head. Holden rushes away, to wonder later whether he had done the right thing, whether Antolini was really a "flit"—or a genuine friend in a generally hostile world. This self-questioning sets off a chain of events that brings Holden to a confrontation with his own death as he descends into the Egyptian tomb at the museum, sees again the ubiquitous obscene phrase he has rubbed off of Phoebe's school walls, and envisions his own tombstone with his name, the years of entry and exit, and the phrase pursuing him into imagined death—

"Fuck you" (p. 204). It is shortly after this that Holden, refusing to agree to Phoebe's running away to the west with him, announces that he has decided to stay—to rejoin the human race. As he watches Phoebe going around and around on the carrousel, grabbing for the gold ring, he realizes that he cannot shield her from experience: "If they [the kids] fall off, they fall off, but it's bad if you say anything to them" (p. 211). And the action of the novel closes as Holden feels so "damn happy" that he is "damn near bawling" watching Phoebe going around and around: he has fallen and survived, and he has discovered that he can be happy in the presence of an innocence he no longer has—without being a catcher in the rye.

The Ohmanns consider that the "shortcomings of [*Catcher's*] awareness and its art" are manifest in its failure to show that Holden had an option of working for a better society. It is not at all clear, however, that Holden refuses this option. Mr. Antolini, in one of the novel's deepest moments, quotes Wilhelm Stekel to Holden: "The mark of the immature man is that he wants to die nobly for a cause, while the mark of the mature man is that he wants to live humbly for one" (p. 188). The comment comes at a critical turning-point for Holden, and is certainly lodged firmly in his psyche. But of course it is true that Holden does not turn his face into the sunrise at the end of the novel, expressing his determination to overthrow the bourgeois capitalistic society in favor of a socialist utopia. Indeed, the whole thrust of the novel seems to suggest that there is no social or political or economic structure that could insure sexual tranquility, banish pimples, outlaw old age, abolish death—or that would relieve Holden or any other human being of the tragic implications of his physical, sexual, emotional nature: to these he must reconcile himself, recognizing not only the "shortcomings" of man but also the "shortcomings" of himself.

But Holden is not so shortsighted, I think, as the Ohmanns suggest. In the closing lines of the novel, he confesses of the tale he has told: "I'm sorry I told so many people about it. About all I know is I sort of *miss* everybody I told about. Even old Stradlater and Ackley, for instance. I think I even miss that goddam Maurice. It's funny. Don't ever tell anybody anything. If you do, you start missing everybody" (p. 214). The Ohmanns consider this confession an overlay of "nostalgia." If it strikes them as naive or sentimental, it is hard to understand how they can believe so fiercely in a socialist utopia that must surely be based on some kind and measure of the human love—agape, not eros alone—Holden has attained at the end of *Catcher*. If a utopia is established without this kind of mutual love and understanding, is it not likely to turn into the kind of dictatorship with which the twentieth century is so familiar? In any event, the Ohmanns might have recognized that Holden has been awakened to a precondition of a better society—love of fellow human beings—before condemning Salinger for not instilling Holden with a vision of the kind of ideal state that has never existed before and seems not to exist now.

Would we really want Salinger to recycle the visions of *Looking Back-*

ward or *A Traveler from Altruria?* The experience of the twentieth century has forced the literary imagination to portray the dark underside of such bright visions—as in *Brave New World* and *1984*. Holden joins a long succession of American "heroes" (Hawthorne's, Melville's, James', Twain's, and more) in discovering that experience is inevitably made up of good and bad, love and hate, light and dark. The Ohmanns have censured previous critics for removing *Catcher* from history. Do they not propose at the end to carry Holden out of baffling, muddled history into a tidy and clear-cut ideology?

Note

    1. *The Catcher in the Rye* (New York: Little, Brown, 1951; rpt. Bantam, 1964), pp. 6–7. All further page references appear after quotations in the text.

Universals and the Historically Particular

Carol Ohmann and
Richard Ohmann*

    James E. Miller, Jr., in "*Catcher* in and out of History" (*Critical Inquiry*, Spring 1977) records that our article on Salinger's novel ("Reviewers, Critics, and *The Catcher in the Rye*," *Critical Inquiry*, Autumn 1976) came along as something of a shock, returning once again to a text whose pages had been leaved so often and so often written about that there seemed little news left to tell about it. "I clearly reckoned," Miller writes, "without the Ohmanns and what might be termed a Marxist or neo-Marxist approach" (p. 600). He goes on to argue that the news we bring is bad news, a misinterpretation of *Catcher*.

    Miller holds that in deriving as we do Holden's pain (with only some qualifications) from a dehumanizing and competitive society, we have been "simplistic" and "myopic": we have naively assumed that a "utopian socialistic society (even were [one] to grant its possible creation) [would] miraculously erase all the problems Holden faces" (p. 601), whereas "the problems of a sensitive and perceptive adolescent moving painfully to maturity can never be solved by restructuring society politically and economically" (p. 601). Neither can "the decrepitude of the aged, the physical repulsiveness of the pimpled, the disappearance and dissolution of the dead, the terrors (and enticements) of sex, the hauntedness of human aloneness, the panic of individual isolation" (p. 601).

    First, we want to note that Miller, witness the sentence above, brings to the novel a vocabulary of universals; the particularities of *Catcher* do not

*Reprinted by permission from *Critical Inquiry* 3, no. 4 (Summer 1977): 773–77. © 1977 by the University of Chicago.

inevitably press such a category of interpretive concepts upon us. Miller has assumed a critical methodology and assumed it as if it were, necessarily, *the* critical methodology, proper to this fiction and to others. Implicit in these assumptions is a further one: Miller's very methodology implies a reading of history, and that reading amounts to a denial that history happens. But it does happen, and literature both reflects and helps to create historical change. The pain of adolescence, for example, does not figure as a subject or a concept in English or medieval literature. Youth does, of course, but how? As a time to hawk and to hunt, to joust and to fight, to be gay and loving, for if pimples there were (and presumably there were), they were held as nothing compared to the enviable fact that in youth you had your health. There was a danger to the soul, to be sure, in living light-hearted; priests and poets warned of that.

> Yyng men that bern hem so gay,
> They think not on domysday,
> Quan they xul stonde in powre aray
> And for here dedes damnyd be.[1]

But how different that is from our notion of adolescence, which surely arises long after the time when, say, a youth of fifteen in Kent could inherit his father's farm and frequently did; adolescence as we experience and think of it is tied, we would argue, to historical changes that have placed Holden Caulfield's real counterparts in schools, peripheral to social responsibilities, and in a position of prolonged dependence on their parents, from birth until the age of twenty-one or beyond.

To address, as Miller does, the text of *Catcher* particularly, we would argue that Holden's experiences of old age, physical repulsiveness, sex, aloneness and isolation, and even death are embedded in his full experience of society, and that his responses, moment by moment, bear the imprint of his total response to the competitive, dehumanizing world he is in the process of rebelling against and rejecting. He finds old Spencer pathetic (and very touching) not just because he is elderly and arthritic and snuffy with flu, but because he is relatively powerless, not very well off, and naive (though uncomfortable) in urging upon Holden his teacherly prescriptions for life: be sensible, do your lessons, take care for your future—as if with one's own efforts alone one could guarantee one's worldly future. (Ours is, of course, a society where the worth of people is primarily defined by their ability to earn and/or exercise power; in the war of all against all, old age is a handicap and hence a cause for disrespect; it has not always been so in our culture and is not everywhere so today.) Ackley's unloveliness derives from more than his unruly teen-aged hormones. He *won't* brush his teeth, he *won't* wash his ears, he *will* squeeze his pimples with his hands, he *will* cut his fingernails right on to the floor. All this is part of a defensive-aggressive mind set, Ackley's response to the invidious little society of Pencey Prep, in which Stradlater, who is not only handsome and athletic but rich and conceited, is a

Year Book boy, a hot-shot, and Ackley is just the reverse, not so rich (he habitually insults the possessions of Holden and Stradlater, by fingering them and tossing them about), and sincere in the practice of his minority religion, Catholicism. Ackley's neglect of his person is a continual assertion of his person—analogous to old Marsalla's famous fart.

Holden responds not to the timeless terrors of sex but to the exploitation of girls and women by such types as Stradlater; Stradlater "snows" them,[2] not so much seduces them as overwhelms them, and to him Jane Gallagher, precious to Holden, is virtually nameless; Stradlater refers to his last girl as "that pig."[3] "Fuck You" on walls is a reminder not simply of sex but of sex as aggression, and to this particular phenomenon in his competitive and patriarchal society, Holden responds with nausea and anger. And he sees the danger that he, too, may separate feeling from sex and turn girls into objects in the scramble for status. One of Holden's most intense and poignant statements of his loneliness (which Miller quotes) occurs after Stradlater's date with Jane. Holden has assaulted Stradlater, been laid low, and stands in Ackley's room; Ackley can be, if not a chum, company at least, but not at this moment, not in this matter of Holden's anxiety and pain over Jane, for even Ackley participates in the attitude toward women Stradlater enacts, if only vicariously by inventing interminable lies about his, Ackley's, sexual exploits last summer. Holden's panic and confusion over Antolini's caress (whose nature, we think, Salinger deliberately leaves ambiguous) is likewise reflective of sexual politics, indeed of politics, in his society. To be a "flit," to be touched by a "flit," is a shameful, terrifying departure from the aggressive, self-assured masculine norm of a society in which the hot-shots are Stradlaters, the winners in the game, which is, for those on the other side, "no game" at all.[4] It is, of course, a society that does not approve of, and so usually precludes, the expression of tenderness between man and man.

Death, it is true, cannot be abolished; it can come early even to the rich and comes to everyone sometime. But its meaning, to the dying and the survivors, differs from one epoch to another and one society to another. (Chaucer and Dante were different from us.) We would only suggest that the metaphysical centrality assigned to death by many of our critics and philosophers has something to do with the near removal of death from social life, the segregation of the old and dying, and the unparalleled place, in our culture, of individual goals.

Miller's universalizing terms, far from being universals of critical interpretation, are a special vocabulary of bourgeois thought. They assign to unchanging human nature or "the nature of life itself" (p. 601) what is changeable and historically defined. In doing so, they work to reduce human nature to what is least distinctively *human* about us—our bodies, aging, death. One of Marx's great achievements was to see that, on the contrary, as our species entered into productive relations and so into history, it liberated itself from the mere repetitiveness of biological life. A human society reproduces itself biologically, but at the same time it is always altering its relationship to nature, its capacity for further reproductions, and the consciousness of its members.

The same materialist outlook shows us that not all members of a society will have the same consciousness. In a society where one group produces value for another, the two are likely to see things differently. Yet there is nothing automatic about this: exploited classes, in particular, must struggle for consciousness. As Marx put it in *German Ideology* "The ideas of the ruling class are in every epoch the ruling ideas: i.e., the class, which is the ruling material force of society, is at the same time its ruling intellectual force." And literary criticism is not exempt from this principle. That (in Miller's word) our "physical, sexual, emotional nature" has "tragic implications" (p. 602) that "experience is inevitably made up of good and bad, love and hate, light and dark" (p. 603)—these are useful or comfortable ideas for any ruling class, for they say in effect that things as they now are cannot be modified by any social structure: and they have been the ruling ideas of the bourgeois university. Miller shares this vocabulary and its ideological position with very many of our critics, who deal in the same set of "eternal" (or "modern" or "American") verities that deny history and deflect attention away from the precise nature of our society.

The critical disagreement here—there is no begging it—is a sharp one, and has implications reaching well beyond critical practice. We are not arguing simply that Marxism leads to a better reading of *The Catcher in the Rye*, or any other text, than New Criticism does, or myth criticism or psychoanalytic criticism, though we certainly believe that to be so. We believe that Marxist criticism has priority over, and in fact explains, these criticisms, because Marxism—not as dogma grounded in scripture, but as a dynamic and self-critical method—offers a better understanding of the world than any other body of thought and practice. The Marxist critic is committed to persuading others that Marxism is the truest knowledge of ourselves and our history, and the best framework within which to struggle for a human future, rather than simply to supplying and defending a reading of this or that work, rather than to securing a respected place for Marxism alongside the other isms represented in a department or a discipline.

Of course, this conflict of ideology can't be settled by a set of assertions like the ones we've just written. Within the pages of journals like this, it can only be settled case by case. We have tried to show that Miller's reading is inadequate to *Catcher*, and that it is so not for any personal failure of insight or wit or sympathy, but because it rests on a scheme of history that will not stand up to scrutiny. Further, we have suggested (but not proved) that Miller's reading (like ours, of course) is itself an historical act that historical materialism explains.

The ideological character of Miller's argument is especially evident when he speaks directly of politics. When he argues, for instance, that Holden (and Salinger) do make a political move in fixing on agape as "a precondition of a better society" (p. 603), his thinking is recognizably bourgeois in character. That is to say, he argues from the ideological assumption that individual human consciousness is prior to material history—that without a billion changes of heart nothing can change. But agape, apart from solidarity and politics, has always been and will remain impotent; our society can happily tolerate it since it leads to no action: distant love for everyone, like Zooey's for the Fat Lady, is *in effect* love for no one. For another instance, Miller reads us as blaming everything on "the evils of a capitalistic society" (p. 601) (whereas socialists hold that capitalism has contributed immeasurably to human possibility, though with immeasurable suffering along the way), and he sees us as positing a socialist "utopia" that we never mention and in which we do not believe. This, too, is a familiar movement of bourgeois ideology: to paralyze striving for change by presenting what-could-never-be as the only alternative to what-is. These arguments, and more, in Miller's comment show it to be an instance of a false consciousness that we recognize because we too have labored within it.

Notes

This essay is a reply to disagreements raised by James E. Miller, Jr. (Spring 1977) to the Ohmanns' "Reviewers, Critics, and *The Catcher in the Rye*" (Autumn 1976).

1. Richard Leighton Green, ed., *The Early English Carols* (Oxford, 1935), no. 363. M. Y. Offord, ed., *The Parlement of the Thre Ages* (London, 1959); Carleton Brown, ed., *Religious Lyrics of the XIVth Century* (Oxford, 1924), no. 6, and *Religious Lyrics of the XVth Century* (Oxford, 1939), no. 147, help to round out this little picture. We are grateful to our colleague William Ian Miller for refurbishing our (now faded) memory of medieval literature, for aiming us right at suitable texts, and for telling us some points of medieval minority law.

2. *The Catcher in the Rye* (New York: Little, Brown, 1951; rpt. Bantam, 1972), p. 49.

3. Ibid., p. 30.

4. Ibid., p. 8.

Holden Caulfield: "Don't Ever Tell Anybody Anything"

Duane Edwards*

Salinger's admirers have responded in a variety of ways to *The Catcher in the Rye*, but most have something in common: they idealize Holden. In order to do so, they play down the seriousness of his ambivalence, exhibitionsim, and voyeurism and assign the blame for his severe depression entirely to society, to the world of perverts and bums and phonies. Failing to respond to the first person narrator as ironic, they assume that Holden should be taken at his word; that he is right and the world is wrong; that

*Reprinted by permission from *English Literary History*, 44, no. 3 (Fall 1977): 556–67. © 1977 by the Johns Hopkins University Press.

there is a sharp dichotomy between Holden and the world he loathes. Charles H. Kegel, for example, refers to Holden's "absolute hatred of phoniness."[1] Carl F. Strauch cites "the violent contrast between . . . society and Holden's world."[2] Ihab Hassan views Holden's "retreat to childhood" as "an affirmation of values."[3] What these writers ignore is that Holden shares in the phoniness he loathes; that he lives by his unconscious needs and not the values he espouses; that he withdraws from rather than faces the challenge of personal relationships.

It's not difficult to understand why readers have ignored, or have failed to perceive, Holden's grave deficiencies as a person. After all, he is very appealing—on the surface. He genuinely appreciates brief and isolated instances of kindness and accurately pinpoints phoniness in both high and low places; he is witty and his love for Phoebe is touching. But he himself is phony at times, and he has virtually no self-awareness. Furthermore, he has no intention of gaining self-awareness. Offered good advice by the psychoanalyst Wilhelm Stekel (through Mr. Antolini), he becomes "so damed *tired* all of a sudden" and is unable to concentrate (188).[4] Confronted with the charge that he cannot name one "thing" he likes "a lot," he again cannot "concentrate too hot" (169). Of course he can't; he's too busy repressing the truth. So he rambles on about two nuns he met briefly and will never see again, and he tries to convince Phoebe—and himself—that he likes James Castle, a boy who is dead. But he cannot name one *living* person, or even one occupation, that he likes. Nevertheless, he believes he is a lover of people in general because he wants to be the catcher in the rye.

When Holden says that he wants to be the catcher in the rye, he reveals a great deal about himself—a great deal more than he knows. He reveals that he does not seriously want to learn about himself. He simply won't make the effort. After all, he hasn't bothered to read Burns's poem; he isn't even able to quote accurately the one line he heard a small boy recite (173); he doesn't know that Burns's narrator contemplates kissing the "body" he meets in the rye field. So when Holden changes the word "meet" to "catch"[5] and talks not of love but of potential death (falling off a cliff), he reveals his willingness to distort the truth by ignoring—or even changing—the facts. He also reveals his use of displacement: he substitutes one response for another. He focuses on danger and potential death instead of love and a personal relationship. Ultimately, he reveals his unreliability as the narrator of his own life's story.

Fortunately, the fact that Holden distorts doesn't matter to anyone concerned with the *significance* of the events and dialogue recorded in *The Catcher in the Rye*. Like the psychoanalyst analyzing a dream, the reader can analyze what matters most: the distortions. What emerges from this analysis is an awareness that Salinger's narrator is ironic: he doesn't understand (or know) himself, but he unwittingly lets the reader know what he is like. In fact, he does so at the very beginning of the novel when he promises to give the reader "none of that David Copperfield crap" about his "lousy childhood" (1).[6] Normally, such a statement would be innocent and unrevealing, but Holden isn't "normal": he's a severely depressed adolescent telling the story of his youth while in a mental institution. He is, by his own admission, sick (213).[7] So his refusal to talk about the incidents of his childhood signifies that he will remain ill, as does his chilling advice, "Don't ever tell anybody anything," at the end of the novel (214).

Elsewhere in the novel there is evidence that Holden will remain ill because he refuses to assume responsibility for his own actions. For example, when he is "the goddam manager of the fencing team," he leaves the "foils and equipment and stuff" on the subway. Although he admits that he left them there, he hastens to add: "It wasn't all my fault" (3).[8] Here and elsewhere he simply will not or can not let his mind rest without ambivalence or qualification on a conclusion.

Ambivalence is, in fact, characteristic of Holden and the surest evidence of his mental instability. If he loathes what he loves and does so intensely, he is by no means well. He is also not what he and many readers assume he is: an anti-establishment figure whose disgust is directed entirely at other people.

It's easy to demonstrate that Holden is ambivalent since he is ambivalent toward so many people and things. He hates movies and the Lunts but attends movies (137) and takes Sally to a play starring the Lunts (125). He is contemptuous of Pencey but is careful to emphasize that it has a "very good academic rating" (4). He claims to loathe the perverts he sees through his hotel window but makes a special effort to watch them and even admits that "that kind of junk is fascinating" and that he wouldn't mind doing it himself "if the opportunity came up" (62).[9] He criticizes phony conversations but engages in them himself—with Mr. Spencer (8) and Ernest Morrow's mother (54–55), for example. He criticizes "old Spencer" (and others) for using a phony word like "grand" (9), but he himself uses equally phony words such as "nice" (1) and "swell" (124).[10] He loathes Ackley and Stradlater but misses them as soon as they're gone. He wants to see people—Mr. Antolini, Mr. Spencer, and Carl Luce, for example—but doesn't like them when they're in his presence. Obviously, then, Holden is ambivalent, and ambivalence is a certain indication of mental instability.

What is Holden's problem? Whatever it is in specific form, it's reflected in his inability to relate sexually to females. Holden himself suggests this when he says, "My sex life stinks" (148). But even when he speaks the truth he fools himself: he believes that he cannot "get really sexy" with girls he doesn't like a lot whereas, in reality, he cannot get sexy with a girl he does like. In fact, what he likes about Jane Gallagher is that a relationship with her will not go beyond the hand-holding stage. In his other attempts to establish connections with girls or women, he fails sexually and, in fact, deliberately avoids both affection and serious sexual advances.[11] He kisses Sally Hayes— but in a cab where the relationship cannot go beyond "horsing around" (125). He consents to have a prostitute sent to his hotel room but asks her to stop when she starts "getting funny. Crude and all" (97), that is, when she proceeds from words to action. Aroused by watching the "perverts" in the hotel, he does call up Faith Cavendish (64), a woman he has never seen, but at an impossibly late hour and so ensures that she will refuse his request for a date. Clearly, Holden has a problem with females.

This problem is reflected in his response to Mercutio in *Romeo and Juliet*. Acting in character, Holden identifies with Mercutio, the character in the play he has most in common with. As Strauch has pointed out,[12] both Holden and Mercutio are associated with foils. But the two have much more in common than weapons. To begin with, Mercutio assigns the role of lover to Romeo (I.iv.17) just as Holden assigns the role of lover to Stradlater. Then, too, both young men ramble on when they talk. Mr. Antolini reminds us that this is true of Holden (183 ff.); Romeo calls Mercutio's long speech (I.iv.53–94) "nothing" and Mercutio himself admits that he talks of "dreams / Which are the children of an idle brain, / Begot of nothing but vain fantasy" (I.iv.96–98). Finally, both Mercutio and Holden like to "horse around." Holden does so repeatedly; Mercutio does so even when he's dying.

What these two characters have in common at the level of speech and overt behavior reveals how they are alike in subtler ways. For example, both talk about, but do not engage in, sexual love. Both are more enamoured of words than facts. Both are victims—from Holden's point of view. Mercutio is the victim of the Capulets and of Romeo's desire to live at peace in the world; Holden sees himself as the victim of snobs, perverts, and phonies. Since Holden identifies with victims in general and, in fact, projects his suffering onto them, he has sympathy for the ducks in Central Park (13), for Selma Thurmer (3), and for the lunatic in *Mark V* (99). It follows logically that he likes Mercutio.

It also follows logically that he did not like "Romeo too much after Mercutio gets stabbed" (111). Clearly, Romeo is the antithesis of both Mercutio and Holden. He is passionate; he speaks without irony; he goes to bed with Juliet. He is by no means sexually shy although he, like Holden, is very young. In contrast, Holden is sexually shy; paradoxically, he also has an exhibitionistic attitude, that is, he has a *need* to attract attention to himself by attempting "to amuse, to stir, or to shock others."[13] Acting on this need, he performs for Stradlater in the men's room (29); he pretends to have a bullet in his stomach (103–04; 150); performing for Ackley, he pulls his hunting hat over his eyes and says in a hoarse voice, "I think I'm going blind" (21); he wears a red hunting cap in the streets of New York. He even calls himself an exhibitionist to attract attention to himself (29).

It's true that each of these examples of exhibitionism is, in itself, both harmless and normal, especially for a boy of Holden's age. (Holden himself would say that he was simply "horsing around.") But Holden has a need to show off, and he has more serious problems eventually. After all, he does end up in a mental institution. Consequently, his exhibitionistic attitude serves as a clue to his state of mind; it also helps to explain why Holden "got sick and all." Since he himself won't tell us, this clue is especially important.

Other important clues to Holden's problem are included in Chapter 25, the chapter following Holden's flight from Mr. Antolini and preceding the one-page concluding chapter which reveals that Holden is in a mental institution. Near the beginning of Chapter 25, Holden's mental breakdown (which is not recorded in the novel) is anticipated: Holden has a headache and feels "more depressed than [he] ever was in [his] whole life" (194). He also has the desire to catch what he assumes is "some perverty bum that'd sneaked in the school late at night to take a leak or something and then wrote [an obscenity] on the wall" (201). And, finally, he notices—and comments on—a little boy who "had his pants open" (202). Since Holden likes children more than adults and dead people more than the living, he is in character when he enters the tombs of the mummies with the little boy and his brother. He is also in character when, left alone in the tomb, he finds peace among the dead—at least temporarily. But then the words "Fuck you" written in red crayon on the wall remind him that he has not escaped from people, not even from the "perverty bums." Furthermore, he realizes that there is no escape even in death: some day someone will write this same obscenity on his tomb, he assumes. So when he leaves the tomb he is not cured but is, in fact, very ill: he "sort of had diarrhea" and finally passes out.[14]

Commenting on this scene, Strauch stresses that Holden feels better after he faints and "is reborn into a world of secure feelings and emotions, with himself fulfilling the office of catcher in his mature view of Phoebe."[15] Since Holden is reconciled with Phoebe and says that he felt "so damn happy all of a sudden" (213), there is some basis for this statement. However, Holden is not "reborn." Instead, by his own admission, he "got sick" (that is, mentally ill) *after* the fainting incident and the expression of happiness and is *subsequently* in an institution. Furthermore, his identification with the lunatic in *Mark* V prepares us for this.

Although Carl F. Strauch sees in Holden's response to the lunatic an anticipation of the fact that Holden "will subsequently break his morbid psychological fetters,"[16] there is too much evidence to the contrary. It's true that Holden and the lunatic have something in common: both spend time in tombs; both suffer; both are mentally ill. But they are also unlike one another in some important ways. To begin with, the lunatic participates in his own cure by running up to Jesus, adoring him, and calling out to him. In contrast, Holden withdraws from people, including Phoebe. (Significantly, she isn't mentioned or referred to in the concluding chapter although characters peripheral to Holden's existence are.) He watches her "going around and around" on the carrousel, but he remains at a distance and stands apart from "the parents and mothers and everybody" who seek shelter from the rain under the roof of the carrousel. It's true that he, like the lunatic, does go home, but the lunatic goes home cured while Holden goes home only to leave in order to enter an institution. Finally, whereas the lunatic tells everybody what has been done for him, Holden regrets having told anybody anything (214). So it's not surprising that when Holden says he likes the lunatic "ten times as much as the Disciples" (99), he refers to him as "that poor bastard" who "lived in the tombs and kept cutting himself with stones" (99) and does not refer to the lunatic's cure or his re-entry into the world of people, including adults. Acting consistently, he responds to *Mark V* the way he responds to Burns's poem: he cites what pleases him and ignores what doesn't.

This subjectivity and tendency to distort explains a great deal about Holden. Specifically, it explains his interest in the "perverty bum" and the little boy whose pants are unbuttoned. Both appeal to him because of his voyeuristic tendencies.

That Holden has voyeuristic tendencies should surprise no one. He himself admits that he finds it "sort of fascinating to watch" (62) bizarre sexual activity through his hotel window. Besides, anyone "who in the unconscious is an exhibitionist is at the same time a voyeur" in psychoanalytic terms.[17] So it is not surprising that Holden is interested in the "perverty bum" and the little boy. What is surprising is the degree of his response. In the first instance he responds with extreme hostility; he wants to catch the bum urinating and/or writing on the wall (Holden is a bit ambiguous here) and "smash his head on the stone steps till he was good and goddam dead and bloody" (201). In the second instance he responds with extreme concern and embarrassment; he says the boy's behavior "killed" him and adds that he wanted to laugh when the boy buttoned his pants without going behind a post, but he didn't dare to; he was afraid he'd "feel like vomiting again" (202–3).

What is happening is that looking is becoming a perversion for Holden: it is beginning to be concentrated on the genitals and associated with the function of excretion. It also does not prepare for the normal sexual act[18] and is the logical, although not "normal," outgrowth of his sexual shyness, of his reluctance to go beyond holding hands. It also follows quite naturally from the fact that Holden is sexually ambivalent; he hasn't lost interest in females and cannot acknowledge his sexual interest in males.

Many critics writing about homosexuality in *The Catcher in the Rye* assume that Holden is the victim of homosexuals, but there is a great deal of evidence to the contrary. To begin with, Holden fails to complete most of his phone calls to females, but he easily completes phone calls to two homosexuals: Mr. Antolini and Carl Luce. Secondly, *he* seeks *them* out; he is the aggressor if there is one. In fact, his first two remarks to Luce reveal his unconscious desire to make sexual contact with his former Student Advisor. "Hey, I got a flit for you," he says first of all, and then asks him, "How's your sex life?" (144). Thirdly, Salinger links Holden to the two homosexuals by letting the reader know (through the narration) that all three of them respond sexually to older women:[19] Luce is dating a woman in her late thirties (145); Antolini is married to a woman who "looked pretty old and all" (185); Holden responds sexually to Ernest Morrow's mother (56). But nothing reveals more about Holden's relationship to homosexuals than his response when he wakes up in the middle of the night in Mr. Antolini's house. Consider his exact words:

> I woke up all of a sudden. I don't know what time it was or anything, but I woke up. I felt something on my head, some guy's hand. Boy, it really scared the hell out of me. What it was, it was Mr. Antolini's hand. What he was doing was, he was sitting on the floor right next to the couch, in the dark and all, and he was sort of petting me or patting me on the goddam head (191–92).

Since Holden tells us that Antolini is there in the dark touching him, we have to assume this is true; there is nothing to negate or contradict or undercut this statement. But what Antolini's intention was we cannot know since even Holden is confused. Antolini was patting *or* petting him, Holden says. But the difference between patting and petting is great: we pat children and pet lovers. Furthermore, nothing that Holden says about Antolini's response to Holden's wild flight in the night suggests that Antolini is guilty of making a sexual advance. Besides, what matters most of all is this incident is Holden's distortion of experience, specifically, his overreaction. Even if Antolini did make an improper move, Holden is safe: Mrs. Antolini is in the adjoining room; Antolini is by no means aggressive; and Antolini has agreed to go to bed.

Why, then, does Holden respond so violently? Why is he sweating and ill when he leaves the house? The answer is that he is projecting his desire for homosexual expression onto Antolini. (This does not mean that Holden himself is a homosexual but that he has not yet made a sexual choice.) In the passage cited above, this is evident. Holden assumes that "some guy's hand" is on his head before he can identify Mr. Antolini or identify the hand as his. Furthermore, in this same scene he acknowledges, as the ironic narrator, that he inspires such behavior. He says, first of all, that perverts are "always being perverty when *I'm* around" (105) and emphasizes that this "kind of stuff's happened to me about twenty times since I was a kid" (193). Naturally. He is attracted to—and attracts—homosexuals.

Unfortunately, Holden isn't conscious of this. In fact, he works hard to repress all knowledge of his latent desires. To begin with, he doesn't seem to be conscious of the significance of his remarks to Carl Luce in the bar even though he admits that he "used to think" Luce was "sort of flitty" (143). But the patting (or petting) incident is more overt and threatens to make Holden conscious of his latent homosexual desires. He reacts by becoming ill. He has a headache, becomes anxious and depressed (194), has sore eyes (195), experiences a mild form of hypochondria when he says he has "lousy hormones" and cancer (195—96), and wishes to negate his identity by "going out West" where nobody would know him (198). But, most important of all, he wants to be unable to hear or speak; he wants to be a deaf mute who marries and lives in isolation with a beautiful deaf mute girl (198—99). In other words, Holden wants to live apart from men and wants to be unable to hear or speak anything. In expressing this Holden expresses his wish to have no reminders through speech or action of his unresolved sexual conflicts.

It shouldn't be surprising that Holden has severe sexual conflicts: his family situation is far from ideal. The father barely exists as far as Holden and Phoebe are concerned, and the mother is not emotionally involved in the lives of her children. This is revealed in the scene in which the Caulfields return from a party. First of all, they are indifferent to Phoebe. Although she is still a child, they have left her home alone. When they do return home late at night, only Mrs. Caulfield bothers to look in on her daughter. But she is by no means greatly concerned. She doesn't object seriously to what she assumes is smoke from a cigarette Phoebe has been smoking; she moves randomly and nervously (like Holden) from one subject to another, including Holden's return from school; she fails to react to Phoebe's statement that she couldn't sleep. In brief, she is a mother incapable of affection.

Meanwhile, the father has gone into another room without bothering to inquire about Phoebe. Since Phoebe has said that he will not attend her Christmas pageant, it's safe to assume that he is generally absent from his children's lives. He is the aloof father whose inaccessibility makes it impossible for his son to identify with him and thus to develop "normally."

But he does have a connection with Holden: he punishes him. Confirming this, Phoebe says repeatedly that Mr. Caulfield will "kill" Holden (165, 166, 172), and Holden himself acknowledges that "it would've been very unpleasant and all" if his father had found him at home (178). Since Mr. Caulfield remains a vague and powerful figure, his effect on his son is inevitably exaggerated and debilitating. He joins forces with his wife to stifle and stunt his son's sexual development.

Because Holden's home situation is so unfortunate, it's easy to sympathize with him. It's even tempting to see the conclusion (Chapter 26) as affirmative. Besides, Holden is very appealing when he criticizes bums and phonies and perverts—so appealing that it's easy to forget that he's a bum, a phony (at times) and a potential pervert. And when he expresses his love for Phoebe, his hostility and egotism seem relatively unimportant. So it's tempting to see Holden as a person who doesn't need a psychoanalyst because he has gone beyond affirmation and denial. But at the end of the novel Holden is depressed and subdued. He has lost interest in life: he doesn't want to think about the past; he isn't interested in his future. When he tells D. B. that he doesn't know what to think about "all this stuff I just finished telling you about," he reveals that he is still confused. And when he says that he misses everybody—even Stradlater and Ackley and Maurice—he reveals that he is still sentimental. Although his sentimentality has often been sentimentalized as love, it is not love at all. It is a symptom of his inability to express his feelings easily and naturally.

Nevertheless, Holden is likable. He also deserves sympathy because, as William Faulkner has said, he "tried to join the human race and failed."[20] But Faulkner is not quite accurate when he says that there was no human race for him to enter. Phoebe loves him; D. B. expresses an interest in him by visiting him in the mental institution; Mr. Antolini offers him shelter and good advice. Ultimately, people are as good to Holden as he is to them. So Holden should not be idealized. It may be true that he is "more intelligent than some and more sensitive than most,"[21] but his response to his own experience results in deep depression and may have culminated in mania.[22] Nor does Holden resist the establishment that makes it difficult for him to love and develop. His rebellion is all fantasy. He tells off no one—not even the prostitute or the phonies at Pencey. And his overt behavior is conventional except when he is acting out his exhibitionistic attitude. He doesn't become a recluse or a beatnik; instead, he returns home, enters an institution, and will *again* return to school in the fall.

He does have what Faulkner calls an "instinct" to love man,[23] but this makes him a typical, rather than extraordinary, teenager. It's what causes him to want to join the human race.

What does make him extraordinary is his special ability to detect phoniness everywhere (except in himself). Of course it's unfair to emphasize, to the exclusion of everything else, that Holden shares in the phoniness he loathes. After all, Holden conforms to phoniness because he wants so badly to join the human race. But in doing so he makes it difficult for others like himself to find a human race to join.

Notes

1. Charles H. Kegel, "Incommunicability in Salinger's *The Catcher in the Rye*," *Western Humanities Review*, 11 (Spring, 1957):189.

2. Carl F. Strauch, "Kings in the Back Row: Meaning Through Structure, A Reading of Salinger's *The Catcher in the Rye*," *Wisconsin Studies in Contemporary Literature*, 2 (Winter, 1961):11.

3. Ihab Hassan, *Radical Innocence: Studies in the Contemporary American Novel* (Princeton Univ. Press, 1961), p. 261.

4. Page numbers which appear parenthetically in the body of this paper refer to the Bantam Books paperback edition of *The Catcher in the Rye*.

5. It's possible that the little boy quoted Burns's poems inaccurately and that Holden is repeating accurately what he heard. Nevertheless, my central point remains valid: Holden is not concerned enough about the truth to gather the facts. Being in the right is much more important to him than being right.

6. In one sense, Holden keeps his promise: he doesn't tell the reader much about his childhood. However, since he reveals his "symptoms" through his speech and behavior, it's possible to infer what his childhood was like. Besides, Holden has something in common with David Copperfield: he's very sentimental. This should surprise no one since Salinger carefully links Holden to David in two ways. First of all, Holden is a Caul-*field* and David is a Copper-*field*. Secondly, both are born with a caul. Caul is the first part of Holden's surname; it is also the name of the fetal membrane David is born with (see the fourth paragraph of Dickens's novel).

7. Unwittingly, he acknowledges this again when he says, "In my *mind*, I'm probably the biggest sex maniac you ever saw" (62). On other occasions he calls himself an exhibitionist (29) and admits that he can be sadistic (22).

8. The significant word here is "all"; it suggests that Holden knows he is at fault but will not assume responsibility for his actions.

9. Carl F. Strauch cites this scene to confirm that Holden contrasts the world he loathes; however, Strauch ignores the fact that Holden finds the perverse behavior attractive. In addition to admitting that indulging in perverse behavior would be "quite a lot of fun," Holden renders a long, detailed account of the women's clothing used by the transvestite (61); he also watches the "perverts" willingly, with obvious interest, and for quite a long time.

10. Holden's use of what Strauch calls "slob" and "literate" language suggests that Holden is ambivalent toward language and toward education in general.

11. It is important to emphasize that Holden has difficulty expressing himself either affectionately or sensually. (Sentimentality should not be mistaken for affection.) For example, he finds even Phoebe "too affectionate" when she puts her arms around his neck (161). This inability to express or receive affection suggests that Holden had difficulty "from the very beginning" with parents who were too cold or too aloof. Since "normal" sexual development depends on the successful fusion of the earlier "affectionate current" of love with the later "sensual current," Holden's chances of maturing "normally" are not good.

For an interesting and informative discussion of the relationship of tenderness to sensuality, see Philip Rieff's *Freud: the Mind of the Moralist* (Garden City, New York: Doubleday, 1961), pp. 174–77.

12. Strauch, p. 15.

13. Any of a large number of psychology or psychoanalytic texts could be used to arrive at an understanding of the term "exhibitionistic attitude." I have quoted briefly from the Laurel *Dictionary of Psychology*, ed. J. P. Chaplin (New York: Dell, 1975), p. 184 because it offers a succinct definition which applies so exactly to Holden without distorting what a more elaborate discussion of the term would include. The definition of the term helps to explain why Holden has a need to amuse Stradlater, to shock Ackley, and to stir Phoebe.

14. If Salinger intended the reader to see Holden's diarrhea and fainting as a cure, D. H. Lawrence is right: novels cannot lie but novelists are often dribbling liars.

15. Strauch, p. 23.

16. Strauch, p. 17.

17. Sigmund Freud, *Three Contributions to the Theory of Sex*, ed. A. A. Brill (New York: Random House, 1938), p. 575.

18. It is instructive to relate what Freud says about voyeurism in *Three Contributions to the Theory of Sex* (especially on pp. 569, 575, and 593 in the Brill edition) to Holden's behavior. Freud may not present the last word on the subject, but what he says fits Holden so exactly that it is difficult not to believe that Salinger knew Freud's essay when he wrote his novel.

19. Salinger likes to link two or more people by means of specific details. As indicated above, David Copperfield and Holden are linked by a caul; Mercutio and Holden are linked by foils; the lunatic in *Mark V* and Holden are linked by tombs and madness. Analogously, Carl Luce, Mr. Antolini and Holden are linked by their sexual interest in older women.

20. Frederick L. Gwynn and Joseph L. Blotner, eds., *Faulkner in the University* (New York: Random House, 1965), p. 244.

21. Gwynn, p. 244.

22. Although Holden does not acknowledge that he was manic between chapters 25 and 26, it is likely that he was. To begin with, he has most of the criteria "required for 'definite' depression": depression, loss of energy, agitation, feelings of self-reproach and guilt, complaints of diminished ability to concentrate, mixed-up thoughts, and recurrent thoughts of death. Furthermore, at the end of Chapter 25, when he is watching Phoebe on the carrousel, he appears to be approaching that state of euphoria characteristic of the manic. He also exhibits at least some of the symptoms which must be present in mania: distractibility, racing thoughts, and

"push of speech." If Holden does become manic, the break between the last two chapters is explained: manics generally cannot remember what they said and did during the manic period.

For a professional presentation of diagnostic criteria of depression and mania, see pp. 199–200 of *Psychiatric Diagnosis* (New York: Oxford University Press, 1974) written by Drs. Robert A. Woodruff, Jr., Donald W. Goodwin, and Samuel B. Guze.

23. Gwynn, p. 244.

A Retrospective Look at *The Catcher in the Rye*   Gerald Rosen*

Now that over a quarter century has passed since the publication of *The Catcher in the Rye*, it is possible to see the book in the light of the enormous body of writing that has been done on it. There are collections of articles and bibliographies to aid the person who wishes to do this.[1] It is also possible to see the book in the context of Salinger's other work, especially the writings about the Glass family, most of which were published after *Catcher*. These stories reveal themes not immediately apparent in a reading of *Catcher* and stem from a side of Salinger that has been of less importance to his critics than to Salinger himself. I refer to the importance of Eastern thought and religion to Salinger, and of Buddhism in particular, especially the form which we in the West refer to as Zen.[2]

The Zen masters have a saying, "Sometimes we go east, sometimes we go west," and it appears that Salinger, after a brief attempt to "go west" in the American army during World War II, became disillusioned with his native culture and society and turned to a study of Eastern thought. This disillusionment can be seen in Holden's approving remark about his brother D. B.: "My brother D. B. was in the Army for four goddam years. He was in the war, too—he landed on D-Day and all—but I really think he hated the Army worse than the War. . . . He said the Army was practically as full of bastards as the Nazis were." Of course I don't mean to identify Salinger with D. B., but like D. B. Salinger himself participated in the Normandy invasion and his story, "For Esme—with Love and Squalor," embodies the vision which Holden attributes to D. B.

In Buddhism one is asked to give up one's illusions. *Catcher* was given final shape in the post-war period, and it is basically a novel of disillusionment. The radical nature of Salinger's portrayal of disappointment with American society, so much like Twain's in *Huck Finn*, was probably as much of the reason that *Catcher* (like *Huck*) was banned from schools and colleges as were the few curse words around which the battle was publicly fought.

After this novel of the death of belief in America, Salinger turned to

*Reprinted by permission from *American Quarterly* 29, no. 5 (Winter 1977):547–62. © 1977 by the American Studies Association.

wrestling with the problems of Eastern thought in the Glass books. In particular, Franny (who is, in many ways, an older female Holden, suffering from the same alienation-nausea of the seer) and Zooey are faced with the problem of reconciling their interest and training in Eastern thought (embodied in the influence of their brother Seymour upon them) with their deep conditioning and tangled loyalties to Western culture and perceptions and to their personal histories as Jewish-Christian Americans from the Upper West Side of Manhattan. "I was *born* here. I went to *school* here. I've been *run over* here—*twice*, and on the same damn *street*," Zooey lectures Franny (and himself as well).

Since Salinger seemed to achieve instant success with the appearance of *Catcher* in 1951, it is important to remember that he was already in his early thirties by this time, had been publishing stories in slick magazines like *Saturday Evening Post* for ten years, and had been working on *Catcher* through much of this decade during which time he was studying Buddhism and working on the beginnings of the Glass family saga as well. ("A Perfect Day for Bananafish," and "Down at the Dinghy," were published before *Catcher*).

The Buddha, like most great ancient religious teachers, now exists at the point where the lines of history and legend cross. But as Christmas Humphreys observes in his study of Buddhism, "Legend is often a poetic form of history. . . ."[3] A Raja of the Sakya clan (he is sometimes referred to as Sakyamuni—the sage of the Sakyas), the Buddha, according to tradition, was born in what is now Nepal in 563 B.C. His name was Siddhartha Gotama. Raised in a protective, affluent environment, the young prince was shielded from the suffering of the world and not taught to deal with it. The turning point in the story of the Buddha's life occurs when he is confronted with old age, sickness, and death. They so shake him he decides to leave the shelter of his surroundings and the distractions of his involvement in his everyday life in order to wander in the world in search of a guide who will teach him to come to terms with old age, sickness, and death. He doesn't find one, is forced to work out his salvation on his own, persists in his detachment and alienation, has a vision of the truth, and returns to the world out of compassion for his fellow living suffering beings.

I would suggest that, in rough outline, and without the Buddha's final conscious mature understanding, this is the form of the story of Holden Caulfield. When we first meet Holden in the affluent, protective environment of a prep school, we are prepared for his lonely journey by immediately being given a picture of his alienation from the non-seeing groups of people around him. (Alienation is the negative side of detachment or non-attachment which the Eastern religions see as a virtue.) Salinger presents us with our first glimpse of Holden on the day of the big football game. Holden's detachment from the game is emphasized by having him view the stadium from a distance where the excitement and involvement of the crowd over "the two teams bashing each other all over the place" appears ridiculous. Holden comments,

"The game with Saxon Hall was supposed to be a very big deal around Pencey. It was the last game of the year and you were supposed to commit suicide or something if old Pencey didn't win."

The reference to suicide is not fortuitous for we soon come to see that it is precisely a continuing preoccupation with death that keeps Holden from participating in the games of those around him. It prevents him from concentrating on those activities like day-to-day school chores which we don't ordinarily think of as games but which, in the presence of death, tend to recede toward the unimportance we usually ascribe to games.

And, in fact, just as in the story of the Buddha, it is sickness, old age, and death, which we the readers, along with Holden, encounter when we begin our journey through the pages of *The Catcher in the Rye*. We meet sickness and old age in the form of Mr. Spencer, Holden's teacher:

> The minute I went in, I was sort of sorry I'd come. He was reading the *Atlantic Monthly*, and there were pills and medicine all over the place, and everything smelled of Vicks Nose Drops. It was pretty depressing. I'm not too crazy about sick people, anyway. What made it even more depressing, Old Spencer had on this very sad, ratty old bathrobe that he was probably born in or something. I don't much like to see old guys in their pajamas and bathrobes anyway. Their bumpy old chests are always showing. And their legs. Old guys' legs, at beaches and places, always look so white and unhairy.

Holden explains to Mr. Spencer that his problem relates to the idea of life as a game. "He [Dr. Thurmer—the headmaster] just kept talking about life being a game and all." To which "old" Spencer responds, "Life *is* a game, boy." Holden agrees with him outwardly, but he tells us, his confidants, "Game my ass. Some game." At this point Holden believes his objection to life as "a game" is that it's only fun for the winners. But he has deeper, unconscious objections to life, since ultimately in life there are no winners, only corpses. And immediately after introducing sickness and old age, Salinger presents us with the third member of the Buddha's problematic triad—death.

Holden, like the young Buddha, is obsessed by death, and by its corollaries, time and change. He has turned Spencer's exam question about ancient Egypt into a short essay which Spencer cannot see as springing out of this obsession: "Modern science would still like to know what the secret ingredients were that the Egyptians used when they wrapped up dead people so that their faces would not rot for innumerable centuries." And Holden flunks, because on this exam, as in his life, no one has ever taught him how to get beyond this primary question, in the shrill light of which all secondary questions are obscured.

From the start, Holden's mind has been filled with images of rot and decay. (Besides "old" Spencer himself, we have also met his rotting bathrobe.) And it is this obsessive concern of Holden's which accounts for the concentration of his narrative upon details of bodily functioning, dirt and decay—filthy fingernails, mossy teeth, smelly socks, a rusty, filthy razor— which our institutions attempt to repress or deny.

Disgust is our culturally conditioned response to these natural data, and when the book appeared many teachers and reviewers—people who are successfully functioning within the culture's institutional system—did, in fact, respond to the mention of these matters in the text with disgust. Holden is also disturbed by much of this. He, too, has been raised in this culture (many critics have pointed out that he still holds some of the middle-class values he attacks) and is sickened by their presence. Yet he can not sweep the evidence of decay and death under the carpet of his mind into his unconscious. He doesn't like what he sees, but he can't help *seeing* it, just as he can't avoid the presence of the central fact of his life, his brother Allie's death, which ultimately sets him off on his quest for an adult guide.

Salinger himself has his present narrator, Buddy Glass, define the artist as seer, and Buddy too seems determined to wrestle openly with death; not only Holden, but the Glass children as well are obsessed by the death of a brother. It was probably a fight against allowing the facts of death and change to get out of his sight and become unconscious that led Salinger to his post-war studies of such philosophies as Taoism and Buddhism which begin with the primary fact of impermanence and change and attempt to teach us to see and accept this central datum of our experience.

Holden has no one to teach him how to cope with death. In a stable culture, one would ordinarily turn to the oldest people for this kind of wisdom. They've been around the longest and presumably would have had the most experience with these matters. But in a rapidly changing culture like ours, the old people and their knowledge appear obsolete to the young. To Holden, the older people he meets are generally all right, but they seem "out of it": "I have this grandmother that's quite lavish with her dough. She doesn't have all her marbles anymore—she's old as hell . . ." and in "old" Spencer's case, "he was a nice old guy that didn't know his ass from his elbow."

Seeking protection himself, Holden is forced to protect the adults he encounters. He forgives Spencer in advance for failing him, writing on his exam, "It's all right with me if you flunk me. . . ." Several critics have noted the contradiction between Holden's hatred of phoniness and his lying to Ernest Morrow's mother when he meets her on the train on his way to New York from Pencey. Yet he lies to her to protect her from having to face the fact that "Her son was doubtless the biggest bastard that ever went to Pencey. . . ." And it is interesting that when he lies to her about his name, he doesn't do it for the usual reason one lies—to aggrandize oneself—but rather he takes on the name of Rudolph Schmidt, the dorm janitor.

After he fails to get the guidance he needs from his teachers or from the other adults he meets, one would expect Holden to turn to his parents. But in the entire novel, his father never appears and his mother appears once and then only speaks to Phoebe as Holden hides in the closet. The absence of Holden's parents (along with the absence of real religious guidance in the form of a school chaplain or family minister) is so important it amounts to a presence. On the failure of religion, Holden tells us, "my parents are different religions, and all the children in our family are atheists. If you want to know the truth, I can't even stand ministers. . . . They sound so phony when they talk." And, about his family, in the first paragraph Holden explains, "my parents would have about two hemorrhages apiece if I told anything pretty personal about them." Here is the genesis of his hatred of phoniness. His parents live in two worlds: the real world and the world of appearances. The surface does not reveal the underlying reality and Holden has been taught not to talk about what lies beneath. Yet, at times, indirectly, he does. When Phoebe suggests he become a lawyer like their father, he says, "Lawyers are all right, I guess—but it doesn't appeal to me. . . . All you do is make a lot of dough and play golf and play bridge and buy cars and drink martinis and look like a hot-shot." This occurs right after Phoebe asks him to replace their father at her play (the father will be in California on business).

Holden's mother, though well-meaning, won't be of much help either. "She still isn't over my brother Allie yet," and "She's nervous as hell. Half the time she's up all night smoking cigarettes." Like the other adults, parents can't be relied upon to see, much less give good advice. Holden says of insensitive Stradlater, the secret slob, "he was mostly the kind of a handsome guy that if your parents saw his picture in your Year Book, they'd right away say, "Who's *this* boy?"

Holden sorely misses being able to turn to his parents in his time of trouble. He doesn't say this, but he reveals it obliquely in his movie-fantasies of being shot by the mob. In the first, he pulls the peak of the hunting cap over his eyes and shouts about being blind. (This is the reverse of the baseball catcher's hat position, in which the peak is *back*, implying the catcher *must* see, and Holden has chosen to be a "catcher.") Then Holden shouts, "Mother darling, everything's getting so *dark* in here," and "Mother darling, give me your *hand*. Why won't you give me your *hand*?" This seems like clowning, but in fact it is a revelation of his terrible anguished isolation from his family. In a later fantasy, Holden reveals, "I didn't want anybody to know I was even wounded. I was *concealing* the fact that I was a wounded sonofabitch." Then he calls Sally and explains the source of his wound: "They got me. Rocky's mob got me." This is clarified three pages later, when he refers to his family at Allie's funeral as "a mob," thereby revealing the source of his wound and the traumatic occasion when he first really felt the pain of it. And he begins to speak of Allie as if he were alive but underground: "I certainly didn't enjoy seeing *him* in that crazy cemetery" [italics added].

So Holden can not get advice on how to leave the world of childhood from the adults around him. Nor can he find suitable models to emulate. The two Pencey alumni we encounter are Ossenburger, a phony undertaker, and an old guy who appears on Veteran's Day and tells Holden that Pencey will prove to be the best years of his life. This does not increase Holden's hope for the future. And as for Ossenburger, "he started these undertaking parlors all over the country that you could have members of your family buried for about five bucks apiece. . . . You should see old Ossenburger. He probably just shoves them in a sack and dumps them in the river." (Again, Holden can't stay away from the subject of the death of family members and the decay of the corpse. Even when he later goes to the Museum of Art, he winds up in the mummy room explaining about preserving the dead to two boys and then getting sick and "sort of" passing out.)

Holden possesses the necessary but painful gift of the novelist—the intuitive ability to perceive that words are instruments used to create effects and have no necessary attachments to non-verbal reality. So he needs more than even good advice, he needs a living adult, a mature person within the culture who, by his or her living presence, will *demonstrate* a possibility that Holden might achieve if he gives up the non-defined personality of his childhood and accepts a role as a mature member of the society. Holden's brother D. B. who once offered this possibility has sold out to Hollywood which produces images such as the great lover with the violin and the courageous guy with romantic wounds. Since the viewer can't hope to live up to these images, they contribute to making him feel small and un-courageous and add to his wounds. As Holden notes, "the goddam movies. They can ruin you. I'm not kidding." And he isn't. And Mr. Antolini, who gives Holden what might seem to be good advice, cancels any effect his words might have had by his actions and his mode of life.

Americans have always found it difficult to accept limits. Even if the chance to head for the frontier was largely mythic, its significance as myth was its denial of limits in the imaginations of those Americans who were stuck in the East. Of course death is the ultimate limit, and Jessica Mitford has shown to what lengths Americans will go to deny its reality. Institutional roles are limits, too, and Holden, in his extended adolescence, is in the position of one who has been left outside the house of the culture's institu-tions for too long, and has become taller than the ceiling. Everyone in the house appears to him to be unconscious of the fact that they are stooping to fit inside because this posture has become habitual to them. They have grown into it. Holden is asked to stoop consciously—to enter the house at a time when, so to speak, he has become too tall for it.

In reaction to this, Holden fantasizes a Thoreau-like existence in the country, outside of the limits of institutional roles and of social norms and manners. He tells Sally, "we could drive up to Massachusetts and Vermont, and all around there, see. It's beautiful as hell up there . . . we could live somewhere with a brook and all . . . I could chop all our own wood in the wintertime. . . ."

Sally, who has been successfully acculturated, explains to Holden about his obligation to fulfill the traditional male role of husband and provider, and then she promises, "There'll be oodles of marvelous places to go." In responding to Sally, Holden gives us the novel of his future which haunts him and which is one more factor preventing him from accepting an adult role and "growing up" into the society:

> I said no, there wouldn't be marvelous places to go after I went to college and all. Open your ears. It'd be entirely different. We'd have to go downstairs in elevators with suitcases and stuff. We'd have to phone up everybody and tell 'em goodbye and send 'em postcards from hotels and all. And I'd be working in some office, making a lot of dough, and riding to work in cabs and Madison Avenue buses, and reading newspapers, and playing bridge all the time, and going to the movies. . . .

It is important to note here that Holden's rejection of an adult role is not a case of sour grapes. He believes he *will* succeed and it is the successful life he fears. And this passage in which he tells Sally to open her eyes and ears, "Open your ears. . . . You don't see what I mean at all," further highlights his desperate isolation. Like the adults, his contemporaries don't see what he sees or hear what he is saying either.

With such a dead-end vision of the trap of adulthood and marriage, it is no wonder that Holden fears initiation into that most adult and most involving and non-detached form of relationship—sex. In a society in which human relationships are infected by market-place values of competitiveness and surface appearance, and humans are measured in terms of social status and money income, Holden is seeking a deeper, more real relationship with someone—a more human relationship. Holden is against many things, but he isn't nihilistic. "Human" is one of his values, as he reveals comically in his preference for the horse over that sacred American object, the automobile: "A horse is at least *human* for God's sake."

Another positive value of Holden's is that it is wrong to hurt people. He reveals this when he says, in attempting to forgive bores, "They don't hurt anybody, most of them. . . ." So Holden is very careful not to use people as a means for his own ends, to try to be certain that he treats each person as a human being and not as a commercial object available for his use in the manner sanctioned by his culture. Yet he is a member of his culture to a degree, so it is not surprising that when he is offered the teenage dream of being indoctrinated into sex in a non-responsible situation, in which all he has to pay is money, he jumps at the chance, and then, when he is confronted by the human reality of the situation, his tremendous empathy surfaces and he feels sorry for the girl. Of course, Maurice victimizes him here, because Holden allows himself to be victimized by virtually everyone who tries; the culture's emphasis on "winning" in encounters with other people is so threatening to him that he plays it safe by always losing—his scissors to Ackley, his coat to Stradlater, his sweater to James Castle, and so on.

Pure sex, like the myth of rural peace, is a romantic good place Holden is struggling to hold onto in the face of the urban-commercial society determined to pollute both. But Holden's mistrust of sex goes deeper than the merely social level. For Holden, sex is the ultimate involvement in the world; it is the final entry into time. Holden cannot accept change and time is the measure of change. Time is the medium in which change lives. Time is the silent partner of death. And sex is the passageway through which one is seduced into entering time. Salinger makes this connection clear when Sunny, the prostitute, first comes to Holden's room and asks him, three times, whether he has a watch. Of course, he doesn't. He is still a virgin. He has not yet left the timeless world of childhood.

At Pencey, Holden equates sex with time when referring to Stradlater's date with Jane Gallagher. At first, he virtually equates sex with perversion when he calls Stradlater "a very sexy bastard" because of his interest in the details of Jane's stepfather running around naked in front of her. And then, obsessed with the idea of Stradlater's copulating with Jane, whom Holden remembers as a young girl, he begins to talk of Stradlater's "giving her the time." The fact that this was a popular expression does not reduce the significance of Holden's repeated use of it—rather it generalizes Holden's identification of sex with time.

Thoughts of sex seem to lead Holden to thoughts of death. After the fight with Stradlater over Jane, Ackley asks Holden what the fight was about, and Holden tells us, "I didn't answer him. . . . I almost wished I was dead." In his New York hotel room, when he is thinking about sex and then considers calling Jane at college, an excuse for the late-night call pops into mind: "I was going to say her aunt had just got killed in a car accident. . . ." And after Sunny, the prostitute, leaves his room he begins to talk out loud to his dead brother Allie.

In both Holden's mind and in his culture, besides the link between sex and death there is a connection between sex and aggression, and aggression is an extremely negative quality to Holden. As in his reaction to the culture's emphasis on winning, Holden is so anxious to avoid aggression that he makes himself defenseless. He fights Stradlater, but loses and tells us, "I'd only been in about two fights in my life, and I lost *both* of them. I'm not too tough. I'm a pacifist, if you want to know the truth."

One reason he loses the fight is that he can't make a fist, and it is interesting to note that he injured his fist, and thereby partially rendered himself incapable of aggression, by punching it through a window after Allie died. Aggression, at its extreme, will lead to someone's death and, as Holden comments about the death of Mercutio, "it drives me crazy if somebody gets killed . . . and it's somebody else's fault." Here we have a clue as to why Holden has crippled himself—he has been so shocked by Allie's death that he is afraid to act in the slightest manner that might implicate him in the injustice of it. At bottom, beneath Holden's quarrel with his culture, there is always his quarrel with God whom Holden can't forgive for killing his brother.

Although his swing at Stradlater would seem to violate his anti-aggressive stance, it is in the name of protecting a non-aggressive person that

Holden attempts it. What he especially liked about Jane was that she kept her kings in the back row in checkers. This has intrigued the critics, but what it seems to me to represent is a holding back of one's aggressive powers and an unwillingness to enter the competitive game and use them against other people; this is one of Holden's cherished values and, in his own case, his bane as well.

The connection between sex and death in the culture surfaces in the famous scene near the end of the book where Holden attempts to erase the "Fuck You" signs in Phoebe's school. The culture uses the same word for its highest aggressive insult and for its term for sexual intercourse. In the culture's mind and in Holden's, sex is something men *commit* on women and it is clear that this view of sex, built into the culture's language and value system, has poisoned it for Holden.

So here we come full circle: Holden fears aggression because it may lead to death, sex is equated with aggression, and, once again, sex is thus connected with death and with its agent, the grim-reaper Time.

In opposition to this vicious circle, Holden dreams of an Edenic world, outside of time, beyond aggression: a world prior to the anxiety caused by the Fall. In his romantic imagination, this world is equated with the prepubescent world of childhood. No one is Holden's world understands natural forces (no adult ever *does* tell him what happens to the ducks in the winter) and puberty resembles death in the way it places man at the mercy of tremendous natural forces which come with one's body and are the price one pays for living in the changing material world. The Hindus, wrestling with these same problems, define this material world as Maya, the veil of illusion, which supposedly keeps one from seeing his ground in the eternal, unchanging, One. The Buddhists see the notion of the unchanging One as one more concept of stability which we manufacture and hold on to to keep from dealing with the reality of change.

Holden holds on to many things to keep from dealing with the reality of change. In the museum, there is glass which keeps things out of time and decay. Holden especially likes the museum for this reason. "The best thing, though, in that museum was that everything always stayed right where it was," and "Certain things should stay the way they are. You ought to be able to stick them in one of those big glass cases and just leave them alone." It is at Allie's funeral that Holden is jolted out of this timeless world that he has seen preserved behind the glass, and, as if in revenge against this fraud, his response is to punch his fist through a window, breaking the glass which has deceived him. Later in the book, beneath the glass in the wall in the Museum of Art, he sees a "Fuck You" scrawled in red crayon and this verbalizes the traumatic insult the timeless world gave him when it broke with Allie's death.

The presence of these "Fuck You" signs in the book points to a crucial difference in attitude between Salinger and his young narrator. The closeness of Salinger and Holden in terms of certain values and aspects of vision is emphasized by Salinger's use of Holden as a first-person narrator. Any distance between them tends to be obscured by Salinger's obvious sympathy for Holden, and by the tone of his writing which succeeds in its scrupulous efforts to get Holden's speech down exactly, creating an intimate effect which is almost like having Holden in the room, telling the reader his own story.[4]

Yet, to ignore the distance between Holden and his creator is to do a disservice to Salinger. In the instance of the "Fuck You" signs, Salinger is doing precisely the opposite of what Holden is attempting to do. Quixotically, Holden attempts to erase the "Fuck You" signs, thereby trying to keep children from learning about sex in this misguided (and even aggressive) context. He is trying to be the catcher who keeps children in their Eden before the Fall. Yet Salinger, by *including* these "Fuck You" signs, is actually scrawling them on the walls of his book, forcing the reader to acknowledge their presence and deal with them. At the time the book was published this caused a controversy and was one reason the book was deemed "dirty" by many readers and was taken from libraries and the reading lists of high school courses. Salinger here is not playing the catcher at all, but is asking the reader to grow up and accept the fallen world in which he finds himself.

Interestingly, the readers who attempted to ban the book from libraries and from the schools of their children were acting in exactly the immature manner which causes Holden so much pain and which Salinger is trying to diagnose and prescribe for in the novel. Yet here we see what must be a conflict in Salinger's own mind: after 1947, he had identified himself with the *New Yorker* magazine, publishing almost all his stories in its pages. *Catcher*, however, was not published in the *New Yorker*, and it is clear it couldn't have been published there because of these same "Fuck You" signs.[5]

Brendan Gill tells us, regarding Harold Ross, the founder of the *New Yorker* and its editor at the time *Catcher* was published, that Ross had "a puritanical determination to exclude even the mildest sexual innuendoes." "He said it was his intention to publish nothing that would bring a blush to the cheek of a twelve year old girl. This was a peculiar standard to set for a magazine universally acknowledged to be among the most sophisticated in existence—a magazine that Ross had founded, moreover, with the stipulation that it was not to be edited for the old lady in Dubuque." As for William Shawn, the editor who succeeded Ross and who was in charge during the publication of the Glass stories which came after *Catcher*, Gill comments. "the harshest expletive I ever heard him utter is a whispered, 'Oh, God!' "

Thus, by serving up a fare that includes "Fuck You" signs, Salinger is rebelling against his literary parents at the *New Yorker*, giving them a dish they can't chew and thereby, by implication, putting them in the position of poor immature Holdens, trying to serve as catchers for their readers. And, by the way, perpetuating the same standards of sex and language which are causing Holden so much of his pain. Brendan Gill tells us, "Ross believed in a double standard of language—one for the publicly printed word, the other for private speech."[6]

"Life is suffering." This is the first "Noble Truth" of the Buddha, and it stands like a neon sign over the entrance to Buddhism, acting like a filter that only lets in those who are willing to accept this premise as the price of admission. By the time Holden goes to see his sister Phoebe, one can certainly say that *his* life is suffering in the true Buddhist sense. (Another translation of "suffering" would be "continued irritation" or "anxiety.") The other of the four Buddhist Noble Truths say there is a cause for suffering and a cure. The cause, most briefly termed "desire" or "selfish craving," is said to stem from the failure to accept change (and the failure to deal with sickness, old age, and death) and the concomitant attempt to avoid change by holding on to things, grasping at false possibilities for stability and illusions of permanence. The cure is to let go of desire and selfish craving for ways out of time, be they promised by public gods or private fantasies.

Holden is holding on to many things besides his virginity. He is holding on to his old character patterns which lead him to be unable to let go of saying yes to virtually everything anyone asks him for, and to losing in almost every encounter with other people (especially where money is concerned). He also holds on to objects, such as Allie's glove, and the broken pieces of Phoebe's record (symbolically so like a corpse—the matter is still there, but not the music). He holds on to old opinions as well, such as his (and Allie's) veneration of the kettle drummer at Radio City Music Hall. By avoiding a meeting or a telephone conversation with Jane Gallagher, he holds on to his old image of her which is clearly no longer applicable since she is dating Stradlater; apparently Holden has been defending this image and avoiding her present reality for quite a while since he doesn't even know which school she goes to.

The Buddha said the greatest source of suffering is the belief in a single, continuous, unchanging personality, and the attempt to hold on to it. By not letting go of his old character traits and images of the world, Holden is doing precisely this. Of course, Holden is most strongly holding on to (is most attached to) Allie. When Phoebe challenges Holden to name one thing he likes, he appears to be at a loss for an answer at first, getting stuck on thoughts about James Castle, the boy who committed suicide. Holden is identified with Castle by Castle's having killed himself while wearing Holden's sweater and by Castle's appearing just before Holden on the roll call at school. This carries the implication that Holden may be next in line for Castle's fate. (The fact that Mr. Antolini attempts to help Castle, but is too late, prefigures Holden's experience with Mr. Antolini.) From this image of the dead James Castle, when Phoebe again challenges him, Holden's mind moves back to the image of his dead brother, which he carries with him wherever he goes, and he responds, "I like Allie."

Many people equate Eastern religions with mysticism, and mysticism with pure subjectivity, but Buddhism, at its highest levels, is empirical and asks one merely to be awake to one's real situation and not to believe anything one hasn't experienced. When the Tibetan Buddhist teacher Chogyam Trungpa was talking about finding "a spiritual friend," he was asked by a student, "Is it absolutely necessary that the spiritual friend be a living human being?" to which he replied, "Yes. Any other 'being' with whom you might think yourself communicating would be imaginary."[7]

After Holden says he likes Allie, he immediately turns to the real world and gives us a hint of what will occur at the end of the book at the carrousel. After Phoebe objects, "Allie's *dead* . . ." he adds, "Anyway, I like it now . . . sitting here with you. . . ." What Phoebe has done here is to pull Holden out of his obsession with the sorrows of his past and direct his attention to the existential situation he is in at present.

Right after this, Salinger directs our attention to the Buddhist underpinnings of the novel by having Holden inform us about Phoebe, "She was sitting smack in the middle of the bed, outside the covers, with her legs folded like one of those Yogi guys." This is the lotus position of meditation, the traditional posture of the Buddha, and if Holden doesn't know it, Salinger certainly does. To quote Chogyam Trungpa on the Buddhist idea of psychotherapy:

> Once you begin to deal with a person's whole case history, trying to make it relevant to the present, the person begins to feel that he has no escape, that his situation is hopeless, because he cannot undo his past. He feels trapped by his past with no way out. This kind of treatment is extremely unskilled. It is destructive because it hinders involvement with the creative aspect of what is happening now, what is here, right now.[8]

Holden's meeting with Phoebe is the turning point of the book. For the first time he admits, "I just felt good for a change." And the reason he feels good is clear. He is with a person who sees. He tries to lie to her about his getting kicked out of school and she sees through his lie immediately. He tells her, "I'll probably be in Colorado on this ranch," and she responds, "Don't make me laugh. You can't ride a horse." She isn't easy, but she *sees*. And Holden quickly begins to pour out what is bothering him, as if she were a little doctor. When her mother returns with a headache, she prescribes a few aspirin. And she lies to protect Holden, taking the blame for his smoking. These upside-down situations, in which the younger person protects the older ones and gives them advice, are in line with the whole pattern of the book. And the failure of the older people to protect and guide the young not only results in botched initiations like Holden's, it also leads the younger people to try to be their own parents, forcing them to act older than they are by cursing, affecting a false cynicism, lying about their age, drinking, and wearing falsies.

The Zen masters say, "Cold eye, warm heart," and besides seeing, Phoebe is also compassionate. The *Dhammapada* says "Let us live happily

then, we who possess nothing," thereby defining Buddhists. Holden includes Phoebe within this definition when he says, "She says she likes to
spread out. That kills me. What's old Phoebe got to spread out? Nothing."

But Phoebe does have a small amount of money, her Christmas money.
Eight dollars and sixty-five cents. It isn't much, but it's all she has and she
gives it to Holden. And this *act* of compassion breaks through the shell of
Holden's fearful isolation: "Then, all of a sudden, I started to cry."

What we have here in miniature, in 1951, is the prescient portrait of an
attempt to create a counterculture. The children, unable to connect with the
prevailing culture, begin to separate from it and to attempt to care for each
other. As the Buddha said, "Brothers and sisters, you have no mother and
father to take care of you. If you will not take care of each other, who else, I
ask, will do so." We also have the reason for the failure of the counterculture.
Holden and Phoebe have charge accounts. The money they give away so
freely still comes from their parents and their parents' culture.

Culture is a form of hypnosis and it dies hard. Holden makes one last try
to connect. He leaves Phoebe and plays his ace-in-the-hole: Mr. Antolini.
Mr. Antolini is full of advice, much of it good, but he is blind to the existential reality of Holden's condition. Once again, when Holden needs a guide,
he gets words. They aren't enough. Phoebe remains the only person who has
seen where he is and who has *acted* truly in his behalf.

So he returns to Phoebe and, in opposition to Antolini's treatment of
himself, Holden *watches* the situation and doesn't chase her away, explaining, "I didn't put my hands on her shoulders again or anything because if I
had she *really* would have beat it on me. Kids are funny. You have to watch
what you're doing." And he accompanies her to the carrousel in Central Park
where he gives up his desire to be a catcher and his craving for an Edenic
world and accepts the world in which he finds himself at present: "The thing
with kids is, if they want to grab for the gold ring, you have to let them do it,
and not say anything. If they fall off, they fall off, but it's bad if you say
anything to them."

In a scene which parallels the one in his parents' apartment when
Phoebe gave him her money and his body responded by beginning to cry,
here Phoebe gives him a kiss and nature itself seems to respond as it begins
to rain. Holden, who has been obsessed with Allie's being out in the rain,
stays out in the rain himself, accepts the rain, thereby identifying himself
with Allie and Allie's fate, accepting his own death and vulnerability to
natural forces. He turns away from what he has lost, letting go of his obsessive vision of the dead Allie, and turns toward the happiness which comes in
seeing what he still has—a living Phoebe, with him, right there in the
present. When Holden says, "God, I wish you could've been there," he isn't
just talking to us. He is talking to God.

One suspects that this resolution is merely a temporary respite for
Holden; that he has a long way to go before he'll be able to extend his
acceptance to include the new phonies he meets. But he has survived to tell

his story, and in this respect he is more fortunate than Salinger's other "seer," Seymour Glass. After a similar "perfect" encounter with a young girl, Seymour has shot himself through the head.

For the epigraph of his *Nine Stories*, Salinger has chosen the famous Zen koan, "We know the sound of two hands clapping. But what is the sound of one hand clapping?" A koan has no "right" answer. A particular koan is given to a particular student to see from many sides and learn from, but ultimately it is something that, however fascinating, must be let go of. I would suggest that this first Glass story, "Perfect Day for Bananafish," is a kind of koan, one whose meaning the Glass children will be meditating on and wrestling with for years to come. Ultimately, the problems faced by Holden and the Glass children have no "answer" that *we* can hold on to. But we must be careful not to ask Salinger or anyone else to provide us with this illusory "answer." As Salinger certainly knows, tradition has it that when the Buddha was dying he was asked for one final piece of advice and he replied, "Work out your own salvation with diligence."[9]

Notes

1. See the articles in *Salinger*, Henry Anatole Grunwald, ed. (New York: Harper and Row, 1962), and *Studies in J. D. Salinger*, Marvin Laser and Norman Fruman, eds. (New York: The Odyssey Press, 1963), the articles and bibliography in *Salinger's "Catcher in the Rye,"—Glamour vs. Criticism*, ed. Harold P. Simonson and Philip E. Hager (Lexington, Mass.: D. C. Heath, 1963), and the bibliography in Warren French, *J. D. Salinger* (New Haven: College and University Press, 1963).

2. Several critics touch upon this briefly, some with condescension. There are exceptions however, one of which is Tom Davis, "J. D. Salinger: 'Some Crazy Cliff' Indeed," *Western Humanities Review* 14 (Winter 1960):97–99.

3. Christmas Humphreys, *Buddhism* (Harmondsworth, England: Penguin, 1951), 30.

4. The assumption which is often made, that Holden is relating his experiences to a therapist while he "rests" at a California sanitorium—like Charlie Parker "Relaxing at Camarillo"—is belied by the first sentence of Chapter 19: "In case you don't live in New York, the Wicker Bar is in this sort of swanky hotel, the Seton Hotel." It is hardly likely that Holden would address this to a California psychotherapist. Holden seems to be addressing *the reader* here, and this is interesting in that it hints at Salinger's own solution to the problem of growing up in America without accepting the limits and blindnesses of an institutional role—becoming a writer. A writer is supposedly paid to see, and "author" tends to be one of the least constricting roles in our society.

5. For example, in *Catcher*, when Sally tells Holden to be reasonable and not run away, he responds, "You give me a royal pain in the ass. . . ." In the original version of this, which *was* published in the *New Yorker* as "Slight Rebellion Off Madison," 22 (December 21, 1946), 86, Holden's reply is amended to the less accurate, "You give me a royal pain."

6. Brendan Gill, *Here at the New Yorker* (New York: Berkley Medallion, 1976), 34, 35, 70–71.

7. Chogyam Trungpa, *Cutting Through Spiritual Materialism* (Berkeley: Shambhala Publications, 1973), 88.

8. Ibid., 88–89.

9. Humphreys, *Buddhism*, 40.

Dostoyevsky's *Notes from Underground* and Salinger's *The Catcher in the Rye*

Lilian R. Furst*

"I love Kafka, Flaubert, Tolstoy, Chekhov, Dostoyevsky, Proust, O'Casey, Rilke, Lorca, Keats, Rimbaud, Burns, Emily Brontë, Jane Austen, Henry James, Blake, Coleridge" Salinger declared in the summer of 1951 at the time of the publication of *The Catcher in the Rye* in the most revealing of the few interviews he has ever granted.[1] That statement alone would form a tenuous basis for a rapprochement of Dostoyevsky and Salinger since Dostoyevsky is only one of seventeen authors named, and it would be hard indeed to plead Salinger's affinity with, say, Jane Austen or Burns, except perhaps in regard to their common mastery of the spoken word. In the case of Dostoyevsky, however, there is other and more cogent evidence of his particular importance to Salinger. Twice within his short stories there are direct references to Dostoyevsky. In "The Last Day of the Last Furlough" Sergeant Babe Gladwaller chooses to spend part of that momentous day "with Father Zossima and Alyosha Karamazov on the portico below the monastery."[2] It seems like a memory of Babe Gladwaller's reading when Sergeant x, in *For Esme—with Love and Squalor,* quotes from *The Brothers Karamazov*. In a copy of Goebbels's *Die Zeit ohne Beispiel* that he finds in the room of a Nazi woman whom he had arrested he sees the inscription in German "Dear God, life is hell."

> Then, with far more zeal than he had done anything in weeks, he picked up a pencil stub and wrote down under the inscription, in English, "Fathers and teachers, I ponder 'What is hell?' I maintain that it is the suffering of being unable to love." He started to write Dostoyevski's name under the inscription, but saw—with fright that ran through his whole body—that what he had written was almost entirely illegible. He shut the book.[3]

Evidently for both Sergeant x and Sergeant Babe Gladwaller Dostoyevsky was of special significance. And so too, it would seem, for Sergeant J. D. Salinger, as he then was, in the light of these reiterated references as well as in the light of his avowed predilection.

Yet hitherto, in spite of their notorious industry in other directions, Salinger critics have hardly ventured to explore this aspect of his work. Only a few desultory comments have linked Salinger and Dostoyevsky. In a phrase that is more striking than illuminating Henry A. Grunwald has issued a warning against turning "Salinger into a sort of Dostoyevsky of the nursery."[4] Arthur Heiserman and James E. Miller Jr in their attempt to classify different types of quest in literature referred to Alyosha Karamazov and the Idiot[5] alongside Salinger's protagonists. But perhaps the most revealing re-

*Reprinted by permission from *Canadian Review of Comparative Literature* 5, no. 1 (Winter 1978):72–85.

mark is one that centres on form rather than on content. *"Seymour: An Introduction,"* James E. Miller Jr has astutely pointed out, "may be said to have the form that conceals form, with all the seeming irrelevancies deliberately designed to create an ever greater illusion of reality—the real reality (a technique, incidentally, not uncommon, as witness Dostoyevski's *Notes from Underground* or Rilke's *The Notebook of Malte Laurids Brigge*)."[6] The same holds true of *The Catcher in the Rye,* as we shall see.

The alignment of *The Catcher in the Rye* alongside *Notes from Underground* may initially seem somewhat surprising. The distance between the two works in both period and location is certainly considerable. Almost a century stands between their respective dates of publication (1864 and 1951), just as almost half the globe divides Russia from the United States. Such external factors are, however, functionally unimportant in the comparative study of literature where works geographically and historically remote from each other are habitually juxtaposed for a reciprocal exegesis. What matters fundamentally is not the outer relationship (closeness or distance in time and space) of the elements in the comparison, but the existence of a truly organic inner link between them. I shall argue in this essay in favor of the presence of such a link between *Notes from Underground* and *The Catcher in the Rye* in regard to form as well as content. In narrative technique and in the characterization of the chief protagonist there is a substantial degree of similarity between the two works.

At first glance admittedly the central characters appear to be quite different. While Holden Caulfield is an adolescent of sixteen going on seventeen, the former government official of *Notes from Underground* is a seedy forty-year-old in Part One of his narrative, though in Part Two he casts back to his crucial formative experiences at the age of twenty-four. Clearly he is more set into the mould of his personality than Holden. The author too suggests the unlikelihood of any further change in him by his final abruptly dismissive phrase: "He couldn't resist and went on writing. But we are of the opinion that one might just as well stop here."[7] In Holden's case on the other hand there would seem to be a greater potential for change, in view of his youth. The problems that he describes may represent merely one phase of his development, a temporary condition which he may outgrow or of which he may be "cured" by the psychological treatment he is undergoing. He himself shows an extraordinary detachment as to his prospects, which hardly bodes well for his future: "A lot of people, especially this one psychoanalyst guy they have here, keeps asking me if I'm going to apply myself when I go back to school next September. It's such a stupid question, in my opinion. I mean how do you know what you're going to do till you *do* it? The answer is, you don't. I *think* I am, but how do I know? I swear it's a stupid question."[8] Holden Caulfield seems here to have written himself off with a tragicomic shrug of apparent indifference in much the same way as the Underground Man.

In fact the disparity in age between the protagonists of *The Catcher in the Rye* and *Notes from Underground,* like their geographical and temporal separation, soon proves of far lesser import than the similarity of the problem with which they are grappling. Both are beset by an acute sense of alienation which becomes manifest in a whole variety of ways ranging from the familiar to the recondite. What is so striking is the parallel pattern that emerges from an analysis of their alienation despite the differences in their outer situation.

To take the most obvious facet first: both have become outsiders by the beginning of their narratives. The Underground Man has, many years ago, we are given to understand, abandoned his position as a government official. Even while he was working, his departure from the norm puzzled and "worried me then: I was unlike everyone else, and everyone else was unlike me. 'I'm all alone while there are a lot of them' I mused" (p. 126). Holden Caulfield too is unlike everyone else and all alone as he is "kicked out" (p. 4) of Pencey Prep, the third successive school that he has left in disgrace. Both therefore stand at a remove from the social station expected of them (i.e. work and school), both moreover do so in a strange self-exclusion that is semi-voluntary. For Holden Caulfield certainly does not lack the intelligence to keep up with the academic requirements at his schools; what he does lack is the will—the will to conform. Like Holden, the Underground Man found neither satisfaction nor meaning in his job: "I entered the service to have something to eat (and for that only). And so, when a distant relative died, leaving me six thousand rubles, I immediately resigned" (p. 92). Each has consciously opted out because life within the accepted framework seemed pointless.

It is here that the personal withdrawal is linked to a protest against the social system as such. The alienation of Holden Caulfield and of the Underground Man stems from their radical rejection of a social order which both perceive as hypocritical, corrupt, and basically askew. Holden's favourite term of contempt is "phony." He sees himself surrounded by "phonies," notably in those prep schools: "You ought to go to a boys' school sometime. Try it sometime," he tells his date, Sally Hayes. "It's full of phonies, and all you do is study so that you can learn enough to be smart enough to be able to buy a goddam Cadillac some day, and you have to keep making believe you give a damn if the football team loses" (p. 131). His repeated failures at school are in effect a practical expression of his deep revulsion against the moral perversity of the code of values represented by the people he encounters there. He himself is fully aware of this:

> One of the biggest reasons I left Elkton Hills was because I was sur-
> rounded by phonies. That's all. They were coming in the goddam window.
> For instance, they had this headmaster, Mr. Haas, that was the phoniest
> bastard I ever met in my life. Ten times worse than old Thurmer. On
> Sundays, for instance, old Haas went around shaking hands with every-
> body's parents when they drove up to school. He'd be charming as hell and
> all. Except if some boy had little old funny-looking parents. You should've
> seen the way he did with my roommate's parents. I mean if a boy's mother

was sort of fat or corny-looking or something, and if somebody's father was one of those guys that wear those suits with very big shoulders and corny black-and-white shoes, then old Haas would just shake hands with them and give them a phony smile and then he'd go talk, for maybe a half an *hour*, with somebody else's parents. I can't stand that stuff. It drives me crazy. It makes me so depressed I go crazy. I hated that goddam Elkton Hills. (pp. 13–14; italics are Salinger's).

Naive, vituperatively *ad hominem* though this outburst is, its indictment of the entire system is perfectly clear. Throughout his wanderings in New York after his flight from school Holden is repeatedly distressed and instantly alienated by further discoveries of "phoniness" wherever he looks. He dreams of running away to Vermont with Sally Hayes for the simple, good life (p. 132), or—grotesquely yet significantly—of a total retreat from human communion into the pose of a deaf mute (p. 198). Only with small children, as yet uncontaminated by spuriousness, does he feel happily at ease.

The Underground Man is a vehement as Holden Caulfield in his condemnation of the dominant social mores of his time. He abhors the self-complacent vanity of Apollon (p. 187) and is incensed by his former schoolfellows' callous worship of success (p. 146) measured primarily in terms of money and status equivalent to the Cadillac that is the symbol of achievement in *The Catcher in the Rye*. But this critique of the established order goes far beyond mere irritation at snobbish vacuity. He questions the very foundations of the currently accepted *Weltanschauung* based on a "scale of advantages on statistical averages and scientific formulas thought up by economists" (p. 106). Such simplistic schematization is anathema to him for he has become convinced that the genuine values of life—whatever they may be—do not "fit into any scale or chart" (p. 106). The "laws of logic" are not "in accordance with human laws" (p. 116). While he agrees "that man is a creative animal" he is acutely conscious also of man's fascination with "chaos and disorder" (p. 116). So "man is a comical animal" (p. 117) "doomed to strive consciously toward a goal, engaged in full-time engineering, as it were, busy building himself roads that lead somewhere—*never mind where*" (p. 116; italics are Dostoyevsky's). The implication is obviously that these roads may in fact lead nowhere, that life is a paradoxical labyrinth rather than a structured system. The paradigm of that purported system is the crystal palace, built to scales, charts, scientific formulas, and allegedly "indestructible" (p. 118). It is as the incarnation of misguided rationalism that it arouses the Underground Man's ironic scorn (pp. 118–19). Though the primary butt of his invective was, as is well-known, Chernyshevsky's blueprint for utopia, *What Is To Be Done?*, the significance of his alternative reaches out far beyond this immediate target. In opposition to the restricted orderliness and artificiality of the reigning organization he defiantly proclaims his own ethos:

So one's own free, unrestrained choice, one's own whim, be it the wildest, one's own fancy, sometimes worked up into a frenzy—that is the most advantageous advantage that cannot be fitted into any table or scale and that causes every system and every theory to crumble into dust on contact. And where did these sages pick up the notion that man must have something that they feel is a normal and virtuous set of wishes; what makes them think that man's will must be reasonable and in accordance with his own interests? All man actually needs is *independent* will, at all costs and whatever the consequences. (p. 110; italics are Dostoyevsky's)

This is a rampant individualism to which Holden Caulfield would willingly subscribe. Although the Underground Man's mode of expression is more abstract and more sophisticated than Holden's direct emotionalism, the tenor of their protest is identical: against a wrong-minded, "phony" order, and for personal freedom and sincerity.

Yet in spite of their deep alienation and their outspoken social criticism, neither the Underground Man nor Holden Caulfield has totally cut adrift from the community around him. Their stance is highly contradictory, torn as they are "between the imperative of involvement and revulsion at involvement."[9] That phrase, written about *The Catcher in the Rye*, is equally apposite to *Notes from Underground*. In both works the tension between communication and non-communication forms one of the major themes.

This is so amply evident in *The Catcher in the Rye* that it hardly requires much elaboration. The novel consists structurally of a series of encounters, a string of conversations or attempted conversations. Holden first discusses his situation with Old Spencer. Discounting his whimsical exchanges on the train with Mrs. Morrow, his next dialogue is with Faith Cavendish who gives him short shrift. He fares hardly better with "the three witches" (p. 70) from Seattle, when he tries "to get them in a little intelligent conversation" (p. 73). Nor is Old Horwitz, the taxi driver, very receptive to his musings on the fate of the ducks in winter so that "I stopped having a conversation with him" (p. 82). The prostitute is even less amenable to his suggestion that she "might care to chat for a while" (p. 95). Things go better at last with the nuns at Grand Central Station: "We sort of struck up a conversation" (p. 109), a tentative human relationship with an element of respect and liking for all its grotesque overtones. With Sally Hayes, however, Holden is back to the old obtuse non-comprehension that is the repeated response to his utterances. A "typical Caulfield conversation," old Luce calls such interchanges without specifying what he means by that phrase, though we may surmise that he is referring to Holden's unconventional, often startling views, his flights of enthusiasm alternating with a deadpan laconicism, his disconcertingly honest probing, as well as his failure by and large to find a sympathetic hearing. Only with his sister Phoebe is there real tenderness and openness. The encounter with Mr. Antolini towards the end of the novel, a parallel to that with the old schoolmaster, Spencer, at the beginning, seems to come no closer to any mutual understanding. If his interlocutors do not grasp his meaning, neither does he theirs. This "incommunicability" at the core of *The Catcher in the Rye*, to use

Charles H. Kegel's term, is illustrated also in the fifteen attempted telephone calls, of which a mere four are completed, "and those with unfortunate results."[10] The very fragmentation of Holden's speech, his frequent recourse to such apologetic approximations as "sort of," "and all," "I mean," show his ineptitude in communication. Nevertheless he does go on trying to talk to people.

So does the Underground Man. His sorties from the retreat of his mousehole represent attempts to re-establish some social contacts. Admittedly his efforts are feeble and not without an admixture of that masochistic perversity that makes him court failure throughout his life. He senses, for instance, that Simonov, a former schoolmate of his, might not welcome his company. Even so, after an interval of almost a year, he visits him because, one Thursday, he suddenly felt "unable to stand my loneliness" (p. 139). It is thus a need for companionship that draws him out into a world that he hates, fears, despises, but also somehow longs for. At Simonov's he runs into several other former schoolfellows who are planning a party, to which he invites himself by offering to contribute seven rubles like the others. Again he takes the initiative despite their evident lack of encouragement, indeed their thinly veiled rudeness. Not surprisingly in the event he is very obviously the intruder on the party. "I didn't sing. All I did was try not to look at any of them. I affected a nonchalant air, waiting impatiently for them to address me first. But, alas, they didn't. Ah, how I longed to make up with them at that moment" (p. 156). Insults, derision, and humiliations do not deter him from following them to the house of pleasure, where he meets Liza. This is his one true opportunity for a human relationship. In place of the scorn he had reaped from his schoolfellows, from Liza he gets at least a modicum of genuine response—sufficient to induce her to call on him a few days later. But the potential evanesces because he has no warmth, no capacity for true feeling. "Why you're . . . just like a book," (p. 174) Liza had already commented on their first conversation. "That was the only way I knew how to speak—'like a book' " (p. 179), he concedes to himself, adding bitterly that often it "was so contrived and such *bad literature*" (p. 200). For, as he realizes, "I wasn't prompted by my heart but by my stupid head" (p. 200) with the result that "I couldn't love her" (p. 199). Though he longs for human relationships as an escape from the lonely misery of his mousehole, he lacks the emotional generosity to sustain them.

The Underground Man is thus as torn between the poles of involvement and non-involvement, communication and non-communication, as Holden Caulfield. In their reactions to this dilemma they differ to some extent. Here more than elsewhere the divergence between them not only in age but also in background is of importance. The Underground Man, brought up, as he tells us, "without a family . . . without feelings" (p. 170), is full of latent hatred against himself and others. His animosity culminates in his conscious cruelty to Liza, but it is manifest throughout in the venom and malice of his vitriolic outbursts. Holden Caulfield on the other hand often sounds an elegiac note in his tragic-comic jumble of emotions. He is by no means without feeling. His tenderness for little children, above all for his sister, is surely connected with his love for Allie, the younger brother who died. It is arguable that in the long run this softer streak in Holden will save him from the fate of the Underground Man, that his confinement in the asylum is only temporary. But there is no cogent evidence in the text to support these hypotheses; they are no more than hopes. And, on the contrary, under unfavourable circumstances of repeated failure and rejection Holden could eventually become as cynical as the Underground Man. Be that as it may, when we see them, both are caught in the paradox of their strong innate urge to involvement and communication, yet with a society that repels and alienates them.

The ambivalence of this situation stems in large measure from the ambiguity of their attitudes towards themselves. For self-alienation, with all its peculiar perplexities, is an essential facet of the total alienation syndrome that besets both the Underground Man and Holden Caulfield. Neither really knows himself; each is in a sense engaged in a quest for his own identity, a scrutiny of himself that of necessity entails investigation of one's relationship to the outer world. But that in turn must inevitably remain in a disturbing state of flux if the pivotal persona is himself still floating in doubt. So the Underground Man laments that everything "disintegrates chemically" (p. 103), while Holden Caulfield constantly has to confess "I don't know."

Accordingly, the search for certainty forms one of the cardinal themes of both *Notes from Underground* and *The Catcher in the Rye*. It surfaces in the recurrent preoccupation with the attainment of truth, and particularly in the dichotomy between "truth" and "lies," which are envisaged not as fixities but as stages on a sliding scale that is itself, moreover, given to perturbing shifts. "I was lying just now" (p. 91), the Underground Man abruptly announces after his self-introduction; "I'm lying like a son of a bitch" (p. 120) he later reiterates. Are these startling assurances of deception to be taken at face value, or are they to be read as an integral part of his characteristic equivocation? There is no way of knowing for sure. Perhaps the Underground Man is playing a game (p. 179) with the reader, as with Liza and indeed with himself, in order to block out "the outline of the truth" because it is "a sordid, obscene truth!" (p. 200). Holden Caulfield too proclaims himself "the most terrific liar you ever saw in your life" (p. 16), a contention borne out in part by his frequent lies about his age—usually in an attempt to obtain alcohol!— and his invention of alleged physical infirmities: a "tiny little tumor on the brain" (p. 58), a recent operation on his "clavichord" (p. 96), and a bad leg (p. 157). These comical tall tales do not seriously undermine his credibility since they serve a specific purpose in extricating him in each instance from an awkward situation. Curiously, however, it is the offer that punctuates his narrative in such profusion, namely "if you really want to know the truth," that causes a vague uneasiness in the reader. It may be simply a case of protesting too much. But as in *Notes from Underground* so also in *The Catcher in the Rye* objective criteria are hard, if not impossible, to establish because the first-person narrative in both stories strictly limits the perspective. Consequently certainty eludes protagonist and reader alike from beginning to end.

The equivocalness of the narrators is further heightened by their common tendency to escape into fantasies. Both patently delight in roles and masks that transport them from grim reality into mirages which render the self more attractive or at least more acceptable to the dreamer. The Underground Man, fully aware that he lacks "the guts to face *reality*" (p. 148; italics are Dostoyevsky's), envisages himself repeatedly as "a hero" (pp. 136, 196), though he knows that he is only playing "a part to save appearances" (p. 194). His principal wish-image is highly revealing in the light of his incapacity either to give or gracefully to receive love:

> But how much love—ah, how much—I experienced in my dreams, when I escaped to "the sublime and the beautiful." Perhaps it was an imaginary love and maybe it was never directed toward another human being, but it was such an overflowing love that there was no need to direct it—that would've been an unnecessary luxury. Everything always ended safely in a leisurely, rapturous sliding into the domain of art, that is, into the beautiful lives of heroes stolen from the authors of novels and poems and adapted to the demands of the moment, whatever they might be. I, for instance, triumphed over everyone, and they, of course, are strewn in the dust, acknowledging my superiority; I'm all-forgiving; I'm a great poet and court chamberlain; I fall in love; I inherit millions and donate them to human causes and take advantage of this opportunity to publicly confess my backslidings and disgrace which, of course, is no ordinary disgrace but contains much that is "sublime and beautiful" in it, something in the Manfred style. Everyone is weeping and kissing me (they could hardly be so thick-skinned as not to); then I leave, hungry and barefoot, to preach new ideas and rout the reactionaries at Austerlitz. Then, a triumphal march is played, an amnesty is declared, the Pope agrees to leave Rome for Brazil, there's a ball for all of Italy at the Villa Borghese on the shores of Lake Como, which lake, for this occasion, is moved to the vicinity of Rome. (pp. 137–138).

Holden's fantasies, the product of his vivid imagination, are even more varied and characteristically mingle the comic with the pathetic. "I'm an exhibitionist," (p. 29) he declares right at the outset before his schoolfellows as he clowns the role of governor's son who wants to be a tap-dancer instead of going to Oxford. Later, taking his cue from "the goddam movies" (p. 104), he repeatedly enjoys the fiction of himself as the guy in the shootout with a bullet in his guts, "a wounded sonuvabitch" (p. 150), dripping blood all over the place until bandaged by his girl. In spite of their apparent adolescent crudeness these dreams express the same craving for attention and affection as the more literary and sophisticated ones of the Underground Man. In both instances, moreover, the alienated outsider in search of himself and of his place is at one and the same time nurturing a more glamorous self-image and pleading for loving attention from others.

This tendency to take refuge in fantasies is but another manifestation of that misrelationship to the inner self as well as to the outer world that equally typifies the Underground Man and Holden Caulfield. A fundamental disruption of the normal responses is at the root of their aberrant and paradoxical behaviour patterns; hence that constant, puzzling ambivalence, that alternation between an alienated rejection of society and latent longing for involvement, between withdrawal and attempted communication, between self-alienation and the quest for identity.

These outward symptoms of disorientation point to a pair of personalities of striking similarity in spite of the differences in their ages, situation and surroundings. For both the Underground Man and Holden Caulfield are, as the former perceives himself, men of "heightened consciousness" (p. 96), or more precisely, of heightened self-consciousness. They are in the grip of an exaggerated self-awareness, and what is more, they tend to see themselves in a dualistic vision that verges on the schizophrenic. It is this that leads to that characteristic set of tensions which dominate their existence and which repeat in their attitudes towards themselves that same ambiguity that bedevils their relationships to others. The Underground Man and Holden Caulfield alike oscillate between solipsism and irony, hope and indifference, the grotesque humour of detachment and the bitterness of lost illusions. The underlying conflict is between the self-esteem that devolves from their proud sense of their own pre-eminence over the average man in intellect and sensitivity on the one hand, and on the other the self-denigration that drives them masochistically to magnify their physical defects and almost gloat over their failures. "I'm a highly developed, civilized man! . . . I'm a well-educated, sophisticated man" (p. 183), the Underground Man assures himself at one moment; yet, he had previously introduced himself with these words: "I'm a sick man . . . a mean man. There's nothing attractive about me" (p. 90). Holden too seems veritably to enjoy belittling himself as he confesses: "I have no wind, if you want to know the truth. I'm quite a heavy smoker" (p. 5) and tells us: "I'd only been in about two fights in my life, and I lost *both* of them. I'm not too tough" (pp. 45–46; italics are Salinger's). But his contempt for the "morons" (p. 84), the "jerks" (p. 85), and of course those notorious "phonies" he sees all around him surely suggests a certain confidence in his own superiority. Holden's combination of individualistic self-assertion with pervasive self-doubt runs largely parallel to that of the Underground Man. Dostoyevsky and Salinger have drawn masterly portraits of figures tortured by a series of uncertainties that threaten to shatter their egos and their whole universe in a maelstrom of bewilderment.

These extensive similarities between the protagonists of *Notes from Underground* and *The Catcher in the Rye* are backed by the far-reaching likeness of literary presentation and narrative technique. While there are arguably a fair number of other characters in the literature of the past hundred years who share certain features with the Underground Man, in no case is the parallelism of form as well as of content as consistent as in this instance.

Both works are cast in the form of a first-person narration that draws on the tradition of the confessional novel. The cues that the Underground Man gives us—half ironically—to his tale: "a chatterbox" (p. 104), "my babble" (p. 92), "I'll talk about myself" (p. 93)—these are just as applicable to Holden Caulfield. The dominant manner in each case is that of colloquial expression, ranging in tone from half-whispered intimacy to shrill hysteria. As Carl F. Strauch has pointed out, *The Catcher in the Rye* "moves effortlessly on the colloquial surface and at the same time uncovers, with hypnotic compulsion, a psychological drama of unrelenting terror and final beauty."[11] That comment holds equally true of *Notes from Underground*.

What is more, the author is in both stories absent from the actual narrative, apart from Dostoyevsky's opening footnote and his brief final comment which really act as an extraneous framework. Salinger, like Dostoyevsky, remains completely hidden behind the persona who carries the story along single-handed and independently as it were. No voices other than his are heard, except in reportage, and that through his perception. This undoubtedly fosters a strong sense of intimacy between the persona and the reader. Indeed the chief protagonist in both *Notes from Underground* and *The Catcher in the Rye* faces the reader repeatedly throughout the story, speaking to him directly. Holden begins his tale with these words: "If you really want to hear about it, the first thing you'll probably want to know is where I was born, and what my lousy childhood was like, and how my parents were occupied and all before they had me, and all that David Copperfield kind of crap, but I don't feel like going into it, if you want to know the truth" (p. 1). That reiterated "you" in the leitmotif phrase "if you want to know the truth" and also elsewhere punctuates Holden's account of himself. The Underground Man reinforces his use of "you" by the formal address "ladies and gentlemen": "Now I want to tell you, ladies and gentlemen, whether you like it or not" (p. 93). Like Holden's "you," that "ladies and gentlemen" recurs frequently. Obviously this technique leads in both works to an acute involvement of the reader through the establishment of a straight link between the persona and the reader as speaker and listener. There is a very real feeling of immediacy and of contact which must surely be linked with the protagonist's urge to communicate.

On the other hand, for all its vividness this manner of narration does raise certain problems, and they are identical for *Notes from Underground* and *The Catcher in the Rye*. Firstly, the question as to the putative audience remains unanswered. Who are the "ladies and gentlemen" that the Underground Man is apostrophizing? Who is, or are, Holden's "you"? There is little internal evidence in either case. The Underground Man at least tells us that he is writing because "I'm bored with constantly doing nothing" and also because "I feel that if I write it down, I'll get rid of it" (p. 123). The same subconscious desire for catharsis may be impelling Holden, or he may even have been encouraged into this self-outpouring in the course of the psychological treatment he is undergoing. But that is mere conjecture. His confession is more plainly oral not only in its phraseology but also in the emphasis on such words as "hear" (p. 1) and "tell" (p. 213), whereas the Underground Man's is purportedly a written document. The audience, however, is in both cases unidentified, and hence a part of the puzzle; and that perplexity is intensified by a corollary of the first-person mode of *Notes from Underground* and *The Catcher in the Rye*, namely the limitation of the viewpoint that inevitably follows from narration by a single person without authorial intervention. Lacking outside correctives and objective criteria either from the author or from other characters, the reader must perforce adopt the persona's own perspective. This in turn, of course, serves to heighten the reader's involvement, in this instance to draw him in both works ever more deeply into the protagonists' gnawing uncertainties.

In structure too similarities exist between *Notes from Underground* and *The Catcher in the Rye*. Both use the device of a retrospective framework in which the protagonist looks back on his life up to that point. The Underground Man begins his review at the age of forty and goes back later to incidents that had occurred when he was twenty-four. Holden's time-span, in keeping with his youth, is much shorter, but he also is retracing bygone events. Both, moreover, undertake their excursions into the past from a kind of retreat: the Underground Man's metaphoric mousehole, and the institution "out here" (p. 1) where Holden is presumably hospitalized. From the temporary safety of these refuges each recalls his successive encounters with the reality of the outer world: the Underground Man's confrontation with the burly policeman, his reunion with his schoolfellows, and his meetings with Liza correspond to the whole series of assorted people that Holden runs into at his schools and during his adventures in New York. Different though they are in actual content, their respective encounters are in the last analysis analogous in their abrasive effect. The outline of both works is circular insofar as the protagonists arrive back at the end in time and space to their starting-points. But the inner movement is surely that of a downward spiral: the Underground Man has sunk irredeemably into his mousehole while Holden Caulfield appears to have regressed into that childhood which he idealizes. The ending of both works is completely open, hanging abruptly, indeed startlingly in the air. In *Notes from Underground*, as in *The Catcher in the Rye*, the final impression is of "a combination of nightmare and burlesque where horror and comedy mix in inexplicable fashion."[12]

What conclusions may be drawn then from this multifaceted, farreaching parallelism between *Notes from Underground* and *The Catcher in the Rye*? It is obviously tempting to posit an influence of Dostoyevsky on Salinger, particularly in the light of Salinger's avowed predilection for the

Russian novelist and his repeated references to his writings. Influence is a slippery concept, difficult to prove with any conclusiveness. What is more, Salinger's well-known personal reticence deprives us largely of the letters and diaries which often provide helpful clues and documentation in the case of other writers. Yet given the massive internal evidence it seems not imprudent at least to conjecture the likelihood of such an influence.

But the affinity between *Notes from Underground* and *The Catcher in the Rye* also leads to more important conclusions and in an area less tentative than that of influence: namely in regard to Salinger's place in literary tradition. Critics have tended to site him predominantly within the American framework. The most common comparison by far has been to Huck Finn[13] as one of the Good Bad Boys of American literature, to use Leslie Fiedler's[14] telling phrase. Other filiations have been drawn too, to Gatsby[15] or Redburn[16] for instance, and Holden naturally always features prominently in studies of the adolescent in American fiction.[17] Some attempts have indeed been made to investigate aspects of Salinger's European background, notably his interest in Kierkegaard[18] and his links to the Romantics.[19] In France he has been presented as "un Alain Fournier américain[20] because Fournier's *Le Grand Meaulnes* is a novel of adolescence like *The Catcher in the Rye*. "Holden is observed to keep company not only with Huck Finn but also with Ulysses, Aeneas, Ishmael, Alyosha, Stephen Dedalus and Hans Castorp," Arthur Heiserman and James E. Miller Jr point out[21]—somewhat tantalizingly since the thesis is not fully explored. Indeed it is Miller himself who has insisted most emphatically that "in spite of this wide scattering of interest and attractions, Salinger is not a Zen Buddhist, or a philosopher or a poet. He is an American novelist writing in the American tradition."[22] The confession of Buddy Glass in "Zooey" that *The Great Gatsby* was his Tom Sawyer when he was twelve reveals, according to Miller, Salinger's "fundamental affinity for the narrative tradition."[23] This is incontestable. But Salinger's own confession: "I love Kafka, Flaubert, Tolstoy, Chekhov, Dostoyevsky, Proust, O'Casey, Rilke, Lorca, Keats, Rimbaud, Burns, Emily Brontë, Jane Austen, Henry James, Blake, Coleridge" shows a writer whose literary horizons extended beyond *The Great Gatsby* and *Huckleberry Finn*. Without denial of Salinger's deep American roots, his place in a wider literary lineage should be acknowledged. The comparison of *Notes from Underground* to *The Catcher in the Rye* shows that Holden Caulfield represents not merely the American adolescent but also a prime example of the anti-hero as he has evolved on both sides of the Atlantic from Dostoyevsky's seminal portrait. As a classic of modern sensibility *The Catcher in the Rye* must be read alongside such works as *Notes from Underground,* Sartre's *Nausea,* Camus' *The Stranger,* Svevo's *Confessions of Zeno*. Salinger's imagination, while drawing on the native American context, rises to universal humanistic truths in his brilliant evocation of a characteristic figure. It is this that accounts for his extraordinary impact and his lasting appeal.

Notes

1. William Maxwell, "J. D. Salinger," *Book of the Month Club News,* Midsummer 1951, 5–6.

2. *Saturday Evening Post,* ccxvii (15 July 1944), 26.

3. J. D. Salinger, *Nine Stories* (Boston: Little, Brown and Company 1948, 5th ed. 1953), 160.

4. *Salinger: A Critical and Personal Portrait,* introduced and edited by Henry Anatole Grunwald (New York: Harper and Brothers 1962), xiii.

5. Arthur Heiserman and James E. Miller, Jr, "Some Crazy Cliff," in Grunwald, ed., *Salinger: A Critical and Personal Portrait,* 196–97.

6. James E. Miller, Jr, *J. D. Salinger,* Pamphlets on American Writers, No. 51 (Minneapolis: University of Minnesota Press 1965), 42.

7. F. Dostoyevsky, *Notes from Underground* (New York: Signet 1961), 203. All subsequent references are to this edition.

8. J. D. Salinger, *The Catcher in the Rye* (New York: Bantam Books 1964), 213. All subsequent references are to this edition.

9. Miller, *J. D. Salinger,* 13.

10. Charles H. Kegel, "Incommunicability in Salinger's *Catcher in the Rye,*" *Western Humanities Review* xi (Spring 1957):188–90. ·

11. Carl F. Strauch, "Kings in the Back Row: Meaning through Structure. A Reading of Salinger's *The Catcher in the Rye,*" *Wisconsin Studies in Contemporary Literature* 2 (Winter 1961):5.

12. Miller, *J. D. Salinger,* 9.

13. See Charles Kaplan, "Holden and Huck: The Odyssey of Youth," *College English* xviii (November 1956):76–80; Arvin Wells, "Huck Finn and Holden Caulfield: The Situation of the Hero," *Ohio University Review* ii (1960):31–42; Levi A. Olan, "The Voice of the Lonesome: Alienation from Huck Finn to Holden Caulfield," *Southwest Review* 48 (Spring 1963):143–50; Edgar Branch, "Mark Twain and J. D. Salinger: A Study in Literary Continuity," *American Quarterly* ix (Summer 1957):144–58.

14. "The Eye of Innocence," in *No! In Thunder: Essays on Myth and Literature* (Boston: Beacon Press 1966), 251–91.

15. Mario L. D'Avanzo, "Gatsby and Holden Caulfield," *Fitzgerald Newsletter* 38 (1966):4–6.

16. Robert L. Gale, "Redburn and Holden—Half Brothers One Century Removed," *Forum* iii (Winter 1963):32–36.

17. See Frederic I. Carpenter, "The Adolescent in American Fiction, "*English Journal* 46 (September 1957):313–19; Ihab Hassan, "The Idea of Adolescence in American Fiction," *College English* xxi (December 1959):140–46; W. Tasker Witham, *The Adolescent in the American Novel* 1920–1950 (New York: Ungar 1964).

18. William Wiegand, "Salinger and Kierkegaard," *Minnesota Review* v (1965):137–56.

19. Carl F. Strauch, "The Romantic Background," *Wisconsin Studies in Contemporary Literature* iv (Winter 1963):31–40. See also Strauch, "Kings in the Back Row." 29.

20. Robert Kanters, "Le mystère Salinger—un Alain Fournier américain?" *Figaro Littéraire* xvi (11 November 1961):2.

21. "Some Crazy Cliff," 196–97.

22. Miller, *J. D. Salinger,* 44.

23. Ibid.

The Eighties

"Flunking Everything Else Except English Anyway": Holden Caulfield, Author

A. Robert Lee*

I

Few self-accounts, whether autobiography or novel, display quite so take-it-or-leave-it a bravura as *The Catcher in the Rye*. From Holden's opening disparagement of his early childhood as "all that David Copperfield kind of crap"[1] through to his last, peremptory "That's all I'm going to tell about" (213), J. D. Salinger has his narrator sound the very model of skepticism about whether indeed we do "really want to hear about it"(1). Yet given the book's spectacular popularity since its publication in 1951, clearly only the most obdurate of readers have proved resistant to "hearing about it" and to Holden's different virtuoso flights of scorn or dismay or selective approval. For however we have come to think of Holden Caulfield—as one of the classic isolates of modern times, as the savvy but endlessly vulnerable witness to crassness and bad faith, as postwar American adolescence itself even—still another figure presses out deep from within. At virtually every turn Holden gives notice of his endemic and unremitting will to a style of his own, to writerliness, to showing himself, knowingly or not, as nothing less than the very author in waiting of *The Catcher in the Rye*.[2]

In part, this identity inevitably has something to do with Salinger's originality in conceiving as his narrator the seventeen-year-old who hovers dauntingly at "six foot two and a half," whose hair has turned its celebrated and premature gray on the right side of his head, and who writes of Pencey Prep and his all but Lost Weekend in New York from a West Coast psychiatric ward in the wake of his nervous breakdown. But, to use a key term from the novel, the "composition" Holden puts before us offers anything but the merely offbeat recollections of a put-upon and precocious teenager. This "composition" is the latest in a career that time upon time has seen Holden "composing" other themes, other selves, and other identities. Each, however, has hitherto been of the moment, a spontaneous if never other than highly particular creation conjured into being to meet a required part, or to

---

*This essay was written specifically for this volume and is published here for the first time by permission of the author.

185

win or deflect attention, or to fill up the spaces of his loneliness, or, often enough, simply to make good on his sheer creative overdrive. Whatever the occasion, these made-up identities are for the most part extraordinarily affecting and often wickedly funny, a kind of inspired ventriloquy on Holden's part, and at the same time a set of rehearsals, a repertoire, to be called back into play by the eventual author-autobiographer.

In this connection, too, it does not surprise that nearly all the values and people Holden most prizes possess a humanity marked out by style, by an authenticity not only of the heart and senses, but also of art. Indeed, these people are like Holden himself—the Holden who can be wilful, contrary, often impossible, yet in a manner insistently of his own making and at odds with whatever he deems dull or conformist. Each "phony," "and all," and "crumby" is reiterated as often as needed to install his own special signature as writer or monologist, a signature that would be impossible to think anybody's but his alone.

The Catcher in the Rye, as often enough noted, does indeed thereby yield a portrait of the artist, but one that, more than other comparable narratives, operates within its own rules. For a start it makes Holden's every authorial tic and habit as much an equal part of the narration as all the supposedly actual events being unfolded. One thinks not only of his use of "phony" and the like but also of the jibes at his own expense: "I'm the most terrific liar you ever saw. It's awful" (16). He automatically assumes that he has the reader's ear: "She's all right. You'd like her" (67), he says, notably, of Phoebe, and in almost the same phrase, of Allie. And in his off-hand way he makes frequent and meanly well-targeted judgments: "Pencey was full of crooks" (4) or "That guy Morrow was about as sensitive as a goddam toilet seat" (55). Holden seems ostensibly to tell the one story that bears on "this madman stuff" only to reveal himself, fugitively, in the margins as it were, also telling another, that in which he writes himself imaginatively into being. Both stories are told by the ultimately larger self of Holden as author, the Holden who can editorialize gloriously, fire off opinions, imitate screen celebrities or his fellow preppies, and even, as it appears, brazenly flaunt his resentment at all the unlooked-to burdens of writing autobiography. But if any one overwhelming clue can be said to indicate his essential vocation, it has to do with his strongest and most symptomatic fear, that of disappearing, be it in crossing Route 202 to see "old Spencer" or Manhattan's Fifth Avenue as he talks to the dead Allie. At the very moment of making that fear articulate, transposing it from life into narrative, it is actually being dissolved and conquered.

Analogies have been much proposed for *Catcher*, particularly Dickens's *David Copperfield*, Twain's *Huckleberry Finn* and Joyce's *Portrait*.[3] Each novel, as a life, rite of passage, or journey, offers clear similarities in terms of type and situation. But Salinger's novel belongs still more precisely to the company of those fictional autobiographies which show their protagonists discovering their truest being in the call to authorship and in the "self" they see themselves shaping as the words precariously, yet inevitably, take sequence upon the page. Memorable as each is, Copperfield, Huck, and Dedalus tell their stories from positions of retrospect (even Copperfield with his teasing "Whether I shall turn out to be the hero of my own life . . . these pages must show"). Holden is altogether more extemporaneous, his account more volatile and rapid, or so Salinger persuades us to feel. Holden's essential styling of things—his every transition, dissolve, off-the-cuff commentary, and wisecrack—could hardly fail to implicate us from first to last in the heady business whereby as for the first time and in the mirror of his own "composition" he sees himself whole and clear. In no way can he ever disappear again, even if he does "sort of *miss* everybody I told about" (214).

To some extent an experiment like Gertrude Stein's *The Autobiography of Alice B. Toklas*, Stein's invention of herself through the persona of her Paris companion and memoirist, bears a resemblance to *The Catcher in the Rye*.[4] Yet Stein's modus operandi never wholly frees itself of the suspicion of staginess or formula. Two other American first-person classics, Ralph Ellison's *Invisible Man* and *The Autobiography of Malcolm X*, however, unlikely as they might at first perhaps be thought, come closer.[5] Both, in an overall sense, obviously tell a more consequential story than Holden's, that of the black American odyssey as against the turnings of white bourgeois New York and its satellite outposts in New Jersey and Pennsylvania. But they do so in a manner and with an improvisational daring greatly of a kind. Each depicts a self, in the face of historic denial, discovering itself as it goes along, a self that, as it moves from blank to identity, marginality to center, does so as though exhilarated and even astonished at its own formulation in writing.

No one would suggest Holden to be some exact fellow traveller of Ellison's black underground "spook" or the oratorical whirlwind who becomes Malcolm X. But the story he offers in *The Catcher in the Rye* delineates a figure who equally, and equally powerfully, draws the energies of self-discovery into his own narrative. This drama of self-inscription, if we can call it so, in and of itself thereby becomes the parallel of all Holden's other doings at Pencey and in Manhattan. Not the least part of it, furthermore, is that whatever Holden's protestations to the contrary, his is a finished autobiography, a story posing as a fragment as may be but wholly complete in its beginning, middle, and end. It would do less than justice to who he is, or at least to who and what he has become, and to Salinger behind him, to think otherwise.

Holden, then, takes to the writer's life out of several kinds of necessity. Despite the contrariness of his signing-off—"I'm sorry I told so many people about it" (214)—his "composition" represents nothing less than a path to psychological health. He has, so to speak, remade himself. Moreover, the privileges of authorship, in addition, have given him his occasion as for the first time to elicit pattern, order, from what throughout his troubled young life has overwhelmingly been flux and loss. Writing, too, has ended his isolation by giving him access to a community that will read and respond to him. Above all, he has achieved his apotheosis, that of an artist writing from the fullest wellsprings of his being and so "unprostituted"—the jokily risqué term he uses about his Hollywood screenwriter brother, D.B.[6] He has made one world into another, one prior self or circle of selves into another. Acknowledging the "author" in Holden thus becomes a critical necessity if we are to get anything like the full measure both of the tale he tells and of himself as teller.

II

From start to finish Holden qualifies as a "performing self," in Richard Poirier's phrase, "authorly" to a degree in how he sets up terms and conditions for his story.[7] Nowhere does he do so more cannily than in the opening of *Catcher*, where his mock brusqueness in saying what he *won't* do—"I'm not going to tell you my whole goddam autobiography or anything" (1)—and his equally mock doubts about any readerly good faith we might be assumed to possess—"If you really want to hear about it" (1)—combine not so much to put us off as positively to commandeer our attention. "Where I was born," "my lousy childhood," and "anything pretty personal" about his absentee parents are to be withheld, though not, apparently, the happenings behind this "madman stuff" and his being "pretty run down." How better, it could be asked, to stir curiosity or lay down guidelines as to what is to follow? His every denial and insistence betrays the "authorly" Holden, a narrator about his duties with all the animus of one who can do nothing to stop the story-telling impulses within him.

D.B., the brother who "used to be just a regular writer" but who on Holden's estimate is "being a prostitute" in Hollywood, similarly helps to position Holden as author. D.B. has forfeited this "regularity" for the movies, for the Jaguar, and, we learn at the end, for "this English babe" who comes with him to visit Holden. But he once wrote "this terrific book of short stories" (1) whose title piece, "The Secret Goldfish," Holden has taken to because it delineates a body of private feeling strongly held—that of "this little kid that wouldn't let anybody look at his goldfish because he'd bought it with his own money" (2). As narcissistic as the "kid" may be, he has made of the goldfish a thing of his own, an icon or even artwork. D.B. also points ahead to remind us that Holden comes from a family of writers, not only himself as the Hollywood "prostitute" but Allie who wrote poems on his baseball mitt and Phoebe who composes her "Old Hazle Weatherfield" detective stories. All the Caulfield siblings, in fact, are compulsive fabulists, imaginers.

A number of selective highlightings, first from the Pencey scenes and then those in New York, will help unravel the rest of the pattern. The interview with "old Spencer" has rightly been admired as a comic tour de force, from the "ratty old bathrobe" worn by Spencer and the Vicks Nose Drops through to "the terrific lecture" about "Life is a game" and the daz-zlingly awful nose-picking. As a parody of dead rhetoric and set-piece counseling, the episode works to perfection. But in addition to the comedy, it also serves to open up another round of perspectives on Holden as author. Whatever else Holden has failed, he has "passed English," or, as he says in his note added to the exam answer written for Spencer on the Egyptians, "It is all right if you flunk me though as I am flunking everything else except English anyway" (12). A boy who can wonder where the ducks in Central Park go in the winter or see through received cliché—"Game, my ass. Some game"—might well "pass English." In the first instance he is about the search for some kind of benign spiritual principle and in the second about the quest for a language untrammeled by inertness or mere hand-me-down phrasing. He seeks an "English" that expresses him, his situation, not that of "phony" institutionalism.

Little wonder, then, that Holden also shows himself as a virtually insatiable reader. If he can "act out" his contrition for Spencer, assuage the history teacher's need to play the stentorian, he has books in plenty to draw upon. Not only has he been exposed to "all that Beowulf and Lord Randal My Son stuff," but to a literary syllabus as extensive as it is various. *David Copperfield* he brings into play in his first sentence. Clad in his red hunting hat while rooming with Stradlater he reads Isak Dinesen's *Out of Africa*—"I wouldn't mind calling this Isak Dinesen up" (18). Within a trice he adds to the roster Ring Lardner, Somerset Maugham, and Thomas Hardy—"I like that Eustacia Vye" (19). On the train to New York he delivers himself of his thoughts on "those dumb stories in a magazine," obviously no fan of tabloid popular culture. The sex book he has read at Whooton, "lousy" as he thinks it with its view "that a woman's body is like a violin and all" (93), comes pressingly to mind as he waits for his prostitute at the Edmont Hotel. He delivers himself about his views of the Bible—"I like Jesus and all . . . " but the Disciples " . . . were about as much use to Him as a hole in the head" (99). With the nuns Thomas Hardy again comes into his mind: "you can't help wondering what a nun thinks about when she reads about old Eustacia" (110), and *Romeo and Juliet* and *Julius Caesar*. He remembers a discussion of *Oliver Twist* in a film seen with Allie, a novel obviously familiar to him. His meeting with Carl Luce has him invoking Rupert Brooke and Emily Dickinson as, incongruously, a pair of "war" poets, and in turn Hemingway's *A Farewell to Arms* ("a phony book") and Fitzgerald's *The Great Gatsby* ("Old Gatsby, Old sport. That killed me," as his eye for style causes him to remark). For good measure, given the novel's title, he throws in Robert Burns, the writer from whose ditty he has conjured up his fantasy of himself being a catcher in the rye. All of these allusions he contrives to wear lightly, passing stopovers as might be in the passage of his own gathering imagination. In fact, they speak to him from within the community he will shortly join, that of authors and artists who have also and at every risk made over the world on their own creative terms.

A key moment in the process manifests itself in "the big favor" solicited of him by Stradlater, namely a "composition" that can be about anything "just as long as it's descriptive as hell." More than a little revealingly, Stradlater instructs him not "to stick all the commas and stuff in the right place." In part, this advice is to cover up Holden's authorship, but as Holden himself realizes only too well, it typifies how neither Stradlater nor much of the rest of Pencey has the faintest appreciation of what "English" means. The date with Jane Gallagher, who for Holden is the girl individualized by keeping her kings at the back at checkers but for Stradlater is no more than another sexual scalp, stirs in him the memory of Allie, live or dead his one dependable imaginative ally alongside Phoebe. Unsurprisingly he chooses to write about the mitt, the poems in green ink "written all over the fingers and the pocket and everywhere" (38). Holden writes, too, in his "pajamas and bathrobe and my old hunting hat" (37), as if he were kitted out for the job like some updated Victorian man of letters. Everything he pours into his "description," predictably, is wasted on Stradlater, flush as the athlete is with sexual conquest and with concerns a universe away from whatever Holden may have encoded about Allie's death—his traumatized night in the garage and the near self-mutilation of putting his writing hand through "all the goddam windows." "I sort of like writing" (39), he confides, almost shyly, as though dimly aware that we have caught him about his most intimate and essential business. Authorship, whether he likes it or not, pursues him.

Literal authorship, however, is one thing. Holden also revels in "authoring" himself in other ways—as the student penitent for Spencer, as the scholar-prince and then canasta player for an uncomprehending Ackley, as the "goddam Governor's son" who prefers tap-dancing to government and then the no-holds-barred pugilist for Stradlater, and as "Rudolf Schmidt," the name he borrows from the dorm janitor to discuss Ernest Morrow with Mrs. Morrow when they part share a compartment on the train journey between Trenton and Newark.

This latter impersonation again helps establish Holden's drive to invention, his relentless and high-speed fabulation. His version of Morrow as "adaptable," "one of the most popular boys at Pencey," "original," and "shy and modest," not only plays to a fond mother's heart, but also shows Holden on a great improvisational jag, one invention barely put forward before another follows suit. His lie, too, about leaving Pencey early on account of needing an operation for a "tumor on the brain" smacks of a matching versatility of invention, alibi-ing as an art—as in turn does his excuse for not visiting the Morrows in Gloucester, Massachusetts, on account of a promise to see his grandmother in South America. He even starts reading the timetable to stop inventing or lying—"Once I get started, I can go on for hours if I feel like it. No kidding. *Hours*" (58). He cannot resist, too, trying on the role of "club car" roué, a man who knows his cocktails and has the chutzpah to ask Mrs. Morrow to join him. This is wit, style, ventriloquy, all to symptomatic good purpose. More "authoring," literary and otherwise, however, lies directly ahead as Holden alights at Penn Station and embarks upon his weekend tryst with New York.

III

"I'm traveling incognito" (60) Holden tells the cab driver who takes him to the Edmont Hotel and who has to field the questions about where the ducks go when the Central Park lagoon freezes over in winter.[8] Much as Holden gamely affects to apologize for the B-movie implications of the phrase—"When I'm with somebody that's corny, I always act corny too" (60)—it again emphasizes his uninhibited and ever-burgeoning passion for invention. Doubtless the "loneliness" that tears at him always, together with his fear of disappearance and sheer nervous fidget, propel him more and more into these impersonations. Yet whatever their cause, they mark him as a peerless and habitual fantasist. And are they not, also, instance for instance, the contrivances of a self that as yet is truly "incognito," that of Holden as yet again the author? Each con-man routine and verbal sleight-of-hand virtually bespeaks authorship, an inventing self as well as invented selves. Is there not, even, a hint of the embryonic author in Holden's subsequent query to the cabbie about which band might be playing at the Taft or New Yorker and about joining him for a cocktail—"On me. I'm loaded"? For this is Holden as returnee Manhattanite, back for a good time, a glad-hander, knowing in the city's ways and willing to say the hell with expense. That he is also under-age to be drinking merely points up the masquerade. But who Holden truly is, here as elsewhere, indeed does lie "incognito."

Yet even *his* role-playing risks eclipse when he witnesses the routines being acted out at the Edmont. One window reveals the transvestite recomposing himself as a woman and then "looking at himself in the mirror." Holden does not fail to note that he is "all alone too." A second window exposes him to the "hysterics" of the couple squirting water in each other's mouth, with a possible third party just out of view. "Lousy with perverts" is Holden's reaction, much as he concedes that this "kind of junk is sort of fascinating to watch" (62). But mere voyeur Holden is not. He wants, indeed needs, to be in the action, the absolute participant observer. To watch this urban cabaret relegates him to consumer not maker. Within a trice he is back to his own efforts, the would-be suitor to Faith Cavendish, burlesque stripper and Eddie Birdsell's "ex." Much as he fails to talk her round—"I should've at least made it for cocktails or something" (66)—it leads him on to the person he knows to have a truly creative center, none other than his fellow writer and infant sister, Phoebe.

"Old Phoebe," Holden muses, "You never saw a little kid so pretty and smart in your whole life" (67). But no sooner has he made an inventory of all that makes Phoebe an object of passionate fondness for him—the straight A's, the short red hair stuck behind her ears, her "roller-skate skinny" body, her ability to speak Robert Donat's lines in *The 39 Steps* and stick up a finger with part of the middle joint missing—than he also adds a detail as close as could be to his own impulses. Alongside D.B. and Allie, "a wizard," Phoebe is a writer. Holden gives the information as follows:

Something else she does, she writes books all the time. Only, she doesn't finish them. They're all about this kid named Hazel Weatherfield—only old Phoebe spells it "Hazle." Old Hazle Weatherfield is a girl detective. She's supposed to be an orphan, but her old man keeps showing up. Her old man's always a "tall attractive gentleman about 20 years of age." That kills me. Old Phoebe. I swear to God you'd like her. . . . She's ten now, and not such a tiny kid any more, but she still kills everybody—everybody with any sense, anyway. (68)

Holden recognizes in Phoebe not just a sister but a figure whose creative quirks amount to perfection. She cannot finish her stories. She gets her proportion all out of joint (the twenty-year-old father). The name "Hazle" is either an inspired abbreviation or a misspelling, not to say an ironic echo of Faith Cavendish's "Cawffle" for Caulfield. And she makes her detective an orphan with a parent. The logic here, of course, is that of a child's imagination, the logic of splendid fantasy more than hard fact or chronology. Holden recognizes in it the same authenticity as in D.B.'s "The Secret Goldfish" or Allie's poems in green ink, a Caulfield energy of imagination by which he, too, is wholly possessed. Nonetheless, his own "compositions" have still supposedly to take written shape, even though they are in fact being realized even as he describes Phoebe and everybody else.

His other "authoring" goes on, however, as unstoppable and fertile as ever. He tells "the three witches," Laverne, Old Marty, and Bernice, with whom he drinks and dances in the Lavender Room, that his name is "Jim Steele," that if not Peter Lorre then he has seen Gary Cooper "on the other side of the floor," and that "sometime" he will look them up in Seattle. But when, once more rebuffed, he again calls to mind Jane Gallagher, it is as another literary ally, another fellow traveler in the ways of the imagination. She may well lose eight golf balls, be "muckle-mouthed," keep her kings at the back, be "terrific to hold hands with," and get hold of his neck at the movies, but she also has a redeeming affinity with "composition" and the written word. Once again Holden alights on aspects of someone else that mirror his own writerly alter ego: "She was always reading, and she read very good books. She read a lot of poetry and all. She was the only one, outside my family, that I ever showed Allie's baseball mitt to, with all the poems written on it. She'd never met Allie or anything, because that was her first summer in Maine—but I told her quite a lot about him. She was interested in that kind of stuff" (77).

Jane belongs in a companionship of style, and Holden responds accordingly. Like D.B. before the "prostitution," Allie, and Phoebe, she recognizes and opens to the things of the imagination. Others, too, will embody this for Holden: the black piano-player at Ernie's—"He's so good he's almost corny" (80); the two nuns (one of whom teaches English); "this colored girl singer" Estelle Fletcher whose record of "Little Shirley Beans" he buys for Phoebe; Miss Aigletinger who took them to the Museum of Natural History; "Old James Castle" who was bold enough to tell Phil Stabile he was conceited, would not take it back, and was driven to jumping to his death at Elkton Hills school (a boy, significantly, with "wrists about as big as pencils"); and Richard Kinsella, who during "Oral Comp" always gets derided for his "digressions" (of which Holden observes, "I mean it's dirty to keep yelling 'Digression!' at him when he's all nice and excited" [184]). Like all of these, Jane appeals to his need for alliances against the dead hand of *un*creativity and "phoniness."

His trip to Ernie's, and the Catch-22 conversation en route in which the cab driver Horwitz tries to find the logic of his question about the Central Park ducks—he unwittingly comes close with "If you was a fish, Mother Nature'd take care of *you*, wouldn't she?" (83)—again call into play Holden's skills as literary impresario. "Old Ernie" he quickly marks down as a "phony," a mere exhibitionist rather than legitimate piano-player who is given to "putting all these dumb, show-offy ripples in the high notes, and a lot of other very tricky stuff that gives me a pain in the ass" (84). He hates the clapping, the instant "mad" applause. He even, teasingly, thinks of himself as "a piano player or actor or something" to the effect that "I wouldn't want them to *clap* for me. . . . I'd play in the goddam closet" (84). As if from instinct, Holden knows that good music—good writing or good art in general—needs a right, intimate, true response and not mere noise. But such surrounds him, especially when he runs into Lillian Simmons who asks him about D.B. who "went with" her for a while ("In *Holl*ywood!," she gushes, "How *mar*velous! What's he *do*ing?") Lillian he can just about tolerate, but not the "Navy guy" with her. In a last stab of invention he designates Lillian's date "Commander Blop or something."

His experiences with "the elevator guy" Maurice and Sunny might be thought a case of art outrunning life. Holden's virginity, his sex-book good manners as he thinks them when the girl gets to the room—" 'How do you do,' I said. Suave as hell, boy" (93)—his parlor-game attempt at conversation in the guise once again of "Jim Steele," and his excuse of having had an operation on his "clavichord" hovers between pathos and French farce. When Maurice returns for the rest of the money, he knows just whom he is dealing with, however—"Want your parents to know you spent the night with a whore?" (102). "A dirty moron" Holden can call him, but he can't "act" his way out of getting slugged. What he can, and does, do, typically, is re-invent himself as a movie hero, a bleeding, tough-guy private eye. He acts out in life what he will go on to act out in his writing:

> About half way to the bathroom, I sort of started pretending I had a bullet in my guts. Old Maurice had plugged me. Now I was on the way to the bathroom to get a good shot of bourbon or something to steady my nerves and help me *really* get into action. I pictured myself coming out of the goddam bathroom, dressed and all, with my automatic in my pocket, and staggering around a little bit. Then I'd walk downstairs, instead of using the elevator. I'd hold on to the bannister and all, with this blood trickling out at the side of my mouth a little at a time. What I'd do, I'd walk down a few floors—holding on to my guts, blood leaking out all over the place—

and then I'd ring the elevator bell. As soon as old Maurice opened the doors, he'd see me with the automatic in my hand and he'd start screaming at me, in this very high-pitched, yellow-belly voice, to leave him alone. But I'd plug him anyway. Six shots right through his fat hairy belly. Then I'd throw my automatic down the elevator shaft—after I'd wiped off all the finger prints and all. Then I'd crawl back to my room and call up Jane and have her come over and bandage up my guts. I pictured her holding a cigarette for me to smoke while I was bleeding and all.

The goddam movies. They can ruin you. I'm not kidding. (103–4)

As pastiche Chandler or Hammett or Erle Stanley Gardner this would take some beating—film noir from an expert. But Holden is also "scripting" his own part, an author-director writing himself into his own text. The way ahead has once more been richly indicated.

It is so, again, in Holden's meeting with the two nuns as he awaits his link-up with "old Sally Hayes." His mind drifts effortlessly across his life present and past, Sally with her flurry of words like "grand" and "swell" and the recollection of Dick Slagle who pretended Holden's suitcases were his own at Elkton Hills (despite Holden's gesture of putting them out of sight under his bed). Slagle has taken refuge in the word "bourgeois," an intended put-down of Holden, but as tired a form of language as Sally's schoolgirlisms. In encountering the nuns, however, Holden again finds himself recharged by their evident genuineness, the one next to him especially with her "pretty nice smile," her warm thank-you for his contribution, her being an English teacher, and perhaps most of all her enthusiasm on hearing "English was my best subject." As much as he cannot resist two "digressions" of his own—on what a nun thinks about the "sexy stuff" in *The Return of the Native* or *Romeo and Juliet* and on his father's one-time Catholicism—he sees in his listeners a decency that all but humbles him. He also upbraids himself for having even to think of money in connection with them and for blowing smoke in their faces. "They were very polite and nice about it" (113), he reports, as unfeignedly charitable about his rudeness as about not bringing "Catholicism" into the conversation. Holden writes of them as of Jane or Phoebe or the hat-check girl, women for whom one of his wilder "performances" would be wholly wrong.

Holden's next foray into a literary arena, or at least something close, arises out of his date with Sally Hayes ("the queen of the phonies") to see Alfred Lunt and Lynn Fontanne in the Broadway benefit show *I Know My Love*. No sooner does he buy the tickets than his mind takes off on "acting," the whole nature of "performance" itself. He thinks as a veteran of bad or unauthentic "performances"—those of Spencer, Stradlater, Ackley, Buddy Singer from The Lavender Room, Old Ernie, and "white girl" singers of "Little Shirley Beans," among others. The latter, who lack Estelle Fletcher's "very Dixieland and whorehouse" feel, can also be compared with the "terrific whistler" Harris Macklin and the "swell" kid he hears "singing and

humming" Burns's lines "If a body catch a body coming through the rye."
The child's obvious unphoniness "made me feel better." Such are his touch-
stones for his dislike of "acting" ("I hate actors") and his irreverent slaps at
Laurence Olivier's Hamlet ("too much like a goddam general, instead of a
sad, screwed-up type guy"). Holden's own touch of Hamletism also, no
doubt, plays into these judgments, his own need to find out how exactly to
"act" for himself. The other touchstone he turns to lies in the exhibits in the
museum, "unactorly" "glass case" art that does not "move," is "warm," and is
free of all the "dog crap and globs of spit and cigar butts from old men" that
deface Central Park. "Performance" as seen in the museum—whether the
Indians rubbing sticks or the squaw with the bosom weaving a blanket or the
Eskimo fishing or the deer and birds—all strike Holden as things that
"should stay the way they are," natural and "forever" as indeed exhibits in a
natural history museum might be expected to be.

His verdict on the Lunts has exactly to do with their unnaturalness.
They overact, or rather "didn't act like people and they didn't act like actors";
theirs are performances whose off-centeredness he rightly thinks "hard to
explain." Matchingly hard for him to explain to Sally is his own "performance": his hatred of the "dopey movie actor" type he sees at the intermis-
sion and of Sally's Ivy League "buddyroo," of conversation about the Lunts as
"angels," and even of Sally herself. On he persists, however, through a
risingly frenetic inventory of New York, taxicabs, Madison Avenue buses,
"phony guys that call the Lunts angels," and his own experience of boys' prep
schools. But when he tries to "author" an alternative, Sally and himself as
pastoral homesteaders in Massachusetts and Vermont, he finds himself
speaking—writing—in the air, cut down by the unimaginativeness of Sally's
response. Their exchange ends in disaster ("I swear to God I'm a madman"),
but as he takes stock he also thinks that at the time of "writing" his script for
Sally and himself "I *meant* it." Holden, once again, has become most alive
and most himself in making an imagined world.

Nor does Holden find his direction from the two would-be mentors he
seeks out, Carl Luce and Mr. Antolini. Both betray him, or at least fail to
grasp the essential human and creative purposes behind Holden's turning to
them. Luce he has been drawn to because he knows or pretends to know the
mysteries of sexual life. He also has "the largest vocabulary of any boy at
Whooton" and "intelligence." But Holden suspects him from the outset of
being a "flit" himself, a mere "hot shot" parader of his own ego and vanity. As
to Antolini, his betrayal cuts even deeper. Yet another English teacher, he
has won Holden's admiration for trying to talk D.B. out of going to Hollywood and for being his "best" teacher. But he also has his not-so-hidden
purposes in calling Holden "you little ace composition writer," in welcoming
him to the Antolini apartment for the night, and for playing the sage with his
citations from William Stekel on "brilliant and *creative* men." The game is
revealed in his homosexual pass, that "something perverty" which for

Holden is not only sexual but also a sell-out of all the "literary" advice he has had served up to him by Antolini. Only in Holden's *own* will to make good on the artist in himself, Salinger invites us to recognize, can lie his salvation.

The pointers in that direction are given in abundance. Holden tellingly casts his mind back to D.B.'s conversation with Allie about war writing and about Rupert Brooke, Emily Dickinson, Ring Lardner, and *The Great Gatsby*. Out in the park again looking for ducks he starts "picturing millions of jerks coming to my funeral and all" (154). At his parents' apartment he goes into his "bad leg" routine for the new elevator boy. In Phoebe's room he experiences a near shock of recognition on reading the entries in her notebooks, one stylist's salute to another. She, in her turn, understands the broken record pieces he is carrying for her; the significance of his "I passed English"; the parable of James Castle and Holden's related "catcher" fantasy; and what they are about in dancing the "four numbers" to her radio. The "something very spooky"—his fear of disappearing on Fifth Avenue—serves to indicate the ebb before the storm, his lowest point. Not only must he erase all the "fuck you"s from the walls in order to make a world worthy of each Allie and Phoebe, he also must write himself back into being and into a health to the other side of the "dizziness" and "crazy stuff" that threatens his very existence. "Mad," euphoric, certainly, though he appears in company with Phoebe on the carrousel (that modern incarnation of a medieval art pageant) as it plays "Smoke Gets in Your Eyes" in the rain, Holden can in fact combat his fear of disappearance only through art, authorship. What greater apprenticeship, after all, could anyone have served?

"That's all I'm going to tell about" (213) may indeed be his parting shot, but it is an "all" of whose variety, drama, or fascination, we have been left in no doubt. Only an author of his vintage, too, could offer the advice "Don't ever tell anybody anything. If you do, you start missing everybody" (214). For in making text of life, "goddam autobiography" of experience, he has separated the observer in himself from the participant. He has become, willingly or not, the person he himself has most sought out from the beginning and who in return has most sought him out, none other than Holden Caulfield, author.

Notes

1. J. D. Salinger, *The Catcher in the Rye* (New York: Bantam Books, 1964), 1. Subsequent page references in the text are to this edition.

2. Oddly, this aspect of Holden has not been much covered in the criticism. But I do want to acknowledge, however, the following: Eugene McNamara, "Holden as Novelist," *English Journal* 54 (March 1965): 166–70, and Warren French, "The Artist as a Very Nervous Young Man" (chapter 8), in *J. D. Salinger* (New York: Twayne, 1963), 102–29. Other criticism with a bearing includes Maxwell Geismar, "The Wise Child and the *New Yorker* School of Fiction," in *American Moderns: From Rebellion to Conformity* (New York: Hill and Wang, 1958), 195–205; Donald P. Costello, "The Language of *The Catcher in the Rye*," *American Speech* 34 (October

1959): 173–81; and Carl F. Strauch, "Kings in the Back Row: Meaning Through Structure—A Reading of Salinger's *The Catcher in the Rye*," *Wisconsin Studies in Contemporary Literature* 2 (Winter 1961): 5–30.

3. See, notably, Charles Kaplan, "Holden and Huck: The Odysseys of Youth," *College English* 18 (November 1956): 76–80; Edgar Branch, "Mark Twain and J. D. Salinger," *English Journal* 44 (September 1957): 313–19; and Malcolm M. Marsden, ed., *If You Really Want to Know: A "Catcher" Casebook* (Chicago: Scott-Foresman, 1963).

4. Fiction that poses as autobiography has, to be sure, a long ancestry, but other American examples would include James Weldon Johnson, *The Autobiography of an Ex-Colored Man* (1912), John A. Williams, *The Man Who Cried I Am* (1967), and Ernest Gaines, *The Autobiography of Miss Jane Pittman* (1971). Given the arguments I make about an analogy between Afro-American fiction and *The Catcher in the Rye*, it will be no surprise that all these were written in fact by black authors.

5. This is not to propose that *Catcher, Invisible Man,* or *The Autobiography of Malcolm X* fall into a single shared category of "fictions of fact." But they do have in common the "dual" aspects of a story being told and the storyteller's recognition of how that "story" helps establish his or her identity.

6. Holden and the movies offers a complementary perspective to Holden as author. Time and again he cites film, film actors, different scenes. In this respect, see Bernard S. Oldsey, "The Movies in the Rye," *College English* 23, no. 3 (1961): 209–15.

7. Richard Poirier, *The Performing Self: Compositions and Decompositions in the Languages of Contemporary Life* (New York: Oxford University Press, 1971).

8. Compare, once again, Ralph Ellison's narrator in *Invisible Man,* typically the following: "I'm shaking off the old skin and I'll leave it here in the hole. I'm coming out, no less invisible without it, but coming out nevertheless. . . . ." Both the prologue and epilogue underscore the narrator's "incognito" status.

The Disappearing Subject: A Lacanian Reading of *The Catcher in the Rye*

James M. Mellard*

I felt like I was sort of disappearing. —Holden Caulfield

Considering the fact that J. D. Salinger's *The Catcher in the Rye* is one of the most popular novels in the history of publishing, as well as once one of the most frequently written about, one may find it surprising that so few psychological, especially psychoanalytic, interpretations have appeared on it. True, not every novel is destined to elicit psychoanalytic readings, but some would seem so destined. Those novels that have an adolescent hero in the midst of an identity crisis, one who is critically without a strong parent of either sex during the crisis, who is suffering from the recent death of a younger brother, who worries about the innocence of a still younger sister, who carries the weight of all the innocent children in the world around on his

*This essay was written specifically for this volume and is published here for the first time by permission of the author.

frail shoulders, and who apparently recounts his story from a psychoanalytic ward somewhere out West—such novels would seem to beg for a psychoanalytic reading. Of course, Salinger's *Catcher* may be the only such novel, but still one finds it hard to imagine that just one sustained effort at a psychoanalytic reading has appeared. Verging near this method is Maxwell Geismar's essay "The Wise Child and the *New Yorker* School of Fiction."[1] Apparently, thinking of Freud's notion of the Oedipal problem, Geismar does mention that though Salinger dedicates the novel to his mother, the mother of the novel's hero—Holden Caulfield—is never more than "shadowy" or "a voice through the wall," and that Holden's father is notable for his "absence";[2] Geismar even speaks of the novel's "neurotic anarchism" and refers to its hero as a "paranoid savior" with an "obsessive affection for little children".[3] But if some of his more illuminating observations come from a Freudian paradigm, Geismar never really initiates a psychoanalytic method. Thus it is left to James Bryan to offer the only sustained psychoanalytic interpretation of any rigor.[4] And that is a shame, for Bryan's reading of *Catcher*, in that it turns Holden Caulfield into a virtually psychotic, would-be violator of little sister Phoebe, is almost a parody of all the worst offenses of Freudianism. Thus Bryan's reading, whatever other virtues it may have, has the virtue of making one appreciate the revision of Freudian theory found in the work of Jacques Lacan.

When Bryan says that "the urgency of Holden's compulsions . . . comes of a frantic need to save his sister from himself,"[5] it is the tactlessness of the tactic, the literalization of Freud's basic metaphor, to which one must object from a Lacanian perspective. A Freudian may be compelled to say it this way, but a Lacanian need only say that Holden has located Phoebe in the place of the mother—that is, in the place of the "other"—and that he must resolve the Imaginary identification with this and additional types of others—"doubles" such as Ackley and Stradlater—in order to incorporate the role made for him in the Symbolic, a role that is located in the place of the father, but that is not specifically *his* father's place. Holden's situation, as Bryan seems to suggest throughout, indeed is Oedipal, but it is not the reductively Oedipal situation the Freudians often literalize as patricide and incest. Rather, it is the Oedipal passage as described by Lacan—the necessity of the protagonist's submitting, Symbolically, to Castration and subjection to the Law, to the rule of the Other named by Lacan in the Name-of-the-Father. The Lacanian reading is that Holden Caulfield must find his place in the structure of relationships established on the pattern of the family and reified in the structures of language. Bryan is quite correct in suggesting that Holden must become an adult, but he is wrong to argue that Holden's becoming an adult is signified by his giving up Phoebe as a sexual object. Perhaps in some impossible "literal" sense that is true (since, as one shall see, Phoebe is indeed a displacement of the mother), but for Lacan becoming an adult means accepting one's place in the structure where the mature subject stands. In Holden's case as the male subject, that place is the place of the father, a place taken not *from*, but *in* the Name-of-the-Father authorized in the Other, in Language, in Culture itself. In Lacanian terms, this development means only that Holden must become a fully realized *subject*. He must complete the passage through the Oedipal phase encompassed in Lacan's concept of the register of the Imaginary in order to incorporate the register of the Symbolic that underlies both Oedipus and Imaginary. It is mature *subjectivity*, not sexuality as such, that is Holden's problem. And that subjectivity is interpretable in terms of those concepts Lacan identifies as *aphanisis*, *l'objet petit a*, and the *moi* within the conflict of Desire and the Law—concepts that will become clearer as one proceeds.

I

Holden Caulfield, whatever other problems he may have, has a problem Lacan considers under the term *aphanisis*, the "fading" or "disappearance" of the subject. The term *aphanisis* is "Freudian," but it was not originally Freud's. It was introduced by Ernest Jones to identify the subject's fear of the disappearance of sexual desire, a fear Jones regarded as more profound than the fear of castration.[6] Lacan reinterprets the term to refer to the "movement of disappearance" that the subject perceives at the advent of mature or Oedipal-stage subjectivity.[7] The concept that Lacan explains here is rather complex. In general, it refers to the "birth" of the subject-as-subject beyond the passage through the mirror phase, in a beyond reached through the Oedipus passage and defined as both the Unconscious and the Other. Lacan teaches that the inchoate subject merely perceives an identificatory "other" in the mirror-phase realization; in the subject's relation to the other—ordinarily the mother—there is a sense (false, Lacan contends) of reciprocity between the subject and the other (the object in which the subject identifies itself as a totality). What the mirror-phase doubling lacks is the mediation of Law, the awareness of meaning's being determined elsewhere, in an unconscious Other located in the place of the Father. The mature subject is realized only upon recognition of the Law of the Father, the recognition that one's meaning, if not one's being, comes from the Other. In the movement through the Oedipal passage, therefore, two related functions take place. Lacan calls them "alienation" and "separation." "What we find once again here," Lacan writes, "is the constitution of the subject in the field of the Other" (*FFC*, 208). But this constitution occurs in the process of an alienation of the subject resulting from the separation of "self" from identificatory "other." The constitution thus entails the "disappearance" of the subject from his or her full consciousness of self. "If he is apprehended at his birth in the field of the Other," says Lacan, "the characteristic of the subject of the unconscious is that of" falling "beneath the signifier that develops its networks, its chains and its history," and thus of being "at an indeterminate place" (*FFC*, 208).

Lacan, by his use of schemas forces one to imagine the birth of subjectivity as the division of an originary object-sphere (one may imagine the process, perhaps, as partial mitosis or cell division) into two spheres that overlap rather than separate entirely. Lacan is interested in the area of the overlapping of the two spheres. He suggests that the left-hand sphere represents the realm of the subject's "being," the right-hand sphere the realm of the Other's "meaning." The area of overlap Lacan calls "non-meaning" (see *FFC*, 211). The "disappearance of the subject" occurs in this area of overlap, the realm of non-meaning, the domain that physicists would call "indeterminacy," the place where at any one time one may "know" only one of two possible functions. In physics, the two are location and velocity; in the psyche, the two are "being" and "meaning." Lacan says,

> Let us illustrate this with what we are dealing with here, namely, the being of the subject, that which is there beneath the meaning. If we choose being, the subject disappears, it eludes us, it falls into non-meaning. If we choose meaning, the meaning survives only deprived of that part of non-meaning that is, strictly speaking, that which constitutes in the realization of the subject, the unconscious. In other words, it is of the nature of this meaning, as it emerges in the field of the Other, to be in a large part of its field, eclipsed by the disappearance of being, induced by the very function of the signifier. (*FFC*, 211)

Thus, says Lacan, interpretation in analysis need not search for meaning so much as for the objects in which the subject hereafter localizes meaning in relation to a "self" that is no longer available to consciousness.[8] In Lacan's words, "Interpretation is directed not so much at the meaning as towards reducing the non-meaning of the signifiers, so that we may rediscover the determinants of the subject's entire behaviour" (*FFC*, 212).

In *The Catcher in the Rye* the problem of the fading of the subject is suggested very early. It is linked to Holden's typical adolescent problems with Oedipal and Narcissistic others. It begins, symptomatically, at a moment of passage, departure, separation. It results from the youth's decision to leave Pencey Prep, and surfaces because of the need to make contact with a figure of the father. Leaving Thomsen Hill, from which he had looked down on the school and the students and faculty collected at the football game, Holden tells us that as he crosses the highway and heads for "old Spencer's house. . . . I felt like I was sort of disappearing. It was that kind of a crazy afternoon, terrifically cold, and no sun out or anything, and you felt like you were disappearing every time you crossed a road".[9] Though at this point in the novel Holden does not perceive the problem *as* a problem, as something to fear or worry about, he persists in concerns connected to his disappearance as a subject, a disappearance necessitated by his becoming—if he ever shall—a mature, post-Oedipal subject. If Salinger's text raises the problem in a rather overt way, it continues the problem in the more subtle way of symbolism, the way of metonymical displacement. In effect, through the symbols the text veils the problem behind associative objects that Lacan calls the signifiers of the unconscious, the Other.

Holden's thoughts about his disappearance are related to those frequent ones about death and suicide. The former—disappearance—overdetermines the meanings of the latter—death thoughts. Thus aphanisis or disappearance is implicit in the apparently ironic comment at the novel's outset that "the game with Saxon Hall was supposed to be a very big deal around Pencey. It was the last game of the year, and you were supposed to commit suicide or something if old Pencey didn't win" (2). It is equally implicit in Holden's comment—a bit later in the scene with Spencer—that concerns about the future, coming too late, "made me sound dead or something" (14). It is even more evident in Holden's remark, later, as he tries to sleep in Ackley's roommate's bed after the fight with Stradlater: "I got up and went over and looked out the window. I felt so lonesome, all of a sudden. I almost wished I was dead" (48). In addition to images of suicide, Holden's thoughts are subjected to related images of what Lacan, in the essay on the mirror phase, calls the "fragmented body" (*Ecrits*, 4). Thus, after the encounter with the pimp/elevator operator Maurice in the hotel in New York, Holden imagines himself, wounded, with a "bullet in my guts." Though in his fantasy he "plugs" old Maurice, the other-directed violence does not cancel out his own problem: "What I really felt like, though, was committing suicide. I felt like jumping out the window" (104). This fantasy, by metaphorical transfer, reminds Holden of a moment when, by identification, he had seen himself dead, a suicide, his body as it were in pieces visible to anyone. "I probably would've done it, too, if I'd been sure somebody'd cover me up as soon as I landed. I didn't want a bunch of stupid rubbernecks looking at me when I was all gory" (104). What is happening here is that Holden is projecting his fear of disappearance and bodily fragmentation into the identificatory image of his acquaintance James Castle, the boy from a former school (Elkton Hills) who indeed had committed suicide and had done so by leaping from a window. He says, "there was old James Castle laying right on the stone steps and all. He was dead, and his teeth, and blood, were all over the place, and nobody would even go near him." Since "he had on this turtleneck sweater I'd lent him" (170), it might have been Holden himself.

Most of these references to death, dismemberment, or disappearance are direct enough not to be called symbolic in a literary sense. But there is a symbolic texture to the novel that exhibits the same themes as they relate to the Lacanian Symbolic. James Castle is such an obvious identificatory image for Holden that it hardly warrants mentioning. The unconscious ordinarily operates much more subtly, for the simple reason that it *means* to hide its significations from consciousness. So here one must look for the less obvious symbolizations. The novel's subtlest, most important symbolization occurs in a metonymical displacement of the aphanitic concern. It lies in Holden's thoughts about the ducks in Central Park. The ducks are what Lacan would call an algebraic sign whose meaning lies elsewhere than in themselves. They appear first, not coincidentally, in Holden's thoughts in the scene with Spencer. "I was sort of thinking of something else while I shot the bull. I live in New York, and I was thinking about the lagoon in Central Park, down near Central Park South. I was wondering if it would be frozen over when I got home, and if it was, where did the ducks go. I was wondering where the ducks went when the lagoon got all icy and frozen over. I wondered if some guy came in a truck and took them away to a zoo or something. Or if they just flew away" (13). Holden's thoughts about the ducks recur frequently enough for one to realize that the ducks stand for something about which he is concerned regarding himself. He mentions them again to two different cab drivers once he is in New York City. The first driver merely asks Holden if he is trying to kid him (60), but the second one turns the question into a metaphysical issue of the sort that on a deeper level also troubles Holden. The driver implies that, like the fish in the lagoon, the ducks must do whatever it is in their nature to do.

> "They live right *in* the goddam ice. It's their nature, for Chrissake. They get frozen right in one position for the whole winter."
>
> "Yeah? What do they eat, then? I mean if they're frozen *solid*, they can't swim around looking for *food* and all."
>
> "Their *bodies*, for Chrissake—what'sa matter with ya? Their bodies take in nutrition and all, right through the goddam seaweed and crap that's in the ice. They got their *pores* open the whole time. That's their *nature*, for Chrissake. See what I mean?" (82–83)

But it becomes increasingly evident that Holden's concern about the ducks is related to his concerns about himself. Obviously, those concerns regard his persistence, as opposed to his disappearance, as a subject. Plainly, the ducks' disappearance is related to those nagging questions Holden has about death. He is concerned not merely with his own, but the deaths of others as well. The metonymical associations are clear, for when he speaks of the ducks again, he moves from their disappearance directly into thoughts of his death, and from there to thoughts about his dead brother, Allie. "I thought probably I'd get pneumonia and die. I started picturing millions of jerks coming to my funeral and all. My grandfather from Detroit, that keeps calling out the numbers of the streets when you ride on a goddam bus with him, and my aunts—I have about fifty aunts—and all my lousy cousins. What a mob'd be there. They all came when Allie died, the whole goddam stupid bunch of them" (154–55). Salinger effects an intricate psychoanalytic transition here. In Holden's imagination of his own death, one sees immediately that the fundamental issue is his relation to his parents, on the one hand, and to his dead brother, on the other. The child's fantasy of his own death, Lacan tells us, is just another way of combatting aphanisis, the problem of the subject's disappearance. Lacan explains that the child, recognizing his disappearance beneath the signifier in the Other, projects the desire of the Other (the parents) into a denial of the disappearance. In answer to the question, "What does the parent desire?" the child says, "The parent desires me." "The subject," writes Lacan, "brings the answer of the previous lack, of his own disappearance, which he situates here at the point of lack perceived in the Other. The first object he proposes for this parental desire whose object is unknown is his own loss—*Can he lose me?* The phantasy of one's death, of one's disappearance, is the first object that the subject has to bring into play in this dialectic, and he does indeed bring it into play." But the real issue is parental love. "We also know," says Lacan, "that the phantasy of one's death is usually manipulated by the child in his love relations with his parents" (*FFC*, 214–15). In the novel, Salinger writes, "I kept worrying that I was getting pneumonia, with all those hunks of ice in my hair, and that I was going to die. I felt sorry as hell for my mother and father. Especially my mother, because she still isn't over my brother Allie yet" (155). In sum, Lacan says, "One lack is superimposed upon the other" (*FFC*, 215), the lack the subject perceives in himself is superimposed upon the lack the subject perceives in its relation to the parents, this lack being the gap in the subject's knowledge of the desire of the parent. Moreover, this move by the subject, Lacan contends, is absolutely fundamental to the constitution of the subject as a consciousness, for without the move into a relation to the Other, a move that inevitably creates a gap, a lack, a fading or disappearance of something cherished of the subject (Lacan says this "thing" is, in essence, the phallus), the subject can never become aware of signification, the translation of being into meaning, of metonymical objects into signifiers, a translation that is at the heart of Desire, itself the heart of the normally constituted subject.

II

The other focus of the passage in which Holden imagines his death and funeral is the focus on his brother Allie. The passage referring to Allie's funeral goes on much longer than the summary above suggests, but the theme it regards remains the same: aphanisis, Holden's disappearance. It is less Allie's disappearance than his own that concerns Holden. Holden needs something—an object, another subject—in which to find himself not merely as projected into an Imaginary double, but as a *moi* incorporated into the Symbolic. The distinction here between the register of the Imaginary and that of the Symbolic is manifested in the difference between what Lacan regards as "ideal *ego*" and what he regards as "ego *ideal*." Doubles such as Ackley and Stradlater belong to the false consciousness of the former, while Allie belongs to the true, but unconscious domain of the latter. Allie, of course, stands in the place where Holden would stand in the relation to the parents, for there is a powerful identification of Holden with his brother. Lacan's distinctions between the two forms of ego-identification are related to the distinction he makes between the functions of "alienation" and "separation." The form of identification based on alienation is founded on the mirror-stage process of identification of an Imaginary other, the one Lacan calls the subject's ideal *ego* or ideal *imago*.[10] "I have described," he says, "the sight in the mirror of the ego ideal, of that being that he first saw appearing in the form of the parent holding him up before the mirror." Thus, Lacan contends, the ego *ideal* is first identified with the parent who gazes lovingly at the child. But in this exchange of gazes, the ideal *ego* also takes shape in the child. "By clinging to the reference-point of him who looks at him in a mirror," says Lacan, "the subject sees appearing, not his ego ideal [which is the parent], but his ideal ego, that point which he desires to gratify himself in himself" (*FFC*, 257). The one—the ideal *ego*—is located in the place of the other; the second—the ego *ideal*—is located in the place of the *moi*. It is at this latter point that Allie is located. In Holden's structuration as a subject, Allie stands in the place of the *moi*, the place in the structure of the subject where the ego *ideal* stands. This place, Lacan says, is in the field of Desire; identification, to which Lacan refers in Freud's thought as the "enigmas in identification" (*FFC*, 256), is thus not subsumed entirely in Imaginary narcissism, as one may think. Rather, like the subject himself, identification itself is also divided, existing on the one side as an Imaginary, narcissistic *projection*, and on the other as an *introjection* in the realm of the Other in the Symbolic.

The form of identification located in the ego *ideal* is related to—in fact, forms—the *moi* of the subject. It is observed in analysis in the objects—the *objets petit a*—in which the unconscious subject finds himself or with which he unconsciously identifies himself. Lacan refers to the inauguration of the "kernel of the ego ideal" as the "stroke" that marks an original libidinous inscription that will permit the separation of ego *ideal*—*moi*—from ideal *ego*. "The single stroke, in so far as the subject clings to it, is in the field of desire, which cannot in any sense be constituted other than in the reign of the signifier [the phallus], other than at the level in which there is a relation of the subject to the Other. It is the field of the Other that determines the function of the single stroke, in so far as it is from it that a major stage of identification is established in the topography then developed by Freud— namely, idealization, the ego ideal" (*FFC*, 256). Lacan describes the ego *ideal*—the *moi*—that separates itself from the Imaginary others and becomes localized in *objets a* in a metaphor of a darning egg. The *objet a* is a "privileged object," "that object whose very reality is purely topological" as it is "that object that rises in a bump, like the wooden darning egg in the material which, in analysis, you are darning" (*FFC*, 257). In effect, claims Lacan, the *objet a* permits one to discover the outlines of the *moi*, to discover that the *moi* is the stocking that is shapeless until given discernible shape by the *objet a*. "Through the function of the *objet a*, the subject separates himself off, ceases to be linked to the vacillation of being, in the sense that it [the *objet a*] forms the essence of alienation" (*FFC*, 258). Lacan calls this form of identification one "of a strangely different kind" (*FFC*, 256), "strange" perhaps because it not only is related to the meanings of sex, but it is also related to the significance of death. For man, Lacan says, "because he knows the signifi-ers," the objects in the unconscious symbolizing birth, love, procreation, and death, "sex and its significations are always capable of making present the presence of death" (*FFC*, 256).[11]

Now one may begin to see why the dead brother is so critical to Holden's sense of himself. Allie is a figure of Holden's ego *ideal*, the *moi* or ideal self that is unknowable except through the objects in which it is in-scribed. Again, the identification of Holden with Allie is almost too obvious to mention; moreover, since it lies close to consciousness, that identification is likely to be rather misunderstood in itself. Thus, because of the uncon-scious function of repression, the deeper significance of Holden's relation to Allie lies in an object, not in Allie himself. The one object in which Holden's unconscious identifies Allie—the one that represents perhaps the most touch-ing element of the novel—is Allie's baseball mitt. One suspects that the mitt becomes an *objet a* for Holden not merely because it is a part-object that may stand for Allie; it is virtually necessary as an object of extreme signification to Holden because it is related, metonymically and metaphorically, to the hand. And not just any hand, either, but the right hand, since it is a left-hander's mitt. Nor is it even Allie's hand that is the source of importance. Allie's mitt leads one to Holden's broken hand—the hand broken at the time of Allie's death and the hand for which the mitt must stand as much as it stands for Allie. The hand becomes identified with the loss of the brother, and so becomes related to the lost object of mourning. It is clear that one of Holden's psychological problems, of the type that Lacan addresses in his essay "Desire and the Interpretation of Desire in *Hamlet*," is incomplete mourning.[12] Holden was never able to complete the process of mourning his dead brother because he was not present with his family. "I wasn't there," Holden says. "I was still in the hospital and all after I hurt my hand" (155). Furthermore, this broken hand is related to the subject's problem of castra-tion, inasmuch as castration is itself related to the signification of death, Holden's death as much as Allie's. "I slept in the garage the night he died," Holden says, "and I broke all the goddam windows with my fist, just for the hell of it. I even tried to break all the windows on the station wagon we had that summer, but my hand was already broken and everything by that time, and I couldn't do it" (39). As the death of the brother becomes associated with Holden's awareness of finitude, limitations, and therefore of castration, so also does the broken hand become identified with Holden's sense of the limits of himself, his ego, his *moi*. It means that he cannot be just anything anymore. "I can't make a real fist any more—not a tight one, I mean—but outside of that I don't care much. I mean I'm not going to be a goddam surgeon or a violinist or anything *any*way" (39).

Allie's mitt is mentioned first in the novel in a context that reveals some of its multiple significations for Holden. To begin, the mitt is the subject that Holden chooses to write about in response to Stradlater's request he write a "descriptive" essay for him. "I wrote about my brother Allie's baseball mitt.

It was a very descriptive subject. It really was. My brother Allie had this lefthanded fielder's mitt. He was left-handed. The thing that was descriptive about it, though, was that he had poems written all over the fingers and the pocket and everywhere. In green ink. He wrote them on it so that he'd have something to read when he was in the field and nobody was up at bat. He's dead now" (38). It is clear enough, in this passage, that Allie represents an ideal of some sort for Holden. That he represents the ego *ideal*, rather than the specular ideal *ego*, is suggested in Holden's description. He describes Allie as both smart and decent, "terrifically intelligent," but also "the nicest" member of the family (38). If Holden's admiration of Allie itself suggests the younger brother's relation to Holden as ego *ideal*, their relation as virtual alter egos is suggested in another part of the passage, one that in passing implicates the other important *objet a*—the red hunting cap—that dominates Holden's consciousness and exposes his unconscious. The reference is to Allie's bright red hair. Holden mentions the red hair as if it were the reason for his having once become aware of Allie's presence far behind him, but the awareness seems more mystical than physical. "I'll tell you what kind of red hair he had," says Holden. "I started playing golf when I was only ten years old. I remember once, the summer I was around twelve, teeing off and all, and having a hunch that if I turned around all of a sudden, I'd see Allie. So I did, and sure enough, he was sitting on his bike outside the fence—there was this fence that went all around the course—and he was sitting there, about a hundred and fifty yards behind me, watching me tee off. That's the kind of red hair he had. God, he was a nice kid, though" (38). The significant detail here, perhaps, is that Allie stands in the position of the *moi* in relation to Holden. He stands behind the subject—Holden-as-I—and at a distance, and in Holden's description one thus perceives that the "I" sees itself being seen by this Other self that locates the *moi*, the ego *ideal* lying on the plane of the unconscious. In this relation, therefore, as Lacan argues, Holden's conscious "I" is in fact now constituted by the Other mediated through his younger, idealized—and idealizing—brother, or, to play off Lacan, (br)other.

III

Holden's suitemate Ackley and roommate, Ward Stradlater, represent different sorts of ego relationships for Holden. They are specular "doubles," though they represent different aspects of the double. Ackley is the negative image of self—ugly, pimply, self-absorbed. Stradlater is the somewhat—only somewhat—more positive double—handsome, clear-featured, albeit equally narcissistic. Of the two, Stradlater is more important, for he raises Oedipal problems near to the surface of the novel's text. The functions of Stradlater and Allie suggest once again the differences Lacan notes between alienation of the subject and separation of the subject, the one functioning in the Imaginary, the other in the Symbolic. These differences, moreover, illustrate Lacan's distinction between the ideal *ego* (in the Imaginary) and the ego *ideal* (in the Symbolic). Whereas Allie seems located now in the realm of the Symbolic, and becomes from there the object in which Holden identifies his *moi*-self, Stradlater represents a mirror-figure of narcissistic identification within the Imaginary. That means Holden's relation to him will be rather ambivalent, marked by admiration as well as hostility (just as his relation to Ackley is hostility marked by grudging admiration). Clearly, Stradlater represents to Holden one whom he might imitate, but at the same time he is one with whom Holden shall enter into conflict. The difference between these two functions—imitation and aggression—is brought out by one of Holden's *objets a*. What is more, the difference between these two functions suggests the difference between the Imaginary and the Symbolic as registers, as, that is, fields which in their own ways determine signification. Signification operates through triangular relationships within each register. The relation in the register of the Imaginary between Holden and Stradlater pivots on a series of third objects or persons, really, on the difference in the reaction of each to the third point in the triangle. The failure of Stradlater to understand how much the mitt means to Holden suggests the difference between the ideal *ego* found in the Imaginary and the ego *ideal* found in the Symbolic. When Allie's baseball mitt is the third point of the triangle, the signification arises from the difference between Holden and Stradlater in relation to the subject about which Holden writes.

> All of a sudden, he said, "For Chris*sake*, Holden. This is about a goddam *base*ball glove."
> "So what?" I said. Cold as hell. (41)

In giving Stradlater the composition about Allie's mitt, Holden is offering— via a mediation from within the Symbolic—a piece of himself to his roommate. But Stradlater, as blind, Imaginary other rather than knowing, Symbolic Other, does not understand any of this deep personal significance. Holden, for that matter, does not understand it consciously either, but the Other, his unconscious, understands enough at this moment to force Holden to act. For when the point of the triangle is filled by yet another figure—a figure of the other who stands for the mother—the relationship between Holden and Stradlater shifts suddenly from Imaginary to Symbolic, and becomes Oedipal in the transfer.

Thus, crucial as this moment is, more crucial in Salinger's development of Holden's psychological structure is the consequence of this moment. For following upon Stradlater's rejection of Holden's *objet a* comes the fight between the two youths. Ostensibly, the fight is over Jane Gallagher. One suspects that if Stradlater had been sympathetic at all to the topic of the composition Holden had written, Holden would not have gotten into the fight with Ward over what Holden imagines the handsome youth to have done on the date with Jane. Jane is involved, in the same ways as the baseball mitt, in a series of triangular relations involving Holden and another male. But where in the former Imaginary structurations the person stands in the place of the identificatory other and the object stands in the place of the *moi*, here in the transition into the register of the Symbolic, one of the persons will stand in the place of the (m)other and the other person in the place of the father, a term, incidentally, one would like to call (f)other for the sake of non-sexist symmetry with what Lacan often calls (m)other. The third point on the triangle—the one the subject would fill with the self—the *moi*—is precisely the one that *disappears* when the subject moves into the register of the Symbolic. That *moi* can be observed only in its symbolic displacements, in the objects in which the subject inscribes its ego. By seeing the parallels in these two structurations, one may begin to see why Lacan regards the Oedipal relation as a problem of subjectivity rather than sexuality as such. The fact that one may displace the mitt by a person such as Jane Gallagher in the triangular structuration suggests that though the relation is fundamentally Oedipal, the desire that both object and person represent is not itself sexual. The desire is a desire for that which the subject lacks. It is not that the person or object in either the symbolic place of the *moi* or the Imaginary place of the other stands for the mother; rather, both places are taken by the object of the subject's desire. It is that which the subject desires, namely, the phallus, for the phallus represents the desire of the Other, and, says Lacan, man's desire *is* "the desire of the Other" (*Ecrits*, 289).

Thus Jane Gallagher, like the mitt, is merely a relay, but Jane is a relay in the triangular circuit between Holden and the figure—Stradlater—who stands in the place of the father. Salinger's text makes it rather evident that the fight takes place in a different register for Holden. The event occurs in a threshold realm, an area of the liminal, the transitional. The fight between the two takes on, in consequence, much of the significance of a dream for Holden. Indeed, since he says repeatedly he does not remember precisely what happened in the incident (40–45), the repression is distinctly like that involved in one's memory of dreams: "This next part I don't remember so hot. All I know is I got up from the bed, like I was going down to the can or something, and then I tried to sock him, with all my might, right smack in the toothbrush, so it would split his goddam throat open. . . . It probably would've hurt him a lot, but I did it with my right hand, and I can't make a good fist with that hand. On account of that injury I told you about" (43). Thus it becomes fairly plain that the incident functions to draw together the congruent significances of the mitt, Jane Gallagher, and Holden's damaged hand—objects representing in turn *moi*, (m)other, and phallus. For each is observable in—or inferrible from—a conflict that occurs because Holden wants to believe that Ward had made out with a girl in whom Holden has invested the sort of significance one ordinarily sees invested by the Oedipal subject in the mother. But the most important lesson for Holden—one not yet clear here—is that the mother does *not* have that for which the subject longs. As Lacan has said, the "test of the desire of the Other is decisive not in the sense that the subject learns by it whether or not he has a real phallus, but in the sense that he learns that the mother does not have it" (*Ecrits*, 289).

In Lacanian terms, it is in the place of the mother that little sister Phoebe returns in relation to Holden as a subject-consciousness. Phoebe brings one back to the theme of Holden's "disappearance." That disappearance is related both to the disappearance of the phallus as a real object in its becoming "merely" a signifier, and to the disappearance of Holden's "being" in his assumption of Oedipal "meaning." This latter, the "identity" theme, brings the *moi* back into the picture, and thus brings Holden's favored *objet a* into the equation as well. That favored object is Allie. As it happens in the novel's beginning, so it happens in its ending. When Holden feels his disappearance, he seems always to be crossing some threshold—a highway earlier, now street intersections. "Everytime I came to the end of a block and stepped off the goddam curb, I had this feeling that I'd never get to the other side of the street. I thought I'd just go down, down, down, and nobody'd ever see me again" (197). The feeling that Holden describes here is precisely that about which Mr. Antolini had told Holden. Its significance—interestingly enough, given Lacan's emphasis on "*l'instance de la lettre*"[13]—is represented to Holden in a letter (187). Antolini earlier had said to Holden: " 'This fall I think you're riding for—it's a special kind of fall, a horrible kind. The man falling isn't permitted to feel or hear himself hit bottom. He just keeps falling and falling. The whole arrangement's designed for men who, at some time or other in their lives, were looking for something they thought their own environment couldn't supply them with. So they gave up looking. They gave up before they ever really even got started. You follow me?' " (187). The "letter" that Antolini gives Holden—the piece of paper, at least, on which he had written a saying of Wilhelm Stekel and which Holden still keeps (188)—makes a statement that fits well with the teachings of Lacan, particularly those connected with the phallic signifier.[14] "The mark of the immature man is that he wants to die nobly for a cause," Stekel says, "while the mark of the mature man is that he wants to live humbly for one" (188). Lacan would say that the immature man would assume that all that he has to give—his signifiers ("money") or his life—is capable of filling the gap between the desire embodied in the cause and the law embodied in the failure. This gap is located precisely where the phallus-as-signifier-of-plenitude would be, but that is precisely the gap one cannot fill. The mature man, Lacan would say, is the one who lives humbly because he knows that the gap between desire and law cannot ever be filled by the subject, living or dead. But when Holden first experiences that feeling of falling, of his disappearance, after having bolted from Antolini's apartment, he had turned to Allie as his Symbolic bulwark against his fading self. "Every time I'd get to the end of a block I'd make believe I was talking to my brother Allie. I'd say to him, 'Allie, don't let me disappear. Allie, don't let me disappear. Allie, don't let me disappear. Please, Allie.' And then when I'd reach the other side of the street without disappearing, I'd *thank* him" (198). But upon successfully negotiating the passage across many street corners, Holden decides to take his disappearance into his own hands. He falls into a fantasy in which he vows never to go home again, deciding, instead, to hitchhike out West and to build a "little cabin somewhere," there to live with "this beautiful girl" he would marry. Himself only pretending to be a deaf-mute, she would in fact be one, and, in a very Lacanian twist, they would communicate only by letter, at least in letters. "She'd come and live in my cabin with me, and if she wanted to say anything to me, she'd have to write it on a goddam piece of paper, like everybody else" (199). The fantasy excites Holden, but he decides he must do one thing before heading West; he must say goodbye to Phoebe. On his way to meet with her, however, he passes through the museum and visits the Egyptian tomb, the room of the mummies. It is in the movement through the place of death, the symbolic place of absence and negation, the ritualized place wherein culture hallows one's disappearance, that Holden articulates to himself much of the meaning of his experience. That experience, as perhaps it must be, is also captured in letters, really in the letters of two words, the epithet that ambiguously embodies the double meaning of sexuality.

> I was the only one left in the tomb then. I sort of liked it, in a way. It was so nice and peaceful. Then, all of a sudden, you'd never guess what I saw on the wall. Another "Fuck you." It was written with a red crayon or something, right under the glass part of the wall, under the stones.
> That's the whole trouble. You can't ever find a place that's nice and peaceful, because there isn't any. You may *think* there is, but once you get there, when you're not looking, somebody'll sneak up and write "Fuck you" right under your nose. (204)

IV

Having in effect now moved into the domain of the Symbolic, the domain of the letter, Holden must now exercise his place vis-à-vis Phoebe in her place as a child and as a sister, roles that are defined not by the animal or biological Real, but by the human and cultural Symbolic. Holden must himself speak from the place of the father in relation to her. That means he must speak the word of the father in the name of the Law of the Father. He must say "No." Holden says "No" emphatically when Phoebe shows up for their presumably final appointment with her suitcase in hand, ready to go West with her brother and to set up housekeeping in the place of that beautiful deaf-mute about whom Holden fantasizes. Were Holden still in the grip of the Imaginary, he would see that his fondest dream is now on the verge of realization. There is in fact a moment when Holden must see this, and he is made dizzy by the sight. When Phoebe says, "I'm going with you. Can I? Okay?" Holden recounts, "I almost fell over when she said that. I swear to God I did. I got sort of dizzy and I thought I was going to pass out or something again" (206). But knowing now that one cannot ever fulfill the dream for which she has been the symbol, he tells her she cannot go. "No," he says. "You're not *going*. Now, shut up! Gimme that bag" (206). Later, at the carrousel at the zoo, where he has taken Phoebe to soothe her feelings, Holden thinks of the gold ring pursued by the children. The ring is a symbol of phallic plenitude and as such is related to the imminence of castration. Thus Holden thinks here in terms consistent with the realization of one's Symbolic castration, a term that in Lacan means primarily one's want, lack, finitude, limitation, or, in a word, one's *mortality:* "All the kids kept trying to grab for the gold ring, and so was old Phoebe, and I was sort of afraid she'd fall off the goddam horse, but I didn't say anything or do anything. The thing with kids is, if they want to grab for the gold ring, you have to let them do it, and not say anything. If they fall off, they fall off, but it's bad if you say anything to them" (211). His remarks suggest clearly that Holden now internalizes the Oedipal law, and that his realization prepares him for a fully mature subjectivity. He is now a properly divided subject, forever alienated from the images of the other, and separated from, but implicated in, the *objets a* forming the *moi*—the ego *ideal*—that functions now in compliance with the Law of the Other. In effect, by his disappearing act, Holden has achieved a new identity, assumed a new "self," and it is only appropriate that Phoebe, the former symbol of the (m)other, should give him back the object that shall represent that identity. It shall, moreover, by its metonymic associations, bring back the dominant symbol of Holden's *moi*-being, his dead brother, redheaded Allie, as well as those foils (shades of Lacan's Hamlet) that first marked his loss of the phallus. The object, of course, is the red hunting hat that Holden had bestowed on Phoebe, that she had returned to Holden, and that now she grabs out of Holden's coat pocket and places back on his head (212).

Restored to the only sort of fullness that shall ever be available to one who has acceded to the Symbolic, Holden is gripped by joy at this moment. Sitting on a bench in the sudden rain, watching Phoebe go around on the carrousel, at this final moment of the main narrative Holden feels unbounded pleasure, perhaps a Lacanian *jouissance*. "I felt so damn happy all of a sudden, the way old Phoebe kept going around and around. I was damn near bawling, I felt so damn happy, if you want to know the truth" (213). It may take a while for others to perceive it, but Holden's Other knows: he's okay now. Though the last, very brief chapter of *The Catcher in the Rye* leads one to surmise that Holden is in psychotherapy in California, where his brother D. B. lives, it would seem that on the evidence of the story he tells he no longer has any real need of therapy. He would appear to be as healthy, as "whole," as sane as anyone might ever be. All that remains, perhaps, is for Holden to understand fully the significance of the story he has told. This significance is the significance of the Symbolic itself. Holden's final words suggest clearly he has grasped that significance. Not only has he acted on his new perceptions of the Symbolic, but he also seems to know the truth of Lacan, that it is the fate of the human to miss those things—especially, and always, *that* thing—one desires. Much of the sense that he has now grasped the Symbolic order lies in the significance of his narrative *as* narrative. His story belongs to the Symbolic, and while the Symbolic permits him to tell his story, it does not permit him to retrieve its events and people as such. So his story, like all stories, is simply a displacement of desire; it simply becomes another way of missing something, of knowing something that is missing and of knowing that something is missing. "About all I know," Holden concludes, "is I sort of *miss* everybody I told about. Even old Stradlater and Ackley, for instance. I think I even miss that goddam Maurice. It's funny. Don't ever tell anybody anything. If you do, you start missing everybody" (214). Even one's self, Lacan would say.

Notes

1. Maxwell Geismar, "J. D. Salinger: The Wise Child and the *New Yorker* School of Fiction," in *American Moderns: From Rebellion to Conformity,* ed. Maxwell Geismar (New York: Hill and Wang, 1958), 195–209. Reprinted in *Salinger: A Critical and Personal Portrait,* ed. Henry Anatole Grunwald (New York: Pocket Books, 1963), 95–111.

2. Grunwald, *A Critical and Personal Portrait,* 102, 98, 102.

3. Ibid., 99, 100, 101.

4. James Bryan, "The Psychological Structure of *The Catcher in the Rye,*" *PMLA* 89 (October 1974):1065–74. For another type of challenge to Bryan, see Dennis Vail, "Holden and Psychoanalysis," *PMLA* 91 (January 1976):120–21. For a very complete and annotated bibliography of criticism and other writings on or by Salinger, see Jack R. Sublette, *J. D. Salinger: An Annotated Bibliography, 1938–1981* (New York: Garland, 1984).

5. Bryan, "The Psychological Structure," 1068.

6. Ernest Jones, "Early Development of Female Sexuality," in *Papers on Psychoanalysis,* 5th ed. (London: Bailliere, Tindall & Cox, 1950), 438–51. See also Jean Laplanche and J.-B. Pontalis, *The Language of Psycho-Analysis,* trans. Donald Nicholson-Smith. (New York: Norton, 1973), 40.

7. Jacques Lacan, *The Four Fundamental Concepts of Psycho-Analysis,* trans. Alan Sheridan, ed. Jacques-Alain Miller (New York: Norton, 1978), 208; hereafter cited parenthetically in the text as *FFC*.

8. To make easier the comprehension of the discussion, here is Lacan's basic schematization of the splitting of the subject that leads to those two forms of *aphanisis* that he calls "separation" and "alienation" (*The Four Fundamental Concepts,* 211):

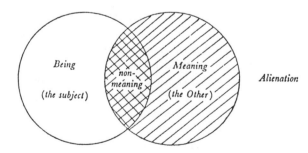

What Lacan wishes to illustrate here is the way in which the subject, upon becoming a self-*conscious* subject (truly a *subject*, in other words), loses something either way he or she turns, whether toward meaning, in which case being is lost, or toward being, in which case meaning is lost. Lacan further illustrates the principle of separation/alienation by use of the threat (based on the familiar Jack Benny joke), *Your money or your life*. Lacan says, "If I choose the money, I lose both. If I choose life, I have life without the money, namely, a life deprived of something" (212), a something he would call the phallus, the very signifier that constitutes the subject-as-subject at the same time it constitutes the Other of the unconscious. For some of Lacan's variations of the so-called Schema L, which shows the quaternary structure of the fully constituted subject, see his *Ecrits: A Selection*, trans. Alan Sheridan (New York: Norton, 1977), 193, 197; hereafter cited parenthetically in the text as *Ecrits*.

9. *The Catcher in the Rye* (New York: Bantam Books, 1964), 5; hereafter cited in the text. The novel was originally published by Little, Brown, in 1951.

10. These concepts will be clarified somewhat by another of Lacan's schemas, the one he calls "R" (see *Ecrits*, 197):

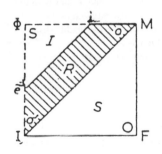

SCHEMA R:

Schema R is an extension of the basic schema "L," which is shaped essentially like a large Z and displays the four positions of the subject (I, other, *moi* or ego ideal, and Other) at the points, starting at the top left and moving to top right, then to bottom left, and finally to bottom right. Schema R complicates this basic schema by opening up a space Lacan regards as the Real (R), a "register" that balances the register of the Imaginary (the top left triangle) and the register of the Symbolic (the bottom right triangle). One might say that it is the Real of human experience that causes all our problems by causing the split spoken of above, the problems of separation and irreparable alienation. The symbols on the corners on the outside of the square represent the basic signifiers of the subject: the symbol Phi is the phallus, the M is the Mother or the "primordial object," the F is the Father, and the I is the ego Ideal or "that which is reflected of his form in his objects" (*Ecrits*, 194). The symbols on the corners inside the square represent the four elementary perspectival positions of the subject: the S is the I or speaking subject (*je*, in French), the o is the other (the figure or figures of the specular double), the O is the Other (also the Unconscious), and the o' is the *objet a* that represents the *moi* or ego *Ideal* to consciousness. In principle, the subject may look at anything from any of these subject positions, though not all, of course, are equally available to consciousness. The e and the i represent, respectively, the ego and the specular image, those *topoi* Lacan calls "the two imaginary terms of the narcissistic relation" (*Ecrits*, 197). The R, in the shaded area, represents the Real, the I in the top triangle represents the Imaginary register, and the S in the bottom triangle represents the Symbolic register, each of which has a characteristic imprint on the cognitions of the subject.

11. See Ellie Ragland-Sullivan, *Jacques Lacan and the Philosophy of Psychoanalysis* (Urbana: University of Illinois Press, 1985), viii, 38, 145, for comments on the basic signifiers.

12. Jacques Lacan, "Desire and Interpretation of Desire in *Hamlet*," *Yale French Studies* 55/56 (1977):11–52.

13. See "The Agency of the Letter in the Unconscious or Reason since Freud," in *Ecrits*, 146–78.

14. It seems that the question of the phallus is especially important where Antolini is concerned in the text. Holden believes that the teacher has made a homosexual advance toward him, and that judgment—which Holden later questions—may seem to compromise the functional truth of the advice Antolini gives the youth. Really, it should not, for in fact the man is in search of the same thing—phallic plenitude—as the boy; Holden, in his "normality," simply seeks it in women, the other of male heterosexuality. Lacan speaks of homosexuality in the essay on the phallus: "male homosexuality, in accordance with the phallic mark that constitutes desire, is constituted on the side of desire, while female homosexuality, on the other hand, as observation shows, is orientated on a disappointment that reinforces the side of the demand for love. These remarks should really be examined in greater detail, from the point of view of a return to the function of the mask in so far as it dominates the identifications in which refusals of demand are resolved" (*Ecrits*, 290–91). Lacan means, one surmises, that the desire of one such as Antolini is invested in the male—in Holden, for example—because he desires, still, to *have* the phallus, represented in the male, rather than to *be* the phallus for the female, as in heterosexual attachments. From a Lacanian point of view, heterosexuality is never so solidly entrenched that the subject can—or should—too readily dismiss homosexuality as merely an alien otherness. In his defense, Holden is not at all prepared simply to dismiss Mr. Antolini, though, clearly, Holden exhibits a "normal"—culturally defined—homophobia.

Salinger in Continental Jeans:
The Liberation of Böll and
Other Germans
Siegfried Mandel*

Nineteenth-century translators were commissioned by the droves to satisfy public curiosity and tastes, as well as launch commercially successful ventures for publishers. After mediating between the original and the new language and producing facsimiles, translators would then retreat into anonymity and never be heard from again. All that has changed in our modern and "queer world of verbal transmigration," an apt coinage by Vladimir Nabokov,[1] when in the case of a controversial work translators became as much of an issue as the original author. Some European versions of J. D. Salinger's *The Catcher in the Rye* not only invite discussion of the art of translation but also of cultural receptivities, literary influences of the translated work, and the motivations of translators as artists and thinkers.

The spontaneous evidence for the high marketability of Salinger's novel in America stirred publishers worldwide to action, but contrary to their expectations—especially in Europe—response in the 1950s was lethargic. Yet, in a changing world that also saw a new generation of restless young

*This essay was written specifically for this volume and is published here for the first time by permission of the author.

looking for different, nontraditional "heroic" prototypes, the reading market for the Salinger novel dramatically reversed itself. In the mid-1960s it was not unusual for American visitors to Europe to be asked if they knew J. D. Salinger and what his new book, after *The Catcher in the Rye*, was going to be be about. Although this is still a moot question, Salinger's first novel eventually garnered not only a large market but an unusually responsive reading audience in England—where it was severely bowdlerized at first—and in France, Germany, Italy, Finland, Poland, Russia, as well as in Israel, South Africa, and Australia.[2] For a short time it was banned in the last two countries mentioned—on moral grounds—but censorship only whets the public's appetite. While reviewers' fanfare and immediate public attention boosted the novel into an American orbit, the European publicity machinery was scarcely engaged. Robert Laffont, a Paris publisher, was not disheartened by apathy toward Salinger, however, despite a fine translation of the novel into French, and he persisted by also publishing Salinger's *Nine Stories* and urging booksellers to publicize the author. One problem was gathering information about the mysterious author, and the United States Information Service in Paris no doubt added to the confusion by supplying a photo of the chubby, smiling Pierre Salinger, a White House spokesman at the time.[3] Within a decade, the novel by the real Salinger, however, gained firm ground.

Cultural contexts, of course, count for much in readers' identification with figures and themes in translated fiction, yet the Salinger reception in Europe generally has common features. These are implicit in German responses as well, though here we can see more clearly than anywhere else the interplay of social and literary experiences. Initially, German-reading audiences in West Germany and Switzerland showed more interest in *The Catcher in the Rye* than did the French. The Swiss publishing house Diana issued a translation by Irene Muchlon in 1954,[4] but in a nine-year span it did not manage more than 5,000 sales. The picture began to change when Kippenheuer publishers commissioned Heinrich Böll to take a hand. He was an experienced translator, who, with his wife, Annemarie, had already tailored German versions of novels, plays, and stories—some of which also became theater and movie features—by Kay Cicecellis, Paul Horgan, Patrick White, Brendan Behan, John M. Synge, Bernard Malamud, as well as three Salinger stories that had appeared in the *New Yorker*. Muehlon's old title *Der Mann im Roggen* (literally, the man in the rye) was transformed by Böll into the more accurate *Der Fänger im Roggen* in 1962 and the Muehlon version was refashioned—not always for the better stylistically—but with the contents unimpaired. Several gears then meshed to give the novel prominence: the growing cultural readiness of German-reading audiences to identify with key features and issues and to engage in self-analysis; its publication in paperback by Rowohlt in 1972, with immediate sales of 300,000 that indicated its middle-class and student appeal; and, tangibly, it paralleled Böll's burgeoning reputation as a writer and winner of the Nobel Prize for Literature in 1972.

During interviews with journalists and critics, Böll graciously and appreciatively discussed the association early in his career with Salinger's fiction. It gave him an opportunity to articulate his special indebtedness and to discuss the postwar social and literary situation in Germany.[5] It should be recalled that from a practical point of view many German writers depended upon supplementary free-lance earnings to make a living. The translation of works from foreign literature was one of several avenues, and it was quite popular because that had been cut off during the Nazi years. But for Böll there were other considerations as well. In 1967 he was asked by the journalist-critic Marcel Reich-Ranicki why he had been prompted to devote a considerable part of his working time to translations from English. Böll responded: "First of all, the pleasure of working with the substance of language. And secondly, the pleasure of collaborating with my wife."[6] With his wife, Annemarie, he later translated Salinger's *Franny and Zooey*.

To the query as to what the task of translation meant to Böll, he replied: "For someone who himself writes novels and stories, translating is an event in which giving and taking is simultaneous. It also is an act that requires justness because it founders on so many inadequate translations. Aside from that, it is an act of liberation: the translation of Salinger's books constitutes such an act of liberation for me."[7]

From other interviews and personal essays, what Böll meant by "liberation" comes into sharper focus. In essence it meant finding his own voice to represent in fiction the realities of life—past and present—as he saw and felt them. He would be satisfied only when he thought he had gained believability: when his voice coincided with a personal style and aesthetics merged with his moral sensibilities. It was a matter of ingrained disinclination to march in step—prompted perhaps, as he wryly said, by slight corpulence—that kept him from joining a Hitler youth group as a twenty-three-year-old in his native city of Cologne. After being called into the army from 1939 to 1945 and serving mainly on the Russian front, his antagonism toward compulsory activity, blind obedience, and adaption to any and all ossified institutions grew. It was phony functionaries whom he despised, and ordinary people caught in unbearable circumstances with whom he sympathized.

It was natural then for Böll to experience a shock of recognition when he found in Salinger's *The Catcher in the Rye*, "something very much related to an entire generation. . . . I simply felt a certain brotherliness and brotherhood when I read Salinger."[8] And beyond that, he noted with exhilaration, Salinger held out the possibility of "liberation from the insane, deep-rooted German earnestness of which I've not rid myself."[9] Salinger's effect was almost immediately evident in Böll's novel *Ansichten eines Clowns* (1963; *The Clown*, 1965). Just as Salinger's novel might have been subtitled "Holden's View of the World," Böll's title explicitly refers to the picaresque hero Hans's rebellious views (top to bottom "Ansichten"), which, like Holden's, put him on a collision course with a world that promptly defines his angry and comedic tiltings as psychiatric buffooneries. Holden and Hans resist the stamp of conformity that society brandishes and both respond with blasphemous antisocial and antireligious outbursts that outrage their brainwashed elders. Frustration, despair, idealism, and disillusionments drive Holden and Hans to the brink. Both reject the world as they find it. Böll allows Hans to shatter against the walls of convention; Salinger, however, leaves open the possibility for Holden to reenter the world through the fragile communications with a few others like his sister, Phoebe. Salinger's characters have specific name attributes: mythologically, Phoebe possesses an aura of brightness and redemptive female essence, while the family name Caulfield harbors the significance of the lucky caul that attends some births. Salinger's readers are pap fed by a semihappy ending, for Holden, despite all his expressed disgusts, has a life-saving zest and curiosity that makes most episodes adventurous rather than tragic. Böll, on the other hand, works with the problem of having Hans be more than the proverbial Hanswurst of folk genres or a Holdenesque naïf; Hans had to unburden himself of bitter social criticism. Despite the model of Salinger's comic antihero, Böll could not adopt a bantering tone.

Salinger's stories and novel caught Böll at moments when certain artistic problems were worrisome to him. At one point, Böll's Hans expresses the author's dilemma: "I have never succeeded in portraying the human element without producing awful Kitsch."[10] Indeed, the line crossed so frequently by Salinger and Böll from sentiment into sentimentality has bothered critics and artists more than it has readers: what is anathema to the former may be sheer indulgent pleasure for the latter. Böll felt that Salinger had shown him a way out of the trap of sentimentality; like a ventriloquist, he uses Hans to voice a confident authorial self-analysis, "I have succeeded quite well in representing the lyrical features in the life of juveniles through the poetry of everyday language."[11] Therein lies the basic affinity between Böll's and Salinger's fiction—a spontaneous and natural capturing of expressive, rhythmic, and colloquial speech patterns of adolescents. Critics noted that dialogue in Böll's fiction gained in economy and color after his Salinger experience—slang and jargon became literary exponents that created lifelike characters. Salinger's fluent handling of Holden's interior monologues, as well as the boldly minimal plot and action of the novel, also held technical interest for Böll.

Rarely will an author seek models against which to test his own work if they are profoundly different from his own tone, temperament, and intentions. Böll was no exception. He noted that translating Salinger's fiction "gave me extreme pleasure; even the super-mannerism at play did not frighten me off because I had similar manneristic inclinations."[12] Aside from points of style and characterizations, Böll shares Salinger's stark implications that the social environment lies oppressively upon individuals, with twofold effects: the retardation of a maturing development and the tendency to affect emotionally ingrown family relationships. In regard to Holden and Phoebe, and then by extension to Salinger's subsequent stories about the Glass family, Böll observed a common psychological phenomenon: Phoebe, the novel's most sympathetic character, "of course, is quite nearly immunized by society. . . . What we see generally is a refusal to grow up, to become involved with the maturing process. That is even carried farther. It is something I have noted in Salinger's other works, and it has something incestuous about it. This though, apparently, also appears to be present in my own writings. All the relationships in the Glass family—sisters, brothers, father, mother—have something incestuous about them as well."[13] What is suggested is a kind of psychological bonding that intensifies relationships but also severely limits communication with others. But in all cases, inside or outside of the family, the authority figure becomes suspect. Holden sees himself and Phoebe as a Laertes-Ophelia pair who "horse around" while Polonius, the father authority figure is, so to speak, shooting the bull.

The refusal by the young to give up childhood and enter the world of adult responsibilities is universal, but in postwar Germany it took on deeper dimensions. It became entwined with their confronting and questioning the generation of their elders about the role they played during the Hitler era and its attending bankruptcies—themes that occupy serious German postwar fiction and life. The idea of "growing up" meant adapting oneself to the hypocrisies of the establishment. Günter Grass's Oskar in *The Tin Drum* novel was the single most explosive figure to ignite far-reaching controversy about matters of conscience and participatory guilt. The novel caused anxieties as much for its scabrous assaults on conventional proprieties as its insistence upon minutely scrutinizing an undigested past. Böll, however, takes aim at his targets without blunderbuss scatology, and, with Salinger as a model, contents himself with commonplace explicatives and personalized grievances in the voice of vernacular polemics. Hans and Holden vent their emotional stresses against religious observances and tabooed figures as well. Holden often adopts these stances as a pose of sophistication, while Böll explains Hans's outbursts: "Even in blasphemy lies a recognition of God; sometimes, blasphemy is one's only means."[14] Similarly, Holden's blasphemies are self-conscious and cocky assertions of independence rather than absolute convictions; they speak of personal traumas.

The imaged figure of the hero in serious fiction has much to do with the orientation of the author. Böll's literal and figurative disinclination to march in step put him in sympathy with Salinger's Holden who "couldn't even stand looking at the back of the guy's neck in front of me,"[15] during a one-week trial with the Boy Scouts, not to speak of what he thinks happens in the Army. Holden rails against Lieutenant Henry of Hemingway's "phony book" *A Farewell to Arms*, but identifies with the "old sport" in Fitzgerald's *The Great Gatsby*, and he prefers Shakespeare's "old Mercutio," who was "very smart and entertaining" and was killed through no fault of his own, contrary to Romeo and Juliet ("Julius") who "get pretty annoying sometimes" in a play that "gets pretty sexy in some parts." Böll does not impose that kind of literary unsophistication upon his characters. Yet, Böll and Salinger converge in their portrayals of the underdog pitted against the establishment and the futility of the rebellion. The "little man" as hero or antihero is dominant in their fiction. "The word hero," Böll noted in comments about Elisabeth Schnack's translation of Synge's *The Playboy of the Western World,* "in German has indeed also a wide range of meanings between the most serious and the comic."[16] That range of flexibility in the actions and language of Böll's and Salinger's unanchored heroes approximates the flux of natural experiences in the life of readers.

Böll has pointed out that although comparisons between Salinger's work and his own through 1962 are justified and influences are clear, it still must be taken into account that he is a German and Salinger an American: "Simply put, a difference exists between us as individual authors and our historical backgrounds."[17] Salinger's postwar America was vastly different from Böll's postwar Germany. America needed to find out what to do with victory; Germans needed to cope immediately with the physical rubble left by defeat and to bury the heinous past as expeditiously as it had buried its victims. It did not take long for the economy to recover through the miracle of workaholism and for people to sink into memory-screening moral insomnia. Political bureaucracy was again in full bloom—reconstituted and nominally denazified or whitewashed, and the literary market began to respond to varieties of consumer demands, mostly nonfiction and historical fiction, at first. Cultural ties with the world were reestablished as books banned and burned during the Nazi regime were republished, but often exiled authors were not made welcome in person because there was an unspoken resentment that they had abandoned their country, albeit to save life and sanity. Imports from America were a popular mix of translations—classics, bestsellers of quality or entertainment fodder—among them the fiction of John Steinbeck, William Faulkner, Ernest Hemingway, Saul Bellow, Truman Capote, and J. D. Salinger. Of enormous success was Thornton Wilder's stage and book version *The Skin of Our Teeth,* whose German title very clearly expresses the idea that once again we have escaped by the skin of our teeth, bringing to the surface latent fears and a mordantly comic sense of relief. Salinger's novel would also play a special role.

Among serious German writers engaged in fiction other than that designed to entertain and pacify consumers, Böll judged the literary situation between 1945 and 1955 from different perspectives. The German language during that period, said Böll, "was again brought to life." Language up to then had either been polluted by blood and soil slogans and race ideology— the language of official nationalistic incitements—or as a literary language it had been rendered sweetly innocuous by nonpolitical nature lyricism. It is folly, however, to indict the modern German language as an evildoer, a charge levelled by George Steiner and others; language is a means toward an expressed end and like any other tool it is at the mercy of its users. But, in a sense, it was a frozen language, unsuited to all free expression. A vital function was served by the so-called Group 47, a loose association of committed antifascist writers who aimed to thaw the freeze and revitalize German literature.[18] They found models in the fiction of Hemingway, Carson Mc-

Cullers, or Salinger, which was suffused with spontaneity, naturalness, and serious humor. Böll was part of this group and saw the struggle with language and literature firsthand: "for inexplicable reasons the German language of all authors who wrote and published was stuck at rock bottom . . . but inside and outside of various groups something took place that one can really call *new;* it was not communal work . . . and yet during those ten years, a common ground was formed, one that made possible what had not been possible before: experiments."[19]

Most of the writers that Böll had in mind needed first to discover or rediscover the major works of fiction commonly known abroad from Joyce to Faulkner and those proscribed in Germany from Kafka to Hermann Broch. With these as models, the debilitating use of language of the Hitler years could be cured so that "experiment" or revitalization of literature could ensue.[20] Some writers, like Böll, found the work of translation congenial, rewarding, and liberating, in stimulating their own work. An open ideological stance by characters and criticism of societal institutions were permissible, and the choices of fictional forms were limited only by the talents of authors. It was an atmosphere in which the best of translators could be seen, as Nabokov put it, "the professional writer relaxing in the company of a foreign confrere." What the translator would also need was imagination and style, he should have "the gift of mimicry and be able to act, as it were, the real author's part by impersonating his tricks of demeanor and speech, his ways and his mind, with the utmost degree of verisimilitude," as well as have a thorough knowledge of the author's culture.[21] Although the last of these Nabokovian requirements Böll could barely meet, even as a prisoner of war for a few months in an American camp, he possessed ample talents for the other prerequisites. Moreover, how different are rebellious adolescents with their identity and maturing crises in any modern country? In fact, the rampant antiheroes in American fiction of the 1950s are barely distinguishable from their European counterparts in social aggressiveness, antiestablishment sentiments, personal flounderings, and identity-seeking.

Böll's translation of *The Catcher in the Rye* has received criticism—some of it justified and some of it not—from bilingual analysts. In any case, the criticisms do reveal problems inherent in the art of translation, as well as the intrusion of Böll as a translator with strong personal preferences. Walter E. Riedel noted that the first translation by Irene Muehlon, *Der Mann im Roggen*, left much to be desired and that Böll's reworking was more precise.[22] He correctly sees, however, the tone-setting opening paragraph as too formal stylistically. Holden says,

> If you really want to hear about it, the first thing you'll probably want to know is where I was born and what my lousy childhood was like. . . .[23]

> (Böll:) Falls Sie wirklich meine Geschichte hören wollen, so möchten Sie wahrscheinlich vor allem wissen, wo ich geboren wurde und wie ich meine verflixte Kindheit verbrachte. . . .[24]

The highly formal "Sie" ruins the intimate contact Holden's "you'll" establishes with the reader. Muehlon tries to solve the problem in this fashion:

> Falls wirklich jemand die Geschichte hören will, so möchte er wahrscheinlich vor allem wissen, wo ich geboren wurde und wie ich meine Kindheit verbrachte. . . .[25]

> (Muehlon retranslated:) If somebody really wants to hear the story, he will really want to know where I was born and how I spent my [lousy] childhood. . . .[26]

Although Muehlon's "somebody . . . he" transforms Salinger's direct "you'll . . . you" into a third person address, the psychological result is interesting. She sets up a subliminal situation in which a question is implicit: "is *somebody* listening out there?" And, of course, the worldwide response to Holden's nonstop confessions answers that question. Why neither Muehlon nor Böll simply used "Du," a peer address for the egalitarian American "you," is explainable by a reluctance to unbend. Muehlon consistently excises the mildest lowbrow adjectives as in (lousy) childhood. With a measure of fidelity, Böll does reproduce Holden's freewheeling slang, characteristic of him and his adolescent peers, except for the vulgar Anglo-Saxon graffiti Holden twice finds scrawled on walls. An explicit rendering was essential since the graffiti rouses Holden to sincere anger: he possesses an integral core of generosity and, closely tied to the novel's title and theme, he wishes to protect the innocence of those younger than himself and keep them from "falling"—he is the self-styled, moralistic catcher in the rye.

The need for exact replication of language is no quibbling matter. It imbues Holden's character with an urge to share intimacies. Yet this artistic truth is really authorial pretense. Holden tells the reader, "What really knocks me out is a book that, when you're all done reading it you wish the author was a terrific friend and you could call him up whenever you felt like it."[27] Most who have had the urge to contact Salinger have met with an icy silence from the recluse of Cornish, New Hampshire. Böll, for his part, has opened himself to interviews and has been eager to throw himself into West–East literary and political battles and to broadcast his ideas—if not his advice—to the largest possible media audience; but in his fiction sex is treated shyly and language for the most part with a realism hedged by proprieties. These personal manners put Böll poles apart from his countryman Günter Grass who bruises adult readers, and from Salinger who unsettles them.

Although the personality differences between Salinger and Böll as authorial, public, and private personalities are so pronounced, there is one Salinger theme—played vibrato on one string—that is echoed by Böll: the phony system and its functionaries are guilty and not the helpless individual caught in their toils; it is often the young and disenchanted set who speak out against the older generation. German youth had questions about events of the unthinkable past. By extension, Böll formulated similar syllogisms in his fiction, essays, and talks: not the German soldier but the Army establishment must be saddled with the catastrophes and the horrors of the "dirty war." An essay in 1960 concluded that social and political cleansing of Germany must be more expeditious because "all of us have been damaged by the past—and we are survivors."[28]

During a talk given at a PEN congress held in 1974 in Jerusalem, he noted that "we live in a century of exiles," all the oppressed during the past years were exiles. Such simplifications and secular absolutions from the idea of collective guilt were soothing pieties sought by Germans who reacted defensively against foreign criticism and that of the German émigrés. Yet Böll was also insistent on moral scrutinies and was relentless in his exposures of social injustice. As an informal historian of German experience, he was accepted because he had demonstrated what many readers felt was fairness and sympathy. Salinger, while not as extensive a chronicler of the American scene as Böll was of the German scene, did capture the mood and problems of the young generation in crisis and the insulated, noncommunicative older generation.

Böll's sympathies coincided with Salinger's and enabled the translator to find readily the equivalent tone in the German version of *The Catcher in the Rye*. Aside from tone and style, Salinger's narrative techniques eminently suited Böll's search for liberation through experimentation. Böll took note of how the three-day span of Holden's episodic adventures was enlarged by skillful interweaving of interior memory narrations. In the 1950s Böll, on his own and with his wife, also translated the uncomplicated and touching fiction of Pulitzer Prize winner Paul Horgan—*Christmas Eve in San Cristobal*, *Weihnachtsabend in San Cristobal*; *The Devil in the Desert*, *Der Teufel in der Wüste*; but it was *The Catcher in the Rye* that set Böll on course.

Young narrators in some postwar German fiction had an affinity with Salinger's Holden, and we find prime examples in Siegfried Lenz's novel *Deutschstunde*, 1968 (*The German Lesson*, 1971) and in Ulrich Plenzdorf's *Die neuen Leiden des jungen W.*, 1973 (*The New Sufferings of Young W.*, 1979).[29] The Lenz novel had as great a vogue in the divided Germanies as Salinger's novel had in America. With its translation into English, the *Times Literary Supplement* hailed it as probably "the most successful work of fiction to appear in West Germany."[30] It is a well-crafted novel, but applause for it by Germans, it seems to me, was motivated less by its literary qualities than by its welcome narrative about Siggi, a Holdenish youngster who defies strictures about loyalty and duty to help a painter continue his clandestine artwork after it was banned by totalitarian authorities during the Hitler years. Again, it is the quiet and spontaneous humanity of a youngster that is contrasted to the conformism of his elders.

Plenzdorf's work caused an entirely different sensation after it came into being in East Germany, first as a novella in the periodical *Sinn und Form* in March 1972, and then in book form; it was followed by numerous theater performances and a film. Somehow its potential social explosiveness escaped the watchful eye of the censors; after all, its main thrust satirically countered subculture invasions of Western jargon, rock and roll, as well as mod and jean-dress mania. In the body of Plenzdorf's fiction, the paternity of Salinger's *The Catcher in the Rye* and Böll's translation of it are openly discussed—they become intrinsic to the art form and integral to the narrator's multifarious and ambiguous musings. In a short time, the play also crashed theater boards in West Germany. Young audiences on both sides of the Berlin Wall screened out the obligatory authorial obeisance to the work ethics in social realism (East Germany's literary doctrine) and the condemnation of decadent frivolity. Edgar Wibeau, the Holdenesque adolescent, was promptly labeled by a West German journalist a "red Werther in blue jeans."[31] Werther, of course, was the young man in Goethe's *The Sorrows of Young Werther* who put a bullet in his maudlin head when his love was unrequited. That shot was heard around Europe in the late eighteenth century, and many a poetically melancholic youngster followed suit, much to Goethe's embarrassment and chagrin. Thomas Carlyle testily told the young to stop mooning and wallowing in sweet self-pity and to get to work, an injunction Plenzdorf dutifully and loudly echoed and pointed against would-be Werthers and pathetic Holdens. Edgar has abandoned a menial though socially useful job and gorges himself on hip music and art and chooses Salinger's Holden as a favorite literary and live model. Perhaps as comic punishment for his subversion of East German "duties," Edgar dies of a malfunctioning electric spray-gun he has invented. Holden, however, will most likely come out of his juvenile depression by growing up in a less intolerant society.

As a young writer, Plenzdorf dons a mask and plays a game with authorities and readers. The game consists of having his fatalistic Edgar Wibeau say, "No human being can read all books, not even all very good ones. So, I concentrated on two. . . . My favorite books were Robinson Crusoe. . . . the other one was by that chap Salinger. . . . I still turn pale when I think that the book could have slipped by me."[32] Except for the fact that Robinson Crusoe and Holden distance themselves from societal conformity, the difference between the workaholic Robinson and the freedom-seeking Holden is so great that one cannot miss the implicit satire. The response by young German readers to Edgar/Holden gives ample proof, contrary to critical elders who castigated Edgar's vulgar language.

In the quote just given, we can also see how closely Plenzdorf models Edgar's diction upon Holden's, down to repetitions of pet phrases. Edgar, too, rebels against the "dense" older generation, "people over twenty-five." "I think," says Edgar, "that people ought not be allowed to get older than seventeen or eighteen. Afterwards they get jobs, go to college, or join the Army and one can't reason with them anymore. At least, I haven't found anybody to reason with. Maybe nobody understands me. Later you wear bluejeans that you don't have a right to anymore."[33] Edgar, as well, rebels against schooling, runs from home and parental supervision. In seclusion he listens to music, "bluejean music" and not highbrow "Händelsohn Bach-oldy." Adolescent needs and values are portrayed in conflict with uniformity, without the ironic realization that this is simply another type of conformism.

By adopting *The Catcher in the Rye*, Plenzdorf-Edgar assures the authorities that he has nothing against the books of Marx, Engels, and Lenin: "no halfway intelligent person can have any objections to Communism and the riddance of exploitation throughout the entire world."[34] What "gripes" him though is "everything else." What that "everything else" is, Plenzdorf in 1974 explained to his English translator, Kenneth P. Wilcox: Edgar's suffering is a criticism of East German officialdom's insistence upon the "achievement principle" as a means of establishing personal worth.[35]

Without Salinger's Holden novel, Plenzdorf's would have been inconceivable. Like other readers, Plenzdorf is attracted as much to the author as he is to Salinger's fictionalized Holden. Indeed, he conflates them: "That Salinger is a peach of a fellow. How he crawls around in that wet New York and doesn't come home because he dropped out of school where they gave him a pain; I get a kick out of that. If I knew his address, I'd write to tell him to come over here. He definitely was my age. Mittenberg [Edgar's town] naturally was small potatoes compared with New York but with us he'd recuperate splendidly. Above all, we would get rid of his idiotic sexual problem. That perhaps is the only thing I could never understand about Salinger. But that is easy for me to say because I never had sexual hangups."[36] Edgar apparently has more cultural and political constraints and concerns to cope with than Holden in a similarly "phony society."

Edgar is semiliterate, like Holden, and misdates Goethe's *Werther* by a hundred years: "I can't imagine that anyone spoke like that, even three hundred years ago. The whole business was nothing but letters by this impossible Werther to his pals back home. . . . Whoever wrote those should really take time to read my Salinger. *That is genuine people!*"[37] Plenzdorf's novel, play, and movie are derivatives of Böll's version of Salinger's *The Catcher in the Rye*, but the language he gives Edgar is contemporary subculture jargon, which Böll chose not to follow down to the last syllable uttered by "genuine people." Neither version was without self-servings: Böll's most consciously aims for an art form, while by and large Plenzdorf's capitalizes on sociological and documentary realism. Both authors take their eyes off the Salinger novel for their own liberation as writers. By accident of time they also serve their readers: the "genuine people" seek identity through literary models and find their rage and confusion voiced on the printed page.

Notes

1. Vladimir Nabokov, "The Art of Translation," in *Literature and Liberalism*, ed. Edward Zwick (Washington, D.C.: New Republic Book Co., 1976), 264.

2. Robert Gutwillig, "Everybody's Caught *The Catcher in the Rye*," *New York Times Book Review*, 15 January 1961, 38.

3. Lewis Nichols, "In and Out of Books: M. [Monsieur] Salinger," *New York Times Book Review*, 1 July 1962, 8.

4. J. D. Salinger, *Der Mann im Roggen*, trans. Irene Muehlon (Zürich/Stuttgart/ Konstanz: Diana Verlag, 1954).

5. Heinrich Böll as a public figure, unlike the reclusive Salinger, has granted many interviews, so that their contents often tend to be repetitious. For the purposes of this essay, I found the following interview to be most representative: "Interview von Marcel Reich-Ranicki, 1967," in *Heinrich Böll: Aufsätze, Kritiken, Reden* (Stuttgart/Hamburg: Deutscher Bücher-bund, 1967), 543–53. A short series of essay-memoirs by Böll, spanning the years of his youth in Cologne and continuing through postwar times, appear in his *Missing Persons, and Other Essays*, trans. Leil Vennewitz (New York: McGraw-Hill, 1977). The problems and efforts of reconstituting German postwar literature are highlighted in Böll's *Erzählungen, Hörspiele, Aufsätze* (Köln/Berlin: Kiepenheuer and Witsch, 1961).

6. Böll, *Aufsätze*, 552.

7. Ibid.

8. Manfred Durzak, *Das Amerika-Bild in der deutschen Gegenwartsliteratur* (Stuttgart: Kohlhammer, 1979), 153.

9. Ibid., 154. See Durzak's interview with Böll in its entirety, 145–71.

10. Heinrich Böll, *Ansichten eines Clowns* (Stuttgart: Kohlhammer, 1963), 102.

11. Ibid., 103.

12. Durzak, *Das Amerika-Bild*, 156.

13. Ibid., 166.

14. Böll, *Aufsätze*, 546.

15. *The Catcher in the Rye* (New York: Bantam Books, 1964), 140–41; all references to the text are to this edition.

16. "Zur neuen Übersetzung von Synge" [1961], Böll, *Aufsätze*, 112–13.

17. Durzak, *Das Amerika-Bild*, 169.

18. The literary and political activities of writers associated with this informal group are detailed by Siegfried Mandel, *Group 47: The Reflected Intellect* (Carbondale: Southern Illinois University Press, 1973); numerous literary portraits and interpretations of the social scene are well covered by Peter Demetz, *Postwar German Literature* (New York: Pegasus, 1970).

19. Böll, *Aufsätze*, 549–50.

20. Literary and linguistic integrity in postwar German fiction was severely criticized by George Steiner, John McCormack, and Hans Habe, who in turn were vitriolically attacked by some leading German writers and critics; the significant polemics are contained in *Deutsch— Gefrorene Sprache in einem Gefrorenen Land?*, ed. Friedrich Hand (Berlin: Literarisches Colloquium, 1964); see also, S. Mandel, "Postscript," *Group 47*, pp. 202–12. German readers' reception of modern American fiction is detailed in *Literatur nach 1945: Themen und Genres* 18, ed. Jost Hermand (Wiesbaden: Akademische Verlagsgesellschaft, 1979), 108–9, passim.

21. Nabokov, "The Art of Translation," 267.

22. Walter E. Riedel, "Some German Ripples of Holden Caulfield's 'Goddam Autobiography': On Translating and Adapting J. D. Salinger's *The Catcher in the Rye*," *Canadian Review of Comparative Literature* (Spring 1980): 196–205.

23. *The Catcher in the Rye*, 1.

24. *Der Fänger im Roggen*, trans. Heinrich Böll (Köln: Kiepenheuer & Witsch), 7.

25. *Der Mann im Roggen*, trans. Muehlon, 5.

26. This translation as well as all others in this essay, except where indicated, are my own.

27. *The Catcher in the Rye*, 18.

28. Böll, *Aufsätze*, 325, 330.

29. Ulrich Plenzdorf, *Die neuen Leiden des jungen W.* (Frankfurt a.M.: Suhrkamp, 1973). The astonishing impact of Ulrich Plenzdorf's freewheeling adaptation of Salinger's *The Catcher in the Rye* is discussed fully by Manfred Durzak, *Das Amerika-Bild in der deutschen Gegenwartsliteratur* (Stuttgart: Philipp Reclam, 1979); Durzak, *Die deutsche Kurzgeschichte der Gegenwart* (Philipp Reclam, 1980); Walter E. Riedel (fn.22); and Karl-Heinz Schoeps, "Der DDR-Roman" in *Handbuch des deutschen Romans*, ed. Helmut Koopman (Düsseldorf: Bagel, 1983), 566–67. Kenneth P. Wilcox has translated Ulrich Plenzdorf's novel *Die Neuen Leiden des jungen W.*, entitled *The New Sufferings of Young W.* (New York: Ungar, 1979), and has provided sound biographical and background discussions. (My quotes are translated from the original version.)

30. Siegfried Lenz, *Deutschstunde* (Hamburg: Hoffmann and Campe, 1968). Cited from the jacket of the English version, *The German Lesson*, trans. Ernst Kaiser and Eithne Wilkins (New York: Hill and Wang, 1971).

31. "Roter Werther in Blue Jeans," a newspaper heading of a review by Rolf Michaelis in the *Frankfurter Allgemeine Zeitung*, cited in part as jacket copy for the Suhrkamp edition of Plenzdorf's *Die neuen Leiden des jungen W.*, 1973. See also Marcel Reich-Ranicki, "Der Fänger im DDR-Roggen," *Die Zeit*, (11 May 1973): 3.

32. Plenzdorf, *Die neuen Leiden*, 32–33.

33. Ibid., 104.

34. Ibid., 80–81.

35. Plenzdorf, *The New Sufferings*, "Introduction," ix.

36. Plenzdorf, *Die neuen Leiden*, 33–34.

37. Ibid., 37.

Holden Caulfield, C'est Moi   Mary Suzanne Schriber*

If Holden Caulfield set out to study the criticism of *The Catcher in the Rye*, he would find himself the hero of an "awesome" (in today's Pencey Prep idiom) novel that sold a million and a half copies in the ten years following its publication and millions more since 1961.[1] A major figure in what George Steiner referred to, as early as 1959, as "the Salinger industry,"[2] Holden would find himself the subject, by 1981, of 344 essays and reviews, 21 books, 142 references and articles and chapters, and 14 dissertations and theses in the United States alone.[3] Perhaps most phenomenal of all, he would discover that critics have imposed on him and his story an enormous freight of sign value, of significance, in the sense both of meaning and of importance. Holden Caulfield has been construed as a classic American hero, the American adolescent, and the whole of American youth. The novel in which he appears has been associated with the classics of American literature, with the Quest, with the American dream, and with the myth of America. How have

*This essay was written specifically for this volume and is published here for the first time by permission of the author.

critics managed to magnify to such proportions a protagonist who is, after all, but a sixteen-year-old urban, male, WASP preppy? How has it happened that critics have persuaded themselves that this carefully delimited young male is the whole of youth, male and female, and the whole of America as well?

The popularity and magnification of Holden Caulfield and his story are rendered yet more peculiar by the propensity of critics to doubt the importance of the elusive J. D. Salinger, fallen silent since 1965, and of his one novel, *Catcher*. Critics apologize for their industriousness while in the act of producing the criticism that canonizes Salinger. Thus the 1963 Pocket Books collection of critical essays on Salinger begins with this observation by Henry Grunwald: "There is a feeling in many quarters that altogether too much fuss is being made about J. D. Salinger"; sympathetic critics classify him as a "good minor writer" while insisting that he holds the imagination as other good minor writers do not; unsympathetic critics who otherwise relegate those deemed minor to the oblivion of critical silence feel called upon to put this particular "minor writer" in his place at length.[4]

A cynic might note that the wedding of academic tenure and publication accompanied the Salinger industry, and that the flap over the decency of its language conveniently provided axes to grind and arguments to be made in print. Harvey Swados offers as reasons for the massive critical attention that has in turn designated *Catcher* an American epic Salinger's "supposed profundity," his "tantalizing physical inaccessibility," and the "legend of mysterious private suffering cohabiting with a singularly Christian literary morality . . . conducive to excited appraisals of a writer's importance."[5] Or perhaps *Catcher* has been the high school and college novel of choice because of the age of its protagonist and because of its genre: the novel of adolescence. Yet neither sheer pedagogical appropriateness to the interests of the young (if the term includes both males and females) nor literary interest in novels of adolescence (if the term designates a period in the lives of the young of both genders) accounts for *Catcher* being required as classroom reading; there are other contemporary novels of female adolescence, such as Carson McCullers's *A Member of the Wedding* and Ella Leffland's *Rumors of Peace*, that have fared considerably less well both in the marketplace and in academic journals.

The essential ingredient in the phenomenal success and the critical reception of *The Catcher in the Rye* is the propensity of critics to identify with Salinger's protagonist. Holden Caulfield, c'est moi. Falling in love with him as with their very selves, they fall in love with the novel as well. The criticism indicates that they see in Holden, and in themselves through his agency, an incarnation of their youth. Having identified with Holden, critics then engage in a procedure that magnifies him. Undeterred by and apparently oblivious to Holden's gender (and his social and economic class as well), they first assume maleness as the norm. Next, they are reinforced in this assumption by male-identified and gender-inflected theories of American literature, regnant for thirty years, within which more than a generation of readers has been taught to situate American novels. Developed by scholars who have themselves conflated the human and the male, these theories guide critics as they construe and construct the meaning of *Catcher* and its place in American literary history. They enable critics to find in Salinger's novel that which has been defined as archetypally American and thus classic, a literary work of timeless and universal significance.

Describing unabashedly the degree of identification of the male reader with Holden Caulfield, Robert Gutwillig writes: "What was it about the novel that struck Americans so squarely ten years ago and continues to hit the mark still? . . . the shock and thrill of recognition. Many of my friends and this writer himself identified completely with Holden. . . . After reading the novel, several of us went out and bought ourselves red caps and earflaps, and we all took to calling each other 'Ace' and 'Prince.' " What is more surprising is that even as an adult Gutwillig apparently continues to identify with Holden: "I believe that, despite its flaws, it will continue to be read. . . . Holden takes Phoebe to the carrousel. He stands in the rain, watching her 'going around and around in her blue coat and all.' 'God,' he says, 'I wish you could have been there.' We *are* there" (emphasis added), writes Gutwillig in 1961, just as "we" were there in 1951.[6]

Fifteen years later, *c'est la même chanson* is sung by Sanford Pinsker. Pinsker declares that, having early fallen in love with *Catcher*, he has been "trying to figure out what that has meant ever since. . . . Like Holden, I yearned for a world more attractive, and less mutable, than the one in which we live and are forced to compete. . . . Holden was my 'secret sharer,' the part of me that knew, deep down, that whatever Life was, it was decidedly *not* a game. . . . Holden said in bald print [what] I dared only whisper *sotto voce*." Like Gutwillig, Pinsker carries his love for Holden with him into manhood: "Holden Caulfield still has an honored place in the minds of what might well be the last generation to have formed its imagination, its sense of who we were, from the pages of a formative book."[7]

While identifying with Holden in their manhood as well as in their youth, critics have failed "to consider gender a relevant factor in either the configuration of identity or the institution of literature itself."[8] This occurs even when the critic is less than fond of the novel but perceives it nonetheless, like Ernest Jones, as "a case history of all of us," apparently defining "us" as male.[9] Presuming that the male is synonymous with the human, critics absorb the female into the male, particularly in their treatment of Holden and sexuality. Brian Way, for example, writes that in New York Holden embarks "on a dream" that is "universally adolescent": "the offer of unbelievable possibilities of sexual adventure and satisfaction." Way does not perceive this as a male's sense of adventure but, rather, he takes it to be normative; he praises Salinger for going "straight to the fundamental biological situation. [Salinger] sees that all the contradictions, agonies, and exaltations of adolescence stem from the central fact: that the adolescent has newly gained the physical potentialities for sexual experience but has not learnt to integrate them either within himself or in any consistent relation to the demands of society."[10] The notion of a "fundamental biological situation" overlooks the differential development, place, and manifestations of sexuality for males and females in the adolescent years.

On those occasions when critics are forced, by choice of texts, to consider female and male protagonists simultaneously, gender differences are sometimes recognized, but not necessarily sustained. Writing about "The Adolescent Hero" of both genders, James W. Johnson notes that sexual confusion "is nearly always more pronounced when the protagonist is a girl." Using Carson McCullers's Frankie Addams as "a conspicuous example of this bisexuality with her boyish haircut and her silver wedding frock," her calling cards that trace her "uncertainty about her sexual nature" and mark "the stages of her sexual as well as psychological maturation," Johnson insightfully observes that "such overt sexual ambiguity does not appear in their [the young women's] male counterparts, who are aware of their biological nature though they may be unsure as to what that nature involves." Nonetheless, having articulated a significant gender difference in the presentation of experience in novels of adolescence, Johnson backs away from his insight, as if unable to assimilate what he has himself detected. He makes no attempt to account for the difference, to convert it into critical capital. Moreover, and seemingly forgetful by the end of his essay of the heroines he earlier distinguished from heroes, he reinstates the male as adolescence itself, reducing the "new school of adolescence" to "the boy-hero" who "may some day achieve the relatively positive vantage-point of intellectualism."[11]

In the insatiable rhetoric of critics, the male is next made synonymous with the nation itself. Listen to Edgar Branch as he claims that *Catcher* and *The Adventures of Huckleberry Finn* are "brothers under the skin because they reflect a slowly developing but always recognizable pattern of moral and social meaning that is part of the active experience of young Americans let loose in the world, in this century and the last. . . . each author has probed beneath surface facts . . . to the experiential continuity of American life."[12] Branch provides here an unmistakable instance of what Sidonie Smith calls "the naive conflation of male subjectivity and human identity" by assimilating the female into the male, and in tropological terms, he casts Holden Caulfield as a synecdoche of America when he is in fact a metonymy: a part is made to represent a whole as if it included all of the other parts that, like it, are merely parts; male *contains* female rather than existing as just another equal part within a larger unit, such as humanity.[13] Branch's rhetoric here immasculates, or renders male, "young Americans" as well as American life itself.

There are of course those who recognize the boundaries within which Salinger sets Holden Caulfield. Harold L. Roth, for one, describes the novel as an attempt to picture "a boy's analysis of himself," and "a young man's thoughts and actions."[14] Rather than subsuming under Holden all adolescents, from the urban slum to the Kansas farm, Maxwell Geismar recognizes that Holden's "is surely the differential revolt of the lonesome rich child, the conspicuous display of leisure-class emotions, the wounded affections never quite faced, of the upper-class orphan."[15] Yet certain observations that appear to take into account the embedding of Holden in a fictive reality, including that of gender, are insidiously phallic. Carl F. Strauch, for example, seemingly confident that he knows how women talk among themselves, describes Holden's much-heralded language as "the idiom of the American male."[16] While this statement appears to take gender differences appropriately into account, it may in fact stand on a stereotype of women, a throwback to notions of the "lady" and a ladylike idiom that eschews four-letter words. Typically the criticism of *Catcher* begins in the symbiosis of male critics and the boy-hero Holden and takes possession of everything in its path, immasculating the whole of adolescence and the nation itself. Holden now magnified, critics claim for *Catcher* the status of a classic on the traditional grounds of universality.

Female critics have been less inclined, proportionately, to identify with Holden Caulfield and then inflate him to cosmic proportions. Of the 344 essays and reviews of *Catcher* listed in the Sublette bibliography, some twenty-three are the work of women. While this figure may simply reflect the lesser number of women publishing literary criticism, it may also indicate that women readers do not identify as readily as male readers with male protagonists. Several female essayists show a sharp awareness of gender and its bearing on literature. Marjorie G. Perloff, for example, contrasts Sylvia Plath's *The Bell Jar* with *Catcher* and observes that while Holden Caulfield is in flight from his world, Plath's Esther Greenwood is the perfect " 'good girl' who has always played the roles others have wanted her to play. . . . Her dilemma seems to have a great deal to do with being a woman in a society whose guidelines for women she can neither accept nor reject."[17] Sally Bostwick and Carol Murphy take Holden's sexual attitudes toward female characters into account; Murphy notes that "there is no real sex in Salinger stories."[18] Nona Balakian includes Salinger in her study of the anti-heroine and observes that in Salinger's work "there is not a single woman of maturity or stature;" in Salinger "the good angel" invariably "bears the face of a little girl (or sometimes a nun)."[19] Most recently, describing Holden Caulfield as a character in "revolt against the life of an adult male," Josephine Hendin avoids the conflation of the adolescent experience of young men and young women.[20]

Other female essayists, however, identify with Holden and immasculate adolescence as fully as male critics. Nancy C. Ralston sees Holden as the forerunner of "the disenchanted young person of today," and she is joined by Leonora Woodman and Molly Workman in the normalizing of Salinger's protagonist.[21] A prize-winning essay on *Catcher* written by a high school student, Amy Fogel, reveals not simply that female readers learn early to identify with male protagonists, as Judith Fetterley establishes in *The Resist-*

ing Reader,[22] but also that they understand this to be required if a story is to win a reader's assent. Testifying unwittingly to the pedagogical importance of fiction that presents female protagonists with whom women can readily identify, Fogel writes: "To understand the positive values of *Catcher*, it is necessary for the reader to identity with Holden, because Salinger's affirmation of humanity comes through Holden's very existence; in his character is the essence of man's nobility."[23]

The gender of a critic, then, is not the sole determinant of a reader's perspective and the meaning that he or she ascribes to Salinger's novel. In the face of the work of women who have identified with Holden, the success and acclaim of *Catcher* cannot accurately be attributed to the single factor of the anatomy of most of those who make up the critical establishment. Rather, critics have been assisted and even directed in their reading by theories of American literature that privilege the male, assume that he is normative, and make intellectual males of us all. Androcentric criticism, that is, is the child of androcentric literary theories. The deconstruction of the critical frameworks that have governed the reading of American literature, together with the understandings enabled by feminist, structuralist, and reader-response theory, explain the powerful impulse among readers, male and female alike, to identify with Holden Caulfield, expand him to cosmic proportions, and then, completing the hermeneutic circle, claim for him a universality that makes *Catcher* a classic.

There are several explanations of the process whereby the male becomes all of us, male and female. According to Dorothy Dinnerstein it begins in human nurturing arrangements in which babies of both sexes, dependent on their mothers, come to resent them and all females. As a result, even a female child identifies with the male and attempts "to preserve her 'I'ness by thinking of men, not women, as her real fellow creatures."[24] According to this theory, girls as well as boys are, from a very early age, in the process of becoming male-identified and would happily merge with male protagonists.

Whether or not we find this persuasive, we know that girls and boys go off to school and learn to be readers. Until recently, becoming a reader meant becoming mentally a male. Carolyn Heilbrun points out that it was only seventeen years ago, in 1971, that readers were asked for the first time to be other than male-identified, to "look at literature as women; we, men, women and Ph.D.'s, have always read it as men."[25] Examining in that same year the evidence of the literary curriculum to which the female student is introduced, Elaine Showalter established that by the end of her freshman year a woman student, supposedly learning "something about intellectual neutrality . . . would be learning, in fact, how to think like a man."[26] Pursuing shortly thereafter the thesis that what represents itself in education and in literary interpretation as neutral and objective and whole is in fact masculine and subjective and partial, Judith Fetterley analyzed the impact on women of reading like men and concluded: "As readers and teachers and scholars, women are taught to think as men, to identify with a male point of view, and to accept as normal and legitimate a male system of values."[27] All readers become male readers in the process of learning to read, enabling female critics to identify with Holden Caulfield, to immasculate themselves as young Amy Fogel did.

Having identified with Holden, female critics then approach the novel in much the same way as their male counterparts. And what is this way? Structuralism, reader-response theory, and experiments in cognitive psychology, linguistics, and communication theory have drawn attention to the extent to which reading and the construction of meaning are enabled by theories that, far from being transparent, are in fact mediators between readers and texts. Structuralists find the chief mediators in the text itself; a work "has structure and meaning because it is read in a particular way" and is "actualized by the theory of discourse applied in the act of reading"; the readers' understanding of the operations of literary discourse tells them what to look for in a text.[28] Reader-response theorists, on the other hand, contend that the mediators are outside of the text in the reader; "even the simplest understanding and recollection depend on knowledge that the reader brings to the task."[29] While leaving unresolved the vexing question of whether readers control texts or texts control readers, cognition research shows that "comprehension is mediated by generalized knowledge structures, or schemata, that exist in the mind of the reader. The schemata that are activated in the process of understanding a text provide a framework for the construction of meaning."[30]

It is at this juncture that the presumed tendency of human beings of both genders to identify with the male, whether because of nurturing arrangements or schooling, joins theories of American literature that have dominated the American academic marketplace for some thirty years and have become staples in the educational process: the Quest, the Dream, the Rebel, the American Adam, the Romance as quintessentially American. Whether these theories are initially in or out of the text in the mind of the reader, whether they enable the critic to abstract patterns embedded in the fiction or to create and impose patterns from the outside, they nevertheless are now outside American fiction. They have taken on lives of their own, apart from any specific literary work. They are enlisted to situate individual novels in relation to tradition; they are sockets into which novels are routinely plugged in order to be charged with meaning. They are major agents in the construing and constructing of sign value and thus significance. These same theories are unmistakably present in *Catcher* criticism and are unmistakably masculinist, ratifying the identification of readers with that which is male and leading critics to normalize, universalize, and canonize Holden Caulfield.[31]

The regnant theories of American literature and of American literary history, those of such major critics as Lionel Trilling, Joel Porte, F. O. Matthiessen, Daniel G. Hoffman, Marius Bewley, R. W. B. Lewis, and Richard Chase,[32] have located the essence of American culture, and hence of

American literature, in the sort of experience that, thanks to gender roles, has been accessible primarily to the male, is fictionalized primarily by male writers, and appeals to the androcentric bias of our culture. Nina Baym has explained how the quest of critics for "Americanness" and for the "American character," foregrounding fiction "that ignores details of an actual social milieu" and casting female characters as antagonists, has served to deny women's fiction and women writers a canonical position in American literary history.[33] Because these theories of American literature that privilege male fictions have been in the ascendancy in the academic study of American literature, the majority of American fiction to which students are exposed is the work of male writers whose protagonists incorporate that elusive, essential "Americanness" defined by theorists.

Yet there is perhaps a more insidious consequence of the imperialism of these formulations of our literary history. They perpetuate the masculinist status quo. Readers who have been taught to situate fiction within the regnant schemata of American literature are enabled by these schemata to make the most meaning from, and find to be most significant and therefore most important, those fictions that the schemata favor. Consequently, a process of self-selection is set in motion; other and perhaps equally meritorious fictions are rendered invisible in the glare of these masculinized dream and quest patterns. Moreover, features of canonical texts themselves that stand in the foreground of other frameworks are obscured if not rendered invisible because theory directs readers to fasten repeatedly on the matter that theory inescapably privileges; as cognition research demonstrates, "the schema activated determines the particular details that will be recalled, and, in the case of ambiguous passages, the nature of what is understood and remembered."[34]

The criticism of *The Catcher in the Rye* shows the degree to which literary theory is responsible for the attribution of global significance to the tale of a WASP preppy male youth. Critics clearly impose on or find in (as the case may be) Holden Caulfield and his adventures the definitions of essential "Americanness" that characterize the work of Trilling and Bewley and others. The trend began as early as 1956, in Charles Kaplan's essay entitled "Holden and Huck: The Odysseys of Youth." As the title forewarns us, Huck and Holden are about to become "youth" itself, apparently entirely male, as it sets off, in Kaplan's words, on "an adventure story in the age-old pattern of a young lad making his way in a not particularly friendly adult world." Having immasculated "youth," it is easy to immasculate "adolescence" as well, as Kaplan proceeds to do: "In addition to being comic masterpieces and superb portrayals of perplexed, sensitive adolescence, these two novels thus deal obliquely and poetically with a major theme in American life, past and present—the right of the nonconformist to assert his nonconformity, even to the point of being 'handled with a chain.' In them, 1884 and 1951 speak to us in the idiom and accent of two youthful travelers who have earned their passports to literary immortality."[35] Notice how that which is associated with the male, in Kaplan's rhetoric, has progressively absorbed everything in its path. "Youth" and "adolescence" are first implicitly masculinized. Next, that which has been masculinized is expanded into a theme in the whole of "American life," and even immortalized by being projected into both "past and present." Then this all-consuming male, encompassing "youth" and "adolescence" and "America . . . past and present" draws the "nonconformist" into its system. The coup de grace, however, the most chilling manifestation of the insidious power of this androcentric habit over the perceiving mind—insidious because it remains invisible while selecting that which will become visible—occurs in the quote: "handled with a chain."

Kaplan's relentlessly immasculating rhetoric first does its work on "nonconformist" and then, ironically, on Emily Dickinson's "Much Madness Is Divinest Sense." Having assimilated everything into the male, Kaplan's rhetoric then either contradicts the equation of "nonconformist" with the male or manages to immasculate none other than Emily Dickinson. Theories of American literature that implicitly govern Kaplan's reading can be credited with this, theories that conflate American and male experience and proceed to blind the critic even to so strong a female presence as that of Emily Dickinson and to the implicit contradictions in his own critical text.

Perhaps the most anthologized essay on *Catcher*, Heiserman and Miller's "J. D. Salinger: Some Crazy Cliff," manages like Kaplan's essay to place *Catcher* within a frame of reference that, allowing the male to stand for the whole of humankind, turns the whole of America into a company of men. Heiserman and Miller's treatment articulates up front, however, the process whereby a novel like *Catcher* is canonized at the expense of that which is female. These critics place *Catcher* in the "ancient and honorable narrative tradition, perhaps the most profound in western fiction . . . the tradition of the Quest. We use the medieval term because it signifies a seeking after what is tremendous, greater than the love of a woman . . . somewhere on the arc of the Quest, the love of woman must be eschewed or absorbed: the hero must bind himself to the mast, or must seek his Ducalinda because she is Virtue, not because she is Female." Heiserman and Miller could not be more clear: Quest fiction is perhaps the most profound fiction; Quest fiction is male; Quest fiction is about heroes made tremendous by seeking the tremendous, and that which is tremendous is that which is dissociated from woman and her love. Along with Judith Fetterley and others, one wonders how a female reader can possibly identify with such heroes without identifying against herself. In this tradition, questers are the outcast and, according to Heiserman and Miller, "American literature seems fascinated with the outcast, the person who defies traditions in order to arrive at some pristine knowledge, some personal integrity." In the brief compass of two pages, woman has first been excluded from the quest and then from that with which American literature is fascinated. Holden Caulfield, of course, "is one of these American heroes. . . . Salinger translates the old tradition into contemporary terms." In the course of the essay, Holden is ranged with Eugene Gant, Natty Bumppo, Huck Finn, Hans Castorp, Huxley's heroes, Dostoyevski's Idiot, Quentin Compson, Ishmael, Nick Adams, "Stephen Dedalus and Leopold Bloom rolled into one crazy kid."[36] Assisted by genre theories and theories of American literature that encourage the construction of impressive meanings and spectacular family credentials for *Catcher*, small wonder that critics have attributed to Salinger's novel such imposing sign value and significance.

Other favorites of American literary theory, in addition to "American-ness" as nonconformity and as inherent questing, come into play in *Catcher* criticism, most of them inaccessible to a female reader short of the partial lobotomy performed in the educational process. Ihab Hassan, for example, finds in Salinger's novel "the tough western hero" delivering an "embarrassed testament of love" and "the American rebel-victim," as well as "the new look of the American dream."[37] Leslie Fiedler associates Holden with the "good bad boy" tradition, the very epithet ensuring, according to Fiedler, a best-seller: "How much longer it took for a book to be called *Bad Girl* and how different the connotations of the title!" Fiedler claims that the "good bad boy" is America's vision of itself—crude and unruly in his beginnings "but endowed by his creator with a sense of what is right. . . . Sexually as pure as any milky maiden, he is a roughneck all the same, at once potent and submissive, made to be reformed by the right woman."[38] The critical faculties readied and alert for the tradition of the "good bad boy," Fiedler goes on to classify *Catcher* with *Huckleberry Finn*, *Tom Sawyer*, and *On the Road*. Salinger's novel is rendered particularly meaningful and important, that is, by its conformity to unifying theories of the American literary tradition in which critics are steeped. Critics are prepared to tease these patterns out of texts and to acclaim those presumably significant books that fit that old favorite notion of American literature as a "literature of boys. Many of our classics have survived as classics for boys . . . for adolescents."[39] The terms in which critics have created a reputation for *Catcher* testify to the continued viability of that tradition in the academic mind.

Thus the popularity and the ascription of broad significance and exceptional literary importance to *The Catcher in the Rye* can be traced to nurturing arrangements, to assumptions that the male is the normative, and to androcentric theories of American literature in which American fiction is routinely framed and taught. Yet a qualification is in order here. The reading experience of many of us, female as well as male (and rural as well as urban, Catholic and Jewish as well as WASP), is articulated in many of the claims made for Salinger's novel. Reader response, and not just the rhetoric of critics, suggests that *Catcher* is a fiction that *does* capture and express recognizable parts of adolescence. Does Salinger's novel more than "seemingly" escape, somehow, the confines of gender to touch broad if not universal human sensibilities? Perhaps the response to this novel should warn us that "concentrating on gender difference can lead us to slight the affinity of women and men . . . the common ground shared by all humans."[40] Moreover, if the criticism of *Catcher* manages by and large to articulate the intuitions of many readers of both genders, how can that criticism fairly be labeled androcentric and accused of a masculinist imperialism that mistakes part of human experience for the whole? Or on the other hand, have we been duped into finding ourselves in Salinger's novel by the androcentric logic in which we are schooled? Is the reading of *Catcher* an instance in which "androcentricity *may* be a sufficient condition for the process of immasculation"?[41]

Catcher criticism is guilty of androcentricity as charged because it fails to be self-reflexive. It remains oblivious to the possibility of a female perspective; it fails to problematize the male (and the urban and the WASP); it remains shackled to "false and damaging 'universals' that saddle the major intellectual discourses."[42] It does not declare its assumptions and explain where *Catcher* gets "its power to draw us into its designs," whether from an appeal to authentic desires for liberation and maturity or sheer complicity in our androcentric conditioning.[43] *Catcher* criticism arrogantly assumes that the male includes, unproblematically and unquestionably, the female, the adolescent, and the nation itself, as if this were a given in the natural order of things, requiring no comment and no explanation. Having spoken to and for an exceptionally large audience for four decades, *The Catcher in the Rye* perhaps legitimately deserves its popularity and its designation as a "classic." The critical case for *Catcher*, however, remains to be made. Contrary to the silences and assertions of Salinger criticism to date, an adolescent male WASP is not automatically nature's designated spokesperson for us all.

Notes

1. Robert Gutwillig, "Everybody's Caught *The Catcher in the Rye*," *New York Times Book Review*, 15 January 1961, 38; reprinted in *Studies in J. D. Salinger*, ed. Marvin Laser and Norman Fruman 1963), 1; hereafter cited as *Studies*.

2. George Steiner, "The Salinger Industry," *Nation*, 94 (14 November 1959); reprinted in *Studies*, 113.

3. Jack R. Sublette. *J. D. Salinger: An Annotated Bibliography, 1938–1981* (New York: Garland, 1984).

4. Henry Anatole Grunwald, introduction to *Salinger: A Personal and Critical Portrait* (New York: Pocket Books, 1963), ix.

5. Harvey Swados, "Must Writers Be Characters?," *Saturday Review* 43 (1 October 1960); reprinted in *Studies*, 121.

6. Gutwillig, *Studies*, 5.

7. Sanford Pinsker, "*The Catcher in the Rye* and All: Is the Age of Formative Books Over?" *Georgia Review* 40 (1986):953–56, 961.

8. Sidonie Smith, *A Poetics of Women's Autobiography* (Bloomington: Indiana University Press, 1987), 15.

9. Ernest Jones, "Case History of All of Us," *Nation*, 1 September 1951, 176.

10. Brian Way, " 'Franny and Zooey' and J. D. Salinger," *New Left Review*, May–June 1962; reprinted as "A Tight Three-Movement Structure" in *Studies*, 194, 196.

11. James W. Johnson, "The Adolescent Hero." *Twentieth Century Literature* 5 (1959):6–7, 10.

12. Edgar Branch, "Mark Twain and J. D. Salinger: A Study in Literary Continuity," *American Quarterly* 9 (Summer 1957); reprinted in *Studies*, 49.

13. Smith, *Poetics*, 17. I am indebted to my colleague, James M. Mellard, for this tropological observation.

14. Harold L. Roth, "Salinger, J. D. *The Catcher in the Rye*," *Library Journal* 86 (1951):7.

15. Maxwell Geismar, "J. D. Salinger: The Wise Child and the *New Yorker* School of Fiction," in *American Moderns: From Rebellion to Conformity*, ed. Maxwell Geismar (New York: Hill and Wang, 1958); reprinted in *Studies*, 76.

16. Carl F. Strauch, "Kings in the Back Row: Meaning through Structure, A Reading of Salinger's *The Catcher in the Rye*," *Wisconsin Studies in Contemporary Literature* 2 (Winter 1961); reprinted in *Studies*, 146.

17. Marjorie G. Perloff, " 'A Ritual for Being Born Twice': Sylvia Plath's *The Bell Jar*," *Contemporary Literature* 13 (1972):509–11.

18. Sally Bostwick, "Reality, Compassion, and Mysticism in the World of J. D. Salinger," *Midwest Review* 5 (1963):30–43; Carol Murphy, "Some Last Puritans," *Approach: A Literary Quarterly* 53 (1964):24.

19. Nona Balakian, "The Prophetic Vogue of the Anti-Heroine," *Southwest Review* 47 (1962):137.

20. Josephine Hendin, *Vulnerable People: A View of American Fiction since 1945* (New York: Oxford University Press, 1978), 114. While it is tempting to attribute this gender aware-ness to the resurgence of the women's movement and the development of feminist criticism, the facts of publication show otherwise, note the dates of these essays by women: Perloff, 1972; Bostwick, 1963; Murphy, 1964; Balakian, 1962; Hendin, 1978.

21. Nancy C. Ralston, "Holden Caulfield: Super-Adolescent," *Adolescence* 6 (1971):431; Leonora Woodman, "Teaching Literature Thematically," *English Journal* 55 (1966):564–68; Molly F. Workman, "*The Catcher* in the Classroom," *Virginia English Bulletin* 10 (1960):1–6.

22. Judith Fetterley, *The Resisting Reader* (Bloomington: Indiana University Press, 1978).

23. Amy Fogel, "Where the Ducks Go: *The Catcher in the Rye*," *Ball State Teachers' College Forum* 3 (1962):76.

24. Dorothy Dinnerstein, *The Mermaid and the Minotaur* (New York: Harper, 1976), 107.

25. Carolyn Heilbrun, "Millett's *Sexual Politics*: A Year Later," *Aphra* 2 (1971):39.

26. Elaine Showalter, "Women and the Literary Curriculum," *College English* 32 (1971):855.

27. Fetterley, *Resisting Reader*, xx.

28. Jonathan Culler, *Structuralist Poetics* (Ithaca, N.Y.: Cornell University Press, 1975), 113–14.

29. Mary Crawford and Roger Chaffin, "The Reader's Construction of Meaning: Cognitive Research on Gender and Comprehension," in *Gender and Reading: Essays on Readers, Texts, and Contexts*, ed. Elizabeth A. Flynn and Patrocinio P. Schweickart (Baltimore: Johns Hopkins University Press, 1986), 4; hereafter cited as *Gender and Reading*.

30. Patrocinio Schweickart and Elizabeth Flynn, introduction to *Gender and Reading*, xii. E. D. Hirsch, Jr., as well, sets out the importance of schemata in his *Validity in Interpretation* (New Haven, Conn.: Yale University Press, 1967).

31. In Salinger criticism there is an amusing instance of the role of theory in the reader's assessment of a text. Harold Orel, in "What They Think About Teen-Agers in Books" (*College English* 23 [1961]:147–49), reports that students in his high school honors English class accused Holden of lacking good sense. We can assume that some of these same students, once in college and introduced to theory and following in the footsteps of their professors, will learn to see Holden as a hero and his story as a classic.

32. These important studies include studies such as Marius Bewley, *The Eccentric Design* (New York: Columbia University Press, 1963); Richard Chase, *The American Novel and Its Tradition* (Garden City: Anchor Books, 1957); R. W. B. Lewis, *The American Adam* (Chicago: University of Chicago Press, 1955); Joel Porte, *The Romance in America* (Middletown, Conn.: Wesleyan University Press, 1969); Lionel Trilling, "Manners, Morals, and the Novel" and "Reality in America" in *The Liberal Imagination* (New York: Viking, 1950); Daniel Hoffmann, *Form and Fable in American Fiction* (New York: Oxford University Press, 1961); Leslie Fiedler, *Love and Death in the American Novel* (New York: Criterion Books, 1960); F. O. Matthiessen, *American Renaissance* (New York: Oxford University Press, 1941).

33. Nina Baym, "Melodrama of Beset Manhood: How Theories of American Fiction Exclude Women Authors," *American Quarterly* 33 (1981):131.

34. Crawford and Chaffin, *Gender and Reading*, 8.

35. Charles Kaplan. "Holden and Huck: The Odysseys of Youth," *College English* 18 (November 1956); reprinted in *Studies*, 31, 37–38.

36. Arthur Heiserman and James E. Miller, Jr., "J. D. Salinger: Some Crazy Cliff," *Western Humanities Review* 10 (Spring 1956); reprinted in *Studies*, 23–25.

37. Ihab Hassan, "J. D. Salinger: Rare Quixotic Gesture," in *Radical Innocence: Studies in the Contemporary American Novel* (Princeton: Princeton University Press, 1961), and in a slightly different form in *Western Review* 21 (Summer 1957); reprinted in *Studies*, 58, 66, 67.

38. Leslie Fiedler, *Love and Death in the American Novel* (New York: Criterion Books, 1960), 267–68.

39. Van Wyck Brooks, *The Writer in America* (New York: E. P. Dutton, 1953), 64.

40. Schweickart and Flynn, *Gender and Reading*, xxix.

41. Patrocinio Schweickart, "Reading Ourselves: Toward a Feminist Theory of Reading," in *Gender and Reading*, 42.

42. Schweickart and Flynn, *Gender and Reading*, xxix.

43. Schweickart, "Reading Ourselves," in *Gender and Reading*, 42–43.

INDEX

239